Volunteering and Communication

VOLUME 2

This book is part of the Peter Lang Media and Communication list.
Every volume is peer reviewed and meets
the highest quality standards for content and production.

PETER LANG
New York • Bern • Frankfurt • Berlin
Brussels • Vienna • Oxford • Warsaw

Volunteering and Communication

VOLUME 2

Studies in International and Intercultural Contexts

Edited by
Michael W. Kramer
Laurie K. Lewis
Loril M. Gossett

PETER LANG
New York • Bern • Frankfurt • Berlin
Brussels • Vienna • Oxford • Warsaw

The Library of Congress has cataloged the first volume as follows:

Volunteering and communication: studies from multiple contexts /
edited by Michael W. Kramer, Laurie K. Lewis, Loril M. Gossett.
pages cm
Includes bibliographical references and index.
1. Voluntarism. 2. Interpersonal communication.
I. Kramer, Michael W. II. Lewis, Laurie K. III. Gossett, Loril M.
HN49.V64V638834   302'.14—dc23   2012029432
ISBN 978-1-4331-1718-3 (vol. 1, hardcover)
ISBN 978-1-4331-1717-6 (vol. 1, paperback)
ISBN 978-1-4539-0959-1 (vol. 1, e-book)
ISBN 978-1-4331-2463-1 (vol. 2, hardcover)
ISBN 978-1-4331-2462-4 (vol. 2, paperback)
ISBN 978-1-4539-1441-0 (vol. 2, e-book)

Bibliographic information published by **Die Deutsche Nationalbibliothek.**
Die Deutsche Nationalbibliothek lists this publication in the "Deutsche
Nationalbibliografie"; detailed bibliographic data are available
on the Internet at http://dnb.d-nb.de/.

The paper in this book meets the guidelines for permanence and durability
of the Committee on Production Guidelines for Book Longevity
of the Council of Library Resources.

Dedication

To volunteers who cross cultural or national boundaries to serve and to those who want to understand them better

Preface

When we set out to publish our first edited book on volunteers, we wanted to fill a void in the scholarship by publishing a set of studies that demonstrated the breadth of research being conducted on volunteers. We were overwhelmed by the response and were only able to publish 18 of the over 60 proposals we received. We also noticed that there were a large number of studies examining volunteers in international and intercultural settings. We considered the possibility of producing a second volume dedicated to just international and intercultural settings and even suggested it to our editors and publisher. They encouraged us to focus on finishing the first book. I suspect that this response was related to the rather abysmal completion rate of most book projects. My sister-in-law working for a different academic press explained to me one time that about 50% of proposed books are never completed. I suspect that the editors at Peter Lang wanted evidence that we would actually finish the first book before beginning a second one. And so we focused on the first book. Most of the chapters examined the experiences of volunteers from within the United States working in their own or nearby communities, but we included four chapters that involved intercultural or international contexts, two concerning US citizens volunteering abroad and two examining the experiences of volunteers from other countries.

When we finished that book, *Volunteering and Communication: Studies from Multiple Contexts* (Peter Lang, 2013), we were pleasantly surprised when Mary Savigar, Senior Acquisitions Editor in Media and Communication Studies at Peter Lang Publishing, who worked with us on that project, asked us to propose a second book on volunteering in intercultural and international contexts. We immediately began the process of producing this book. The proposal was approved by the editorial board at Peter Lang and we sent out the call for chapter proposals. This time, we received fewer proposals than for the first book, but we were still only able to publish 50% of the proposals we received. There were plenty of scholars doing the challenging work of studying volunteers even in this narrower area of study.

To gain the broadest understanding of volunteering in international and intercultural contexts, we asked for three types of proposals: (1) studies of US citizens volunteering in other places around the world; (2) studies of volunteers from other countries around the world; and (3) studies of volunteers reaching across intercultural lines within their own country to serve specific ethnic or racial groups. We received proposals of all three types; it was not surprising to us that the most proposals were in the first category and the fewest were in the third category. This seems to likely represent the biases we have when we think of international and intercultural volunteers; the first example that comes to mind for many people is the Peace Corps which is well represented in this volume. However, examples of all three types are included.

We hope that that this volume provides a unique focus that the first book lacked by providing a more nuanced examination of some of the unique differences of volunteering in these contexts. We hope that the combination of the two books will stimulate additional research on volunteers and perhaps have a ripple effect of influencing additional volunteering in a multitude of contexts.

ACKNOWLEDGMENTS

We want to thank Mary Savigar. She not only guided us successfully through the process of getting the first book on volunteers published, but she then encouraged us to do this second book and guided us through the process again. We wish to thank the copy editors and Bernadette Shade, the production coordinator for the book, for bringing the book to publication. We thank our departments, peers, families, and friends for supporting us while we worked on this project.

Finally, we are extremely grateful the authors whose work is included in this volume. We hope that they and the readers of the book will benefit from the publication of this book.

The Editors
Michael W. Kramer
Laurie K. Lewis
Loril M. Gossett

Table of Contents

Conclusions

Introduction

CHAPTER ONE

An Introduction TO International AND Intercultural Volunteering

LORIL M. GOSSETT[1]
University of North Carolina at Charlotte

In the spring of 2013, I sent this email message to the Turkish Red Crescent Society (Türk Kızılayı) in the Capitol City of Ankara:

> Hello—My name is Loril Gossett and I am an Associate Professor of Communication at the University of North Carolina at Charlotte in the USA...
>
> I have worked with the American Red Cross for several years. I have studied the ways they motivate, organize, and train their volunteers.
>
> I am currently working on a book that examines volunteers and nonprofit organizations outside of the USA. I will be in Ankara this summer and was hoping I could make an appointment to discuss these issues with someone in your office.
>
> I am interested in understanding the nature of volunteering and charity work in Turkey. I would be particularly interested in talking to someone who is working with volunteers helping with the Syrian refugee effort....

This seemed like a simple and straightforward request. After volunteering with the American Red Cross for several years, I felt I had a decent understanding of how these types of disaster relief societies functioned. The Turkish Red Crescent and the American Red Cross are sister organizations within the International Federation of Red Cross and Red Crescent Societies (IFRC). I was going to be in Turkey for a few weeks in the summer and thought it would be a great opportunity to see how a non-Western IFRC organization operated. Additionally, I had been following the recent Syrian Refugee crisis and knew many of these displaced people were being cared for in Red Crescent managed camps along the Turkish/Syrian border. Given my interest in volunteer management and my previous experience with the Red Cross, I was excited at the potential research opportunities I might be able to develop in Turkey.

The one thing that worried me was that I could not find any volunteer-related information on the Red Crescent website. For my research with the Red Cross, I had relied on volunteer coordinators to serve as my primary organizational contacts. Unable to find such a person in Turkey, I directed my interview request to the organization's general email address and then waited for a response. Several weeks went by and I had not heard from anyone. I sent a few follow up emails to other people identified on the chapter's website (e.g., Human Resources, Donations Department) but never heard back. Months later when I was finally in Turkey, I decided to simply drop by the Red Crescent headquarters to see if I might find someone to interview.

I quickly learned why I never received a response to my email requests.

There was no one at the national headquarters responsible for organizing and training volunteers. The Red Crescent did have volunteers, but these people were not formally integrated into the larger organizational system. My interest in learning how volunteers were working with the displaced Syrians in Red Crescent camps was another non-sequitur request. Through my discussions with various officials, I learned that volunteers were not allowed to have any contact with the Syrians. As one staff member explained, the privacy and safety of these displaced people was of utmost importance. As such, only paid staff members could be trusted to work in the camps because they could be held accountable in ways volunteers could not. Rather than use volunteers, the organization had invested in a large number of paid employees who were trained and able to work on long-term assignments during disasters. None of the issues posed in my email were applicable to the goals or functions of the Turkish Red Crescent. As a result, no one responded to my note.

However, all was not lost. During the two days I spent visiting different Red Crescent offices in Turkey, I learned that people did volunteer for the organization but only at local chapters (not the national headquarters). There was a form people could fill out to indicate their interest in volunteering, but the link to this document was broken on the organization's website, and no one in the national office could find a hard copy. One official confided to me that chapter employees often disliked working with volunteers because they were considered unreliable and did not fit into the formal organizational chart. As such, staff at local chapters had been known to unofficially discourage the involvement of volunteers in the organization's day-to-day activities. The Red Crescent did rely upon spontaneous volunteers during crisis events (e.g., earthquakes, fires), but these volunteers were primarily locals who were not pre-trained or affiliated with the Red Crescent prior to the disaster. Moreover, after the emergency was under control, there was no evidence that the organization tried to remain in contact with these individuals for use in future events.

Everything I learned about volunteer involvement and management within the Turkish Red Crescent was counter to my experiences working with the American Red Cross. One of the primary goals of the American Red Cross is recruiting and retaining volunteers (Gossett & Smith, 2013). As a result, there are over a half million active Red Cross volunteers with 30,000 paid staff members, a 17:1 ratio of volunteers to employees (American Red Cross, 2011, p. 3). Volunteers are trusted to perform nearly all tasks necessary for the operation of the organization. On its website the American Red Cross notes that "we depend on volunteers like you" and claims that "volunteers constitute 94% of the total workforce needed to carry out our humanitarian work" (American Red Cross, 2014, p. 1).

In contrast, the Red Crescent Society of Turkey (Türk Kızılayı) reported having approximately 1,500 active volunteers and 1,600 paid staff members, a 1:1 ratio between employees and volunteers (Turkish Red Crescent Society, 2006). While volunteers are part of the organization, they do not play a central role in humanitarian programs such as disaster relief and community support. My observations of this organization are not unique. Other scholars have noted that the organization "has no policy for recruiting volunteers…Kizilay does not have the system of tools to register and motivate people who want to help as Kizilay volunteers" (Paker, 2004, p. 96). People who do volunteer are typically placed in the blood services department where they recruit donors or assist with youth programs (e.g., summer camps, health education) (Turkish Red Crescent Society, 2013).

It is also important to acknowledge that even if the Red Crescent had a volunteer program in place, the cultural norms in Turkey would make it difficult for them to recruit and retain participants. "Turkish citizens remain disconnected from the civil society movement…only 2.5% of citizens volunteer for social organisations, followed by a slightly higher rate of political volunteering at 4.5% (İçduygu, Meydanoğlu, & Sert, 2011, p. 70). As a point of comparison 26.8% Americans volunteered in 2011 (Bureau of Labor Statistics, 2012).

There are a variety of factors that limit formal volunteering in Turkey. For example, Turkey has the youngest overall population in Europe, with an average age of 29. The culture encourages people to work hard in order compete with the European Union and promote the Turkish economy in the global marketplace. As a result, people typically work six days a week for an average of 52 hours (Wozowczyk & Massarelli, 2011). Additionally, the country's political history has bred a distrust of formal institutions and Turkey has a small population of healthy retirees capable of active civic engagement (İçduygu, Meydanoğlu, & Sert, 2011) With respect to charitable giving, Turks tend to focus their philanthropic activity at the local level, making it difficult for NGOs to engage this population in formal, broad based volunteer programs.

On paper, the American Red Cross and the Turkish Red Crescent appear similar. They are both affiliates of the International Federation of Red Cross and Red Crescent Societies, they both provide humanitarian relief in times of national crisis, and they both provide similar services (e.g., blood donation, emergency preparation, temporary shelters). A key difference between these two groups comes in the way each organization recruits and uses volunteers. Given the cultural norms of Turkey, it makes sense that the Red Crescent organized its programs around paid employees. People in Turkey just don't volunteer the same way they do in the United States.

This experience provided me with the surprising realization that my understanding of volunteerism has been based entirely on my exposure to US-based programs. As a result, I had no way to make sense of the ways in which volunteers were used (or not used) by an organization so seemingly similar to ones I worked with in the United States. I needed to expand my understanding of volunteerism beyond the US context in order to understand what it means to volunteer in other cultures and communities.

To that end, this book was developed to help address a gap in the volunteer literature. It explores how volunteering in other countries is *both* similar and unique compared to volunteering in the United States. The studies included in this volume provide insight into volunteering within three different international and intercultural contexts, individuals from other countries volunteering, individuals from the United Sates volunteering in other countries, and individuals volunteering in their home country to serve a specific cultural or ethnic group, such as recent immigrants. The studies included in this book explore the ways in which different countries and cultures might impact what it means to be or communicate as a volunteer. In doing so, it expands our understanding of international and intercultural volunteerism and provides directions for future research.

In order to provide an introduction and overview of these contexts, this introductory chapter first addresses concepts and definitions associated with volunteerism. Next it explores some of the unique issues connected to international and intercultural service programs, including informal volunteering and embedded volunteering. It then examines how the political, economic, and historical contexts of countries influence the understanding and practice of volunteering in these regions. Finally, it ends with a preview of the studies included in this book.

INTERNATIONAL VOLUNTEERING

Anheier and Salamon, (1999) argue that:

The birth of the modern volunteer movement outside the realm of the state (for example, volunteer armies and work corps), church (for example, laymen) and community (for example, mutual assistance and caring) is closely associated with the creation of the Red Cross in 1864. For more than 100 years, the Red Cross and Red Crescent societies have pioneered volunteering and organized volunteers for humanitarian assistance, to alleviate suffering and poverty. (p. 45)

In the 20ᵗʰ century a number of other non-governmental organizations (NGOs) gained prominence for promoting international volunteerism. Groups such as the US Peace Corps, the UK Voluntary Service Overseas Program, and France's Medecins Sans Frontieres (Doctors Without Borders) mobilized citizens to work across national borders and provide assistance to people in developing countries. The United Nations increased global awareness of volunteerism by declaring 2001 to be the International Year of Volunteers (IYV).

The premise underlying IYV 2001 was that voluntary service makes an essential contribution in addressing problems in areas of social, economic, cultural, humanitarian and peace-building. For this to happen, there was a need for greater recognition and facilitation of volunteer work, more vigorous promotion of voluntary service, and networks to facilitate a drawing upon–the "best practice"–of volunteers. (United Nations Volunteers, 2011, p. 2)

The goal of this 2001 United Nations program was to bring member states and NGOs together to share resources and strategically promote volunteering across the global community. After 2001, the UN continued to support both domestic and international volunteering efforts in order to promote humanitarian aid distribution to underserved communities. In 2012, the United Nations Volunteer Program had sponsored nearly 7,000 volunteers, working in 127 different countries and 159 nationalities, and mobilized 57,000 local community volunteers throughout the world (United Nations Volunteers, 2012).

Rates of volunteer activity vary widely across the globe and different agencies do not always use the same metrics to calculate and compare levels of civic engagement between nations.[2] That being said, these measures give researchers some perspective on the ways people volunteer within different countries and cultures. For example, a 2011 Gallup study of 130 countries found volunteering more common in wealthier and developed nations, with the highest percentage of people engaged in volunteering in Sri Lanka (46%), the United States (43%), New Zealand (39%), and the UK (28%). Countries with the lowest rates of volunteerism were the Balkans and Southern Europe (English, 2011, p. 1). A similar study of 27 European nations found the average rate of volunteerism was 20%. However Denmark, Finland, and Sweden all reported average participation rates of 45%. In contrast "Greece, Malta, Portugal and Spain and the newest Member States–Bulgaria and Romania–the participation rate averages between 10% and 15%" (McCloughan, Batt, Costine, & Scully, 2011, p. 1).

The number of people involved with international volunteerism and their collective economic impact is significant. The Johns Hopkins Comparative Non-profit Sector Project studied data from 37 countries in 2004 and estimated that these international volunteer efforts made a $400 billion contribution to the global economy (International Labour Office, 2011). According to the Center for Social Development, over one million US citizens have reported volunteering internationally. Additionally, transnational organizations such as the European Volunteer Service Organization (EVS), the Centre for European Volunteers (CEV), and the United National Volunteers Program discussed above (UNV) all actively promote international service efforts. While women and retirees tend to volunteer more frequently in the United States, the same does not hold true for volunteers who serve abroad. Research in both the United States and Europe found that international volunteers tend to be white, young, males who are affluent, well-educated and who do not have dependent children (McBride & Lough, 2010; Sherraden, Lough, & McBride, 2008). International service programs may target particular demographic groups over others, resulting in this particular volunteer profile. These types of volunteer opportunities may be less available or attractive for more diverse populations. As such, it is important that scholars examine different cultural attitudes toward volunteerism to better understand why specific populations are not as inclined or able to volunteer in foreign communities.

Lesmeister, Rose, and Barnhart argue "Thousands of organizations worldwide are actively seeking and accepting foreign volunteers to assist with their program delivery and capacity development, yet there is a paucity of research on why organizations might bother seeking or accepting international volunteers in the first place" (2012, p. R15). Indeed, while getting people involved in world affairs through volunteerism may improve global well-being through the sharing of resources and information, these programs can also create problems in the regions where they serve. "Critics contend that [international volunteering and service] tends toward imperialism, reinforcing existing inequities" (Sherraden, Lough, McBride, 2008, p. 396). These scholars argue that volunteer programs can perpetuate social systems of inequality, dividing the helpers and those needing help into two distinct and separate populations. Rather than bringing communities together, outside assistance groups may create or reinforce social divides. It is therefore important for scholars to examine how volunteer efforts may function differently in various contexts. If volunteers are truly to be of service to others, they must understand how to work effectively within their host communities and appreciate different approaches to public service.

While the United Nations and various service groups have turned their attention to examining volunteerism at an international level, the same cannot be said of the academic community. "While people have created their own constructs of volunteering, which are inevitably culturally and socially specific, the dominant representation is of volunteering as the domain of the white middle-class middle-aged female who volunteers (out of altruistic concerns) in social care settings or charity shops" (Lukka & Ellis, 2001, p. 30). Cross cultural comparisons of vol unteer behavior has often been criticized as viewed "through the lens of how the developing (and/or democratizing) country can create new civil society organizations, particularly those engaged in political advocacy, that resemble those found in the 'advanced' West" (Haddad, 2010, p. 34). Recognizing this pattern in the literature, scholars have argued for additional research focused on the unique challenges of international volunteering that is not necessarily based on US or Western European models (Lesmeister, Rose, & Barnhart, 2012).

DEFINITIONS OF VOLUNTEERING

To more fully understand volunteerism within international and intercultural contexts, it is important to first examine what it means to volunteer. The term "volunteer" is derived from the Latin *voluntarius* meaning "of one's free will" and from the French word *voluntaire* used in the context of offering one's service to the military. At the most basic level the term implies a person is freely giving him or herself to serve others or a larger cause. With respect to motivation, volunteerism is often described as an altruistic behavior performed for the benefit others, and without remuneration (Lewis, 2013; Wilson & Musick, 1997). Tilly and Tilly (1994) add that volunteer work is not only unpaid labor, but should also be performed on behalf of people the worker "owes no contractual, familial, or friendship obligations" (p. 291).

Scholars have acknowledged some people volunteer for reasons other than pure altruism. Volunteering may alternatively serve as a means to an end for the worker; a way to learn a skill, form new relationships, gather information about a potential career, or simply increase one's social status (Jorgensen, 2013). This personal investment motivation moves the act of volunteering away from personal sacrifice and frames the behavior in transactional terms. While not compensated through money, some volunteers provide service in exchange for gaining skills, experience, or earning social capital within their home communities. Some people engage in volunteer work in order to promote a set of beliefs; religious missionaries are one such example. Anheier and Salamon (1999) note that "[m]issionary societies, religious orders, and other types of religious organizations have operated internationally for many centuries, particularly so since the early 1900s, carried by the evangelical revival movement that swept the United States and Europe at that time" (p. 45). In addition to providing their labor and resources, these mission-focused volunteers may be motivated to make changes in the communities they are serving (e.g., educational reforms, religious conversion). Mission-based volunteer programs can be particularly controversial, since one group's *community improvement* program may be seen by others as an example of *cultural insensitivity* or *domination*. Regardless of the motivation, a common theme in these definitions is that volunteering is an activity people engage in outside their regular daily activities and interactions. To volunteer is to do something special or exceptional for the service of others.

Even when the meaning of volunteering is consistent across nations, the ways in which volunteering is organized and functions can vary significantly. As illustrated above, although the American Red Cross and the Turkish Red Crescent may share an understanding of what it means to be a volunteer, they have markedly different understandings of the value, organization, and appropriate use of this unpaid labor. Furthermore, most research focuses on behavior and programs consistent with Western definitions of volunteering, without considering the wide range of philanthropic and service-oriented activities that may be more typical in other cultures.

INFORMAL VOLUNTEERING

Offering assistance or help to others informally (outside the confines of a formal service organization) is an example of philanthropic behavior that is not always included in definitions or studies of volunteerism. Wilson and Musick (1997) argue that *volunteering* and *helping* are distinctly different sets of behaviors. Helping is thought to be a private and informal activity directed at close friends and family and born out of a sense of obligation. Indeed, Tilly and Tilly's (1994) definition of volunteering specifically excludes service provided to one's friends and family. This effectively moves individual acts of assistance, such as mowing a neighbor's lawn or babysitting for a relative, to outside the sphere of *real* volunteerism. While there may be reasons to distinguish between these two sets of behaviors, this division effectively removes from scholarly consideration informal activities that serve as a primary form of civic engagement within certain communities.

> [I]nformal volunteering is often underestimated and undervalued in terms of its contribution both to social safety nets and developmental activities. Furthermore, it has also been pointed out that the term "volunteering" may not be recognized by all "volunteers" as applying to them. In other words, there may be established forms of volunteering which are

not even recognized as such in certain cultures or within sectors of the population, despite their invaluable contributions to human development. (United Nations Volunteers, 2002, p. 22)

By limiting the study of volunteerism to formally organized activities, researchers may overlook the ways service and charitable activity is manifest in non-Western, non-industrialized communities. For example,

> In the Andes, for example, mingas or faenas are traditional ways of communities coming together to share labour, usually for the common good. Similar traditions exist in Africa and Asia....These traditions in many countries offer safety nets (especially in times of crisis) and encourage individual voluntary action for the public good. (United Nations Volunteers, 2002, p. 6)

Additionally, Kabelkova (2013) argues that research methods commonly used by volunteer and nonprofit scholars exacerbate this issue because they "often analyze data from the well-known international surveys, such as World Value Survey or Eurobarometer that include few or no questions on informal volunteering" (p. 7). The fact that informal helping behaviors are not included on many of the measures used to assess the level and nature of international volunteerism may prevent scholars from fully understanding the range of activities that may otherwise qualify as civic engagement.

Informal volunteering may have gained popularity in certain regions out of necessity. In countries isolated by physical terrain or politics, assistance from one's family and neighbors may be the only help available. Additionally, people living in small communities may not have a reason to formally organize their volunteer efforts. The value of public service and civic engagement may be strong in these regions but difficult to detect with popular measures of volunteerism.

The preference for local, informal assistance over formal volunteer programs may also reflect a community's value system. For example, Choden's 2003 study of volunteerism in Bhutan found that religious beliefs of this region encouraged citizens to focus inward and help each other in order to remain a self-reliant society. Informal volunteerism in this community is a way individuals demonstrate fealty to their religion and reinforce cultural values to each other.

> [I]t makes sense that volunteerism and the nature of entities that fulfil such functions should be considered in the (Bhutanese) cultural context....If we should go strictly by the idea that such works occur only through legally recognized, non-profit making bodies, then there would be not many that would qualify as voluntary acts in Bhutan. (Choden, 2003, p. 13)

Understanding the significance of Bhutan's preference for informal helping behavior may promote the development of more effective and culturally sensitive assistance programs. Of course, such a move would require that scholars reconsider and potentially expand definitions of what counts as volunteerism.

EMBEDDED VOLUNTEERING

Developing a comprehensive definition of volunteering for international and intercultural comparisons is challenging at best. As previously mentioned, most academic measures have evaluated formal volunteer programs, defined by relatively stable and self-governing organizational structures. This methodological choice may overstate the significance of independent nonprofit programs while overlooking volunteers who serve their communities through embedded civic organizations. Embedded organizations are defined as public service groups that rely on a close relationship with various government bureaucracies in order to function. Examples of embedded volunteer groups include Parent/Teacher Organizations and Neighborhood Associations. Haddad (2006) found that participation in these embedded volunteer organizations is particularly popular in countries where people believe the government should take responsibility to solve the community's social problems. Embedded organizations bring citizens together with officials in order to help the government better serve public interests. Members of embedded organizations work within political channels rather than outside the system. In contrast, non-embedded groups are independent organizations that maintain a self-sustaining structure so they can operate without government assistance. Examples of non-embedded service organizations include Greenpeace and Rotary International. These groups tend to be most popular in countries where people feel individual actors should resolve social problems rather than rely upon government intervention. In these communities, privately funded groups are considered the most efficient way to harness resources present within the community and provide needed services to the public.

Countries where embedded volunteerism is most common include Japan, Spain, and Korea while non-embedded volunteerism dominates in Australia and the United States (Haddad, 2006). The significance of this divide comes when cross-country comparisons of civic engagement and volunteerism emphasize participation in non-embedded organizations and fail to fully account for public participation in embedded groups. Haddad (2006) criticizes many of the most popular civic engagement measures for failing to account for participation in local embedded organizations or combining these groups into an "other" or "miscellaneous" category which effectively obscures their unique nature and impact. Such methodological choices limit the ability of scholars to fully appreciate how volunteerism is understood and performed in particular communities.

Overlooking embedded volunteer organizations in comparative studies of civil society has created a *systematic bias* in favor of certain types of organizations....This bias results in the incorrect conclusion that Japan and other countries with similar volunteering patterns have weak and underdeveloped civil societies, when, in fact, their civil societies may be equally well developed and just taking on a different shape. (Haddad, 2006, p. 1228, emphasis in the original)

While both types of organizations foster civic engagement, they also help illustrate how different cultural values can shape attitudes about the "best way" to engage in public service. As such, it is important that scholars consider what types of activities and organizations are included in various measures and research questions when examining the nature of volunteerism on the international stage.

WHAT DOES IT MEAN TO VOLUNTEER?

Regardless of the motivating factors or organized nature of the behavior, the net result of volunteer efforts has generally been thought to be a societal good, something to be encouraged. What is not to love about free labor for the benefit of others? However, as scholars examine volunteering at an international level, it is important to consider that this activity may not always be viewed in a positive light. What counts as volunteering and its relative value to the society may look or function differently depending on a community's political system, economic status, and social history. Scholars must also consider the role that these various factors have on how people make sense of volunteering across cultural and international boundaries.

POLITICAL STRUCTURE

Parboteeah, Cullen and Lim (2004) hypothesize that socially collectivist societies and liberal democracies are more likely to foster volunteerism among their citizenry: "Because societal collectivism is synonymous with actions that are directed to maximize the well-being of society, it is plausible to expect higher levels of volunteering" (pp. 433–434). Additionally, liberal democracies which allow people to freely associate with each other, increase the likelihood that individuals will form attachments to others and therefore volunteer to help friends and the community at large. Supporting this argument is the fact that most measures of global volunteer activity find the highest rates of volunteerism in democratic countries.

[T]he highest rate of volunteering in democratic countries was found in the United States (66%), South Africa (59%), Philippines (57%) and Sweden (54%), whereas the lowest rates were found in Russia (7%) and in Central-Eastern European countries that used to be Soviet allies, such as Poland (12%) and Hungary (14%). (Kabelkova, 2013, p. 4)

One difference between democratic and more authoritarian governments may be in the ways in which its citizens understand and engage in volunteer behavior. As noted above, most measures of volunteerism emphasize participation in formal service organizations. Informal volunteerism, even if widespread within a community, is not likely to be detected by these tools precisely because of its small scale and unpredictable nature. In countries with a history of civic and political unrest, informal acts of service may be more common than formal volunteerism because these activities are less likely to attract unwanted attention. For example, Pichler and Wallace (2007) argue that "lack of trust in formal organizations in former Communist countries...encourage[s] informal networks to develop since these kinds of reciprocity were a traditional way of managing resources under Communism" (p. 424). During the Communist era it was relatively common practice for citizens to divert goods and provide services to each other outside official channels. These underground networks enabled people to provide assistance to friends in need without alerting authorities to individual stockpiles of goods.

Even as government systems have changed in many of these regions, previously established informal networks used for sharing resources have remained a strong tradition in Eastern and Southern Europe (Pichler & Wallace, 2007). Nistor, Tîrhaş, and Iluţ's (2008) study of volunteerism in post-communist Romania reinforces this point.

> In Romania, as well as in other post-communist countries, survey data show the diminishing social trust, both under its general and institutional form. For the first case the reason lies in corruption, in institutional un-accountability etc. In the same time, people develop trust in informal support networks. The association within family networks, quasi-legal or illegal networks of support etc. serve thus as a complementary regime for the eroded trust in institutions and low levels of participation in formal networks. (p. 172)

With increased availability of social media and other communication channels, neighbors are able to quickly determine who has extra supplies or can help out with various tasks. The means of communication may have changed but the preference for unregulated and informal helping has remained a common form of volunteerism and civic engagement within these communities. Studies that show a low degree of civic engagement in these regions needs to consider that such activity may be occurring outside formal systems. Scholars may need to gain access to informal networks in order to understand when and how volunteerism is manifest within these communities.

In addition to participating in informal helping networks, citizens in many authoritarian countries may also work in state-run public service groups (e.g., women's organizations, youth associations, civil defense units). These government sponsored organizations sometimes call members *volunteers*, but the non-optional nature of participation makes membership an obligation rather than a choice. In such countries the word "volunteer" can become synonymous with government service. In her study of volunteering in the Czech Republic, Kabelkova (2013) argues that four decades of forced participation in government sponsored service groups had fundamentally altered the meaning of volunteerism in the country:

> Given the coercive nature of volunteering during the communist era, there is a presumption that low interest of Czech seniors in volunteering might be influenced by misunderstanding of the word *volunteering*...despite the fact that in the so called Western world its meaning is clear. (p. 11)

Additionally, Wiktorowicz's (2000) study of volunteerism in Jordan found that civic groups in that country tend to be heavily monitored and regulated by the government. By law, the state is allowed to review all volunteer projects and may forbid any activity found to be offensive. "Such discretionary power allows the state to shape the specifics of organizational activity in the kingdom and directs civil society associations into activities approved by the regime" (Witorowicz, 2000, p. 52). While government control over these groups may limit their desirability, participation is strongly encouraged because it limits the time people have outside to engage in activities that might run counter to government interests. As a result Wiktorowicz (2000) argues that Jordan's:

> use of civil society as an instrument of state control and the limits of civic organization in the Middle East challenge social scientists to reevaluate the perspective of civil society as empowerment...[it] does not act as a conduit for freedom; instead, it further extends the state's social control over its citizens. (p. 58)

While people in liberal, democratic countries might consider volunteering to be a way to explore or express personal values, in more authoritarian societies volunteering can effectively suppress the expression of personal interests and encourage social conformity.

Finally participation in independent nonprofit groups may also be impacted by the political climate. For example during the Soviet era, citizens were encouraged to volunteer for the Red Cross, one of the few international NGOs allowed to operate behind the Iron Curtain. However, the fact that the Red Cross was endorsed by the government appears to have fundamentally impacted the volunteer experience. After the fall of the Soviet Union, scholars noted a significant drop in Red Cross membership all across Eastern Europe (Anheier & Salamon, 1999). The fact that people in these transitioning nations stopped working with the Red Cross might be interpreted as a political act rather than a statement against volunteerism. However, Plagnol and Huppert (2010) hypothesize that the rapid decline in formal volunteer activity in these regions might have greater significance.

"[F]orced volunteering during Soviet times largely replaced people's intrinsic motivation to volunteer. Hence, few people may feel the desire to provide assistance to others without specific extrinsic motivation" (p. 175). Along a similar line, Ginga (2010) noted that modern Russians have a learned skepticism toward organizations that purport to be for the benefit of society. He notes that people are reluctant to volunteer in part because of negative public perception of NGOs and low trust in public institutions which have taken advantage of them in the past. Given their political history, efforts to mobilize volunteers in these regions or to have foreign volunteers accepted by local communities might require fundamentally different techniques than used within traditionally democratic countries. The people in these communities may lack trust in any organization asking for or offering assistance; once burned, twice shy. These examples highlight the importance of considering the political context when studying international volunteer practices and rates of participation.

ECONOMIC CONDITIONS

Parboteeah, Cullen and Lim (2004) argue that the relative wealth of a community increases the free time of its citizens which enables them to donate their time and resources to others. In contrast, in communities where people are struggling to survive, citizens may not have the time or energy to donate to others. In addition, in regions where jobs are scarce the presence of volunteers may not be seen purely as a source of relief but also as a source of competition. "The International Labour Organization (ILO) (2011) defines volunteering negatively...voluntary work is not paid, not compulsory, not obligatory, not free work done for household members, and the scope of it is not limited to a particular beneficiary" (Kabelkova, 2013, p. 2). Rather than providing jobs for members of the community, money and resources given to support volunteers—particularly foreign workers from wealthier nations—may be viewed with mixed feelings by the local population. Unpaid volunteer labor may diminish the need for organizations or the government to provide paying jobs that locals are capable of performing (e.g., handing out food to the hungry, providing administrative services).

Indeed, one international aid organization (BOMA) in Africa avoids using volunteers precisely out of fear that introducing free labor may have a negative impact on the already economically depressed communities they serve. As the US based founder of this NGO explained:

> In a country with 40% unemployment, volunteers take jobs away from those willing to work for wages...There are many hardworking people trying to start businesses in everything from the manufacture of malaria nets, to bicycles and books. The constant dumping

of free goods, while well-intentioned, also destroys markets and businesses that otherwise could provide employment and critical incomes for families. (Rungu, 2010, p. 7)

It is not only people in poor communities that might have difficulty accepting volunteer labor. In countries where high tax rates are used to support social services, volunteer labor may be seen as competing with or inferior to government funded programs. In these countries volunteers may be regarded as "... amateurish 'do-gooders' and relics of the past to be replaced by paid professional staff capable of performing tasks more effectively and efficiently" (Anheier & Salamon, 1999, p. 44). These economic systems are designed so that the government has the resources, and thus the obligation, to provide for the welfare of the people. As a result, many of the social service programs that rely on volunteers in the United States (e.g., hospital aides, food banks) are staffed by paid workers who are trained to perform these tasks. There is no labor gap in the system that requires or desires volunteer assistance. To illustrate, a friend of mine moved from the US to Sweden and wanted to volunteer in her son's school. However, when she asked the teacher if she could help in the classroom, her offer was politely rejected. Apparently Swedish schools have enough paid classroom assistants to serve the needs of their students. In fact, the classroom aides might have been offended if the school allowed untrained volunteers to just show up and help. To do so might de-professionalize the position of classroom assistant and imply that *anyone* could do this job.

Volunteering in many socialist countries tends to be focused more narrowly than in the United States. "[I]n Scandinavian countries and Netherlands where governments provide funding for most social welfare, the majority of voluntary work is done in recreational fields (e.g., hunting) or as an expressive volunteering related to civic issues and social movements" (Kabelkova, 2013, p. 5). In countries such as the US, with fewer state-sponsored welfare programs, the nonprofit sector is larger and unpaid volunteer labor is necessary for providing services to the public. Volunteerism has greater breadth and acceptance in communities where paid, professional assistance is not readily available.

HISTORICAL CONTEXT

Although a countries' political structure and economic conditions are partially related to the historical context, there are also situations in which volunteering is deeply rooted in the history of a nation. A case in point is the Japanese volunteer fire fighting program. These traditionally male volunteer groups have existed in Japan since the Edo era in 1629. Initially organized by the Shogun to protect their castles, these groups also protected local neighborhoods from fire damage. At the end of World War II, Japan's military was eliminated and its traditional civil associations were devastated (Pekkanen, 2009). However, the volunteer firefighting brigades were one vestige of Japan's past that remained intact. These groups continued to operate within each neighborhood and served as a subtle reminder of the nation's history. Even today, affiliation in volunteer firefighting units remains a strong tradition in Japan. While profession firefighters have modern equipment that has decreased the need for volunteer groups, these units remain active all over the country and outnumber professional firefighters 6 to 1. "Nearly a million strong, volunteer firefighters continue to serve essential public safety roles, and they provide equally important social capital-building connections among members of society, demonstrating and teaching to others the value of civic responsibility" (Haddad, 2010, p. 43). This volunteer program cannot be fully understood as an act of altruism or social exchange. It also reminds the Japanese people of their history and promotes the values of civil service and commitment to community (Haddad, 2010). This example illustrates that volunteering may have more symbolic than outcome based value. For Japan, people continue to join these volunteer fire departments, even if they never fight a fire, in order to connect the modern era to the country's ancient past.

Another example of volunteerism that might be best understood through historical context is Israel's national service program. Anheier and Salamon (1999) argue that for Jewish people, particularly those who live outside of Israel, volunteering "is intimately linked to the cultural identity and community as a substitute for nationhood...this connection is evident in the long experience of Diaspora and the collectivist voluntary spirit of Zionism" (p. 48). Like many countries, Israel maintains a standing army by requiring military service from all citizens. However Israel also has a national service program available for people who need an exemption from military service (e.g., health issues, educational demands). While service is required of Israeli residents, versions of these programs are also available for non-residents who want to volunteer their services to the country.

> Service—military or national—has been, over the years, the collective route that provided meaning and a sense of identity and belonging to the individual in Israeli society... The contemporary impetus to create a civic service in Israel comes, thus, from two main motives: (a) to promote equality between citizens, both of burden and of opportunity, and (b) to provide arenas for shared experience and dialogue between increasingly separate societies within Israel. (Bar-Tura & Fleischer, 2004, p. 59S)

Voluntary service in this context might be understood as both a political act in support of the Jewish homeland and as a way Jews who live outside of Israel can establish a connection to this larger community. Scholars need to consider the unique historical context of a region in order to understand the significance of particular volunteer programs within a community.

INTERCULTURAL VOLUNTEERING

Studying volunteer behavior in international and intercultural contexts may increase our understanding of volunteer behavior among immigrant or minority populations living within a single country. Wilson's (2000) extensive literature review on volunteerism only cited ethnicity-specific research related to African Americans. Researchers examining intercultural volunteerism within the United States have noted the need for more research on the philanthropic behavior of different racial and ethnic groups. Lukka and Ellis (2001) argue that black, minority, and ethnically diverse members (BME) of US society tend to view volunteering somewhat differently than white Americans. Members of these minority communities tend to describe volunteering as a form of mutual community support rather than as an exchange relationship between the helper and the helped. Additionally, the volunteer work performed by members of these groups is typically done within clearly defined racial or ethnic boundaries.

> BME volunteers regarded their type of volunteering as a specific part of their culture and felt that it was a way to help preserve their children's identity or to reaffirm their own. We can therefore understand how BME volunteering translates into an informal activity that allows closeness to beneficiaries and represents an important expression of identity. This closeness of the beneficiaries is again at odds with the Western construct of volunteering. (Lukka & Ellis, 2001, pp. 34–35)

In addition to preferring to volunteer informally and within homogeneous communities, other research has shown that members of minority groups tend to participate in embedded organizations that focus on solving problems within their immediate communities (e.g., crime prevention task forces, neighborhood associations, fraternal organizations) (Sundeen, Garcia, & Raskoff, 2009). The very types of volunteerism understudied on the international stage (e.g., informal, embedded) may also fall under the radar of scholars studying these activities within the United States. Expanding our definitions and methods for studying volunteerism may improve our ability to study these behaviors in both foreign and domestic contexts.

Researchers have a special challenge when they want to study volunteer behavior among immigrant populations. For example, there are some 40 million immigrants in the US representing 13% of the population (Congressional Budget Office, 2013). Sundeen, Garcia, and Rakoff (2009) argue that there is a "need for greater scholarly attention to the volunteer behavior of these various groups and their respective immigrants, many of whom are not accustomed to the practice of formal volunteering" (p. 930). Immigrants blend the values and norms from their countries of origin with practices they pick up in their new home communities. Sundeen, Garcia, and Wang (2007) note that in addition to language difficulties, a lack of understanding the function of different community groups or purpose of volunteer programs can often serve as a primary volunteerism barrier for first generation immigrants. For people who come from countries where formal volunteering is not common, such as Mexico or parts of Eastern Europe, invitations to join these types of service organizations may not make sense. However immigrants from countries such as Argentina, Japan, and the Philippines, which have strong formal volunteering traditions, may more easily adapt to US volunteering norms.

Additionally, the ways in which immigrants engage in volunteer activities are often shaped by their home culture's norms and traditions. For example Lim's (2012) study of Korean immigrants in the United States found that members of this community were not active volunteers in their children's schools, despite receiving numerous invitations to participate.

> Despite the high value Korean families placed on education, their cultural assumptions about proper family–school relationships differed from the perspective held by mainstream schools rooted in individualistic cultures. In the collectivistic East Asian culture from which the parents came, a school tends to represent an authoritative, separate space demarcated from home by a clear boundary. (pp. 100–101)

Additionally, Lim (2012) explained that the Korean parents were uncomfortable with the highly participatory nature of school volunteer programs because they did not want "to position themselves as teachers' equals due to their cultural value of respect for authority" (p. 105). The value system of this immigrant group's home culture shaped the types of activities they were comfortable pursuing. To that end, gaining a greater understanding of volunteer practices and assumptions in different countries will help scholars and practitioners develop more culturally sensitive ways to reach out and engage immigrants into their new home communities.

ORGANIZATION OF THIS BOOK

Given the range of issues associated with international and intercultural volunteering, the studies in this book have organized into three primary sections. Section One of the book is titled: Volunteers Around the Globe. These chapters examine volunteerism from a distinctly non-US perspective. All of the studies in this section involve volunteers from countries other than the United States who are working in either their own communities or in other nations. The first two studies focus on the way volunteers outside of the US respond to national disasters. The first study illustrates the way Australian volunteers harnessed social media to informally organize their efforts during the Brisbane floods (Chapter 2: McDonald, Creber, Sun, and Sonn). The second study examines volunteers' response to floods in

Thailand (Chapter 3: Kirdnark & Hale). The next study moves away from disaster response efforts and illustrates the ways in which parents in South Korea volunteer in their children's schools (Chapter 4: Lee & Cho). Chapter 5 (Leroux & Saba) examines the experience of Canadian volunteers working in two different countries: Haiti and Senegal. The final chapter in Section One moves the focus away from the volunteers and instead examines how recipients of volunteer assistance make sense of international volunteers who come to their community to volunteer as part of a vacation. This study (Chapter 6: McAllum & Zahra) looks at voluntourism from the perspective of the people being "toured" rather than from the perspective of the volunteers.

Section Two is titled: US Volunteers Abroad. These chapters explore the efforts of volunteers from the United States working in less affluent or less economically-developed countries. Chapters 7 through 10 examine the experiences of volunteers as they learn to cope with the complexities of living and working in different countries. The first two chapters in this section focus on long-term volunteers. These includes Peace Corps volunteers in Southern Africa (Chapter 7: Malleus) and a variety of long-term volunteers including missionaries (Chapter 8: McNamee, Peterson, & Gould). The next two chapters focus on short-term volunteers including voluntourists teaching English in China (Chapter 9: Xu), and short-term mission trips (Chapter 10: Frederick & Mize Smith). The final two chapters in this section consider how volunteering might serve as a means of advancing cultural domination rather than accomplishing the stated humanitarian goals. Craig and Russo (Chapter 11) examine how volunteers in Rotary International struggle to make sense of programs that are intended to empower local communities, but may instead impose Western values on foreign cultures not prepared to embrace them. Finally, Hanchey (Chapter 12) critically analyzes volunteer implicit efforts to export American values to other countries on the grounds that they are exceptional and need to be shared.

The last section of the book is titled: Cross-cultural Volunteering at Home. This collection of studies focuses on volunteers who are working inside their own national borders to provide services to recent immigrants. This context provides an interesting space in which to examine how intercultural factors may impact the volunteer experience. When working in a foreign country, volunteers may lose sight of the cultural norms and values they bring with them from home. However working with immigrants brings intercultural communication challenges directly to the volunteers' own doorsteps and may encourage deeper self-reflection. To that end, the studies in this section explore how volunteers struggle to negotiate between their own cultural and the world view of the people they are serving. The first study examines a mentoring program in Germany where local volunteers mentor Turkish immigrants (Chapter 13: Pfeiffer). The second study examines the experiences of volunteers in Atlanta, Georgia who are working with immigrants from Bhutan (Chapter 14: Kumar & Dutta).

To summarize, this collection of empirical research is designed to help both scholars and practitioners gain a broader understanding of the ways in which volunteering is understood and practiced outside the United States. This book is designed to serve as a companion piece to the 2013 edited volume by Kramer, Lewis, and Gossett, *Volunteering and Communication: Studies from Multiple Contexts*, which primarily featured studies of volunteerism in the US. Taken together, these two books provide a comprehensive look at the current state of research on volunteering within the communication discipline and identify a number of avenues for future research.

NOTES

1. I would like to thank Michael Kramer for his time, patience, and assistance with this chapter. Without his leadership and hard work, this chapter and book would not exist.
2. There are a number of ways volunteerism rates can be calculated (e.g., spontaneous vs. formal volunteering, donations vs. service work). As such, there may be slight differences throughout this and other chapters in the volunteer participation rates reported for the United States and other countries.

REFERENCES

American Red Cross. (2011). *Guide to services*. Publication of the American Red Cross. http://www. redcross.org/images/MEDIA_CustomProductCatalog/m3140117_GuideToServices.pdf. Accessed March 20, 2014.

American Red Cross. (2014). *Ways to volunteer*. Publication of the American Red Cross. http://www. redcross.org/support/volunteer. Accessed February 21, 2014.

Anheier, H. K., & Salamon, L. M. (1999). Volunteering in cross-national perspective: Initial comparisons. *Law and Contemporary Problems, 62*, 43–65.

Bar-Tura, M., & Fleischer, N. (2004). Civil service in Israel. *Nonprofit and Voluntary Sector Quarterly, Supplement, 33*, 51S–63S.

Bureau of Labor Statistics. (2012). *Volunteering in the United States, 2011*. http://www.bls.gov/news. release/volun.nr0.hm. Accessed January 13, 2012.

Choden, T. (2003). *Traditional forms of volunteerism in Bhutan*. The Centre for Bhutan Studies. Thimphu, Bhutan. http://www.bhutanstudies.org.bt

Congressional Budget Office. (2013, May 8). *A description of the immigrant population—2013 update*. Congressional Budget Office: Nonpartisan Analysis for the US Congress. http://www.cbo.gov/publication/44134. Accessed June 24, 2014.

English, C. (2011, January 18). Civic engagement highest in developed countries: People less likely to volunteer time than donate money, help stranger. *Gallup World*. www.gallup.com. Accessed June 4, 2014.

Ginga, I. (2010, July). *Volunteering in Russia: Facts and figures report*. Brussels, Belgium. European Volunteer Center (CEV).

Gossett, L. M., & Smith, R. A. (2013). Spontaneous volunteers: Understanding member identification among unaffiliated volunteers. In M. W. Kramer, L.K. Lewis, & L.M. Gossett (Eds.), *Volunteering and communication: Studies from multiple contexts* (pp. 321–342). New York, NY: Peter Lang.

Haddad, M. A. (2006). Civic responsibility and patterns of voluntary participation around the world. *Comparative Political Studies, 39*, 1220–1242.

Haddad, M. A. (2010). From undemocratic to democratic civil society: Japan's volunteer fire departments. *The Journal of Asian Studies, 69*, 33–56.

İçduygu, A., Meydanoğlu, Z., & Sert. D. (2011, April). *Civil society in Turkey: At a turning point*. Ankara, Turkey: Third Sector Foundation of Turkey (TÜSEV).

International Labour Office. (2011). *Manual on the measurement of volunteer work*. Geneva, Switzerland. ILO Publications.

Jorgensen, H. (2013, June). *Does it pay to volunteer? The relationship between volunteer work and paid work*. Washington, DC: Center for Economic and Policy Research (CEPR).

Kabelkova, M. (2013, May). *Factors influencing volunteering among the elderly in the Czech Republic*. Unpublished Doctoral Dissertation. Clemson University. USA.

Lesmeister, M. K., Rose, P., & Barnhart, E. (2012). Digital R: International volunteer management. In T.D. Connors (Ed.), *The volunteer management handbook: Leadership strategies for success*. 2nd edition. (pp. R1–R19). Hoboken, NJ: John Wiley.

Lewis, L. K. (2013). An introduction to volunteers. In M. W. Kramer, L. K. Lewis, & L. M. Gossett (Eds.), *Volunteering and communication: Studies from multiple contexts* (pp. 1–22). New York, NY: Peter Lang.

Lim, M. (2012). Unpacking parent involvement: Korean American parent's collective networking. *School Community Journal, 22*, 89–109.

Lukka, P., & Ellis, A. (2001). An exclusive construct? Exploring different cultural concepts of volunteering. *Institute for Volunteering Research*. London, UK. http://www.ivr.org.uk/component/ivr/an-exlusive-construct-exploring-different-cultural-concepts-of-volunteering-vaj-2001-vol-3-number

McBride, A.M., & Lough, B.J. (2010). Access to international volunteering. *Nonprofit Management & Leadership, 21*, 195–208.

McCloughan, P., Batt, W. H., Costine, M., & Scully, D. (2011). *Second European quality of life survey: Participation in volunteering and unpaid work*. Luxembourg. European Foundation for the Improvement of Living and Working Conditions.

Nistor, L., Tîrhaş, C., & Iluţ, P. (2008). Linkages between informal and formal social capital and their relations with forms of trust: A focus on Romania. *Transylvanian Review of Administrative Sciences, 34*, 155–174.

Paker, H. (2004, June). *Social aftershocks: Rent seeking, state failure, and state-civil society relations in Turkey*. Unpublished Doctoral Dissertation. McGill University, Montreal, Canada.

Parboteeah, K. P., Cullen, J. B., & Lim, L. (2004). Formal volunteering: A cross-national test. *Journal of World Business, 39*, 431–441.

Pekkanen, R. (2009). Japan's neighborhood associations: Membership without advocacy. In B. L. Read & R. Pekkanen (Eds.), *Local organizations and urban governance in East and Southeast Asia: Straddling state and society* (pp. 27–57). New York, NY: Routledge.

Pichler, F. & Wallace, C. (2007). Patterns of formal and informal social capital in Europe. *European Sociological Review, 23*, 423–435.

Plagnol, A. C. & Huppert, F. A. (2010, June). Happy to help? Exploring the factors associated with variations in rates of volunteering across Europe. *Social Indicators Research, 97,* 157–176.

Rungu, M. (2010, March 22). *This is Africa*: The BOMA project. http://www.bomaproject.org/2010/03/this-is-africa/. Accessed June 24, 2014.

Sherraden, M. S., Lough, B. J., & McBride, A. M. (2008). Effects of international volunteering and service: Individual and institutional predictors. *Voluntas: International Journal of Voluntary and Nonprofit Organizations, 19,* 395–421.

Sundeen, R. A., Garcia, C., & Raskoff, S. A. (2009). Ethnicity, acculturation, and volunteering to organizations: A comparison of African American, Asian, Hispanic, and White. *Nonprofit and Voluntary Sector Quarterly, 38,* 929–955.

Sundeen, R. A., Garcia, C., & Wang, L. (2007). Volunteer behavior among Asian American groups in the United States. *Journal of Asian American Studies, 10,* 243–281.

Tilly, C., & Tilly, C. (1994). Capitalist work and labor markets. In N. J. Smelser & R. Swedberg (Eds.), *Handbook of economic sociology* (pp. 283–313). Princeton, NJ: Princeton University Press.

Turkish Red Crescent Society (2006). *Country Fact Sheet.* International Federation of Red Cross and Red Crescent Societies. http://www.ifrc.org/docs/appeals/06/Logframes/Europe/TR/Prof.pdf. Accessed July 23, 2013.

Turkish Red Crescent Society. (2013). *Volunteering with Turkish Red Crescent Society* http://genckizilaycekmekoy.com/turkish-red-crescent-youth/ Accessed March 1, 2013.

United Nations Volunteers (2002, October). *Volunteerism and Capacity Development.* The United Nations Development Programme (UNDP). http://www.unv.org/en/news-resources/resources/on-volunteerism/doc/volunteerism-and-capacity-development.html. Accessed February 1, 2014.

United Nations Volunteers. (2011). *Marking the international year of volunteers +10: A global call to action.* www.worldvolunteerweb.org/fileadmin/photodb/IYV_10/Resources/Factsheet_GLOBAL%20CALL%20TO%20ACTION_v5-small_01.pdf. Accessed February 1, 2014.

United Nations Volunteers. (2012). *Creating lasting impact: 2012 annual report.* The United Nations Development Programme (UNDP). http://issuu.com/unvolunteers/docs/unv_ar2012_creating_lasting_impact. Accessed January 14, 2014.

Wiktorowicz, Q. (2000). Civil society as social control: State power in Jordan. *Comparative Politics, 33,* 43–62.

Wilson, J. (2000). Volunteering. *Annual Review of Sociology, 26,* 215–240.

Wilson, J. & Musick, M. (1997). Who cares? Toward an integrated theory of volunteer work. *American Sociological Review, 62,* 694–713.

Wozowczyk, M. & Massarelli, N. (2011, March). European Union labour force survey: Annual results 2010. *Population and social conditions: Statistics in Focus.* Luxembourg. Eurostat: European Commission.

Section 1:
Volunteers Around the Globe

Developing Public Disaster Communication FOR Volunteer Recruitment: Understanding Volunteer Motivations

LYNETTE M. McDONALD
University of Southern Queensland

MELISSA CREBER
HUICHUN SUN
LINDSEY SONN
University of Queensland

In January 2011 the Brisbane River burst its banks and inundated the central business district, at least 28,000 homes (Sweet, 2011) and 2,500 businesses in Brisbane, Australia's third largest city. The Brisbane floods became Australia's most expensive natural disaster (van den Honert & McAneney, 2011), causing billions of dollars in damage. As the floods receded, thousands of well-meaning volunteers converged on the worse-hit areas, resulting in confusion and misdirection (Sweet, 2011). Both the local government (the Brisbane City Council) and the Queensland government coordinated volunteer deployment, directing volunteers to register either online via the volunteering organization, Volunteering Queensland, or in person at one of four volunteer registration centers. This resulted in 62,000 registered volunteers (Volunteering Queensland, 2011), many of whom were bussed directly from registration centers to affected areas to help with the clean-up. There was likely triple that number in unregistered volunteers (Vogler, 2011). Dubbed the "Mud Army" by the media, these volunteers cleaned affected houses, businesses, footpaths, and roads (Vogler, 2011) awash with sewage-contaminated mud, armed simply with shovels, brooms, mops, buckets, and scrubbing brushes. The efforts of the "Mud Army," considered by the Brisbane City Council to be the biggest volunteer effort in Australia's history, saved millions of dollars in clean-up costs (Vogler, 2011) for local and state governments and insurance companies.

UNDERSTANDING SPONTANEOUS VOLUNTEERS

Spontaneous volunteers who converge on disaster areas play a critical response role, often being first on the scene and typically trusted by victims. The term "spontaneous volunteers" refers to individuals who provide assistance immediately following a disaster (Lowe & Fothergill, 2003). The sometimes overwhelming number of spontaneous volunteers, from both within and outside the disaster-affected community, poses significant challenges for disaster relief and recovery services (Barraket, Keast, Newton, Walters, & James, 2013). Characteristically, as spontaneous volunteers are seen to hinder relief efforts, government and emergency management agencies resist harnessing this workforce (Drabek & McEntire, 2003). Yet these untrained volunteers are integral to accomplishing many disaster recovery tasks. Indeed, most response work is carried out by community members who are present or nearby during a disaster (Lowe & Fothergill, 2003).

In order to effectively recruit and manage this workforce, understanding spontaneous volunteers and their motivations is critical to establishing effective disaster communication plans (Lowe & Fothergill, 2003). Since disasters often generate powerful emotions and different responses (Beyerlein & Sikkink, 2008), it is important to understand the role of emotions in motivating behavior. Although emotion is intensely researched in other domains (e.g., organizational psychology, management), its influence in volunteering and disaster research has received little attention. Further, as theories (e.g., attribution theory) suggest that feelings of responsibility are requisite for emotion, their role in motivating volunteering requires investigation.

In parallel with volunteer convergence onto physical disaster sites, convergence behavior is now evident online (Hughes, Palen, Sutton, Liu, & Vieweg, 2008). In the 2011 Brisbane floods, many individuals used social media such as Facebook and Twitter not only to exchange information, but for coordinating relief efforts (Knaus, 2011). The actual and potential use of social media in disasters has generated intense interest. Although the use of social media for communication and information exchange in disasters has been studied in the 2011 Brisbane flood research (e.g., Barraket et al., 2013; Cheong & Cheong, 2011), investigation of social media for volunteer recruitment has only recently attracted research attention (e.g., Jones, 2013; Macias, Hilyard, & Freimuth, 2009). The widespread adoption and use of social media by members of the public during disasters (Alexander, 2013) suggest that social media is increasingly critical to future disaster management and relief efforts. Further, it is important to understand how—or whether—social media affect the interpersonal bonds known to influence volunteer recruitment.

Consequently, this research investigated factors motivating the spontaneous volunteering behavior of the "Mud Army" following the 2011 Brisbane floods, specifically, the role of emotions, responsibility feelings, and peer pressure. As anecdotal evidence suggested that many volunteers used social media to coordinate volunteering efforts, such as Facebook, the research also examined the role of social media in volunteer recruitment. This study concludes with implications for disaster communication.

THEORETICAL PERSPECTIVES

Multiple factors influence volunteer actions in disaster situations, including personal motivations (Betancourt, 1990). Motivation as a factor driving volunteering is congruent with Guy and Patton's (1989) belief that altruistic motivations cause individuals to behave in a prosocial manner towards others without thought of intrinsic reward. Several theoretical approaches that have been suggested to understand prosocial behavior and spontaneous volunteers' motivations, both extrinsic and intrinsic, are discussed next.

Intrinsic Factors

Several models of prosocial behavior have been applied to explain the intrinsic or personal factors which motivate helping behavior. The negative state relief model (Cialdini, Schaller, Houlihan, Arps, Fultz, & Beaman, 1987) argues that helping behavior is motivated by negative emotions. In contrast, the empathy-altruism model views prosocial behavior as dependent upon an individual's own emotional experiences of empathy for others combined with responsibility feelings (Batson, 1987). A third perspective is that the divergent effects of distinct emotions mobilize volunteering behavior (Beyerlein & Sikkink, 2008). As disasters often generate powerful emotions and different responses, emotions matter for disaster relief (Beyerlein & Sikkink, 2008) and understanding their function is important. All three behavioral motivators—negative emotions, positive emotions, and feelings of responsibility—were likely associated with volunteering behavior in the Brisbane floods.

Negative emotions. Some scholarship suggests that not all helping behavior is altruistically motivated. According to Cialdini et al.'s (1987) negative state relief model, helping behavior is motivated by an egoistic desire to relieve negative feelings in order to return to a positive emotional state. When we view others in distress, it produces a negative emotional response within us, such as sadness, prompting helping behavior. Thus altruistic behaviors are conducted for the egoistic reason of personal mood management to reduce our own distress (Cialdini et al., 1987).

Negative emotions motivating volunteering during disasters were identified in three studies. In examining emotional responses to the 9/11 New York terrorist attacks, Beyerlein and Sikkink (2008) found that those who experienced sorrow as a disaster response, compared to those not experiencing sorrow, were 46% more likely to volunteer to help. Barraket et al. (2013) also identified negative volunteer emotions in a survey of registered Australian disaster volunteers, and in interviews with registered Brisbane flood volunteers. In the survey, first time Australian disaster volunteers rated "upset at what was happening" higher than more experienced groups, suggesting this as a volunteering motivational factor (Barraket et al., 2013). In the 2011 Brisbane floods interviews, registered volunteers considered that their emotional response to the unfolding crisis was the strongest factor which motivated their volunteering (Barraket et al., 2013). This included feeling guilty about not being directly flood-affected (Barraket et al., 2013). However, specific negative emotions associated with volunteering appears little investigated.

Positive emotions. Batson's (1987) empathy-altruism hypothesis contends that prosocial behavior is contingent upon one's emotional experience of empathy for others. Empathy is characterized by concern for another person's situation (Betancourt, 1990). Empathic emotions, which include feeling sympathetic, compassionate, and moved, enhance helping behavior (Betancourt, 1990). Individuals who are able to empathize with others are driven to help (Betancourt, 1990). Those with this prosocial personality orientation have an enduring tendency to feel concern for others' welfare, driving philanthropic actions (Penner & Finkelstein, 1998). Embedded within this prosocial personality orientation are feelings of personal responsibility for others' well-being, particularly those in distress, which becomes a motivating force to assist those in need (Penner & Finkelstein, 1998). Thus, two intrinsic motivators for volunteering are feelings of empathy and responsibility.

Empathy as a driver of spontaneous disaster volunteering was identified in studies by Safrilsyah, Jusoff and Fadhil (2009), and Barraket et al. (2013). Following the 2004 tsunami which devastated (among other regions) the Indonesian province of Aceh, killing more than 130,000 of its people, the suffering of victims generated empathy amongst Aceh tsunami volunteers, forming the dominant volunteering motivation (Safrilsyah et al., 2009). In the 2011 Brisbane floods, as well as responding with negative feelings, registered volunteers reported positive feelings, such as feeling lucky (Barraket et al., 2013). These two studies indicate that various positive emotions may drive volunteering behavior as a disaster response. However, to date, the variety of positive emotions associated with volunteering behavior appears to be unidentified.

Mixed Emotions. The studies reviewed in the sections on positive and negative emotions suggest that both positive and negative emotions coexist as a disaster response, motivating volunteering behavior. This contrasts with Batson, O'Quin, Fultz, Vanderplas, & Isen's (1983) suggestion that prosocial behavior is contingent on empathy. Yet, observing a person in need usually provokes mixed emotions of empathy and personal distress which occur simultaneously and influence helping behavior (Carrera, Oceja, Caballero, Muñoz, López-Pérez, & Ambrona, 2013). Each emotion set has a very different nature: empathy is an *other-oriented* emotion that evokes the altruistic motivation to reduce the other's need; personal distress is a *self-oriented* emotion that evokes the egoistic motivation to reduce one's own aversive arousal (Batson et al., 1983). These positive and negative emotions therefore drive helping behavior in distinct ways. This is supported by Carrera et al.'s (2013) research results.

Carrera et al. (2013) identified that helping behavior is determined by the emotion which dominates at the end of an unfolding emotional experience, combined with how psychologically easy it is to avoid helping. If empathy is stronger than personal distress, our aim is to alleviate the victim's suffering, no matter whether it is easy or hard to avoid helping (Carrera et al., 2013). Conversely, if personal distress is stronger than empathy, helping behavior will be high only when we think that our discomfort will last unless we help; but if we think that our discomfort will vanish by leaving the situation, helping behavior will be low (Carrera et al., 2013).

These findings suggest that positive, negative, or a mix of both emotions may prompt initial volunteering behavior. Congruent with Beyerlein and Sikkink's (2008) contention that the divergent effects of distinct emotions mobilize volunteering behavior, it is posited that positive and negative emotions are associated both with initial and continuing volunteering behavior in the Brisbane floods. This leads to the first research question:

RQ1: What was the role of emotions in motivating volunteering behavior during the Brisbane floods?

Feelings of responsibility. As noted earlier in discussion of Batson's (1987) empathy-altruism hypothesis, personality factors (the prosocial personality) determine levels of experienced empathy which then drives helping behavior. Embedded within this prosocial personality orientation are feelings of responsibility for those in distress (Penner & Finkelstein, 1998). Individuals' personal feelings of responsibility drive them to help others in need (Beyerlein & Sikkink, 2008) without thought of personal reward. This basic human need to help others is the strongest motivator driving volunteering (Guy & Patton, 1989). Volunteers help others because they believe that they *should* (Tong, Hung, & Yuen, 2011).

Research on Hurricane Katrina (Michel, 2007), 9/11 (Beyerlein & Sikkink, 2008), and the Brisbane floods (Barraket et al., 2013) identified feelings of personal responsibility–the "should" and "ought" to help factors–as motivating volunteering behavior. Following Hurricane Katrina, more than 92 percent of those surveyed (33 percent volunteers/64 percent non-volunteers) felt that they had a personal responsibility to help the victims (Michel, 2007). In response to the 9/11 New York terrorist attacks, those who volunteered, compared to those who did not, felt they had a moral responsibility to help others in need (Beyerlein & Sikkink, 2008). Feelings of responsibility to help also emerged in two studies (survey/interviews) on registered Australian disaster volunteers (Barraket et al., 2013). Although Michel's (2007) results indicates that feelings of responsibility do not always translate into volunteering action, it is expected that personal feelings of responsibility were associated with spontaneous volunteering in this Brisbane flood volunteer study. This leads to the second research question:

RQ2: What role did feelings of responsibility play in motivating volunteering behavior in the Brisbane floods?

Extrinsic Factors

A number of external factors are considered to influence volunteering behavior, including social network ties or peer pressure, and communication factors, specifically social media networks. Their role in volunteering behavior is discussed in this section.

Social network ties. The social networks that develop through friendships with peers can strongly influence volunteer motivations and actions (Jones, 2006). Strong social network ties encourage pro-social behavior in volunteering, creating a "behavior expectation" for members within a social group to help others (Tong et al., 2011, p. 351). Many individuals only volunteer when asked, and there is a strong social pressure to participate when a friend or close acquaintance asks (Freeman, 1997; Jones, 2006). Research on social ties found that the closer individuals are to friends and family, and the more hours they spend interacting with them, the more likely they are to volunteer and to dedicate more hours to volunteering (Jones, 2006; Tong et al., 2011). For this reason, volunteer recruitment is most successfully conducted through asking friends, family, and co-workers to join in volunteering efforts (Freeman, 1997). Congruent with these studies, it is expected that peer pressure from family, friends, or those in other social networks (e.g., religious organizations, youth groups) played a role in motivating disaster volunteer response in the Brisbane floods. This leads to the third research question:

> RQ3: What role did peer pressure from family, friendship, or other social networks (including social media), play in encouraging volunteering behavior?

Communication and social media. With each new disaster, more and more individuals turn first to online sources, including social media, for the most recent information on the disaster and relief efforts (Hughes et al., 2008). Social media includes social networking sites (such as Facebook), blogs, micro-blogs (such as Twitter), social book marking, social networking, forums, and the sharing of audio, photographic and video files (Balana, 2012). During the 2011 Brisbane floods, social networking technologies raised public crisis awareness and kept the public updated (Barraket et al., 2013).

Volunteers use social media not only to receive information, but to organize relief efforts through Facebook, Twitter, Wikipedia (Hughes et al., 2008), and blogging sites (Macias et al., 2009). Social media allows the public to dispense with "information gatekeepers" (Alexander, 2013), including disaster response organizations who traditionally manage the volunteer workforce, as identified in four studies.

Following Hurricane Katrina in 2005, bloggers used the Internet to organize such forms of assistance as manual labor, donations, rescue assistance, and offers of temporary housing (Macias et al., 2009). During the Haiti earthquake in 2010, volunteers used Twitter to create disaster awareness and mobilize help (Yates & Paquette, 2011). During the 2011 Brisbane floods, an analysis of more than 6,000 Twitter tweets highlighted that flood volunteering information was included in re-tweets (Cheong & Cheong, 2011). In the immediate aftermath of Hurricane Sandy in 2012, activists set up their own emergency aid through an informal online movement called "Occupy Sandy," establishing ad hoc feeding and supply stations in New York and New Jersey neighborhoods (Jones, 2013). These studies suggest that social media plays an increasingly important role in volunteering, in particular, in aiding volunteer recruitment. However, what isn't known is the role that social media played in individuals' recruiting of others for volunteering in the Brisbane flood cleanup. This leads to the final question:

> RQ4: What role did social media play in volunteer recruitment in the Brisbane floods?

METHOD

Participants

Four months after the Brisbane floods, 30 volunteers who formed part of the "Mud Army" cleanup crew were interviewed. Participants were initially recruited via purposive sampling. Purposive sampling aims to select interviewees who are most relevant to address the research questions (Bryman, Becker, & Sempik, 2008). To ensure that study participants were "Mud Army" volunteers, a study call for cleanup volunteers was issued first on the volunteer registration website, Volunteer Queensland, then via snowball sampling. Snowball sampling refers to the practice whereby participants are asked to suggest additional individuals who also may be qualified to participate (Horton, Macve, & Struyven, 2004).

Prospective participants were emailed the research information sheet, a consent form assuring interviewee confidentiality, and a brief questionnaire to fill out and bring to their interview. This questionnaire requested details about participants' number of days of flood work, previous volunteer work, whether they were registered or unregistered volunteers, proximity to the flood (home/workplace), and number of days off work due to flooding. Also requested were demographic details (gender, age, education, health, relationship status, number of children, income), which prior research had identified as factors that influenced volunteering behavior.

The participants volunteered for between one to ten days (M_{days} = 3.7) of flood relief work, were aged between 18 to 61 years (M_{age} = 31), earned between US$18,000 to $155,000, and there was an even gender mix. Most were unregistered first-time volunteers who lived adjacent to flooded areas.

Interviews

Questions (available from first author on request) for the semi-structured interviews were pre-tested with six "Mud Army" volunteers recruited via convenience sampling. Semi-structured interviews were used because they facilitate exploration of the subjective meanings and interpretations that people give to their experiences and allow for unexpected and interesting data to emerge (Horton, et al., 2004). Congruent with Horton et al.'s (2004) recommendation, interviews were digitally sound recorded for accuracy, with the participants' permission. The interviews lasted 20 minutes on average.

Analysis

The data were analyzed using thematic analysis following Boyatzis' (1998) guidelines. Thematic analysis encodes qualitative information and so requires the use of an explicit "code" or list of themes (Boyatzis, 1998). A theme is a pattern found in information and may be generated deductively from theory and prior research, or inductively by developing new themes (Boyatzis, 1998). In this case, themes were generated from theory, with new themes also emerging.

The data analysis took an iterative approach, cycling back and forth between the transcripts to identify themes from the literature: emotions, responsibility, social networks and peer pressure, social media and others. To sort emotions into relevant categories, mainstream psychology research on emotional lexicon was applied. Shaver, Schwartz, Kirson, and O'Connor's (1987) list of 135 emotion words was used to sort articulated emotions into six commonly-accepted emotion categories: positively-valenced emotions of joy and love, negatively-valenced emotions of anger, fear, and sadness, and an emotion often considered neutrally-valenced, surprise. For extra words not on Shaver et al.'s (1987) list, Storm and Storm's (1987) cluster of 193 semantically-homogeneous groups of emotion terms, in categories highly similar to Shaver et al. (1987), was used. To elucidate results, quotations are provided with indications of those that exemplified typical statements and those which were exemplars of less commonly held opinions.

RESULTS

RQ1: The Role of Emotions

RQ1 considered the role of emotions in motivating volunteering behavior during the Brisbane floods. The volunteers recalled a variety of emotions which occurred both before and during five situations: while viewing flood damage via media reports and on-site, towards flood victims, experienced as part of the cleanup crew, towards the cleanup work, and in response to work recognition. For each situation, reported emotions were a mix of positive, negative, and neutral emotions; no one situation elicited a single category of emotions. Participants articulated 46 different emotion words across the six emotion categories. For negative emotions, participants used ten sadness words, six fear words, and four anger words. For positive emotions, participants used eighteen joy words and five love words. Three surprise words (neutral emotion) were used. Table 1 lists the emotion words used, with asterisks next to words repeated by multiple volunteers. The situation that elicited the vast majority of emotion words (overwhelmingly positive) was the cleanup work.

Table 1. Elicited Emotion Words.

	Negative emotions			Positive emotions		Neutral
Situation	Anger	Fear	Sadness	Joy	Love	Surprise
Viewing floods on TV or firsthand	Frustrating	Concerned Distressed Worried Disturbed Frightened	Sorry* Sad* Upset Bad Awful Guilt Embarrassed			Shocked* Amazed Surprised
Towards flood victims			Sorry* Sad * Awful		Compassion* Empathy Sympathetic	
As part of the cleanup crew	Despise			Proud* Happy Enjoyment Good Nice	Compassion* Lovely	Amazed
Towards cleanup work	Disgusting Frustrated	Fear Worried Distressed Con-cerned	Sad Depressing Down Disap-pointing (not being called up)	Happy* Good* Pleased* Proud* Fun* Satisfied Elated Rewarding Gratifying Glad Excited Warm Light-hearted Nice Amusing Upbeat		Surprise Amazed
In re-sponse to work recogni-tion			Embar-rassed*	Proud* Grateful	Appreciated*	

Negative emotions. The majority of negative emotion content, predominantly sadness and fear, was primarily felt in response to viewing the floods on TV and firsthand, and towards the flood victims. Just a few anger words were used. Towards the flood damage, volunteers reported primarily sadness and surprise category words, exemplified by a male university student's response: "I felt pretty bad…pretty upset and in shock as well. I never thought it would be so bad." Others, particularly those whose neighbors were flooded, felt guilty or embarrassed (sadness words) about not being affected. Fear words applied to personal distress at the situation.

The situation garnering the second most negative emotion words, mainly fear and sadness category words, was the cleanup work. A number of volunteers used fear words in relation to concerns about becoming ill from sewage-contaminated mud, but all who raised this also light-heartedly downplayed it. Anger words (disgust, frustrated, despise) were used mainly to describe cleanup situations. For example, disgust was used to describe feelings of being covered in filth, but volunteers even provided a lighter take on that. For example, one young woman volunteering with friends said, "It was really good–the volunteers that were doing the cooking would actually hand-feed the people working, because you couldn't pick anything up by hand."

Some registered volunteers used sadness and anger words (disappointment, frustration) when they were not called upon to help. They still found their own sites to work on. Volunteers turned away from helping in some suburbs reported the same emotions in the aftermath of the flood, when it became evident that not all suburbs received the same degree of assistance. Volunteers blamed the media for focusing coverage on particular suburbs, with these suburbs attracting more volunteers.

As part of the cleanup crew, an older married male volunteer voiced anger stating, "There were lots of interesting community dynamics…a clear separation between onlookers versus those who gave help. Onlookers were despised."

Several volunteers linked their helping behavior with pre-empting potential negative emotion states. For example, one young female volunteer who volunteered with her friends said, "If I didn't start helping, probably I would feel a little bit hopeless and guilty."

Positive emotions. The majority of positive emotion category (love, joy) words reported were in response to the cleanup work (far more than for any other situation), for being part of the cleanup crew, in response to recognition for volunteer work, and towards the flood-affected. The cleanup work, and seeing its results, elicited a very high number of joy category words. Most volunteers highlighted the general positive spirit on the streets, the socializing amongst volunteers, and the sense of community spirit. As one male university student said:

Among the volunteers it was ridiculously positive, I've never seen so many positive people in such a confined area...and it's good to know that...if help is needed that people will show up and that they are very friendly...(we were) sharing some interesting stories and conversations, pulling out some jokes...then there were the sausage sizzles....

As part of the cleanup crew, participants also reported a strong sense of pride and other joy emotions. As one said, "...everyone got in and did what they had to do and were happy to do that...(there was) a sense of pride and fulfillment."

In regards to recognition for their work, all volunteers spoke about feeling appreciated for help provided to home and business owners, with several even embarrassed by it. For example, a young female volunteer in casual employment said she felt, "Almost too appreciated...I wished I could have helped more that I almost felt bad (that) I was so appreciated. It seemed like such a small thing to do." Others mentioned how touched they were by that appreciation.

Neutral emotions. The cleanup work also evoked words of surprise among several volunteers in regards to the difference that a small number of people could make. Others felt surprise upon arrival at flooded sites. As one young female volunteer said, "You don't get smell through television and social media. That's what really hits you...the smell and the mud."

Overall, although each situation attracted a variety of emotions, there was a clear divide between situations attracting strong positive or negative emotional responses. Negative emotions were experienced in response to viewing flood damage and the plight of those affected, in response to non-volunteers, and was reported by registered volunteers not being called to help. In contrast, the cleanup work attracted an overwhelmingly positive emotional response, and by far the largest number and variety of emotions words.

RQ2: Feelings of Responsibility

RQ2 considered the role of feelings of responsibility in motivating spontaneous volunteering behavior. Most volunteers explicitly stated that they felt no obligation or expectation from others to help. Instead, most stated that it was something they "just had to do," indicating they felt either an innate need to help or a sense of responsibility. One said, "You're responsible to help because you're part of the community. You couldn't sit there and not help."

Three volunteers linked flood proximity to feeling greater responsibility to help. One said, "I think generally you should help if you can....But if it's somewhere closer, the feeling's stronger." These comments suggest that innate feelings of responsibility, boosted by flood proximity, motivate volunteering behavior.

RQ3: Family and Friendship Networks

RQ3 considered the role that peer pressure from family or friendship networks (including social media networks) played in encouraging volunteering behavior. As noted earlier, although most volunteers stated that they experienced no expectation from others to help, five younger volunteers either explicitly or implicitly mentioned feeling peer pressure to volunteer from friends or family. For example, a young female student stated that both her father and boyfriend pressured her to help:

> I definitely felt a duty to help—it was coming from my dad more than anything else—like the whole time my dad kept saying, "C'mon get down there and help...you should be getting out to help...And also my boyfriend was helping out and was really eager to get going and if I did go, then I wouldn't feel bad. It's like peer pressure.

However, no volunteers mentioned other social groups, except Facebook friends with another female university student indicating that her friends' Facebook postings prompted her volunteering. For those not strongly motivated by innate responsibility feelings, peer pressure from family and friends, including the Facebook forum, appeared to play a role in driving volunteering.

RQ4: The Role of Social Media

RQ4 asked about the role that social media played in organizing volunteer recruitment. At least half the volunteers used social media to obtain flood information, particularly through the Queensland Police Service Facebook page and Twitter site. A smaller number of others used social media to find out which areas needed volunteers, and to liaise on flood relief action plans. As one said:

> On Facebook we were contacting friends, reading their updates of what was going on, where they were, going through photos and videos they were uploading...Going through Facebook and seeing which areas were massive disaster zones and which were still okay to get to. It played a huge role; it told me exactly where to go. I had friends logging on saying 'my house is completely destroyed, I live here, let me know if you can come,' and we'd just hit reply and go "we're on our way. "

However, one volunteer (a married man in his 30s) who used both Facebook and Twitter suggested that Twitter was the more effective forum to match up victims with volunteers noting, "With Twitter, it was so much easier; you just search for a hash tag and immediately it would come up."

In separate interviews, two young female volunteers speculated about the role of ego involvement in motivating volunteers to post social media status updates about their volunteering. One said, "...people might want to volunteer so they can post it on Facebook....A lot of people would have been like, 'Going to volunteer today, good for me,' kind of thing." The role of ego involvement is discussed further in the next section. Overall, the interviews made it clear that social media, specifically Facebook and Twitter, were used as tools for both information-gathering and volunteer recruitment and organization during the Brisbane floods.

DISCUSSION

It is well known that, following disasters, people will converge en masse onto disaster sites to help others. Therefore understanding the multiple influences that drive this assistance is critical for disaster response organizations to communicate with, mobilize, and direct the massive spontaneous volunteer workforce that emerges following disasters. To aid this understanding, this study examined the role of emotions, feelings of responsibility, social network pressures, and social media in motivating volunteer behavior in the 2011 Brisbane floods.

First, results indicated that volunteers reported the experience of both positive and negative emotions, rather than one emotion set, but that different emotions were elicited by different stimuli. These recalled emotions were reported as occurring prior to and during the volunteering experience, indicating that they were neither fixed nor stable. Strong negative emotions, mainly sadness and some fear and surprise, were recalled in response to flood images experienced either first-hand on-site or second-hand via the media. However, positive empathic emotions were also felt towards flood victims. Both positive and negative emotions were associated with initial volunteering behavior. This is congruent with Beyerlein and Sikkink's (2008) 9/11 study results which found that both empathy and sorrow were associated with the initial drive to volunteer. Consequently, neither the empathy-altruism model (which states that positive emotions motivate helping), nor the negative state relief model (which states that negative emotions motivate helping) fully explain volunteers' reported emotion response. Instead, this implies that a new model encompassing both emotion categories is needed to explain initial disaster volunteer motivation.

In contrast to flood- and victim-emotion responses, strong positive emotions, particularly joy, dominated volunteers' reports of their flood cleanup work. This centered on three situations: towards the work itself, being part of the "Mud Army" cleanup crew, and in response to work recognition. During the cleanup work, despite the grueling effort and long hours spent in uncomfortable situations, volunteers spoke of the strong sense of community, of the positive atmosphere with everyone helping everyone else, of the fun of socializing, and the innate sense of pride that was elicited for their own personal role in making a difference in flood recovery efforts. These findings suggest that positive emotions play a role in encouraging continuing volunteering behavior, overriding negative emotions and concerns. They indicate that volunteers experienced a dynamic positive emotional response during the clean-up activities which differed considerably to those prompting the initial volunteering.

Results also indicated that volunteering behavior may be used to avoid or preempt potential negative emotions that would occur if no help was provided. This was articulated by the young woman earlier reported who stated that, "if I did go, then I wouldn't feel bad." These feelings appeared to be tied to peer pressure to volunteer from family and friends, including social media friends.

In sum, this study demonstrated that a variety of emotions played a role in mobilizing volunteering behavior, extending knowledge of the volunteer emotion experience. Emotions, both positive and negative, prompt volunteering behavior and specific emotions appear linked to different behaviors. Further, positive emotions, apart from empathy, are involved in extended volunteering, and volunteering may be used as a strategy to avoid negative emotion experience.

But there is a need to explain why the volunteer mood during the cleanup was, as noted earlier, "ridiculously positive" with a street party-like atmosphere prevailing. The negative state relief model (Cialdini et al., 1987) states that helping behavior increases self-esteem. As an extension to this model, it is suggested that the greater the time and effort invested by volunteers, the greater the personal return in the form of higher self-esteem. That is, longer periods of volunteering may result in greater feelings of pride, which in turn, increases self-esteem. An alternate explanation may come from the socialization literature about harsh fraternity "hazing." Hazing refers to the abuse of new or prospective group members whereby initiates endure a harsh ordeal and, in turn, value that group membership to explain why they suffered the ordeal (Cimino, 2013). Thus, the volunteers who endured dreadful cleanup conditions may have made sense of it by becoming part of the fraternity that was the highly regarded "Mud Army."

The second finding that feelings of responsibility created a strong innate drive to help matched other research. Similar to studies on Hurricane Katrina (Michel, 2007), 9/11 (Beyerlein & Sikkink, 2008), and the Brisbane floods (Barraket et al., 2013), these volunteers said they "should" and "ought" to help, indicating that they felt an urgent, moral responsibility to find "someone, anyone" they could help. Registered volunteers, frustrated by not being called upon, sought out their own volunteering opportunities. In line with Batson (1987) and colleagues' empathy-altruism hypothesis, this suggests that feeling responsible to help is primarily driven by internal forces, rather than external pressures. Further, three volunteers explicitly linked living adjacent to flooded areas to greater feelings of responsibility.

From a volunteer:

(If) somebody needed help...you just do it. You help that house to a certain point, and you move on to the next house....I took work off for two days...then an additional three days flood leave....I shoveled mud, I dug roads, I scraped mud from footpaths, I helped empty out houses—that was for about the first three to four days—and ended up with blisters and cuts on my hands....(There was) a very strong sense of community, a strong sense of fun and enjoyment...people (were) just coming from everywhere. They were positive...getting in, having a laugh, and getting it done as quickly as possible. Then two other ladies with me...we started up a food store, driving around the area...providing food and drink...I was driving around, handing out food, and this woman chases me down the road....she said, "I've got nothing else to give, but I have to thank you," and she gave me a small bottle of moisturizer....I burst into tears because she had nothing left...it was the last thing she had to give. I feel proud (about) what I did...and almost...embarrassed. (Volunteering was) fantastic, heart-breaking, wonderful, sad.

A non-registered woman in a flood-affected suburb who volunteered with her husband

Data, like the volunteer quote included in the insert, suggested the link between responsibility feelings and mixed emotions. Additional research is required to establish the existence of any emotion-responsibility-action causal model.

The third finding was in regards to participants experiencing peer pressure from family and friends to volunteer. The investigation of social networks' role in encouraging disaster volunteering yielded similar results to studies by Tong et al. (2011) and Jones (2006) who found that close personal ties encourage civil volunteering. Although the previous section indicated that most volunteers felt an innate responsibility to help, a small number of younger volunteers were encouraged to volunteer either via subtle peer pressure, usually via social media, or by more directly voiced expectations from friends and family. Previous research on Gen Y has indicated that they rank comparatively lower than other age cohorts in both their commitment to social responsibility and desire to have a strong social impact (Ng, Schweitzer, & Lyons, 2010). Further, many people would prefer to let others volunteer in their stead, but feel morally obligated to help when asked to do so (Freeman, 1997). These two findings may explain why responsibility feelings did not motivate all volunteers.

The fourth finding was in regards to the role of social media in volunteer recruitment. A number of younger volunteers promoted volunteering among their friendship networks or accessed social media for up-to-date information on areas requiring assistance, allowing them to bypass volunteer registration and to determine for themselves their helping behavior. Although (Bruns, Burgess, Crawford, & Shaw, 2012) noted the high use of Twitter during the Brisbane floods, only one participant mentioned its use in assisting volunteering behavior. With the increase in online disaster convergence behavior (see Macias et al., 2009), and the little existing research on the use of social media in volunteer recruitment, the use of various forms of social media as a tool for volunteer mobilization, as well as its use in creating peer pressure, require further research.

An additional factor that may have motivated volunteering, yet does not appear to have attracted research attention, is an ego-serving motivation. It was earlier noted that two young female volunteers ascribed to others a "look what I did" motive, noting use of Facebook as a tool for self-promotion of volunteers' altruistic behavior. This ego-serving motivation has been described in the social psychology literature as "competitive altruism." Competitive altruism is a social phenomenon whereby individuals attempt to out-compete each other in terms of generosity (Hardy & Van Vugt, 2006). Future research might assist with uncovering these motivations. In sum, the research findings indicate that theory in disaster volunteering may need to consider a model that encompasses the role of positive and negative emotions, feelings of responsibility, the importance of peer pressure and the role and self-serving motivations for volunteering.

This study had a small sample size, an age group skewed to the younger demographic, and made some use of snowball sampling, all of which limit data generalizability. As participants' volunteer work occurred several months prior to the interviews, thoughts and feelings that occurred were recalled and, most likely, revised and reconstructed. Thus post hoc "sensemaking" about motivations and feelings may have occurred. Further, a social desirability bias in the data is likely as participants may have presented their "best face" to the interviewer.

CONCLUSION AND RECOMMENDATIONS

Although volunteer convergence onto disaster sites may be problematic for relief efforts, we agree with Lowe and Fothergill's (2003) call for a reframing of spontaneous volunteers as a resource for proactive engagement in disaster response and recovery. This section summarizes the key disaster management and communication lessons emerging from this research.

Disasters evoke emotions that are ubiquitous and dynamic, motivating an outpouring of community help. In line with Barraket et al.'s (2013) findings that first-time disaster volunteers experienced more sadness than more experienced volunteers, the findings from this study suggest that negative emotions act to motivate first-time volunteers. Volunteer recruitment communication therefore needs to highlight the distress and suffering of disaster victims to evoke sadness to prompt volunteering behavior as a coping mechanism. As Carrera et al.'s (2013) studies demonstrated, helping behavior is also determined by how psychologically easy it is to avoid helping, noting the importance of strong empathy to overcome this inertia. It suggests the importance of arousing empathy for victims as well as feelings of responsibility to help. Thus, key messages should emphasize that this is happening in *your* community to people like *you* who are now doing it tough. Carrera et al. (2013) also noted that, if observers are aware that the victims' suffering will continue after they leave the situation, no matter what the dominant emotion elicited, they are driven to help. Particularly in the aftermath of the disaster, as volunteer numbers start to wane, it is suggested that key media announcements need to highlight that victims' continuing distress will only be speedily resolved with ongoing assistance, and that each individual's help can make a real difference.

Some ego involvement was evident via reports of volunteers posting status updates on Facebook about their volunteering. This may have been encouraged via the media's strongly positive portrayal of "Mud Army" volunteers. Although no research on ego-driven volunteering was identified, it suggests that communicated messages may be able to encourage ego-driven volunteering via stories portraying volunteers as "local heroes."

As this and other research (e.g., Bruns et al., 2012) emphasizes, social media is important not just as a communication tool, but because it can provide subtle peer pressure to volunteer, particularly for younger participants. Highlighting recommendations to volunteer with groups of friends may form a useful recruitment strategy, particularly for the younger demographic. It may be helpful to identify for the media examples of such groups to provide evidence of the positive effects of volunteering and the "can do" spirit. In particular, the focus on volunteers' pride in their achievements may help to extend the duration of volunteering.

To avoid a tsunami of spontaneous volunteers descending upon impacted sites to help "somebody, anybody," harnessing and directing this volunteer workforce is a critical first imperative. In an information vacuum, volunteers are increasingly likely to bypass disaster management organizations and use information from social media to select their own sites to assist. Disaster response organizations therefore require coordinated efforts providing key messages that instruct, direct, and deploy volunteers to sites where their efforts are most needed. These key messages need to be communicated using integrated mass media and social media communication strategies. This requires that emergency service organizations review both their current media and social media practices and online presence. In particular, comprehensive, flexible strategies using the most popular social media platforms (e.g., Facebook, Twitter) of the time need to be established providing highly frequent disaster updates. Further, in line with Bruns et al.'s (2012) recommendation, coordination between different emergency and government services and the media, plus disaster response organizations' use of one Twitter hashtag (rather than each organization providing one) as the source of volunteering and recovery information, will minimize conflicting messages and correct inaccurate rumors, while disseminating crucial emergency information. This was exemplified in the campaign "Occupy Sandy" which mastered the call-to-action: each tweeted message indicated exactly how interested volunteers could help (Jones, 2013).

Brisbane flood reports suggested that most volunteers, like those interviewed, were unregistered, converging on areas receiving strong media attention. Anecdotal evidence suggests that TV news coverage focused on areas closest, and most road-accessible, to news stations. These areas attracted so many volunteers that flooding evidence was rapidly eradicated, even though many other areas struggled with on-going recovery efforts weeks, and even months later. This suggests that continuous evaluation of social and mass media disaster coverage should include identification of areas receiving most disaster attention in order to re-deploy volunteers to other areas needing help.

REFERENCES

Alexander, D. E. (2013). Social media in disaster risk reduction and crisis management. *Science and Engineering Ethics*, December, 1–17.

Balana, C. D. (2012, June 15). Social media: Major tool in disaster response. *Philippine Daily Inquirer*. Retrieved from http://technology.inquirer.net/12167/social-media-major-tool-in-disaster-response

Barraket, J., Keast, R., Newton, C. J., Walters, K., & James, E. (2013). *Spontaneous volunteering during natural disasters*. Working Paper No. ACPNS 61. The Australian Centre for Philanthropy and Nonprofit Studies, Queensland University of Technology, Brisbane, Australia. Retrieved from http://eprints.qut.edu.au/61606/

Batson, C. D., O'Quin, K., Fultz, J., Vanderplas, M., & Isen, A. M. (1983). Influence of self-reported distress and empathy on egoistic versus altruistic motivation to help. *Journal of Personality and Social Psychology, 45*, 706–718.

Batson, C. D. (1987). Prosocial motivation: Is it ever truly altruistic? *Advances in Experimental Social Psychology, 20*, 65–122.

Betancourt, H. (1990). An attribution-empathy model of helping behavior: Behavioral intentions and judgments of help-giving. *Personality and Social Psychology Bulletin, 16*, 573–591.

Beyerlein, K., & Sikkink, D. (2008). Sorrow and solidarity: Why Americans volunteered for 9/11 relief efforts. *Social Problems, 55*, 190–215.

Boyatzis, R. E. (1998). *Transforming qualitative information: Thematic analysis and code development.* Thousand Oaks, CA: Sage.

Bryman, A., Becker, S., & Sempik, J. (2008). Quality criteria for quantitative, qualitative and mixed methods research: A view from social policy. *International Journal of Social Research Methodology, 11*, 261–276.

Bruns, A., Burgess, J., Crawford, K., & Shaw, F. (2012). #qldfloods and @QPSMedia: Crisis communication on Twitter in the 2011 southeast Queensland floods. *ARC Centre of Excellence for Creative Industries and Innovation.* Brisbane, Australia: Queensland University of Technology. Retrieved from http://eprints.qut.edu.au/48241/

Carrera, P., Oceja, L., Caballero, A., Muñoz, D., López-Pérez, B., & Ambrona, T. (2013). I feel so sorry! Tapping the joint influence of empathy and personal distress on helping behavior. *Motivation and Emotion, 37*, 335–345.

Cheong, F., & Cheong, C. (2011, July 9). Social media data mining: A social network analysis of tweets during the 2010–2011 Australian floods. *Proceedings for the Pacific Asia Conference on Information Systems (PACIS)*, paper 46. Retrieved from http://aisel.aisnet.org/pacis2011/46

Cialdini, R., Schaller, M., Houlihan, D., Arps, K., Fultz, J., & Beaman, A. (1987). Empathy-based helping: Is it selflessly or selfishly motivated? *Journal of Personality and Social Psychology, 52*, 749–58.

Cimino, A. (2013). Predictors of hazing motivation in a representative sample of the United States. *Evolution and Human Behavior, 34*, 446–452.

Drabek, T. E., & McEntire, D. A. (2003). Emergent phenomena and the sociology of disaster: Lessons, trends and opportunities from the research literature. *Disaster Prevention and Management, 12*, 97–112.

Freeman, R. B. (1997). Working for nothing: The supply of volunteer labor. *Journal of Labor Economics, 15*, S140–S166.

Guy, B. S., & Patton, W. E. (1989). The marketing of altruistic causes: Understanding why people help. *The Journal of Consumer Marketing, 6*, 19–30.

Hardy, C. L., & Van Vugt, M. (2006). Nice guys finish first: The competitive altruism hypothesis. *Personality and Social Psychology Bulletin, 32*, 1402–1413.

Horton, J., Macve, R., & Struyven, G. (2004). Qualitative research: Experiences in using semi-structured interviews. In C. Humphrey & B. H. K. Lee (Eds.), *The real life guide to accounting research* (pp. 339–357). Online access via Elsevier.

Hughes, A. L., Palen, L., Sutton, J., Liu, S. B., & Vieweg, S. (2008). "Site-seeing" in disaster: An examination of on-line social convergence. *Proceedings of the 5th International ISCRAM Conference*, Washington, DC, USA.

Jones, K. (2006). Giving and volunteering as distinct forms of civic engagement: The role of community integration and personal resources in formal helping. *Nonprofit and Voluntary Sector Quarterly, 35*, 249–266.

Jones, C. (2013). *Activism or slacktivism? The role of social media in effecting social change.* School of Engineering and Applied Science, University of Virginia, Virginia, USA. Retrieved from Google Scholar.

Knaus, C. (2011, January 14). Facebook and Twitter the new centres of disaster relief and connection. *Sydney Morning Herald.* Retrieved from http://www.smh.com.au/technology/technology-news/facebook-and-twitter-the-new-centres-of-disaster-relief-and-connection-20110113-19pwk.html

Lowe, S., & Fothergill, A. (2003). A need to help: Emergent volunteer behavior after September 11th. In J. L. Monday (Ed.), *Beyond September 11th: An account of post-disaster research* (pp. 293–314). Boulder: Natural Hazards Research and Applications Information Center, University of Colorado.

Macias, W., Hilyard, K., & Freimuth, V. (2009). Blog functions as risk and crisis communication during Hurricane Katrina. *Journal of Computer-Mediated Communication, 15*, 1–31.

Michel, L. (2007). Personal responsibility and volunteering after a natural disaster: The case of Hurricane Katrina. *Sociological Spectrum, 27*, 633–652.

Ng, E., Schweitzer, L., & Lyons, S. (2010). New generation, great expectations: A field study of the Millennial generation. *Journal of Business and Psychology, 25*, 281 292.

Penner, L. A., & Finkelstein, M. A. (1998). Dispositional and structural determinants of volunteerism. *Journal of Personality and Social Psychology, 74*, 525–537.

Safrilsyah, J.K., Jusoff, K., & Fadhil, R. (2009). Prosocial behavior motivation of Acehness volunteers in helping tsunami disaster victims. *Canadian Social Science, 5*, 50–55.

Shaver, P., Schwartz, J. Kirson, D. & O'Connor, C. (1987). Emotion knowledge: Further exploration of a prototype approach. *Journal of Personality and Social Psychology, 52*, 1061–1086.

Storm, C., & Storm, T. (1987). A taxonomic study of the vocabulary of emotions. *Journal of Personality and Social Psychology, 53*, 805–816.

Sweet, M. (2011, January 18). Australia faces huge rebuild after devastating floods. *BMJ, 342*. Retrieved from http://www.bmj.com/content/342/bmj.d362

Tong, K. K., Hung, E. P., & Yuen, S. M. (2011). The quality of social networks: Its determinants and impacts on helping and volunteering in Macao. *Social Indicators Research, 102*, 351–361.

van den Honert, R. C., & McAneney, J. (2011). The 2011 Brisbane floods: Causes, impacts and implications. *Water, 3*, 1149–1173.

Volunteering Queensland (2011, January 16). *Update from Volunteering Qld.* Retrieved from http://qldfloods.org/article/update-volunteering-qld-sunday-160111.

Vogler, S. (2011, February 8). Brisbane flood cost City Council $440 mil. *The Courier Mail.* Retrieved from http://www.couriermail.com.au/news/brisbane-flood-cost-city-council-440-mil/story-e6freon6-1226002095929

Yates, D., & Paquette, S. (2011). Emergency knowledge management and social media technologies: A case study of the 2010 Haitian earthquake. *International Journal of Information Management, 31*, 6–13.

CHAPTER THREE

Volunteering IN THE Thai Context: Rising Above THE Waters

TREEPON KIRDNARK
Bangkok University

CLAUDIA L. HALE
Ohio University

The tropical climate of Thailand contributes to flooding problems, especially along the Chao Phraya and the Mekong, as well as the Chi and Mun Rivers. The monsoon season of 2011, however, brought historic levels of flooding to the country famously known as the "Land of Smiles." Beginning in October of that year, floodwaters inundated portions of Bangkok, the capital city, with the flooding persisting until mid-January, eventually affecting more than 65 of Thailand's 77 provinces. Nindang and Allen (2012), in a report published by *The Asia Foundation*, noted that the 2011–12 floods killed more than 800 people, left millions homeless or displaced, and created an economic loss that was estimated by the World Bank as exceeding $45 billion dollars, equal to more than 1,425 billion baht, the Thai currency (see also Wikipedia.org). To put this in perspective, these figures represent approximately 30% of the 2012 Thai GNP (GNP figure obtained from tradingeconomics.com).

In times of crisis, whether that crisis is created by a natural disaster, such as a flood, or by a man-made disaster, such as political upheaval or an act of terrorism, effective communication is essential. Individuals living in the area affected by the crisis fervently desire information and assistance that can guide their ability to cope, and the family and friends of those affected just as fervently desire contact with their loved ones or at least information concerning the efforts being made to help their loved ones cope with the situation. Nindang and Allen (2012) shared the sentiments of Ruengrawee Pichaikul, a senior program officer with the Asia Foundation, who wrote about her experience in the blog, In Asia:

> Though frustrating, I continued to examine the murky, and at times contradictory, statements from the political rivals to stay informed. Serving as substitutes for conventional media, Facebook and other social networking sites were buzzing with more useful and essential information—much of which was provided by experts and environmental NGOs. (para. 3)

This study explored a segment of volunteer culture that has emerged in response to the floods that affect Thailand—not only the 2011–12 flooding—but also the flooding that preceded that particular disaster. The research questions posed draw attention to the values shared by Thai volunteers and the role of the volunteer in Thai culture.

BACKGROUND

Ganesh and McAllum (2009) defined volunteerism as "an overall framework which engenders particular types of economic and political structures, discourses, practices, and contexts for connecting individuals with society that are identifiable either in terms of activity (volunteering) or personhood (volunteers)" (p. 345). Citing the work of Clary and colleagues as well as a variety of other scholars, Ganesh and McAllum observed that "volunteerism discursively emphasizes individualism over collectivism....Indeed, the very term *volunteer*-ism emphasizes *voluntas*, or individual will (Habermas, 1984), which implies agency—the ability to make free, rational, and unencumbered choices" (p. 347).

Many organizations in Thailand have organized their activities around the work of volunteers or a combination of volunteers and paid staff members. The focus here is on the volunteerism that has been sparked by the flooding that perennially affects Thailand. One group serving as a special focus for this study was "Roo Soo Flood." This group is embedded in the Thai Public Broadcasting System and became well-known during the flooding of 2011–12.

While the focus is not exclusively on Roo Soo Flood, the work of the members of this group and the motivations underlying their volunteer efforts were instructive. Their work involved communicating with the public about how to prepare for floodwaters, and if an area was already flooded, informing residents as to what they should do. Specifically, this group sought to help victims to be proactive rather than passive. Along with developing "infographics"—animated graphics or pictorials designed to explain complicated information—that were then disseminated via television, Roo Soo Flood utilized social media, such as Facebook and Twitter, to make flood-relevant information more accessible and rapidly available.

An understanding of the Thai culture is central to this research. The most basic question concerns those values that are part of the culture and that encourage, or do not encourage, volunteer engagement. Hofstede (1994) argued that culture is not about an individual but is shared by a group of people living in the same circumstances. Hofstede concluded that there are dimensions of culture, such as collectivism versus individualism, masculinity versus femininity, and a strong desire to avoid uncertainty versus a comparatively weaker desire to avoid uncertainty (i.e., a willingness to engage in more risk) that characterize any culture. These dimensions influence the communication dynamics present within the culture and, in the case of volunteer organizations, influence the communication of and with volunteers.

The reference to "value" in this paper is informed by the work of Kluckhohn (1951) and Rokeach (1973), among others. Both defined values in terms of "preferred states," with Rokeach offering the following explanation:

> To say that a person "has a value" is to say that he [sic] has an enduring belief that a specific mode of conduct or end-state of existence is personally and socially preferable to alternative modes of conduct or end-states of existence. (pp. 159–160)

Specific to the Thai culture, Komin (1990), who cited Kluckhohn, Rokeach, and Williams as influencing her understanding of the concepts of value and value systems, examined "work related values" in Thai governmental and non-governmental organizations. Komin found that some characteristics were different from the characteristics associated with Western organizations. Komin attributed these disparities to socio-cultural differences, concluding "the *Thai social system is first and foremost a society where individualism and interpersonal relationships are of utmost importance*" (pp. 690–691, emphasis in original). Based on her research, Komin outlined nine "value clusters" that are of importance within the Thai culture. Listed from most influential to slightly less influential, those value clusters were: (1) ego orientation, (2) grateful relationship orientation, (3) smooth interpersonal relationship orientation, (4) flexibility and adjustment orientation, (5) religio-psychical orientation, (6) education and competence orientation, (7) interdependence orientation, (8) fun-pleasure orientation, and (9) achievement-task orientation. Each of these clusters is briefly described and their possible relevance to engaging in volunteer activities is considered. Admittedly, this latter consideration is speculative as no research could be found concerning Thai volunteers that spoke to this issue.

Komin described the value cluster of "ego orientation" by asserting that "Thai people have big egos and a deep sense of independence, pride and dignity" (p. 691). The "root values" of ego orientation were identified as face-saving, criticism avoidance, and "Kraeng cai," meaning "to be considerate" or to not impose. These qualities seem to argue against volunteering and/or, more specifically, against seeking assistance from others as that might be considered as imposing upon another individual.

Grateful relationship orientation is characterized by the Thai concept of "*bhunkun*" and its two elements: *ru bhunkun* and *tob tan bhunkun*. In general, *bhunkun* refers to reciprocity of favors. More specifically, *ru bhunkun* instructs Thais to be cognizant and appreciative of acts of kindness that might be directed toward them. *Tob tan bhunkun* instructs Thais to reciprocate acts of kindness whenever it is possible to do so. This value would appear to emphasize an "other-focus" considered to be part of volunteering and, thus, to encourage volunteer efforts.

Komin contrasted the value cluster of smooth interpersonal relationship orientation with the American focus on self-actualization. The smooth interpersonal relationship orientation places emphasis on being "other-focused." Similar to "grateful relationship orientation," this orientation toward interpersonal relationships seems to encourage volunteerism.

In explaining the value cluster of flexibility and adjustment orientation, Komin argued "*the Thai are situation-oriented, not principle nor ideologically-oriented, neither are they system-oriented*" (p. 692, emphasis in original). Komin further explained, "It is always the 'person' and the 'situation' over principles and system" (p. 692). The emphasis here is on flexibility and adjusting responses to fit the situation. Clearly, the situation of a flood brings extraordinary demands/needs and a clear recognition on the part of those called to be volunteers that there is a need to be of assistance.

The religio-psychical orientation ties into the religious orientation of the Thai culture. This orientation implicitly references the fact that Thailand is a predominantly Buddhist country, with approximately 95% of Thais professing Thervada Buddhism. With Buddhism comes the concept of *karma* (with *bun wassana* referring to "good" karma and *kam* referring to "bad" karma). One could conceivably argue that the negative experiences of today are a product of one's karma based on past wrongdoings, i.e., *kam*. This construction would seem to discourage efforts intended to help the person as he or she is reaping a just reward for past wrongdoing. At the same time, to the extent that any time spent volunteering today will lay a foundation for positive karma (*bun wassana*) tomorrow, the religio-psychical orientation should clearly support a volunteer culture within Thailand.

The education and competence orientation, according to Komin (1990), involves an effort to climb the social ladder as opposed to an end-value in itself. The relationship of this value to volunteerism is unclear. In some instances (and cultures), it certainly might be possible that an individual would define volunteering as a mechanism for networking and possibly moving up within society. However, it is not at all clear that this would be the case for Thai volunteers.

The seventh value orientation, according to Komin, is that of interdependence. This orientation is reminiscent of smooth relationship orientation and interdependence orientation. Komin explained that "this orientation reflects the community collaboration spirit through the value of co-existence and interdependence" (p. 693). This value would seem to be clearly relevant to volunteering within Thai society.

The eighth value orientation is that of fun-pleasure. Komin explained, "This orientation is characterized by the seemingly easy-going, fun-loving pleasant interactions, joyful behaviors, and the 'light' approach towards things and events, to the extent that Thailand has gained the stereotyped image of the 'land of smile'" (p. 694). When it comes to explaining volunteer behavior, to the extent that volunteering is seen as a "fun" activity, it might reasonably be anticipated that this value orientation plays a positive role in prompting Thais to share of their time and abilities. However, if an individual defines volunteering as an "obligation" or as a distraction from other, more desirable activities, then it might be expected to reduce motivation to volunteer.

Finally, the ninth value orientation identified by Komin was achievement-task orientation. Komin explained this orientation as emphasizing an "internal drive towards achievement through hard work" (p. 694). One might reasonably expect that a volunteer would be drawn to volunteering by this value.

The foregoing establishes a foundation for our two research questions:

RQ1: Which of the values identified by Komin are cited by Thais volunteers as prompting/supporting their efforts as volunteers and which values work against those efforts?

RQ2: What other aspects of the Thai culture do Thai volunteers identify as supporting or not supporting the work of the volunteer in Thailand?

We turn now to our approach for addressing these two questions.

METHOD

Data were collected via one-on-one interviews conducted by the first author who is a native Thai. Since, at the time of this research, he was living in England and all of the participants in this research were living and working in Thailand, all of the interviews were conducted via phone. Identification of potential participants began with the first author's personal circle of friends and acquaintances. Using the snowball technique, individuals who participated in the interviews were asked to identify other potential participants. Eventually, eight different volunteers (four men and four women) were included within the research. This is, admittedly, a modest number of participants. Participant statements were, in large part, very similar, particularly with respect to the issues relevant to this research. As such, we were comfortable in believing that a reasonable level of saturation was achieved.

At the time of the interviews, our youngest interviewee was 26-years-old and our oldest was 40. Their occupations included a researcher and part-time university lecturer, a doctoral student and part-time university lecturer, a labor union officer, a factory worker, a volunteer coordinator, a coordinator of a labor communication network, and a business owner. One participant did not identify his occupation. All of the interviews lasted at least 40 minutes, with the longest taking 70 minutes. All of the interviewees are native Thais. All volunteered during at least one and possibly more times of flooding in Thailand, with two of the interviewees specifically mentioning the 2004 tsunami as marking the beginning point of their volunteer efforts. Five were involved as volunteers, at some point in time, with the Thai Public Broadcasting System (TPBS).

Each interview began by having the interviewee describe how he/she first became involved in volunteering during a time of flooding in Thailand. The interviewee was asked to describe his/her initial responsibilities, and if those responsibilities changed over time, how they changed. Interviewees were then asked what the biggest personal reward was as a volunteer, including what kept the person coming back. The intent of this particular line of questions was to explore the values they saw as supportive of their work as volunteers. Counterbalancing the positive, interviewees were asked about any experiences or interactions that caused them to question their commitment to volunteering. Finally, they were asked to reflect on the role of volunteering within the Thai culture and whether they would continue to volunteer in the future.

Following the interviews, the first author translated the conversations, which had been conducted in Thai, into English and provided summaries to the second author. Analysis of the data was conducted using a constant comparative approach (Glaser & Strauss, 1967; Kelle, 2007). Our intent with this approach was not so much to develop a formal grounded theory given our reference to Komin (1990) as a guiding framework, but to adopt an approach that would allow us to be sensitive to not only the dimensions identified by Komin but to other values that might emerge within the conversations. Both authors read and re-read the transcripts, consulting with each other concerning their assessments of the similarities and differences in the perspectives of the interviewees, the extent to which statements made by or stories shared by the interviewees could be seen as reflecting one of the value clusters identified by Komin or another possible value. The first author returned to the tape recordings as needed in order to verify what had been said originally and to return statements back to the full context of the specific interview. To the extent that we "unitized" data, the units were the claims offered by our interviewees. These claims were, however, typically embedded in stories that were essential not only to an understanding of the initial claim but that often provided additional insight as to the motivations underlying our interviewees' involvements as volunteers. What follows reflects our identification of the themes that emerged as a result of this process.

FINDINGS

We begin the discussion of our findings by looking at what motivated our interviewees to become volunteers. From there, we address our research questions, exploring whether the values identified by Komin (1990) were reflected in interviewee statements and, then, identifying other values that emerged in our conversations. Pseudonyms have been employed to identify the interviewees whose statements or stories are being shared.

Interviewee Volunteer Motivation

The interviewees came to their roles as volunteers in a variety of ways. For at least three (Mim, Noom, and Ked), volunteering was characterized as a "natural" outgrowth of self. Prior to the flooding, Mim (a 32-year-old female) was the coordinator of a volunteer network. As she explained in her interview, "Since I work with volunteers on a regular basis, it seemed only natural to volunteer myself when the flooding started." Noom (a 26-year-old male), who was a researcher and part-time lecturer, has been involved in volunteer efforts since his days as an undergraduate student. He explained that a friend who was aware of his past volunteer activities knew he would be open to volunteering and, thus, approached him about helping during the flooding. Ked (a 36-year-old female who was a doctoral student and part-time university lecturer) began volunteering in response to the 2004 tsunami in the South of Thailand. There, she met people from all walks of life who truly enjoy their activities as volunteers. These individuals have become a close network of friends who marked the 2004 tsunami as a starting point in a trend of more volunteering among Thais.

For the remaining five interviewees, two individuals (Ton, a 36-year-old male factory worker, and Tum, a 29-year-old male and owner of an advertising agency) played a role in each other's decision to volunteer. Both had worked together as part of a factory union and knew they wanted to somehow be involved in efforts to respond to the flooding. Ton explained, "When my friend [Tum] told me what the volunteers were doing at TPBS, I knew I wanted to be involved."

With the remaining three, Kai (a 33-year-old female and labor union officer) mentioned the loss of her factory job in the floods as a motivation for becoming involved. Wat (a 40-year-old male who did not identify his profession) also began volunteering following the 2004 tsunami. Wat's efforts as a volunteer were motivated, in part, by observing a government system that he did not think was well organized or adequately responsive to needs. As Wat explained:

> During the 2004 flood, the government got tons of donations in the form of clothes and food, but there was a problem how to unload and distribute them to people in need. I kept thinking that we needed to learn from those problems and do better when the flooding started in 2011.

Wat indicated that he believed his prior experience could be of value in guiding efforts that would lessen, if not avoid, the problems of the past.

Finally, Lek (a 35-year-old female who is a coordinator for a labor communication network) began her volunteer efforts by trying to help factory workers who were affected by the flooding. She was especially moved by the situation faced by non-Thai laborers who, in her view, were largely ignored by local politicians given that they (the non-Thai laborers) could not vote in Thai elections. This particular observation was also mentioned by Ton in our conversation with him.

Looking across the stories and explanations shared by each of the interviewees, communication and community membership can be seen to have played key roles in the decision to volunteer. For Ked, Noom, Ton, and Tum that communication was with a community of friends who shared their desire to make a difference and were supportive of their decisions to volunteer. Ton, Lek, Kai, Mim, and Wat expressed felt obligations to communities affected by the flooding. Ton, for example, explained that he identified himself as a member of the Ayuthaya region which was hit hard by the flooding. Rather than simply accepting the status of victim, Ton sought, through volunteering, to exercise a measure of agency. Ton explained, "Being a volunteer is part of my conscience now; when I see people in trouble, I have to help." All of our interviewees acknowledged that they had skills—as organizers and as communicators—that could be employed in a meaningful manner.

Thai Cultural Values Cited as Supportive of Volunteer Efforts

The Thai cultural values that were either explicitly or implicitly mentioned by interviewees as supporting their efforts as volunteers are presented next. Attention was paid, first, to those values identified by Komin (1990) as characteristic of Thai organizational culture and then to other values identified in the interviews. Initially, we had thought to move through each value, one at a time, beginning with "ego orientation," listed by Komin as the most dominate of the nine values. That approach, however, seemed to be problematic as it would result in a mixing of the least mentioned values with more frequently cited values. Eventually, the decision was made to adopt an order to the discussion that better reflected the voices of our participants.

Another challenge existed in the distinctions among values. While overlaps existed in several areas, in particular, the distinctions among "grateful relationship orientation, "smooth interpersonal relationship orientation," and "interdependence orientation" seemed not always clear in the reality of the statements made by interviewees. All eight interviewees spoke to one or more of these orientations. While we tried to respect the nuanced differences across these three orientations, based on our constant comparison method, we have chosen to combine their discussion under the single label: "the importance of relationships/community."

The Importance of Relationships/Community. All of the interviewees cited either friendships or a sense of membership within a community as part of what motivated them as volunteers, invoking either explicitly or implicitly the interdependence orientation. One of the most neglected groups during the flooding was that of the migrant laborers. In part because of her own previous role as a factory worker, Lek was particularly sensitive to the plight of this group. She explained, "Some workers who are not Thai citizens were in the worst situation because they were largely ignored by local politicians who just wanted to favor their voters."

For Lek, Ton, and Kai, their membership in labor unions was part of their volunteer motivation. As Kai explained, "Everybody is like brothers and sisters. The experience from being in the union makes me realize about the problems of other people and the need to help." These interviewees sought to address the needs of workers in a variety of ways by, for example, writing about the needs of the workers and, thus, trying to keep the workers' situation in the public eye (Kai), delivering needed food and other supplies to affected areas (Ton), and serving as an information conduit between those in need and those wishing to give (Lek).

Ton's efforts were focused largely on his home region–Ayuthaya. At first, Ton traveled by car, but eventually, he had to shift to a boat, sometimes needing to coordinate with the provincial administration to obtain access to that form of transportation. In his interview, Ton alluded both to the grateful relationship orientation and the interdependence orientation. At one point, he explained, "When you help other people, later those people reciprocate the help" (i.e., grateful relationship orientation). Later, he noted "if there is a disaster in the future, we will survive if people gather in a network and help the affected people" (interdependence orientation).

Mim spoke, in particular, to the value of networking as essential to being able to help each other. During the flooding, Mim organized a website whose aim was to link interested volunteers with communities in need of assistance. She explained:

> We found there was a gap between the government and local communities. During the flood crisis, when volunteers wanted information about a particular community affected by the flood, they didn't know where to get that information or who to go to. What they have

to do is build a volunteer network and connections at a local level in order to help people more effectively.

In all of these interviewees' accounts as well as others that could be shared, the need for relationship building, for supporting and being supported by a community was preeminent. The interviewees spoke of their concern about the plight of those affected by the flooding, in particular, groups, such as laborers, who were viewed as largely being ignored. They spoke to their membership within a community of like-minded individuals who were or had become their friends. And they spoke to the concept of reciprocation, giving voice to the belief that, when they needed help, others would be there for them.

Flexibility and Adjustment Orientation. The next orientation, mentioned by seven of the interviewees, was that of flexibility and adjustment. Komin (1990) described this orientation as emerging from a Thai tendency to focus on the needs of the particular situation at hand as opposed to trying to adhere to an over-arching principle or set of rigidly established practices. In this regard, perhaps the most striking commonality across the interviews was the tendency to describe either their efforts or their motivation as filling in a gap. This is, perhaps, not at all surprising as most volunteers, no matter the culture or context, would define themselves in this way. At the same time, this particular orientation emerged as both a strength and a weakness in that the interviewees expressed justifiable pride in their ability to respond to the shifting demands of the situation but were also critical of what they described as an ad hoc or inadequate response to what is a frequent problem given that flooding occurs at some level almost every year, albeit the floods of 2011 were extraordinary in their severity.

Kai wrote articles about those affected by the flooding. When, as part of her research, Kai became aware of an area or community that had been overlooked, she took survival kits to those areas. Tum noted a lack of correspondence between the information being broadcast by traditional media (e.g., what the Prime Minister was wearing on a visit to an affected area) and what people actually needed to know. Based on personal conversations and questions/comments posted to websites, Tum and his friends came to realize that not everyone understood traditional reports concerning the flooding. As a result, they began developing and broadcasting infographics to try to more effectively convey information.

Similarly, Mim, Lek, and Wat noted that the management of information was a major problem during the crisis. The complaint seemed to be that, although there was a surfeit of information, not all of that information really addressed the issues that were of interest or importance to those living in the flooded areas. Each of these interviewees, in his or her own way, sought to address the problem: for Mim, it was organizing a website; Lek played a liaison role, finding out what the problems were and seeking answers to residents' concerns.

Noom described himself as a liaison (i.e., "communicator") but with special responsibilities. Part of his role involved learning how to evaluate the quickly changing situation, assessing whether people needed to be evacuated or helped to "live with the flood and manage your community with the flood." Reflecting the need to remain flexible and adapt to changing situations, he explained that, "in the last stage, we were concerned more about how to bring water to the sea via coastal areas without damaging too much agricultural products." Given the significance of agriculture to the Thai economy, this was an extremely important task.

Early in the process, Wat discovered how essential it was to be flexible and to be a problem solver. For Wat, "[what volunteers needed to do] changed every three days....At first, volunteers have to produce sand bags and prepare food, but then most areas were flooded, so they had to produce a boat made of used drinking water bottles." Invoking the smooth interpersonal relationship orientation, Wat summed up the situation by asserting that "this job is about giving."

As previously noted, there did appear to be a negative component to the flexibility and adjustment orientation. Ked noted that the outcomes of a volunteer's efforts are not always given careful thought. Ked, Noom, Ton, Mim, Wat, and Tum all described logistical and organizational problems that plague Thai disaster relief organizations. Mim explained that "even now, in some volunteer organizations, there is no registration system. This system will help track backgrounds of volunteers and this would be very beneficial for volunteer organizations."

Lek and Ton both drew comparisons with Japan. When it came to responding to natural disasters, they characterized the Japanese as being very organized and proactive. Thais (and Thai organizations), on the other hand, were described as being "ad hoc." Noom and Wat spoke of the need for volunteers and volunteer organizations to reflect on what they have learned and to make those changes that would contribute to a more effective and efficient response in the future.

Religio-Psychical Orientation. Seven of the interviewees (Wat, Kai, Noom, Ton, Mim, Ked, and Tum) either explicitly or implicitly referenced the religio-psychical aspect of the Thai culture as they mentioned the concept of "making merit" (*tham boon*). Mim specifically stated "the foundation of Thai culture and religion is collectivism, so this is good for volunteer work since you have to work with other people." Noom explained that "Thais love to give," a sentiment echoed by Wat. Lek, Kai, and Wat also described Thais as "gentle, patient, and kind, all qualities that contribute to the desire to help others" (Lek). For Noom, Mim, Wat, and Tum, the fact that strangers were coming together to help others was the true reward of their volunteer efforts and contributed to a great sense of pride in their country and their fellow Thais.

At the same time, the interviewees did note some problems. Describing a situation that is certainly not unique to Thailand and Thai volunteers, Noom explained that some Thais are happy limiting their help to donating various items but are unconcerned about the logistics involved in distributing those items where they might do the most good. Noom argued that, while Thais are givers, their efforts are not always guided by an understanding of those in need, a situation that leads to a devaluation of the voices and concerns of the victims of the disaster, essentially creating an additional form of victimization.

Fun-Pleasure Orientation. It was unclear whether the fun-pleasure orientation would work in favor of or against the desire to volunteer. Six of our participants (Wat, Ton, Lek, Kai, Ked, and Tum) specifically referenced "enjoyment," "fulfillment," and/or "fun" as not only outcomes of, but motivations for volunteering. Kai stated simply that she was happy to help. Tum argued that the volunteers were rewarded through the pride that they could take in their work and the feeling of being worthwhile. Noom provided a somewhat confusing picture. While expressing some reservations about volunteering in the future, in response to a specific question, Noom said "yes," that he would volunteer again. He admitted that he did "feel good" about his time spent as a volunteer. On a slightly different note, Wat observed that organizations that rely on volunteers need to find ways to make the work environment fun if they are to keep those volunteers.

Ked used the Thai phrase "*pae dan bon*" (literally translated as "the upper ceiling") to describe her experience as a volunteer. Essentially, through volunteering, she became part of a community that helped her to achieve a personal level of efficacy and efficiency. Ked admitted that "the first time of being a volunteer, I felt very good because I thought my life was valuable and could contribute to other people." At the same time, she recognized the difference between personal achievement as a volunteer and actual effectiveness in helping those in need. She was among the interviewees who noted that, despite the good done by volunteers, "it doesn't really fix the cause of the problem."

Achievement-Task Orientation. In some respects, Ked's statement spoke to a variety of cultural values, including not only fun-pleasure orientation but achievement-task orientation as she referenced feeling that, through her volunteer work, she had been able to help others. Mim, Noom, and Lek also offered responses to questions that fell within this cultural orientation, although that classification was often based on the interviewee questioning his/her own activities.

For Mim, "good intention is not enough; the method of volunteering is also important." While describing her efforts to make a positive difference in the lives of those affected by the flooding, Mim also admitted:

> Many times I question what I am doing—is this kind of volunteer work compatible with Thai society? Is it ready?...Volunteers do not only good things; they must have a goal in solving social problems as well.

Noom admitted that: "Until today, I do not know what I get from being a volunteer. I feel good when I do it, but I can't claim anything that is my achievement as a volunteer either." He expressed the belief that people in affected areas need to learn how to manage for themselves.

Education and Competence Orientation. Based strictly on Komin's (1990) description of the education and competence orientation, this particular cultural value was one of the two least referenced values. Within her research, Komin identified the education and competence orientation as involving efforts to climb the ladder within society. Strictly speaking, only Lek offered any comments that could arguably be classify as falling under this orientation, and even then, the "climbing" that Lek spoke of was not for herself but for others. In response to a question concerning challenges, Lek stated: "In terms of laborers, the major challenge is communication. Laborers' voices are not 'loud.' I am trying to make their voices heard by training factory workers to do news reports."

If the education and competence orientation is redefined as embodying a desire to learn and to develop and/or share personal competence, then Mim, Wat, Noom, Kai, Ked, and Tun all spoke to the personal process of learning as a result of their volunteer activities. They also spoke to the need (obligation) to use one's knowledge for the betterment of others. Mim explained:

> Someone asked why I like being a volunteer. I replied that I didn't do it because I feel good about it but because I could change myself. I used to be very introverted and I did not trust anyone. Being a volunteer, I have become more open-minded and learned new ways of life.

Ked argued that "competency is a motivation for keeping me involved. If people have competency, they should use it."

Ego Orientation. We had not thought that ego orientation would play a role in our participants' decisions to volunteer or their characterizations of Thai volunteers. A statement offered by Tum indicated recognition of the problems associated with ego. In explaining why a Thai might volunteer in response to a disaster, Tum stated:

> A volunteer is rewarded once he has decided to be a volunteer....Volunteers are rewarded by doing what they want to do. For other volunteers, the reasons may include to be proud of their work, to feel that they are worthwhile....And sometimes rewards can create a problem because it became a competition for doing a good thing for society—competing on who can do better. Sometimes, it is about an ego.

Statements concerning feeling pride and self-worth suggest a focus on self rather than others. In addition, a competition to do more than others appears to be ego-focuses rather than other-focused.

Other Values Revealed. The second research question concerned whether values not identified by Komin would be cited by our participants. An area of criticism emerged across comments offered by five of our participants (Mim, Wat,

Noom, Ton, and Ked) that suggested "organization" is not a value subscribed to within Thai society.

Wat explained that poor coordination, including poor communication, results in volunteers and/or volunteer organizations focusing only on their own efforts with little attention given to the activities of other volunteers or volunteer organizations. Wat described a lesson he had learned from his 2004 volunteer efforts:

> Volunteer efforts were not very well managed. Thais like to help each other, but effective coordination of efforts is not always done. In the tsunami [2004], we did not have a central information hub, and some communities were helped multiple times while others not so much. I tried to coordinate efforts so that help went to each community and was not repetitive.

Wat noted trying to bring the lessons learned in 2004 with him to his 2011–12 volunteer efforts.

Similar to Wat, Ked initially volunteered in 2004. Even more specifically, both had begun their efforts at the Don Muang Airport where they were first-hand witnesses to government efforts to respond to the crisis. Wat characterized those efforts as "not working," whereas Ked claimed volunteers left the airport site because "it didn't work and many truths were concealed by the government." Together, this suggests that government ineptness in past efforts was a motivating factor for some volunteers.

DISCUSSION

This project began with two questions in mind: 1) Which of the values identified by Komin are cited by Thai volunteers as prompting/supporting their efforts and which values work against those efforts? and 2) What other aspects of the Thai culture do Thai volunteers identify as supporting or not supporting the work of the volunteer in Thailand? Looking across Komin's (1990) list of nine value clusters describing the Thai culture, there were elements of at least seven of the nine that support volunteering one's efforts to help another person. The remaining two value clusters—ego orientation and education/competence orientation—were present only in very limited ways and/or in ways that suggested a different conceptualization than that offered by Komin.

With respect to ego orientation, remember that our participants were all volunteers. We did not seek input from individuals who chose not to respond to a crisis created by a natural disaster. Arguably, individuals who choose not to respond might be motivated by any number of Komin's value clusters, including but not limited to ego orientation, but at least among our group, "independence, pride and dignity" (Komin 1990, p. 691) were neither impediments to nor motivations for volunteering. As for education and competence orientation, Komin's description of this value concerned moving up the social ladder. While it is impossible to rule out the potential for a social desirability bias to be at work, at least among our interviewees, no one cited networking and social mobility as a reason for volunteering, though helping others to have voice and some measure of agency within the situation was mentioned. There was an element of networking present, but that was the need to network in order to accomplish the mission of the volunteer (present in statements made by Mim, Wat, Ton, and Lek).

From a volunteer:

When the big flood started to cover the wider area of central Thailand, my friends and I decided that we should do something, so we volunteered at Thai PBS. At first, I was responsible for preparing information about the flood, especially distinguishing truth from rumors. People were overwhelmed with information from everywhere. I came to believe that many people really did not understand what was going on. My friends and I decided that an infographic approach would do a far better job at communicating complex information in a clear and engaging manner. This was the origin of the "Roo Soo Flood" group.

For volunteers, the work itself is the reward. For me, working with friends in a small studio was a magic moment. Sometimes we stayed overnight. Management specialists might say that, if you want an organization to be effective, job descriptions have to be clear, but in this case, the goal was the most important element. We all worked together without boundaries. We all did more than we were asked, and this was crucial.

In my personal life and work, I embrace an idea of doing good for society. I run an advertising agency. All of my clients are non-profit organizations. So doing good can be part of someone's personal life and professional life. This is the way I choose to live. Being a volunteer has magic moments. Those magic moments will bring me back again and again.

Tum

As they addressed their motivations for and satisfactions with volunteering, the participants cited "community," in a variety of forms, as a primary motivation. Three volunteers (Noom, Ton, and Tum) mentioned friends as having played a role in the decision to volunteer. Two others, Wat and Ked, explained that the friendships formed through volunteering had resulted in a significant network. All five were united through the commitment to make a difference in their community. Noom acknowledged liking the atmosphere created when strangers come together to solve problems. Lek described her activities as "picking up the phone" and getting answers to questions posed by members of her community (factory workers) who felt they were being ignored. Mim saw herself as a member of a community of volunteers, responding to their needs by creating a website that provided them with information that helped them (the volunteers) to more effectively direct their efforts toward helping the community.

While the research questions did not focus specifically on communication, the emphasis the participants placed on community as well as statements they offered concerning the roles played by friends in their decisions to volunteer and the friendships formed as volunteers all spoke to the importance of communication. Added to that are the volunteers' own efforts, as communicators, to reach out to flood victims, either providing information intended to help victims cope or responding to questions or helping them to find their own voices in the situation, and the importance of communication for Thai volunteers is clear.

While all of the interviewees shared the desire to somehow constructively respond to the disaster created by the floodwaters, there were some differences in expectations. Noom, Lek, Mim, Ked, and Wat gave voice to the need for "change." Mim, for example, argued that there is a need to "fine tune expectations" on the part of both volunteer organizations and volunteers. Noom noted that there was a need for volunteers and the organizations they served to look back on their activities, reflecting critically on what worked and what did not work. Noom admitted that he was not sure what he could point to as a clear achievement—a "product"— emerging from his efforts as a volunteer. He argued that people in areas traditionally affected by floodwaters needed to be able to manage that situation for themselves.

Ked echoed Noom's sentiments concerning the need for critical reflection. Ked observed that many of the individuals who volunteered during the crisis did so because volunteering made them feel good; however, the efforts of the volunteers did not really "fix" the cause of the problem. She nonetheless planned on continuing to volunteer because of the competencies she has developed. She likened volunteering to an addiction—when she sees a problem, if no one else is stepping in to help, she will happily do so. What all of them seemed to be pointing to, not only here but in other statements made, was in a failure, post-disaster, to take the time to treat disaster response as a learning opportunity, making those changes that might either help to mitigate problems in the future or make the efforts of volunteers more worthwhile.

It was initially thought that Komin's (1990) fun-pleasure orientation might work against the desire to volunteer. Admittedly, had we interviewed individuals who were in a position to volunteer but chose not to do so, we might have discovered that the fun-pleasure orientation played a role, i.e., that volunteering was not thought to be a means of having fun in one's life. Our interviewees, however, were all volunteers and had experienced the joy that comes from helping others. Their enthusiasm about continuing to volunteer in the future, despite the frustrations that they identified, was typically described as emerging from the fact that they truly enjoyed helping others and had discovered, in other volunteers, a like-mind ed community. In many respects, fun–pleasure served as a reason to *continue* to volunteer more so than as an initial motivation for volunteering.

The achievement-task orientation was not originally identified as a value that would be acknowledged by interviewees as relevant to their volunteer efforts. However, for seven of the eight interviewees, achievement-task orientation was a motivation. The single outlier–Noom–while acknowledging that he felt good when volunteering, nonetheless confessed that "I still cannot claim that I actually achieved anything as a volunteer." While Noom was an outlier in one respect, as already noted, he was not alone in observing the need for critical reflection on the part of volunteers and the Thai organizations that used their services when responding to disasters. Mim, in particular, argued that if constructive changes were not made, it would be very difficult for volunteers and organizations to work together in the future.

In reflecting on what was learned through the interviews, there are the similarities and the differences between the experiences of these volunteers and the experiences of volunteers in other countries. As previously noted, two of the interviewees (Lek and Ton) drew comparisons with Japan's responses to natural disasters. In the view of both Lek and Ton, Thai relief organizations were best characterized as ad hoc in nature. The problems appeared to not be limited to non-governmental organizations. Ked and Wat were among the interviewees who were critical of what they had observed in terms of the government's response to the flooding, characterizing the response as disorganized and, in some of the information released, misleading.

In their calls for reforms in organizational practices, these interviewees appeared to recognize that some of the changes needed would definitely challenge the Thai culture. In Wat's view, Thais were enthusiastic about volunteering, but not particularly good at organizing the efforts of others. There was also the issue of selectivity in whose needs were being met and whose were being ignored. Lek, Ton, and Kai were among interviewees who spoke about neglected segments of the population, particularly non-Thai laborers. Added to this was the challenge of insuring that volunteers understand more clearly what has been accomplished through their personal efforts. Noom's statement–"Until today, I do not know what I get from being a volunteer"–spoke in its own way to the need for a sense of personal achievement if volunteers were to continue sharing their time and talents. Through all of these comments as well as other information shared, we found ourselves thinking back to Hurricane Katrina and the many criticisms that emerged concerning the disorganized handling of that disaster (see, for example, Bumiller, 2005). Clearly, each instance of a natural disaster brings its own unique set of challenges. We share with our interviewees the belief that there is a need for flexibility when responding to disasters and then for reflection once the time is available to step back and engage in a critical assessment. We also share with them the belief that the voices involved in that reflection need to include not simply the elites, but the volunteers and those actually affected by the disaster (in Thai, the "*chao baan*" or "ordinary citizen").

REFERENCES

Bumiller, E. (2005, September 2). Democrats and others criticize White House's response to disaster. The *New York Times* (late addition, East Coast), p. A16.

Ganesh, S. & McAllum, K. (2009). Discourses of volunteerism. In C. S. Beck (Ed.), *Communication yearbook 33* (pp. 343–383). New York, NY: Routledge.

Glaser, B. G., & Strauss, A. (1967). *The discovery of grounded theory: Strategies for qualitative research.* Chicago: Aldine.

Habermas, J. (1984). *The theory of communicative action: Reason and the rationalization of society* (vol. 1, T. McCarthy, Trans.). Boston: Beacon Press.

Hofstede, G. (1994). *Culture's consequences: International differences in work-related culture.* Los Angeles, CA: Sage.

Kelle, U. (2007). The development of categories: Different approaches in grounded theory. In A. Bryant & K. Charmaz (Eds.), *The Sage handbook of grounded theory* (pp. 191–213). Thousand Oaks, CA: Sage Publications Inc.

Kluckhohn, C. (1951). The study of culture. In D. Lerner & H. D. Lasswell (Eds.), *The policy sciences* (pp. 86–101). Stanford, CA: Stanford University Press.

Komin, S. (1990). Culture and work-related values in Thai organizations. *International Journal of Psychology, 25*, 681–704.

Nindang, S., & Allen, T. (2012, August 8). In Asia: Weekly insight and features from Asia. The Asia Foundation. http://Asiafoundation.org/in-asia/2012/08/08/ahead-of-flood-season-thailand.

Rokeach, M. (1973). *The nature of human values.* New York, NY: Free Press.

Trading Economics. www.tradingeconomics.com/thailand/gpa.

Wikipedia. 2011 Thailand floods. http://en.wikipedia.org/wiki/2011_Thailand_floods.

CHAPTER FOUR

Exploration OF THE State AND Nature OF Korean Parents' Volunteering IN School: Who Volunteers, FOR What, AND Why?

H. ERIN LEE
Hankuk University of Foreign Studies

JAEHEE CHO
Chung-Ang University

South Korea is well known for its high education fever [*gyo-yook-yeol*] which is continuously fueled by society's and parents' increasing demands for greater educational outcomes and for more prestigious educational status. These demands have stimulated immense involvement and investment of parents in their children's education (Seth, 2012). According to Hoover-Dempsey et al. (2005), parental involvement in children's education can occur both at home and at school, and it generally takes on three different forms–home-based involvement, school-based involvement, and parent-teacher communication. Research on home-based involvement has examined activities such as parent-child discussions about school, helping with homework, monitoring child activities, and arranging private education opportunities. School-based involvement has been studied in terms of school volunteering, participation in PTA activities, and parent-teacher communication, (e.g., Hoover-Dempsey et al., 2005; Kim & Hwang, 2012; Lee, 2003; Muller, 1993; Park, Byun, & Kim, 2011).

These different forms of parents' educational involvement are also present in Korea. However, a review of the literature on the Korean context shows that there is an imbalance between school-based and home-based involvement activities.

Korean parents tend to be more actively involved in their children's home-based educational activities, while they are less likely to be engaged in the activities that take place at their children's schools (Kim, 2002; Kim & Hwang, 2012; Lee, 2008). This phenomenon is both encouraging and problematic. It is encouraging because the abundance of research conducted on parents' educational involvement shows that, in general, parental involvement is associated with a number of positive outcomes for students, such as teacher evaluations of student competence, student grades, and higher retention and lower dropout rates (Hoover-Dempsey et al., 2005). However, it is problematic because many of these outcomes are also a result of active school involvement. According to Sohn and Wang (2006), research has shown that parents' school involvement, specifically, can lead to increased motivation toward school and schoolwork and increased self-esteem among students. Further, school involvement has been shown to have benefits for the parents as well in that such involvement can heighten understanding of school curricula and programs and can increase opportunities to work closely with the teachers (Sohn & Wang, 2006). This latter aspect is a particularly notable outcome that must be considered in the Korean context, where teachers are still widely believed to be an authority figure in relation to the parents, and the school and the classroom is thought to be a space led solely by the teachers with minimal parent intervention.

Considering such positive functions of parental school involvement, the current study provides a comprehensive evaluation of the current state and nature of school involvement among parents in Korea. Although there exist diverse forms of school involvement, this study pays particular attention to parental school volunteering. This is because, first, school volunteering is a highly voluntary form of school involvement, compared to that occurring in the form of parent-teacher communication that is required through scheduled conferences on a regular basis. Therefore, the exploration of school volunteering will enable a more valid understanding of proactive forms of parental involvement. Second, previous research has often addressed cultural differences in volunteerism across different countries (Eisner, Grimm, Maynard, & Washburn, 2009; Finklestein, 2010; Kemmelmeier, Jambor, & Letner, 2006; Parboteeah, Cullen, & Lim, 2004), and an exploration of parental volunteerism in Korea is expected to broaden understanding in this area. Interestingly, previous studies have presented contradictory findings in regards to cultural differences in formal volunteerism. While Parboteeah et al. (2004) found that countries of collectivistic cultures had higher volunteering rates, Finklestein (2010) found the opposite. Therefore, it is meaningful to further investigate the patterns of parental school volunteering in Korea, well-known as a country strongly characterized by a high collectivistic culture. In addition, considering the greater demand and necessity of parental involvement during the elementary school years (Eccles & Harold, 1993), this study examined the basic patterns of school volunteering among parents of elementary school students in

Korea, in terms of who is participating, in what form, and with what kinds of motivations.

BACKGROUND AND THEORETICAL PERSPECTIVE

Parental Involvement in South Korea's Educational Context

Korean parents are a uniquely vigorous group in terms of being involved in their children's education (Kim & Hwang, 2012). They are heavily invested in their children's education, but their patterns of involvement show a relative imbalance between school and home involvement activities (Kim & Hwang, 2012; Park et al., 2011). As is discussed in more detail below, Korean parents tend to be actively involved in home-based educational activities, such as private tutoring through private academic institutions or personal tutors, while they tend to be relatively less engaged in the activities that take place at their children's schools. The following sub-sections discuss the unique educational culture of Korea, in order to provide a contextual understanding of Korean parents' educational involvement, and the general trends in Korean parents' school and home involvement.

Korea's Educational Fever

Education has been considered one of the most critical components of Korea's national culture, primarily owing to the cultural roots of Confucianism. During the Joseon Dynasty (1392–1910), educated scholars wielded the strongest political and social power, and the most effective resource for social success was educational achievement (Seth, 2012). The social demand for education and emphasis on educational achievement heightened after the collapse of the Japanese occupation and continuously grew throughout Korea's tumultuous modern history (Seth, 2012). Korea's emphasis on education has become so excessive that the entirety of education processes involving the various parties (e.g., schools/colleges, parents, students, private tutoring industry, government institutions) is considered a contentious social phenomenon, referred to as "education fever [gyo-yook-yeul]" or "education heat wave [gyo-yook-yeul-poong]." This education heat wave is focused on producing strong academic performance with the ultimate goal of students' entrance ideally into top-ranking four-year colleges in Seoul. Indeed, Korea has witnessed a great amount of boastful academic outcomes which is easily evidenced through the nation's internationally competitive scores in reading, math, and science (OECD, 2010, 2014) and the many titles won in various international education competitions, including the first place title in the 2012 International Mathematics Olympiad (IMO) (Kim & Shin, 2012).

One of the major reasons for Korean parents' preoccupation with prestigious colleges can be found in the critical role of school ties in social success (Y. H. Kim, 2002). In Korea, there are three types of personal ties which are considered to be the most important for leading a successful life. They are family/blood ties, regional/hometown ties, and school ties (Kim, 2002). While it is impossible to alter the first two types of ties, school ties—particularly college ties—are malleable and can be personally achieved. Having prestigious school ties is important in Korean society because they enable an individual to get a head start in terms of opportunities in the job market, the workplace, and various domains of social life. Essentially, in Korea, reputable school ties based on such distinguished academic background become efficient means of mobilizing an individual upward.

For example, Kim (2014) found in their review of data on college hierarchy that, in the past five years, approximately 70 percent of the passed candidates of the high-rank public-officials exams were graduates from the top three universities in Korea. More recently, a report from the Korea Development Institute (2013) showed that college background directly influenced employment, income, promotions, and both life and job satisfaction (as cited in Song & Park, 2014). Korean parents are also clearly aware of this trend. According to a study conducted by the Korean Educational Development Institute, in 2010, approximately 50 percent of parents of school-age students responded that school background and connections were most important to social success (as cited in Song & Park, 2014).

In this way, there is a strict hierarchy among educational status as well as among higher education institutions in Korea. Therefore, entering and graduating from a prestigious university is considered to be a fundamental condition for leading a successful life in Korea. For this reason, Korean parents are likely to endure any physical, financial, and even mental sacrifice for their children's education (Kim, 2013). This sacrifice, or intense involvement of parents, starts when the children are very young, in many times during the preschool years (Lee, 2013).

Korean Parents' School Volunteering

Based on the small amount of research that has been conducted on parents' educational involvement in Korea, it is known that parental school volunteering does take place, but at a relatively smaller level than the educational involvement occurring at home or outside of school. For example, Park et al. (2011), among other items primarily regarding home-based involvement, measured how often parents contacted the school about volunteer work during the school year and it was close to "never." Lee (2003) also observed, among parents of elementary and middle-school students, that participation levels in school events, school committee meetings, and school volunteering were very low—rates for "no participation" in these capacities were 42.1 percent, 63 percent, and 66.6 percent, respectively.

Similarly, Lee (2008) found that while the majority of parents was actively involved in home involvement and agreed on the need for parental school involvement, only those of high socioeconomic status actually volunteered at their child's school. This is mainly because such high socioeconomic group of parents tend to have relatively higher levels of educational fever regarding their children, sacrificing and investing various resources, such as time, energy, and money.

As such, it can be commonly observed that there is an imbalance in Korean parents' educational involvement, with more emphasis given to home-based involvement than volunteering at school. Therefore, in order to stimulate volunteering at school, it becomes all the more important to understand the current patterns of parental school volunteering in terms of who is volunteering, in what form, and with what kinds of motivations. It must further be noted that previous studies mostly had examined middle-school and high school parents. There is a dearth of studies that discuss the patterns of school volunteering among elementary school parents. In general, elementary schools tend to demand the most assistance from parents, and parents of younger children tend to more actively and easily provide assistance (Eccles & Harold, 1993).Therefore, the first research question of this study explored the basic ways in which parents' school volunteering occurs among parents of elementary-school students:

RQ1:   In what ways does volunteering at school among parents of elementary-school students occur in Korea?

CONTINGENT AND MOTIVATIONAL FACTORS OF SCHOOL VOLUNTEERING

There are many potential factors that help us understand parents' decisions to volunteer at their child's school. Hoover-Dempsey and Sandler (1997) discuss three main factors that motivate parents' school involvement in general. According to the researchers, along with socioeconomic status (SES), parents' school involvement, including volunteering, is significantly related to the parents' internal psychological characteristics—such as parental role construction and educational efficacy—as well as external communicative demands for school involvement (Hoover-Dempsey & Sandler, 1997). Many follow-up studies have found abundant empirical evidence supporting the influential roles of those factors (Hoover-Dempsey et al., 2005; Green, Walker, Hoover-Dempsey, & Sandler, 2007; Walker, Wilkins, Dallaire, & Sandler, 2005). Based on the main findings from previous research, this present study also focused on the functions of parents' SES and the motivational factors that guide parents' school volunteering.

Parents' Socioeconomic Status and School Volunteering

Socioeconomic status, which is often represented by level of education, employment status, and/or income, has been found to be associated with levels of parental educational involvement (Green et al., 2007; Hoover-Dempsey et al., 2005; Shumow, Lyutykh, & Schmidt, 2011). Overall, parents of higher socioeconomic status have been observed to more actively be involved in their children's education (Green et al., 2007).

First, previous studies in Korea consistently found that among parents of all school-age students, those with higher levels of education were more often involved in a wide range of volunteering activities at schools (Byun & Kim, 2008; Lee, 2003; Lee, 2008). Lee (2003) explains this pattern in terms of the higher levels of educational efficacy, educational involvement, and more communication with the teachers among those highly educated parents.

Next, in terms of employment status, especially that of the mother, there has been some conflicting observations. While Lee (2003) found that mothers who were employed full-time were less likely to be involved in volunteering at school than those who were not employed, Y. H. Kim (2002) found that the mother's employment status had no effect on volunteering.

Lastly, household income is another socioeconomic variable that has been found to lead to differences in school involvement, including volunteering. For example, Park et al. (2011) found that parents of higher household income families had a higher tendency to contact their middle-school children's school. Similarly, Byun and Kim (2008) observed that higher household income predicted more active volunteering in school events.

As described above, there exist differences in levels of school involvement or volunteering across certain socioeconomic characteristics of families. However, as mixed findings from previous studies show, it is difficult to conclude that these socioeconomic factors themselves cause or permanently determine the attitudes or behaviors related to parental school involvement. Rather, these demographic factors can be considered to be tangible and objective forms of the array of resources—such as money, time, knowledge, skills, and social networks—that define how and how much a parent is involved in their children's education or school (Byun & Kim, 2008; Hoover-Dempsey & Sandler, 1997). Because of these reasons, there have been inconsistent findings in regards to the roles of parents' SES on school volunteering (Hoover-Dempsey et al., 2005; Green et al., 2007). Thus, the present study explored the following research question:

RQ2:   How is Korean parents' socioeconomic status associated with their school volunteering?

MOTIVATIONAL FACTORS OF PARENTS' SCHOOL VOLUNTEERING

In order to understand parents' decision-making processes in regards to educational involvement, Hoover-Dempsey and Sandler (1995, 1997) provided a theoretical model of the relationships among various cognitive, psychological, and social variables. Regarding the individual-level factors from their model, the researchers assert that the decision-making process is primarily affected by three constructs. These three constructs are: "(a) the parent's construction of his or her role in the child's life, (b) the parent's sense of efficacy for helping her or his child succeed in school, and (c) the general invitations, demands, and opportunities for parental involvement presented by both the child and the child's school" (pp. 8–9). These three constructs are considered to be the main motivational factors of school involvement and have been investigated by many follow-up studies (Hoover-Dempsey et al., 2005; Green et al., 2007; Walker et al., 2005). Thus, in order to comprehend the motivations behind parents' school volunteering in Korea, the current study also examined the patterns of these three constructs. The constructs are reviewed below in more detail.

Parental Role Construction

According to Hoover-Dempsey and Sandler (1995, 1997) and Green et al. (2007), parents' construction of their parental role refers to the parental beliefs regarding the appropriate behaviors that should be undertaken by parents in relation to their children's education. These beliefs serve as the fundamental criteria which set the range of activities that parents will consider to be "important, necessary, and permissible" (1997, p. 9) for themselves and their children. This role construction is influenced by the expectations of the significant, influential groups of which one is an active member (e.g., families, workplace, and religious and school communities) (Walker et al., 2005). Through observations and modeling of the parental involvement behaviors of significant others, parents come to learn what constitutes acceptable and appropriate behaviors as a parent (Hoover-Dempsey & Sandler, 1995). It is also claimed that parental role construction is influenced by parents' beliefs about the processes and outcomes of child development and of child-rearing. Based on this basic concept of parental role construction, research has observed positive effects of this variable on parents' overall school involvement (Sheldon, 2002; Walker et al., 2005).

Parents' Educational Efficacy

According to Hoover-Dempsey et al. (2005), another construct that influences parental school involvement is parents' educational efficacy. This motivational factor is related to how much parents believe that, "through their involvement, they can exert a positive influence on children's educational outcomes" (Hoover-Dempsey & Sandler, 1997, p. 17). In arguing the role of parents' efficacy in educational involvement, Hoover-Dempsey and Sandler largely rely on the main concept of Bandura's (1989) self-efficacy theory. In short, based on Bandura's theory, it can be reasonably assumed that the educational involvement choices that parents make will be informed by outcome expectations regarding their child's education and overall development. This decision-making process will also be affected by one's self-evaluation of one's knowledge and skills applicable to the educational situation; the more strongly positive one's self-evaluations are, the higher the established goals and level of commitment will be. In regards to this motivational factor, previous research's findings supported the positive role of parents' educational efficacy for increasing parents' school involvement (Grolnick, Benjet, Kurowski, & Apostoleris, 1997; Hoover-Dempsey et al., 2005; Shumow & Lomax, 2002).

Demands and Opportunities for School Involvement

Parents' decisions regarding educational involvement may also be influenced by their perception of others' demands and invitations for parental involvement (Green et al., 2007; Hoover-Dempsey et al., 2005). These demands and invitations tend to be communicated through external sources such as a child, school, teacher, or parent. For instance, in regards to children's demands, children can directly ask their parents to come to school, or they may indirectly express their demands through the excitement they show when their parents visit their classroom. The friendly, inviting environment of the school or school newsletters sent home with information regarding volunteer opportunities can also present themselves as demands and opportunities. Empirical research has shown that the communication of these demands and opportunities are positively associated with levels of parental involvement (Deslandes & Bertrand, 2005; Green et al., 2007; Simon, 2004). The current study focused on three particular communicative sources of demands: school, other parents (e.g., room parents), and child.

In this way, previous studies have found strong evidence supporting the positive effects of these motivational factors on parents' overall school involvement. Thus, based on those findings, this study explored the following research question in relation to school volunteering in particular.

RQ3: How are the three motivational factors—parental role construction, parents' educational efficacy, and demands for school volunteering—associated with Korean parents' school volunteering?

METHODOLOGY

Participants

For this study, we depended on a purposeful sampling method to collect data from parents of elementary school students—1ˢᵗ to 6ᵗʰ graders. We contacted two elementary schools located in one small-sized and one mid-sized city. To obtain higher external validity in regards to SES, we selected two public schools that were located in the most highly populated residential neighborhoods of each city—neighborhoods that were not too close to the downtown area nor in the periphery. With permission from the school principals, surveys were sent home to the parents of all students in grades 1ˢᵗ to 6ᵗʰ. A total of 499 usable surveys were collected.

The majority of participants were female (n = 460, 93.1%), most likely mothers. Participants' ages ranged from 28 to 51, with a mean of 38.1 years (SD = 3.98). The average number of children in the participants' families was 2.2 (SD = .67). The median annual household income was $30,000–$40,000. The majority of participants were employed in permanent (n = 225, 46.4%) or non-permanent (n = 86, 17.7%) work, or were housewives (n = 188, 35.9%). Most participants (n = 469, 95.5%) were currently married. According to the Korean Statistical Information Service (2013), the median household income of the province in which the two cities are located was approximately $33,000. Moreover, the same report also indicated that 42.8% percent of households had permanent jobs. Based on these national statistical indicators, the sample for this present study can be viewed as being quite representative of the areas from which they were selected.

Instruments

All of the scales were measured through a 5-point Likert-type scale (e.g., *1 = Strongly disagree, 5 = Strongly agree*). Reliability tests for most of the composite measurements indicated acceptable Cronbach's alpha scores (higher than .70).

Parental role construction. In this study, parental role construction was measured in terms of the extent to which one believed that their school volunteering helped their various roles as a parent. To measure this factor, we created six items. Exploratory factor analysis revealed that the following four items formed a coherent factor: a) I believe that school volunteering is a fundamental responsibility for parents;

b) Through school volunteering, I feel that I am doing my best for my children's school achievement; c) Through school volunteering, I feel that I am doing my best for my children's emotional development; d) Through school volunteering, I feel that I am doing my best for my children's personality development. The reliability for this measurement was strong (M = 2.83, SD = .83, α = .90).

Parents' educational efficacy. Bandura's (2006) scale for self-efficacy was modified to measure parents' educational efficacy. In total, seven items were used to measure this variable. Examples of those items are: a) When others criticize my educational philosophy and pedagogy, I can defend myself; b) I am grateful to have enough resources and abilities to handle unexpected events regarding my children's education; c) Because I believe in my own abilities, I can manage any difficulties facing my children's education; d) I can solve any problems with my children's education. The reliability test showed a very good Cronbach's alpha (M = 3.45, SD = .56, α = .86).

Demands for school volunteering. In this study, we focused on three different dimensions of demands for school volunteering, based on three different sources of the demands: school, other parents, and the child. In order to measure the three factors, we created four items that measured demands for school involvement and applied them to the three different sources, thus resulting in a total of twelve items. The basic item formats were as follows, with "my child's school, other parents," and "my child" inserted in the blank spaces: a) ___ emphasize(s) that parents' school volunteering positively influences children's learning; b) ___ emphasize(s) that parents' school volunteering improves the school environment; c) ___ emphasize(s) that parents' school volunteering is helpful for the general advancement of the school; d) ___ actively encourage(s) parents' school volunteering. Although school's demands for school volunteering produced a relatively low Cronbach's alpha (M = 2.92, SD = .54, α = .65), the other two sub-factors showed high reliability scores—other parents' demands for school volunteering (M = 2.93, SD = .80, α = .90) and child's demands for school volunteering (M = 3.45, SD = .87, α = .91).

Parental school volunteering. In order to identify the specific volunteering activities available to Korean parents, the researchers informally spoke with three mothers of elementary-school students and one elementary-school teacher. In total, twelve different volunteering activities were identified: (1) guest teacher, (2) general classroom assistance, (3) school beautification, (4) library volunteering, (5) assistance for class special-events (e.g., parties), (6) assistance for school special-events (e.g., school festivals), (7) traffic monitoring, (8) assistance for field trips, (9) lunchtime supervision, (10) school meal inspections, (11) school/classroom cleaning, and (12) participation in PTA meetings.[1] All twelve activities were listed in the survey, and participants were asked to respond with either a Yes or a No to indicate whether they had experience with each. When applicable, they were further asked to report the total number times they participated in an activity during the past semester. The sum of frequencies for all twelve school volunteering activities was used to represent an individual's extent of school volunteering.

RESULTS

Descriptive Results

One of the main goals of this present study was to explore the characteristics of school volunteering in Korea. In general, 32 percent of participants had experience with school volunteering. In terms of the specific activities they engaged in, as summarized in Table 1, parents most often volunteered for traffic monitoring (15%), and least often volunteered in the library (2%) and in the cafeteria for lunchtime supervision (2%).

Table 1. Frequencies of School Volunteering Activities.

	Frequencies	Percentage
Traffic Monitoring	77	15%
Participation in PTA Meetings	73	14.6%
Assistance for School Special-Events	48	10%
School/Classroom Cleaning	39	8%
School Meal Inspections	33	7%
School Beautification	23	5%
Assistance for Class Special-Events	22	4%
Guest Teacher	20	4%
General Classroom Assistance	20	4%
Assistance for Field Trips	16	3%
Library Volunteering	9	2%
Lunchtime Supervision	8	2%

Socioeconomic Factors and School Volunteering Experiences

In this study, we focused on four variables in relation to participants' socioeconomic status: education level, partner's education level, employment status, and annual household income. For this analysis, four different cross-tab analyses were conducted, and chi-square statistics were checked. First, Table 2 and Table 3 present the differences in school volunteering experiences by parents' education levels. As Table 2 and Table 3 present, a greater portion of participants with a college or higher degree were involved in school volunteering (39.8%) than participants who had a high school or lower degree (26.1%); similarly, a greater portion of participants whose partners held a college or higher degree were involved (39.1%) than participants whose partners did not (25.3%). Such differences were statistically significant for both the participant's ($\chi^2(1)$ = 10.27, p = .001) and partner's education level ($\chi^2(1)$ = 9.91, p = .001).

Table 2. Results for Participants' Education Level.

	HS Degree or Lower	College Degree or Higher
No Volunteering Experience	198 (73.9%)	130 (60.2%)
Volunteering Experience	70 (26.1%)	86 (39.8%)
Total	268 (100%)	216 (100%)

Table 3. Results for Partner's Education Level.

	HS Degree or Lower	College Degree or Higher
No Volunteering Experience	165 (74.7%)	143 (60.9%)
Volunteering Experience	56 (25.3%)	92 (39.1%)
Total	221 (100%)	235 (100%)

Next, Table 4 presents the relationship between employment status and school volunteering. Although parents who were not employed were more often motivated for school volunteering than parents who were, this difference was not found to be statistically significant ($\chi^2(1)$ = .34, p = .20).

Table 4. Results for Employment Status.

	Employed	Not Employed
No Volunteering Experience	215 (69.1%)	113 (64.9%)
Volunteering Experience	96 (30.9%)	61 (35.1%)
Total	311 (100%)	174 (100%)

Lastly, Table 5 presents how school volunteering experiences are related to parents' annual income. As this table indicates, participants in families of higher annual household income—especially those of $60,000–$70,000 (46%) and of more than $70,000 (42.9%)—more often participated in school volunteering, compared to participants with a lower annual household income. This difference was statistically significant ($\chi^2(5)$ = 15.85, p = .007).

Table 5. Cross-Tab Results for Annual Household Income.

	Under $20,000	$30,000-$40,000	$40,000-$50,000	$50,000-$60,000	$60,000-$70,000	More than $70,000
No School Volunteering Experience	45(84.9%)	76(72.4%)	74(64.3%)	67(68.4%)	27(54.30%)	32(57.1%)
School Volunteering Experience	8(15.1%)	29(27.6%)	41(35.7%)	31(31.6%)	23(46.0%)	24(42.9%)
Total	53(100%)	105(100%)	115(100%)	98(100%)	50(100%)	56(100%)

Effects of Motivational Factors on School Volunteering

This study also aimed at examining the effects of five different motivational factors on school volunteering—parental role construction, parents' educational efficacy, and three dimensions of demands for school volunteering. For this examination, we conducted five logistic regression analyses. First, parental role construction was found to strongly predict parents' school volunteering ($\beta = .77$, $p < .001$, Cox & Snell's $R^2 = .08$). Second, educational efficacy moderately predicted school volunteering ($\beta = .33$, $p = 0.06$, Cox & Snell's $R^2 = .01$). Lastly, in terms of the three dimensions of demands for school volunteering, school's demands for school volunteering was not a significant predictor. ($\beta = .14$, $p = .17$, Cox & Snell's $R^2 = .004$). However, the variables other parents demands ($\beta = .40$, $p = .001$, Cox & Snell's $R^2 = .02$) and child's demands ($\beta = .49$, $p < .001$, Cox & Snell's $R^2 = .04$) were significant predictors.

Next, a bivariate correlation analysis was conducted to explore how the five motivational variables were related to the extent of school volunteering. Table 6 shows the correlation matrix with the six variables. As the table indicates, among the five variables, parental role construction ($r = .226$, $p < .001$) was most strongly correlated to the extent of school volunteering. Although the three dimensions of demands for school volunteering were statistically significantly correlated to the extent of school volunteering, in particular, parent's educational efficacy was most weakly correlated ($r = .098$, $p < .05$). There was no significant correlation between parents' educational efficacy and the extent of school volunteering ($r = .072$, $p > .10$).

In addition to the correlation analysis, we conducted a hierarchical regression analysis to further investigate the effects of the five motivational factors on the extent of school volunteering. For this analysis, we controlled for the effects of SES—education, annual household income, and employment type. We entered the three control variables into the first block of the regression model. Then, considering the two groups of variables—internal and external factors—we entered the three types of demands for school volunteering (external factors) into the first block and added the two internal factors—parental role construction and parent's educational efficacy—into the model. As Table 7 shows, after controlling for the effects of SES, child's demand (β = .579, p = .014) and parental role construction (β = .728, p = .002) significantly and positively predicted the extent of school volunteering.

Table 6. Correlations among Motivational Factors and Extent of School Volunteering.

	1	2	3	4	5
1 Extent of School Volunteering	1				
2 Parental Role Construction	.226***	1			
3 Parent's Educational Efficacy	.072	.197***	1		
4 School's Demands for School Volunteering	.098*	.378***	.086†	1	
5 Other Parents' Demands for School Volunteering	.115**	.532***	.125**	.611***	1
6 Child's Demands for School Volunteering	.178***	.640***	.155**	.531***	.682***

Notes. † p < .10, * p < .05, ** p < .01, *** p < .001.

Table 7. Results from Hierarchical Regression Analysis.

Predictor Variables	Block 1	Block 2	Block 3	R^2	ΔR^2
Education	.383				
Annual Household Income	.583†				
Employment	.542†			.017	
School's Demands for School Volunteering		.205			
Other Parents' Demands for School Volunteering		-.095		.05	.033**
Child's Demands for School Volunteering		.579**			
Parental Role Construction			.728**		
Parent's Educational Efficacy			.203	.074	.024**

Notes. † p < .10, ** p < .01, *** p < .001.

DISCUSSION

Parents' school volunteering has continuously received much attention from scholars and practitioners over the recent years (Hoover-Dempsey et al., 2005). According to Hoover-Dempsey et al., in general, parents' educational involvement, including school volunteering, plays an influential role in children's academic and psychological development. However, despite the high level of interest in home involvement among Korean parents and researchers, there is a relative lack of emphasis given to school volunteering in Korea's educational context. Therefore, the current study aimed to understand this understudied aspect of parents' educational involvement by examining patterns of school volunteering in terms of types and levels of volunteering, school volunteering differences across socioeconomic characteristics, and motivations for volunteering among Korean elementary-school parents. This section discusses some of the noteworthy findings from the study.

From a volunteer:

I have tried my best to attend all class field trips for my son. I know that the teachers are going to have their hands full trying to keep twenty-two excited 7- and 8-year-olds in line outside of the school grounds. So I want to help, out of concern not only for the teachers but also for my son and other kids. I do think it helps. I don't think that volunteering necessarily helps increase my son's test scores or his teacher's evaluation of his work; or maybe it does indirectly and maybe I secretly hope that it does. But I have indeed experienced that my frequent volunteering encourages his teachers to treat him with more care and attention. Also, I get more opportunities to hear about how my son is doing at school. The teachers always have something new to tell me every time I attend the field trips. I can see that my son enjoys my presence as well. I think it makes him feel safe and secure when I am around on the field trips. Also, the smile on his face when I arrive at school tells me that he is proud that his mom is there to help out the teacher. It is mostly that smile that keeps me going back.

Volunteer mother of second-grade student, Seoul, Korea

First, this study explored the different types of activities of school volunteering among Korean parents. A notable finding was that, compared to other activities, only 4% of the parents were involved in general classroom assistance. Moreover, a very small portion of parents had experience as a guest teacher or a volunteer for classroom events (e.g., parties). In other words, compared to the other types of school volunteering activities, Korean parents were quite reluctant to be involved in the classroom. This can be explained by Koreans' extremely high respect for teachers, rooted in Confucian culture. In other words, traditionally, Koreans believe that teachers should be respected at the same level of the king and father.

Korean parents tend to confer to teachers the total authority to teach and supervise their children and consider the classroom to fundamentally be the teacher's own territory. In addition, it is noteworthy that Korean teachers also have a tendency for maintaining their own territory and being hesitant to receive help from the parents. In other words, they may consider parents' involvement in classroom activities as interfering with and undermining the teachers' rights and authority.

Additionally, in regards to teachers' reluctance to parents' volunteering in classroom activities, a Korean teacher addressed an interesting point. During an informal conversation with one of the researchers to discuss data collection, this teacher mentioned that he did not want to receive help from students' parents because he did not want to hear any complaints in regards to unfair treatment of students. In other words, parents occasionally complained about teachers' favoritism toward students whose parents actively volunteered and, thus, this particular teacher wanted to avoid any potential complaints. Related to this point, a survey participant voluntarily wrote down an unexpected comment in the paper-pencil survey. Her note read (translated from Korean): "I think parents' school volunteering is not good because it exacerbates unfair treatment of students whose parents cannot volunteer for their children's school." This message clearly indicated the potential complaints that can be made against the injustice created from unequal levels of school volunteering among parents. Furthermore, the grading system for the Korean elementary schools is also useful in understanding this argument. These schools are reliant on a relative grading system that is based on exams as well as teachers' evaluation of students. All students in a class are ranked from first/top to last. Any suspicious and seemingly unfair rankings are likely to be disputed by the parents. Therefore, it makes sense that teachers would want to avoid such potential conflicts by refusing parents' involvement in classroom activities.

These findings are quite different from previous findings in regards to Western society, where school volunteering occurs routinely and is highly encouraged. In countries of high-context and Confucian cultures like Korea, school volunteering tends to be devalued and underestimated, even though it can have potentially positive outcomes in terms of students' school achievement as well as emotional development. Related to this, it must be considered that in Korea, educational background, especially graduation from top, prestigious universities, is a highly decisive factor of one's success in life. Therefore, trivial and minute details related to students' school grades can trigger significant conflicts between parents and teachers as well as among parents. Unfortunately, this implies the difficulties in changing the values associated with school volunteering in Korean society. In this way, the value of school volunteering is bounded by cultural value systems as well as social structures. In this sense, the study's findings contribute to widening scholars' perspectives in regards to the roles of parental school volunteering.

Next, this study analyzed the relationships between the socioeconomic characteristics of parents—educational level, annual household income, and employment status—and their school volunteering. Results indicated that parents with higher levels of educational attainment and annual household income were more likely to be involved in their child's school. These findings are consistent with patterns observed in Western societies (Green et al., 2007; Hoover-Dempsey et al., 2005) and reaffirm the importance of parents' SES in understanding school volunteering. Considering the academic benefits of parental school volunteering (Hoover-Dempsey et al., 2005), this finding implies that there can be a negative consequence, where inequalities in education can be reproduced through parents' participation in school activities. This further suggests that more differentiated levels and scopes of volunteering activities—such as activities that can take place at home, at one's own spatial and temporal convenience—need to be identified and communicated to parents, in order to encourage and encompass participation from parents of differing resources.

Third, it was quite interesting that, while school's demands for parental involvement did not significantly determine parents' school volunteering, it was significantly correlated to the extent of school volunteering. This implies that, although school's demands for parental volunteering may not create new volunteers, they are likely to encourage experienced volunteers to participate more frequently. Based on this finding, schools will need to contemplate how they can strategically target both new and experienced volunteers in order to maximize school volunteering. For example, if schools communicate a desire to have new parents involved, they may need to seek the help of experienced parent volunteers to encourage other new parents, rather than directly asking them to participate. Particularly, experienced volunteer parents need to actively inform new parents of how much enjoyment and personal satisfaction they can experience from school volunteering, how valuable and beneficial parental school volunteering can be for students' school achievement and emotional development, and how effective such volunteering can be for expanding personal networks through interactions with other parents. However, it must be considered that, as the results of the hierarchical regression indicate (see Table 7), the effect of school's demands for parental volunteering on the extent of school volunteering was suppress by the variable child's demands for parent volunteering. This implies that parents must pay closer attention to their children's direct and indirect communicative cues regarding school volunteering.

Finally, it was considerable that there was no significant relationship between parents' educational efficacy and the extent of school involvement. This is interesting because previous studies have consistently found efficacy regarding children's education to play a positive role in increasing parents' school involvement (Grolnick et al.,1997; Hoover-Dempsey et al., 2005; Shumow & Lomax, 2002).

To thoroughly interpret this result, we need to consider that parents' educational efficacy tends to be stronger among parents of younger students and that it may diminish as students get older (Eccles & Harold, 1993; Lee, 2003). That is, as children advance in grade level, many parents decrease in levels of resources that they may employ to help their children. For example, except for a number of parents with high education levels, it is quite difficult for most parents to help high school students with their schoolwork, such as that involving algebra or physics. The elementary school parents participating in this study also showed relatively high levels of educational efficacy (M = 3.45). This implies that a large portion of Korean parents are highly confident in educating their children and believe that they are competent enough to efficiently and appropriately handle any education-related problems. Such commonality in regards to educational efficacy across the entire sample might have oppressed its effect on parents' school involvement.

In this way, this study produced a number of interesting findings related to parental school involvement in Korea. While some findings echoed previous studies conducted in Western societies, others were quite different and reflected the unique educational context of Korea. As such, these findings are expected to broaden our understanding of parental school involvement, especially in the sense that it shows us that school involvement is also characterized by specific cultural contexts.

FUTURE DIRECTIONS

Although this study identified several interesting and meaningful findings, the following points are recommended for future research. First, one of the most critical issues in regards to primary and secondary education in Korea is the regional and locational inequalities in educational quality. According to a 2013 report from the Korea National Statistical Office (KNSO), compared to the average monthly expense of private tutoring for the five largest cities in Korea (approximately $229), Seoul's was much larger (approximately $312). A noteworthy point is that the quality of private tutoring often influences schools' educational curricula. This is mainly because the level of prerequisite learning is heightened by the quality of private tutoring. For example, it is not uncommon for middle-school students to complete high-school curricula through private education even before entering high school. As the portion of such students increase, the schools find it necessary to establish higher standards for evaluating the students. Eventually, this leads to the exacerbation of educational inequities in terms of educational quality. For instance, the costs for private tutoring are much higher in the affluent areas of Seoul, especially in the general Gangnam area. The mothers of students in the Gangnam area are commonly referred to as "*Gangnam Umma* [mom]," and they have a notorious reputation for being obsessively involved in both home-based and school-based educational activities. These highly-involved parents arduously provide input for the academic curricula of their children's schools, eventually assisting their children's school performance. Due to private tutoring and strong parental involvement, the quality of schools in the Gangnam area is much higher than those in other areas across the nation. Although Gangnam is an extreme case, it will be valuable for future research to compare how school involvement differs across locations in Korea.

Further, future research will benefit by conducting cross-cultural comparisons between parents in Korea and Korean immigrant parents in the US, and possibly with native US parents as well. Although there is a significant amount of research on Korean first-generation immigrant parents in the US (Lee, 2005; Sohn & Wang, 2006), understanding of this literature would increase with data simultaneously collected from the home-country or, in other words, the cultural context from which these immigrant parents emigrated. A comparison of this data would help us understand where immigrant parents' attitudes toward and behaviors of school involvement originate from as well as how the cultural adaptation process affects their ideas about parental involvement.

CONCLUSION

This study explored the patterns of parental school volunteering in Korean elementary schools. It explored the quantity and quality of Korean parents' school volunteering and further examined the effects of parents' socioeconomic status (SES) as well as five motivational factors on the extent of school volunteering. Data analyses showed unique patterns in parental school volunteering activities as well as in the relationships among motivations and school volunteering in the context of Korean elementary schools. These findings meaningfully address the necessity of evaluating the roles of cultural value systems and social structures in understanding the value of parental school volunteering. The findings further suggest that more efficient communication among the main three actors—parents, school, and child—may help increase the extent of parental school volunteering in Korea.

NOTE

1. In the US literature, participation in PTA meetings and activities tends to be identified as an activity independent from school volunteering—both are considered to be dimensions of school-based involvement (Hoover-Dempsey & Sandler, 1997). However, based on our conversations with informants, in the current Korean context, engagement with the PTA was understood as a form of school volunteering rather than an independent form of school involvement.

REFERENCES

Bandura, A. (1989). Regulation of cognitive processes through perceived self-efficacy. *Developmental Psychology, 25*, 729–735.

Bandura, A. (2006). Guide for constructing self-efficacy scales. In F. Pajares & T. C. Urdan (Eds.), *Self-efficacy beliefs of adolescents* (pp. 307–337). Greenwich, CT: Information Age Publishing.

Byun, S-Y., & Kim, K-K. (2008). Parental involvement and student achievement in South Korea: Focusing on differential effects by family background. *Korean Journal of Sociology of Education, 18*, 39–66.

Deslandes, R., & Bertrand, R. (2005). Motivation of parent involvement in secondary-level schooling. *Journal of Educational Research, 98*, 164–175.

Eccles, J. S., & Harold, R. D. (1993). Parent-school involvement during the early adolescent years. *Teachers College Record, 94*, 568–587.

Eisner, D., Grimm Jr., R. T., Maynard, S., & Washburn, S. (2009). The new volunteer workforce. *Stanford Social Innovation Review*, 32–37.

Finkelstein, M. A. (2010). Individualism/collectivism: Implications for the volunteer process. *Social Behavior and Personality, 38*, 445–452.

Green, C. I., Walker, J. M. T., Hoover-Dempsey, K. V., & Sandler, H. M. (2007). Parents' motivations for involvement in children's education: An empirical test of a theoretical model of parental involvement. *Journal of Educational Psychology, 99*, 532–544.

Grolnick, W. S., Benjet, C., Kurowski, C. O., & Apostoleris, N. H. (1997). Predictors of parent involvement in children's schooling. *Journal of Educational Psychology, 89*, 538–548.

Hoover-Dempsey, K. V., & Sandler, H. M. (1995). Parental involvement in children's education: Why does it make a difference? *Teachers College Record, 97*, 310–331.

Hoover-Dempsey, K. V., & Sandler, H. M. (1997). Why do parents become involved in their children's education? *Review of Educational Research, 67*, 3–42.

Hoover-Dempsey, K. V., Walker, J. M. T., Sandler, H. M., Whetsel, D., Green, C. L., Wilkins, A. S., & Closson, K. (2005). Why do parents become involved? Research findings and implications. *The Elementary School Journal, 106*, 105–130.

Kemmelmeier, M., Jambor, E. E. & Letner, J. (2006). Individualism and good works: Cultural variations in giving and volunteering across the United States. *Journal of Cross Cultural Psychology, 37*, 327–344.

Kim, D., & Shin, J. (2012, July 17). Ranked #1 in International Mathematics Olympiad: All Korean participants won gold medals (in Korean). *Seoul Shinmun*. Retrieved from http://www.seoul.co.kr/news/newsView.php?id=20120717002011

Kim, D. (2014, January 11). University composition of successful candidates for higher civil service examination: 7 out of 10 candidates from top three universities. Veritas α. Retrieved from http://www.veritas-a.com

Kim, H. (2013). *Entrance examination family: Middle-class family's use of entrance examination* (in Korean). Seoul, Korea: Sae Mul Gyul.

Kim, S., & Lee, J. (2010). Private tutoring and demand for education in South Korea. *Economic Development and Cultural Change, 58,* 259–296.

Kim, S. D. (2002). Korea: Personal meanings. In J. E. Katz & M. Aakhus (Eds.), *Perpetual contact: Mobile communication, private talk, public performance* (pp. 63–79). New York, NY: Cambridge University Press.

Kim, Y. H. (2002). A study of adolescent's school adjustment in poor families: With the mediating role of maternal involvement. *Korean Journal of Community Living Science, 13,* 1–14.

Kim, Y-H., & Son, J. (2003). Trust, cooperation and social risk: A cross cultural comparison. *Anthology of Korean Studies. UNESCO, 38,* 623–643.

Korea National Statistical Office (KNSO) (2012). *Private education expenditure survey 2012.* Seoul: KNSO.

Korean Statistical Information Service (2013). *2013 Survey of household finance and social welfare.* Seoul: KOSIS. Retrieved from http://kosis.kr/statisticsList/statisticsList_01List.jsp?vwcd=MT_ZTITLE&parmTabId=M_01_01

Lee, D. H. (2008). A study on parental culture: Focused on parents' educational support activities for children (in Korean). *Korean Journal of Sociology of Education, 18,* 135–165.

Lee, H. (2013, March 8). 30 out of 71 most expensive kindergartens are located in Gangnam: University-affiliated or private kindergartens (in Korean). *The Kyunghyang Shinmun.* Retrieved from http://news.khan.co.kr/kh_news/khan_art_view.html?artid=201303080600165&code=940401

Lee, J. (2011). Education and family in conflict. *Journal of Studies in International Education, 15,* 395–401.

Lee, Se. (2003). Influence of parents' school participation on evaluation of teachers (in Korean). *Korean Journal of Sociology of Education, 13,* 185–208.

Lee, So. (2005). Selective parent participation: Structural and cultural factors that influence school participation among Korean parents. *Equity & Excellence in Education, 38,* 299–308.

Muller, C. (1993). Parent involvement and academic achievement: An analysis of family resources available to the child. In B. Schneider & J. S. Coleman (Eds.), *Parents, their children, and schools* (pp. 77–113). Boulder: Westview Press.

OECD (2010). PISA 2009 results: What students know and can do: Student performance in reading, mathematics and science (Volume I). PISA, OECD Publishing. Retrieved from http://dx.doi.org/10.1787/9789264091450-en

OECD (2014). PISA 2012 results: What students know and can do (Volume I, Revised edition, February 2014): Student performance in mathematics, reading and science. PISA, OECD Publishing. Retrieved from http://dx.doi.org/10.1787/9789264208780-en

Parboteeah, K. P., Cullen, J., & Lim, L. (2004). Formal volunteering: A cross-national test. *Journal of World Business, 39,* 431–441.

Park, H., Byun, S., & Kim, K. (2011). Parental involvement and students' cognitive outcomes in Korea: Focusing on private tutoring. *Sociology of Education, 84,* 3–22.

Seth, M. (2012). Education zeal, state control and citizenship in South Korea. *Citizenship Studies, 16,* 13–28.

Sheldon, S. B. (2002). Parents' social networks and beliefs as predictors of parent involvement. *Elementary School Journal, 102,* 301–316.

Shumow, L., & Lomax, R. (2002). Parental efficacy: Predictor of parenting behavior and adolescent outcomes. *Parenting: Science and Practice, 2,* 127–150.

Shumow, L., Lyutykh, E., & Schmidt, J. A. (2011). Predictors and outcomes of parental involvement with high school students in science. *The School Community Journal, 21,* 81–98.

Simon, B. S. (2004). High school outreach and family involvement. *Social Psychology of Education, 7,* 185–209.

Sohn, S., & Wang, X. C. (2006). Immigrant parents' involvement in American schools: Perspectives from Korean mothers. *Early Childhood Education Journal, 34,* 125–132.

Song, H., & Park, J. (2014, January 3). Society of school ties is confirmed by numbers (in Korean). *The Kyunghyang Shinmun.* Retrieved from http://news.khan.co.kr/kh_news/khan_art_view.html?artid=201401030600065&code=940401

Walker, J. M. T., Wilkins, A. S., Dallaire, J. P., Sandler, H. M., & Hoover-Dempsey, K. V. (2005). Parental involvement: Model revision through scale development. *Elementary School Journal, 106,* 85–104.

CHAPTER FIVE

Knowledge Sharing in International Volunteering Cooperation: Challenges, Opportunities and Impacts on Results

MARIE-PIERRE LEROUX
TANIA SABA
School of Industrial Relations, University of Montreal, Canada and Interuniversity Research Centre on Globalization and Work (CRIMT)

International development cooperation strives to contribute to capacity building in the developing countries where programs are implemented. Capacity building is commonly understood as a process aimed at enhancing the capacities of individuals, organizations and institutions (UNDP, 2010). Most development cooperation programs rely on technical assistance to achieve their objectives. Technical cooperation comprises human resource deployment activities aimed at transferring and sharing skills, capabilities and know-how. These human resources come mainly from donor countries and include paid expatriates and volunteers who are recruited to carry out specific assignments. Typical assignments can cover a wide range of areas, such as advising a school's management on how to develop an academic curriculum or a federation of producers on how to better commercialize their products. Whatever the field of practice, there is a need for research on the process of knowledge sharing in the context of international development programs implemented in the developing world.

The purpose of the present study was to gain a better understanding of the experience of volunteers working in technical cooperation in developing countries. It looked closely at the relational processes that evolve during international assignments (IAs) in the specific context of international development projects. In particular, it aimed to explore the factors that impede or positively influence the process of knowledge sharing between Canadian volunteers and their local counterparts working in community-based organizations in two developing countries, namely Haiti (Central America) and Senegal (West Africa). This study adopted a micro-level perspective, focusing on the personal experiences of the individuals involved. First, it strove to understand the communication and relational mechanisms underlying the exchange process. Second, it sought to explore how interpersonal relations impacted the results of knowledge sharing initiatives. Third and lastly, it aimed to identify some communication strategies that Canadian volunteers and their local counterparts used to achieve their objectives.

A review of the literature revealed a dearth of research addressing these specific relational aspects with regard to volunteers. Exploring this avenue of research should shed light on the set of human factors, such as cognitive and social practices, that promote or limit the success of knowledge transfer (Hislop, 2009; Nonaka & vonKrogh, 2009). The study first describes what volunteers working in international technical cooperation are expected to achieve in the course of their duties. It then presents the main literature on knowledge sharing and the factors that impede or facilitate this process. This is followed by a presentation of the theoretical framework developed for this study and the underlying research questions. The last section presents and discusses the results of the study.

LITERATURE REVIEW

Technical cooperation in international development dates from the post-Second World War period under the Marshall Plan, which aimed to help rebuild war-devastated countries. In the present day, technical cooperation remains a component of the international aid system. CIDA, the cooperation branch of the Canadian government (now merged with the Ministry of Foreign Affairs, Trade and Development) defines technical cooperation as the transfer, adaptation or facilitation of ideas, knowledge, technologies or skills to improve development (CIDA, 2011). Hence activities in technical cooperation encompass consulting initiatives and other actions aimed at developing human resources. In terms of investments, technical cooperation activities are included in the $133 billion allocated to international aid by donor countries every year (OECD, 2011). Human resources, specifically Canadian volunteers in the context of this study, contribute to the implementation of technical cooperation initiatives.

According to Land (2007), these volunteers can endorse four main roles. What is expected from them varies significantly. First, their role can consist of substitute functions, whereby they carry out tasks in a local organization in the place of a local employee. Second, they can act as advisors, meaning they provide expert advice in a context where no local expertise is available. Third, they can be responsible for capacity building, meaning they assist individuals and local organizations in developing their capacities and enhancing performance. This specific role encompasses on-site learning, change management, dialogue and facilitation processes. Fourth and lastly, they can also be responsible for project management and the financial control of the resources allocated to local organizations by donors. Land (2007) points out that a person carrying out a technical cooperation assignment is likely to perform more than one role.

In 2012, nearly 7000 volunteers, through the UN alone, served in local communities (UNDP, 2013). Many countries run volunteer programs, as does Canada through its many international cooperation programs. Many Canadian NGOs recruit volunteers to fulfill mandates with their local partners. However, assessing the results of these endeavors remains a challenge. In fact, there is a need to measure how volunteers contribute to capacity building given that many observers and analysts have expressed doubt and criticism regarding the impacts of technical assistance (e.g., Carlsson & Wohlgemuth, 2001; Heizmann, 2008), especially with regard to capacity building, where results are expected in terms of the transfer or adaptation of ideas, knowledge and skills. Among the many problems and criticisms raised since the 1960s, Morgan and Baser (1993), in particular, wondered whether any thought had been given to the utility of such knowledge transfers, and raised questions regarding the understanding of the factors that contribute to the acquisition and assimilation of knowledge. Surprisingly, studies in international cooperation have yet to answer these questions. Hence the pertinence of the present study exploring how volunteers contribute to the process of knowledge transfer and knowledge sharing in technical cooperation.

Knowledge transfer and sharing is "the communication of knowledge from a source so that it is learned and applied by the recipient" (Ko et al., 2005). From this perspective, knowledge transfer is seen in terms of processes and results. However, many factors impact the results of knowledge transfer processes. These factors can be divided into four sets. The first set concerns the nature of the knowledge to be transferred. The more complex the knowledge (Zander & Kogut, 1995), the more difficult its transfer. This complexity, also known as causal ambiguity, refers to knowledge that cannot be explained easily, such as when too many variables are involved, thus increasing the barriers affecting the exchange process (Grant, 1996; Simonin, 1999; Spender, 1996; Suzlanski, 1996). The second set of factors relates to the multiple contexts in which knowledge transfers occur. The main contextual factors cited in the empirical research are the global environment, the organizational context (Reagan & McEvily, 2003), and cultural and institutional distance (Kostova & Roth, 2002; Lia et al., 2007). The third and fourth sets of determinants of knowledge transfer refer to the individual characteristics of the parties involved (e.g., Minbaeva, 2007) and the evolving relationship between them. This latter relational characteristic involves determinants such as trust (Argote et al., 2003; Ko, 2010), social ties (Granovetter, 1973), power relations (Frenkel, 2008), absorptive capacity, defined as the ability to identify, assimilate and exploit knowledge gained from external sources (Cohen & Leventhal, 1989), and shared language (Davenport & Prusak, 1998). Clearly, communication between the parties and other relational factors have proven to be important in the process of knowledge sharing. These factors can contribute to the success of the knowledge transfer, but they can also be important barriers to its realization. The conceptual model developed for the present study of knowledge sharing between Canadian volunteers and their local partners in international cooperation focuses on this relational dimension of the knowledge sharing process.

CONCEPTUAL FRAMEWORK AND RESEARCH QUESTIONS

Knowledge management theories are frequently mobilized in studies on international knowledge transfer (e.g., Bonache & Zaggara-Oberty, 2008; Mäkelä et al., 2011). The model constructed for the purpose of this study aims to establish links between relational factors, such as communication processes, and the results of knowledge sharing, particularly in the context of international development programs. The model consists of four dimensions. The first two refer to the personal characteristics of the volunteers and members of the local team, respectively. The third dimension refers to cognitive, relational and communication aspects. The fourth and last dimension concerns the results of knowledge sharing and covers knowledge internalization, enhanced capacity to act and innovation.

The theoretical foundations of this model highlight the fact that, once in contact, international volunteers and their local partners develop interpersonal relationships through communication, wherein intersubjective processes create outcomes. These outcomes lead to some results. These results do not depend only on the nature of the knowledge transferred, but are influenced by the exchanges between the parties involved, while the exchanges are themselves influenced by the parties' personal characteristics.

In particular, the model emphasizes the intersubjective processes leading to results. During the establishment of interpersonal relationships, cognitive determinants come into play (Gooderham, 2007). The absorptive capacity of the recipient of the knowledge transfer is one determinant of its success (e.g., Szulanski, 1996). If the distance between the parties undermines their ability to evaluate, assimilate and use the knowledge, the transfer will fail. Very little research in this area has focused on the absorptive capacity of the volunteer. Yet, knowledge transfer happens only in a communication exchange. It is a bidirectional process wherein the expatriate is both a source and a recipient of knowledge (Mäkela et al., 2011). To explore whether the absorptive capacity of the parties has an impact on the process of knowledge transfer between volunteers and their local partners, the study explores the following two questions:

> RQ1: Does the absorptive capacity of the volunteer have an impact on the quality of the interpersonal relationship between the latter and his/her local partner and on the results of the knowledge sharing process?

> RQ2: Does the absorptive capacity of the local partner have an impact on the quality of the interpersonal relationship between the latter and the hosted volunteer and on the results of the knowledge sharing process?

Another factor, shared language, is central to the study of knowledge transfer. Speaking different mother tongues is the most obvious obstacle to successful knowledge transfer. In addition, values and beliefs, mental models and schemas may differ between the parties. The cultural and cognitive background of the individuals makes the meaning they give to situations and the sense they make of them unique. The greater the distance between their languages, the greater the challenges facing them (Easterby-Smith et al., 2008). Kostova (1999) and Kostova and Roth (2002) explored the same idea with their concept of "institutional distance," while Frenkel (2008) and Cummings (2003) used the term "cultural distance" in their discussion of elements impeding the transfer process. Sharing the same language or striving to develop common ground helps to establish a cooperative climate, which is central to the process of knowledge creation and transfer. Boland and Tenkasi (1995) illustrated the link between perspective-making and perspective-taking in communication processes. It appears that when individuals show a capacity to understand their partners' different ways of thinking, knowledge sharing is facilitated. This leads to the third and final research question:

> RQ3: Does shared language have an impact on the quality of the interpersonal relationship between volunteers and their local partners and on the results of the knowledge sharing process?

METHOD

The relational processes involved in knowledge sharing activities are central to these questions. It was thus necessary to observe the environment in which the partner organizations evolved and to seek an in-depth understanding of the perceptions of the participants involved. To explore these research questions, the case study method was used, combining multiple sources of information to allow for triangulation of the data (Yin, 2003). Flyvberg (2001) and Rossman and Rallis

(1998) also point out the benefits of a qualitative inquiry when a new angle of observation is required.

As part of the research project, a Canadian NGO that works with volunteers in international development was contacted. Every year, this organization sends approximately 400 individuals abroad following pre-departure training. Over a six-month period, the researcher conducted research for this micro-level case study inquiry with the approval of the managers of the Canadian NGO and the university's institutional ethics committee. The flexible method used allowed her to grasp the personal experience of the Canadian volunteers and their local counterparts (Liamputtong, 2010).

A total of eight case studies out of twelve were retained for the purposes of this study. Each case (four from Haiti, four from Senegal) involved a local organization that hosted volunteers for short and long-term periods, that is, from 2 weeks to 24 months. The non-random sampling technique was used. Starting with the Canadian NGO, which worked in technical cooperation projects, we selected a number of its partner organizations in two developing countries (Miles & Huberman, 2003). All the technical cooperation initiatives studied aimed to enhance the economic conditions of the beneficiaries, through the intervention of volunteers serving in various functions within local organizations.

A case study protocol was developed to guide the data collection. All interviews were conducted in French, recorded with all quotes later translated into English. Two sets of semi-structured interview questions (one for volunteers and one for local partners) were drawn up as guidelines to encourage spontaneous expression on the part of all participants. This interview guide allowed us to gather complex information and showed respect for the participants, who could chose what they wished to share (Fortin, 2006; Liamputtong, 2010). A total of 38 interviews (with 15 volunteers and 23 local partners) were conducted in the eight selected case studies. During coding, all respondents were given alpha-numeric codes. Then pseudonyms were assigned for reporting the findings.

The first field period was in Haiti, Central America, where the researcher conducted several interviews with volunteers and their partner organizations. The same process was applied for the case studies located in Senegal, West Africa. Being in the field allowed us to conduct non-participant observation, meeting participants at their place of work or in their homes. We also met with former volunteers in Canada, who had returned from assignments with local partners.

The content of the interviews were analyzed using Sonal, qualitative data analysis software used to collect, organize, transcribe and analyze audio files. As the case study protocol and interview guidelines covered the major subjects emphasized in the research, themes were identified in accordance with the concepts explored in this study (e.g., personality, intention to share, motivation, language barrier, interpersonal trust, power based on knowledge, etc.). All interview segments were codified. Because a segment often contained multiple themes, each segment could figure in several themes. General themes were first identified and cyclical analysis and coding made it possible to combine and merge some themes, divide other themes, and create new themes, ultimately leading to 46 themes (Glaser & Strauss, 1967; Thyer, 2001). The interviews lasted between 50 minutes and 2.5 hours and the theme segments represent over 86 hours of recording.

FINDINGS

RQ1: Absorptive Capacity of the Volunteer

The volunteer's ability to understand the context in which he/she was operating was a form of absorptive capacity. For example, for one volunteer carrying out an assignment in the area of communication on behalf of a partner organization working in rice production, it was a real challenge to learn the whole production process. This volunteer, named Evelyne, claimed that contextual assimilation was her biggest challenge when it came to proposing communication tools and techniques pertaining to this domain. She described the cognitive process she used, which demonstrated her ability to assimilate information. Eight other volunteers described a comparable approach. The first step in this approach was to communicate in order to understand the needs of the partners with whom they were matched. They then had to assess the partners' level of knowledge and estimate their weaknesses in order to propose a program that would be adapted to their needs and level. Sometimes, volunteers had to refrain from sharing knowledge:

> I would say it's levels of knowledge that I didn't transfer because it wasn't adaptable to their situation. Like picture editing. I showed them in Word instead of Photoshop…which is professional software, and nobody in the organization would have been able to manage it, even with training. It's really advanced software; it's for professionals. (Evelyne, a Canadian volunteer in communication)

Many volunteers described similar steps, emphasizing that they were there for the benefit of their partners. They considered themselves to be advisors and wanted to help and to make a difference. They began by helping their partners carry out a diagnosis of the situation and identify better solutions with them. This cognitive ability was described by Joseph, a Haitian-Canadian volunteer: "…you always need to adapt to their capacity level, it's really variable. There can be well-equipped participants and others who are weaker." The partners also mentioned the absorptive capacity of volunteers who performed well during their assignments:

> (Marc) was able to take in what we told him so as to be able to improve our processes… He said that his Canadian reality was different from the Senegalese reality, so he asked

> us to tell him what we were doing and how we were doing it… He was really bright. He understood things quickly… He had the ability to reflect and understand things. (Ibrahim, a Senegalese partner)

The above extract also shows another characteristic of some volunteers that was related to their absorptive capacity: their openness to listen to their partners. These volunteers accepted new information and were willing to listen to different perspectives and change their own stand.

Conversely, volunteers who were unable to receive external information and grasp the context of the intervention, failed. In some cases, the relationship between the volunteer and his/her partners was preserved but the assignment did not produce the targeted outcomes, as mentioned by the participants from a Senegalese organization working in agriculture. These participants were expecting multiple outputs, such as new proposals to bid for international funding. In other cases, the volunteer's incapacity to absorb information was perceived by the "locals" as incompetency and led to his/her isolation from the group, as explained by a partner working for vegetable producers in Senegal, where Diane, a former volunteer, would not agree to let men participate in the design of the new outlet. Likewise, Marie-Therese, a member of a Haitian organization working to improve women's conditions, said that the whole team ignored a volunteer named Michele to make her understand that she was not welcome there anymore.

RQ2: Absorptive Capacity of the Partner

> They showed a fantastic openness. These people don't get scandalized or discouraged easily, or give up. They often accept the recommendations. They have this tendency, this facility, to learn. They've developed a capacity to absorb things. (Claude, a Canadian volunteer in orgnizational management)

The above extract was representative of half the case studies, which were equally distributed both in terms of the country in which the initiatives took place and in terms of gender. However, the results suggest that those volunteers who acknowledged their partner's absorptive capacity had, by far, communicated with well-educated partners.

Also, some volunteers acknowledged and valued local competencies; they did not label the partner organizations as organizations suffering from the not-invented-here syndrome, a concept expressing a tendency to reject external solutions just because they are not internally developed (Jensen & Szulanski, 2004). The partners themselves generally argued that they wanted to make the most of the presence of the volunteer. They wanted to learn: "There is a legitimate thirst for this knowledge." (Arnaud, a Haitian partner)

The other half of the interview segments pertaining to the absorptive capacity of the partners revealed that sometimes good will was not enough for the process to be successful. The gap in knowledge was sometimes too great to break through this cognitive barrier. However, in these segments, the volunteers mostly mentioned the quality and level of education of the partners rather than their personal attributes. They were unable to assess or speak about the absorptive capacity of individuals. Rather, they spoke in general terms:

> What surprises me is encountering individuals who don't always have the basics, the training, the ABCs required to be able to receive the information. They sometimes have university degrees, but their training doesn't match their responsibilities. (Claude, a Canadian volunteer in orgnizational management)

Even with motivated partners, some volunteers didn't completely achieve their objectives. They had to lower their expectations in terms of the quantity of outputs and the level of knowledge, and attempt to reduce the gap. Annie explained that even when she used educational tools, she had to adjust to the partners' level. She said she felt that her partners were listening to what she was saying, but were unable to conceptualize it. Her perception corroborated that of her partner: "It appears to be difficult because we don't really know...everybody talks about hygiene and safety. We do it, but we don't really understand...why we're doing this" (Martine, Haitian school principal). The same barrier came up when volunteers were sent on assignment to a partner organization that had no knowledge of the subject in question. An example of this was an assignment dealing with the environment at a partner organization that had never heard of this issue before.

The last set of obstacles related to the absorptive capacity of the partner concerning the means taken. Often, the partners mentioned that the assignments were too short for them to be able to absorb all the knowledge they needed to absorb. Yero, a general secretary in a Senegalese agriculture federation, said that smallholder farmers need to practice techniques, to get concrete things done. He also pointed out that some organizations do not have the capacity to absorb new knowledge, due to organizational and structural weaknesses. In fact, many organizations do not have the financial resources to pay for the salaries and tools needed to perform appropriate tasks, leading, among other things, to poor coordination mechanisms and a lack of employee motivation and efficacy.

RQ3: Shared Language

The volunteers developed expectations regarding the results they aimed to achieve during their mandates. In one successful experience, where both sides expressed their satisfaction with the achievements, the parties said that pre-departure contacts had helped establish an initial understanding of the mandate such that the individuals involved shared the same expectations and hopes.

Once in the field, Claude, a volunteer in organizational management, was quickly introduced to his partner and they soon began the work. Claude said that they had a shared understanding of the reason he was there and his partner acknowledged that the earlier communication by virtual contact had established the basis for this common ground. Minor adjustments had to be made to the schedule, but the general orientation and objectives of the assignment were clear and well understood by all the parties concerned. They said that 90 percent of the deliverables were completed and that the partners still see the impact today. For example, the management of this organization promoting youth entrepreneurship uses the tools and techniques proposed and they understand and can now develop and implement a strategic plan. Lastly, the management feels that the employees are now more engaged and autonomous and that communication between field offices is more fluid.

However, unfortunately, not all initiatives were successful. A first barrier sometimes emerged when the volunteer and his/her local partner did not share a common understanding of the mandate. In some cases, misunderstandings evolved through a new formulation of the mandate when the parties were not willing or could not accept to change their perceptions or modify the objectives initially set. This situation sometimes led to the volunteer being isolated from the local team members. Communication broke down and the parties could not find a way to get their views across to one another. Michele, a female retiree on an assignment in communication, had this to say:

> The description wasn't clear. Something about feeding their web site... Last year, there was another volunteer in communication, and she did all these things... I think they would have liked me to do things without them being there. That's not... sharing knowledge... Them giving me things to do and me doing them... If it had been clear, if that had been my mandate, I would have done that. But it wasn't. It was, no, don't do things for them. If that had been my mandate, that would have been the assignment I'd applied for, you know? (Michele, a Canadian volunteer)

The volunteers also talked about the difficulty of not mastering the local language or, on the contrary, the positive impact of being fluent in the language of the host country. The mother tongue of most of the volunteers was French. Both Haiti and Senegal officially recognize French as a national language. However, in the field, many volunteers faced the problem of not being completely understood by their partners. Some of the volunteers who had been posted in Haiti said that many of their partners spoke and wrote in Creole and had a very limited knowledge of French. Most were able to communicate in French, but when it came to the technical aspects of the volunteer's mandate, it was not easy to present concepts and make them clear. One volunteer, a male retiree who originally came from Haiti, explained the context this way: "For many inspectors, [French] is a foreign language, not a second language. So generally, I talked to them in Creole...I know I couldn't have achieved much with them [otherwise]" (Joseph, a Canadian-Haitian volunteer).

Speaking different languages also created a barrier to the socialization process. In some cases, when the entire work environment was in Creole or Wolof, the volunteer did not feel welcome, or well-integrated into the group. On the other hand, volunteers who did not master the local language but were making an effort to speak it said that doing so helped them build a friendly relationship with the locals. Babacar, a volunteer working in the area of the environment said that when he spoke Pular, a Senegalese dialect, it helped him gain his partners' trust and facilitated his integration. Participants from at least four partner organizations said they appreciated the efforts of volunteers to communicate in the local language (other than French). They felt that it showed respect for the host culture. One participant, the coordinator of the vegetable producers' organization, explained it this way:

> I asked her... I told her that it's good to sometimes say a couple of words in Wolof. It can create an opening. Because I know, each time you come, you speak French and I translate, but in the translation I can sometimes miss or not exactly translate what you want to say... so if you already know some words, you can catch the people's attention. Then when you continue, your message will be well received. It's really important. (Mohamed, a Senegalese partner)

Communicating in a common language is a subject that came up often in the interviews, such that "common language" emerged as a theme during the analysis. However, the volunteers and their partners also identified other cognitive sources that influenced their relationships and consequently the results of their assignments. The first refers to cultural artifacts. Sometimes the volunteers did not share the same view as their partners even though they spoke the same language. For example, a young professional woman who was working in communication at a Haitian organization promoting women rights said that cultural differences had led to a profound misunderstanding between herself and her partner: "There was a real culture clash... Our perceptions were much too far apart. It's cultural, I don't blame them" (Evelyne).

Another experienced volunteer who was working in the same field said that despite her volunteering experience, she would not apply for another assignment in Haiti. She expressed bitterness when telling her story. For her, the culture clash was too great to overcome the barriers, and it resulted in her mandate ending prematurely. Her local partner shared the same view, except that bitterness and pessimism gave way to anger in reporting about this volunteer who "could never understand what we were telling her" (Marie-Therese). Communication clearly failed in this example: one party, the volunteer, stopped believing in the concept of developing capacity in a "failed state" and felt powerless. The other party came to doubt the volunteer's mental health and described her as ethnocentric.

However, although cultural distance sometimes had a negative effect on the relationship, it did not necessarily lead to failure. There were sources of creativity and inspiration when the partners could talk about the differences observed. Volunteers and partners who were curious about one another's cultures took the time to listen to one another's views. They could then find a way to adapt. However, reaching a common understanding, when possible, required that volunteers and their partners show a willingness to negotiate their positions. One participant explained that even if you master French, differences of origin matter. After first stating that her relationship with Frederick was excellent, she later shared the difficulties:

> The truth is, we didn't understand each other. I thought he was treating me like a liar. That's what I was thinking… The problem was that I'm Senegalese and he's Canadian. He's not Senegalese and I understand that. There are things I don't understand about him and there are also things that he doesn't understand…He said "No Aya, I heard you saying that it was organic, but you have to tell them the truth…" I was like, "Ah, are you saying that I'm a liar?" I think it was a communication problem and a misunderstanding. I think it was due to our different origins. (Aminatou, a commercial agent in a Senegalese organization)

Cultural backgrounds influenced the communication processes even when the volunteer was experienced. In the above example, the volunteer, a young man who specialized in agribusiness, was half-way through his mandate, and had previously accomplished three missions in Senegal. After this altercation, he and his partner had to step back and analyze what was happening. The next day, they sat down together to explain their points of view and reconcile their differences.

Meanings sometimes differed based on the participants' cognitive backgrounds. The expression "lost in translation," to quote one participant (Evelyne), took on its full meaning. People did not share the same references. This facet of semantics was sometimes even problematic for volunteers with dual nationality. They also had to find a way to arrive at a shared language with their partners. Sometimes, the task was more complex than they had expected, particularly when some partners did not master the basic terms. They spent time articulating their ideas, trying to find expressions or terms that were more accessible. One participant related his communication experience this way:

> I was astonished. I was talking about communication, and the concept of giving relevant information. I think that most of them didn't get the term relevant. During the discussion, I understood that it was the term that was really causing trouble…In Creole, irrelevant

means rude, so relevant would mean polite… After 15 minutes, I saw by the participants' answers to my question that they hadn't understood anything at all. Language differences… they're really only a minor barrier but you can spend 15–20 minutes stuck in an awkward situation. (Joseph, a Haitian-Canadian volunteer in educational administration)

Sharing the values of the partner organization contributed to positive outcomes in terms of the volunteer's integration and the results of the assignment. Many volunteers expressed the view that cultural differences could be overcome if they believed in their partner's mission. The expression "we're as thick as thieves" came up twice by enthusiastic volunteers who shared the same values as their part ners. Sharing the same values generated a sense of belonging and ensured that efforts would be combined and go in the same direction. Sometimes, bringing values in line presented a way out of a deadlock situation. One volunteer expressed it this way:

> Often, even after you work on your values, it can happen that, at the activity level, you don't reach a consensus. If you go back to your values, and ask yourself what you believe in, after that, it goes well. It can be key to resolving a situation. (Jocelyne, a Canadian volunteer in vocational training)

Mohamed, a partner from a Senegalese organization of vegetable producers, said that he was convinced that volunteers who could work on values with their partners would succeed in the mission. He still recalled what was by far his most memorable experience with a Canadian volunteer. Everyone in the village still talked about this volunteer 20 years later. He had reached right into the local culture of the people and designed his interventions based on their values, which were sometimes incompatible with his own. He had observed the village's lifestyle and learned the local language so well that he was able to understand and use local proverbs to have an impact. This was his strategy for succeeding in his mission and convincing the partners to adopt changes and new practices.

Other strategies in the cognition repertory were also used to overcome barriers in communication. The most frequent approach involved the use of diagrams or pictures and drawings when language alone was not enough. This approach had many benefits, such as simplifying complex concepts, finding new ways to translate knowledge, or validating the understanding of the different participants. Prior to the implementation of activities, most volunteers took the time to settle in and observe their work environment. Another communication strategy described by Frantz and Emmanuelle, from a Haitian partner organization, was explained this way:

> Before starting to work with us, on what he was here for, he always prepared a short training session to explain things. So it was easier, after this training, to work for three- or four-hour periods because we understood. We were on the same page. (Frantz, a Haitian partner)

DISCUSSION

This study mobilized knowledge transfer approaches to explore how relational processes between volunteers and their local partners impact the assignments of volunteers working in international cooperation. Specifically, this study emphasized dimensions that presumably facilitate the development of positive relationships through communication. While it is difficult to claim a causal link between cognitive or relational factors and the results of knowledge transfer, the findings suggest that the absorptive capacity of the people and organizations involved, combined with the development of a shared language, have direct impacts on the quality of communication between the parties and consequently, under certain circumstances, influence the outcome of knowledge transfer processes.

The following points will be highlighted in the next section. First, for the partners, it appeared to be important that the hosted volunteers communicate that they could make sense of the partner's different organizational and environmental contexts. Second, the findings suggest that there is a need to review the problem of the partner's absorptive capacity from a different perspective than has previously been adopted in the literature. Third, the levels of cognitive barriers that impeded communication and mutual understanding between the parties will be addressed, and some of the successful strategies adopted to overcome these obstacles will be discussed in light of Carlile's integrative framework for managing knowledge across boundaries (2004). Lastly, some recommendations for further research will be addressed, taking into account the limitations of this study.

With regard to the absorptive capacity of the volunteer, the study clearly shows that successful communication was characterized by individuals (e.g., volunteers) with a reflexive ability and sensitivity towards the local context. Knowledge sharing and transfer were observed on different levels. While local partners were asked to absorb and adapt technical knowledge in order to perform better, successful volunteers demonstrated openness and adaptive behaviors which were reflected in the solutions they proposed to plan and implement together with their partners. Their capacity to absorb contextual knowledge was a prerequisite for a successful interpersonal relationship with their partners, with the local team supporting their integration, and led to outputs that were tailored to local settings. In fact, the volunteer's ability to adapt was the most widely-cited characteristic related to successful integration into the local team and effective knowledge sharing.

Second, although previous studies in knowledge transfer often attribute the failure of such transfers to a lack of absorptive capacity on the part of the recipient, this study suggests other explanations. Indeed, many volunteers attributed the failure of their assignment to their partner, but hardly ever criticized their partner's absorptive capacity or linked this failure with the partner's poor or insufficient knowledge. On rare occasions, volunteers may have felt that their expertise was hard for individuals with few conceptual skills to grasp. However, the gap in technical knowledge between the volunteers and their partners was presumed and anticipated by both parties.

On the one hand, the local partners appeared to expect the volunteers to be highly knowledgeable in their fields of expertise, which was the main reason they had asked for their help. One partner clearly explained that his level of education was no match for the kind of skills that an agricultural engineer could provide. The cognitive challenge here was not linked to a lack of absorptive capacity on the part of the partner, but rather to the ability to communicate and interpret the goals of the assignment. On the other hand, analysis identified many types of volunteers, in line with the typology developed by Land (2007). Most of the volunteers saw their assignment as an educational process to be undertaken with their partners. They were aware that this kind of assignment requires excellent communication strategies. They described themselves as advisors whose goal was to contribute to better organizational performance and they strove to develop solutions in accordance with local capacities, as expected by the NGO that had recruited them. They were sometimes surprised by the low level of local knowledge regarding their expertise, but they made an effort to adjust accordingly. Other assignments operated in substitution mode, where the volunteers carried out tasks without sharing their knowledge. This group of volunteers could not speak about the local absorptive capacity, or if they did, they criticized the organization for the lack of available resources to carry out their mandate.

From a volunteer:

It's a continuous intersubjective negotiation, until we reach a state of equilibrium. Therefore, perceptions will not be the same. There are negotiations–sensitive, tacit, or direct negotiations–until we find targets and reference points... For example, when I came, what I was hearing, what I wanted–when I looked at the organization's performance level, the perception I had at that particular time was not the same as his. Because he's from the inside, he lives it day to day. He even ends up trivializing it. And then I come from outside with explosive ambitions, so it's different. I would put it this way: I have to downsize my ambitions, over and over, resize them. Then he comes and gets closer until we reach a common language, a similar perception–not the same perception, but similar.

Omar, a Canadian volunteer in his forties, originally from Senegal, working in international development

Third, communication issues between Canadian volunteers and their Haitian and Senegalese partners often fell into the realm of shared language. Boundaries arose between them for many reasons. As the results suggest syntactic barriers were common, but communication strategies to overcome them appeared to be effective. The parties also had to develop a common lexicon, as suggested by Carlile (2004). The volunteers who faced this challenge took the time to observe and adopt a participative and active listening mode. Generally speaking, lexical barriers were the easiest to overcome. The parties developed communication tools and strategies to enable them to arrive at a shared meaning. Some volunteers created a reference and lexicon, so that the team could work from the same bases. Others needed to work with an interpreter such that the process of sharing involved a third party. When knowledge was not overly complex, such as when a volunteer had to explain the steps involved in drafting a press release, the process of transferring knowledge succeeded.

However, even when a common lexicon was shared by the parties, the goal of the knowledge transfer was sometimes not achieved. Shared language boundaries sometimes arose when the planned output was not interpreted the same way by all the parties involved, or to put it simply, when the volunteer's perception and the local partner's perception were too far apart. This is where communication strategies became crucial, because the parties needed to translate their tacit knowledge into more explicit forms. The semantic boundary, to employ Carlile's (2004) term, was more difficult to overcome because each of the parties had to translate their knowledge. Only when they succeeded in this bidirectional translation process, could they create common meanings.

Perhaps the most difficult barriers the volunteers faced during their mandate were linked to values. However, the volunteers who embraced local values and based their proposals on these values developed positive communication with their partners, which led to sustainable results. Problems arose when the goals of the assignment were contradictory to the interests of the leaders on site. In these cases, the challenge was to create common interests. Barriers were political and cultural, and communication strategies required volunteers to show political tact, patience and an ability to negotiate and convince their partners that changing existing practices would benefit all parties concerned.

Lastly, based on the results presented in this study, it cannot be concluded that effective communication and a positive relationship between volunteers and their partners will lead to expected outcomes. Further analysis is needed on this subject. However, it is clear that the dimensions explored (absorptive capacity and shared language) contribute to achieving the goal of sharing and transferring knowledge between parties who do not share the same background.

The fact that the researcher was North American constitutes the first limitation of this study. This fact may have increased the bias of the local participants, who may have thought of her as a program evaluator or a potential donor. A second limitation is related to the reliability issue. A cross-checking design, with multiple researchers, would have increased the reliability of the results. However, the procedures and methods were meticulously noted and followed the case study protocol (Thyer, 2001). Also, some participants read a copy of the results pertaining to their case and attested to its credibility.

This exploratory study, to our knowledge, is one of the first studies that has aimed to understand what happens during the process of knowledge transfer and sharing in this particular context. Moreover, the constructivist approach adopted gave space for the "locals" to express their perceptions. This chapter contributes to a better understanding of the many communication challenges faced by volunteers and partners during foreign assignments. The practical implications pertaining to communication issues for NGOs, in terms of managing volunteers, are multiple. NGOs could adjust their predeparture training and insist on language training. Lastly, the recruiting processes used by international NGOs could be made more effective by adapting or adding selection criteria, such as evaluating the absorptive capacity of potential volunteers rather than focusing solely their adaptive capacity.

REFERENCES

Argote, L., McEvily, B., & Reagans, R. (2003). Managing knowledge in organizations: An integrative framework and review of emerging themes. *Management Science, 49*, 571–582.

Boland, R. J., Jr., & Tenkasi, R. V. (1995). Perspective making and perspective taking in communities of knowing. *Organization Science, 6*, 350–372.

Bonache, J., & Zarraga-Oberty, C. (2008). Determinants of the success of international assignees as knowledge transferors: A theoretical framework. *International Journal of Human Resource Management, 19*, 1–18.

Browne, S. (Ed.). (2002). *Developing capacity through technical cooperation: Country experiences*. London: Earthscan.

Carlile, P. (2004). Transferring, translating, and transforming: An integrative framework for managing knowledge across boundaries. *Organization Science, 15*, 555–568.

Carlsson, J., & Wohlgemuth, L. (Eds.). (2001). *Learning in development co-operation*. Stockholm: Almqvist & Wiksell International.

CIDA. (2005). *Le pouvoir du volontariat: examen du programme canadien de coopération volontaire*, Rapport d'évaluation, 125p.: Agence canadienne de développement international.

CIDA. (2011). Rapport statistique sur l'aide internationale: année financière 2009–2010. Gatineau: Agence canadienne de développement international.

Cohen, W. M., & Levinthal, D. A. (1990). Absorptive capacity: A new perspective on learning and innovation. *Administrative Science Quarterly, 35*, 128–152.

Cummings, J. (2003). Knowledge sharing: A review of litterature. In T. W. B. O. E. Department (Ed.), (p. 57): The World Bank Operations Evaluation Department.

Davenport, T. H., & Prusak, L. (1998). *Working knowledge: How organizations manage what they know*. Boston, MA: Harvard Business School.

Easterby-Smith, M., Lyles, M. A., & Tsang, E. W. K. (2008). Inter-organizational knowledge transfer: Current themes and future prospects. *Journal of Management Studies, 45*, 677–690.

Flyvberg, B. (2001). *Making social science matter*. (S. Sampson, Trans.). Oxford, New York: Cambridge University Press.

Fortin, M-F. (2006). *Fondements et étapes du processus de recherches*. Montreal: Chenelière Éducation.

Foss, N., & Pedersen, T. (2002). Transferring knowledge in MNCs: The role of sources of subsidiary knowledge and organizational context. *Journal of International Management, 8*, 49–67.

Frenkel, M. (2008). The multinational corporation as a third space: Rethinking international management discourse on knowledge transfer through Homi Bhabha. *Academy of Management Review, 33*, 924–942.

Glaser, B.G., & Strauss, A. L. (1967). *The discovery of grounded theory: Strategies for qualitative research*. Chicago, IL: Aldine Publishing Company.

Gooderham, P. (2007). Enhancing knowledge transfer in multinational corporations: A dynamic capabilities driven model. *Knowledge Management Research & Practice, 5*, 34–43.

Granovetter, M. S. (1973). The strength of weak ties. *American Journal of Sociology, 78*, 1360–1380.

Grant, R. M. (1996). Toward a knowledge-based theory of the firm. *Strategic Management Journal, 17*, 109–122.

Harzing, A. W. (2001). Of bears, bumble bees and spiders: The role of expatriates in controlling foreign subsidiaries. *Journal of World Business, 36*, 366–379.

Heizmann, H. (2008). Knowledge sharing in international NGOs. *The International Journal of Knowledge, Culture and Change Management, 7*, 65–72.

Hislop, D. (2009). *Knowledge management in organizations* (2nd ed.). Oxford, New York: Oxford University Press.

Jensen, R., & Szulanski, G. (2004). Stickiness and the adaptation of organizational practices in cross-border knowledge transfers. *Journal of International Business Studies, 35*, 508–523.

Ko, D.-G. (2010). Consultant competence trust doesn't pay off, but benevolence trust does! Managing knowledge with care. *Journal of Knowledge Management, 14*, 202–213.

Ko, D.-G., Kirsch, L., & King, W. R. (2005). Antecedents of knowledge transfer from consultants to clients in enterprise system implementations. *MIS Quarterly, 29*, 59–85.

Kostova, T. (1999). Transnational transfer of strategic organizational practices: A contextual perspective. *Academy of Management Review, 24*, 308–324.

Kostova, T., & Roth, K. (2002). Adoption of an organizational practice by subsidiaries of multinational corporations: Institutional and relational effects. *Academy of Management Journal, 45*, 215–233.

Land, T. (2007). *Joint evaluation study of provision of technical-assistance personnel: What can we learn from promising experiences?* (Discussion paper # 78). Maastricht: ECPDM.

Leach, F. (1990). *Counterpart relationships on technical cooperation projects: A Sudanese study*. (D.Phil), University of Sussex, Sussex.

Lia, L., Barner-Rasmussen, W., & Björkman, I. (2007). What difference does the location make? A social capital perspective on transfer of knowledge from multinational corporation subsidiaries located in China and Finland. *Asia Pacific Business Review, 13*, 233–249.

Liamputtong, P. (2010). *Performing qualitative cross-cultural research*. New York: Cambridge University Press.

Mäkelä, K., Andersson, U., & Seppäla, T. (2011). Interpersonal similarity and knowledge sharing within multinational organizations. *International Business Review. 21*, 439–451.

Mäkelä, K., & Brewster, C. (2009). Interunit interaction contexts, interpersonal social capital, and the differing levels of knowledge sharing. *Human Resource Management, 48*, 591–613.

Miles, M.B., & Huberman, A.M. (2003). *Analyses des données qualitatives.* Paris: De Boeck.

Minbaeva, D. (2007). Knowledge transfer in multinational corporations. *Management International Review, 47*, 567–593.

Morgan, P., & Baser, H. (1993). *Making technical co-operation more effective: New approaches by the international development community.* Gatineau, Canada: CIDA.

Nonaka, I., & vonKrogh, G. (2009). Tacit knowledge and knowledge conversion: Controversy and advancement in organizational knowledge creation theory. *Organization Science, 20*, 635–652.

OECD. (2011). *Perspective Note: Technical Cooperation for Capacity Development,* 24p. Retrieved from: http://www.oecd.org/dac/governance development/48260262.pdf

OPM. (2006). *Technical Cooperation for Economic Management* (pp. 107). London, UK: Department of International Development: Oxford Policy Management.

Reagans, R., & McEvily, B.(2003). Network structure and knowledge transfer: The effects of cohesion and range. *Administrative Science Quarterly, 48*, 240–267.

Rossman, R.B., & Rallis, S.F. (1998). Revisiting Foucauldian approaches: Power dynamics in development projects. *The Journal of Development Studies, 40*, 1–29.

Simonin, B. L. (1999). Ambiguity and the process of knowledge transfer in strategic alliances. *Strategic Management Journal, 20*, 595–623.

Spender, J-C. (1996). Making knowledge the basis of a dynamic theory of the firm. *Strategic Management Journal, 17*, 45–62.

Szulanski, G. (1996). Exploring internal stickiness: Impediments to the transfer of best practice within the firm. *Strategic Management Journal, 17*, 27–43.

Szulanski, G. (2000). The process of knowledge transfer: A diachronic analysis of stickiness. *Organizational Behavior and Human Decision Processes, 82*, 9–27.

Thyer, B. (2001). *The Handbook of Social Work Research Methods.* Thousand Oaks, CA: SAGE.

UNDP. (2010). *Annual Report 2008.* Retrieved from: http://www.undp.org/content/undp/en/home/librarypage/corporate/undp_in_action_2008.html

UNDP. (2013). *UN Volunteers Annual Report 2012,* 58p. Retrieved from: http://www.unv.org/news-resources/resources/annual-report-2012.html

Yin, R. K. (2003). *Case study research: Design and methods* (3rd ed.). London: Sage.

Zander, U., & Kogut, B. (1995). Knowledge and the speed of the transfer and imitation of organizational capabilities: An empirical test. *Organization Science, 6*, 76–92.

CHAPTER SIX

Constructing "Them" AND "Us": Host Communities' Perspectives OF Voluntourist Identities

KIRSTIE McALLUM
Université de Montréal

ANNE ZAHRA
University of Waikato

Increasing numbers of young Western tourists traveling to less economical-ly-developed countries are trading in sun, sea, or safari for opportunities to interact with local communities in more meaningful ways. One option is volunteer tourism or *voluntourism*, whereby individuals utilize "discretionary time and income to travel out of the sphere of regular activity to assist others in need" (McGehee & Santos, 2005, p. 760). Since 1990, the voluntourism sector has expanded significantly worldwide, with around 1.6 million people participating in environmental conservation or community development projects annually (Wearing & McGehee, 2013). Community development initiatives can range from 24-week programs constructing rainwater catchment systems and building vegetable gardens in Fijian villages (Global Vision International, 2013) to six weeks spent working with toddlers in South African day-care centers (Wingham, 2013). Despite variation in the duration and intensity of projects, advocates maintain that through such niche tourism experiences, voluntourists are more likely than mass tourists to build authentic intercultural relationships with their hosts (McIntosh & Zahra, 2007). Their argument runs along the lines that voluntourism displaces the unreflective consumption of a commodified tourism product with an "interactive space where tourists become creative actors who engage in behaviours that are mutually beneficial" (Lyons & Wearing, 2008, p. 6). Higgins-Desbiolles (2003), who subtitled her article on the opportunities afforded by engaged tourism experiences for reconciliation between aboriginal Australians and Australians of European descent *Tourism Healing Divided Societies!*, epitomizes this positive perspective of voluntourism as a "force for peace" (p. 35).

Critics counter these claims, arguing that the relatively short time span spent in host communities, or what Callanan and Thomas (2005) call shallow tourism, means that the development of cross-cultural competence is seldom realized (McGehee & Andereck, 2008). Indeed, they posit that voluntourists' narcissistic desire to explore and clarify personal values, which occurs through *othering* or making comparisons with the host culture, only leads to a heightened awareness of their own cultural background (Wearing & McGehee, 2013) and the embedding of more sophisticated cultural stereotypes (Osland & Bird, 2000). That is, although sophisticated stereotyping replaces negative generalizations with conscious attempts to describe cultural practices, using categories such as power distance or the tendency toward individualism or collectivism, these dimensions still fail to capture the complexity of a cultural group.

Critics have also raised questions about voluntourism's economic and socio-cultural sustainability (Mostafanezhad, 2013). Voluntourists may well return home with glossy photos showing them "making a difference" (Wearing, 2001), after carrying out work that has unwittingly undermined community development (Barbieri, Santos, & Katsube, 2012). Their imported volunteer labor risks creating dependence on foreign aid, supersedes or ignores the development of indigenous solutions and approaches, reduces employment for local people, and may simply be of poor quality, requiring repairs and additional work later on (Guttentag, 2009).

What is common to both sides of the debate about the impact of voluntourism is the tendency to position the host community as passive. This study focused instead on the agency of host communities who actively interpret and give meaning to intercultural encounters. Specifically, it examined how village residents of three voluntourism destinations in the Philippines and representatives of grassroots Filipino non-governmental organizations (NGOs) actively constructed voluntourists' identities that specified visitors' position within and relationship to the community. These identities were not fixed and coherent, but emergent, dynamic, and splintered according to stakeholders' vision and goals for their community. Since ascribed identities were worked and re-worked through actions, reactions, and interactions, it considers the strategic intent of various identity constructions as well as their unintended outcomes.

LITERATURE REVIEW

Identity is conceptualized as the "reflective self-conception or self-image" (Ting-Toomey, 2005, p. 212) that each person develops as a result of interactions with others. As individuals belong to multiple collective groups according to culture, ethnicity, gender, religion, class, occupation, and language, identity is multi-faceted, with communication partners influencing which identity assumes salience in a particular context. Collier (2005) also focuses on the socially constructed nature of identity when he proposes that identity results from the twin "processes of avowal (self-views) and ascription (views communicated by others)" (p. 240). Individuals' ability to craft a preferred identity, or to control the "sets of 'meanings' applied to the self in a social role or situation defining what it means to be who one is" (Burke, 1991, p. 837), depends to a large extent on the power that they have. Voluntourists, who are usually young, white, Western, and economically comfortable, have multiple layers of privilege that allow them to exercise considerable agency over their identity construction.

This study linked two different perspectives on how meanings are created and assigned to the literature on voluntourists' identities. The first perspective views identity as the result of a decision about attachment (Cheney, 1983) and considers to whom voluntourists attach themselves. Despite the physical journey involved in voluntourism, individuals can remain rooted in and attached to their own cultural context. In this case, voluntourists who construct themselves as "lucky" and "fortunate" (Simpson, 2004) due to their superior economic, educational, and cultural background can take on a "savior" identity (Stritch, 2011). In this case, voluntourits view the host community through a deficit lens, with voluntourists' philanthropic service based on the "presumption that [their] ... presence will somehow help to redeem a desperate situation" (Heron, 2007, p. 43). Raymond and Hall (2008) noted that these voluntourists frequently adopt a paternalistic attitude and present themselves as "experts" or "teachers" who are determined to share the skills they have imported, irrespective of local needs (p. 531).

Alternatively, voluntourists' engagement with the hosting community can lead to attachment to the host community's values and changes in how voluntourists relate to their own communities on their return. Wearing's (2001) claim that voluntourism causes value change seems borne out by the data as multiple studies have documented shifts in voluntourists' values, practices, and relationships (Grabowski, 2012; Zahra & McIntosh, 2007). As they make comparisons between life at home (their former personal identity) and life within the host community (interpretations of the host community restructure voluntourists' evolving personal identity), voluntourists frequently move from one identity claim to its polar opposite (e.g., from selfish to generous). A volunteer in Zahra's (2006) study, for example, reported that her rejection of an inwardly-focused, hedonistic identity resulted from her voluntourism experience:

I reflected on my superficial life: the binge drinking, the marijuana that was becoming a habit, just seeking a good time .... Already during the project I started thinking about others, being a selfish cow was getting me nowhere. (p. 96)

The return from abroad was marked for many of her participants by long-lasting identity changes which included sharp critiques about the consumer society, a search for transcendence and spiritual experience, and engagement in local development initiatives. Although in this latter case, voluntourism becomes a vehicle for creating a new, more humble and socially aware self, each of the identity positions continues to reinforce differences between the host and home countries. An adoption of a less materialistic outlook on life, for instance, is made after comparing one's current lifestyle choices with hosts who are assumed to be constantly happy despite their poverty (Caton & Santos, 2009). This identity perspective is relatively psychologized, considering primarily voluntourists' reactions and decisions, and also suggests incompatibility between competing identity positions. In both cases, to either remain embedded in one's own culture or to use the intercultural experience to re-examine one's values, host communities play a relatively passive role, acting as a sounding board for voluntourists' identity constructions.

The second identity perspective considers identity as the development of an "I" which is a "unique combination of partially conflicting corporate 'we's'" (Burke, 1937, p. 264), formed and re-formed through interaction. As Weick (1995) explained, the individual is "an ongoing puzzle undergoing continual redefinition, coincident with presenting some self to others and trying to decide which self is appropriate" (p. 20). Before engaging in the voluntourism experience, many travelers frame their journey as a manifestation of solidarity with the host community. On arrival, however, voluntourists can feel overwhelmed by the scope of the problems they encounter and, in light of guilt about their previous or current spending habits, abandon their identification as a socially conscious traveler as misguided (Mize Smith, 2013). Identification with the community stimulates a sense of suffering while simultaneous dis-identification causes shame.

Voluntourists can also undergo identity challenges and even an identity crisis when faced with misunderstandings or clashes with the host community, which is made up of multiple referents "whose opinions matter to the individual" (Scott, Corman, & Cheney, 1998, p. 311). As Salazar (2004) highlighted, individuals "can afford to be curious of that which is new and strange, tolerant of that which is 'Other'...only...when the tourist is clear about whom he/she is him/herself" (p. 102). Tiessen and Heron's (2012) study of Canadian youth involved in international development projects showed that participants' retrospective sense-making about their role was marked by considerable uncertainty: "They were not sure they had a meaningful impact ... and some realised that they may have had very negative impacts on individuals even if they felt they were acting to address community-level issues" (p. 53). Other voluntourists who had hoped to share expertise reported that their interventions were inappropriate or childish in an unfamiliar cultural context (Collins, DeZerega, & Heckscher, 2002).

Evidently, it is imperative to bring in hosts' perspectives when evaluating how individuals decide to "link themselves to elements in the social scene" (Cheney, 1983, p. 342). Unfortunately, compared to research on voluntourists' motivations, values, and experiences, studies of host community' views of volunteers are relatively scarce, due to the challenges associated with research access and decisions about relevant community stakeholders (Wearing & McGehee, 2013). Moreover, community-focused analyses tend to focus exclusively on either voluntourists' positive potential (e.g., Singh, 2002) or negative impact (e.g., Palacios, 2010; Tomazos & Butler, 2010). Only a few studies have considered the possibility of fragmented or shifting responses to voluntourism. Gard McGehee and Andereck's (2009) study of voluntourism in Tijuana, Mexico, for example, found that locals' evaluations of voluntourists varied widely, depending on their mission and purpose. Although community members viewed voluntourists favorably in general (3.9 on a five-point Likert scale), they rated faith-based voluntourists negatively. In an area where church attendance was already relatively high, residents did not welcome the "God talk" that seemed to be the "expected price that they will pay in exchange for the volunteer work" (McGehee & Andereck, 2008, p. 21). McIntosh and Zahra (2007) also highlighted changes in community elders' perceptions of the adolescent voluntourists who ran children's holiday programs in a socio-economically deprived community with significant gang problems. Initially cautious, most were relieved that the "volunteers came in with no 'airs'; 'hey we are better than you', 'you can learn from us' etc." (p. 552).

However, hosts' interpretations of volutourists' identities may be not just reactive but active. Since both one's own and others' identities are mutually constituted through communication, it follows that diverse community stakeholders might strategically use voluntourists' stay to promote their own goals and preferred identities. Hence, this study explored the following research questions:

RQ1:   What kinds of identities did the host communities strategically ascribe to the
        voluntourists?
RQ2:   What was the impact of these ascribed identities on host communities?

METHOD

The data for the project is drawn from a larger study on voluntourists' contribution to the development of community capital, including cultural, social, financial, environmental, and built capital (Zahra & McGehee, 2013). This study, by contrast, did not assume that voluntourists would necessarily make a positive impact but documented the multiple identities that community members and directors and workers in local NGOs ascribed to voluntourists during the various phases of community engagement. We begin by describing the cultural context and the participants and then explain our data collection and analysis procedures.

The Cultural Context

The Philippines offers an interesting intercultural perspective on voluntourism, due to what Rosaldo (1988) called "cultural invisibility" or shared cultural, historical, organizational, and linguistic practices. A long history of cultural borrowing, resulting from almost four centuries of Spanish colonization and evangelization and American political control for the first two-thirds of the twentieth century, means that Western voluntourists tend to feel relatively comfortable on arrival in the Philippines. The use of English is widespread, with three-quarters of the population reporting they understand English and half speaking it (Gonzalez, 2004). Filipinos also have a reputation for friendliness: Cariño and her research team (2001) identified "*pakikipagkapwa* or holistic interaction with others, the root word of which is *kapwa*, or shared inner self" (p. 9), as a core cultural trait.

Despite these cultural parallels and openness to others, however, Filipino culture contains numerous paradoxes. One such paradox is the co-existence of a collectivist orientation and apparent tolerance for high power distance and the development of ground-roots "people power movements" that have ousted two dictatorships since 1986. Openness to relationship building is also context-dependent. Ness' (2003) ethnography documented a resort owner's disdain for "tourists" who occupy idealized fantasy landscapes and purchase activities that are "superficial, temporary,…and for sale" (p. 6). Volunteerism, in contrast, appears to be welcomed far more warmly. Large-scale, top-down government initiatives have promoted local and international volunteerism as a key rural development strategy (Virola, Ilarina, Reyes, & Buenaventura, 2010). In 2013, the government agency recruited 510 volunteers from large foreign sending agencies such as the United Nations Volunteers and the Japan International Cooperation Agency, as part of its International Volunteer Program (Philippine National Volunteer Service Coordinating Agency, 2014). Approximately 1,600 Philippine development-oriented NGOs, including the three NGOs in this study, also use volunteer labor (Caucus of Development NGO Networks, 2009).

The Participants

The three communities in the study were chosen purposively. Both authors have been voluntourists in at least one of the communities, and the second author, who has visited the communities multiple times and coordinated voluntourism projects, has established ongoing relationships with all three communities spanning more than twenty years. Two of the communities are rural; in the rural community in the Luzon region, most participants are squatters who live in poor quality housing with little or no provision for sanitation, while in the other rural community in the Visayas, members own the land on which their homes are built, but due to limited employment opportunities, many men leave the community for extended periods of time to look for work in urban centers or overseas. The third community in the Visayas is urban, with high unemployment, crowded living conditions, and poor sanitation. The NGOs working in the communities provided medical services and micro-finance opportunities for small businesses, constructed basic infrastructure, and engaged in health promotion.

The voluntourists, who appear in the data through the accounts of community members and NGO representatives, were university students and early career professionals from Australia, Hong Kong, Japan, and New Zealand who worked directly with NGOs on projects that combined development and welfare-related work. Activities included building infrastructure such as community toilets, drainage systems, and playgrounds; developing community gardens; maintaining community halls and libraries; organizing street clean-up drives; teaching hygiene and nutrition classes; participating in the NGO feeding programs for malnourished children; and conducting data collection (program needs assessment) for the NGO. At the request of the Filipino NGOs, which focus on women's development, all voluntourists were women.

Data Collection

Focus groups were chosen as the data collection method for two reasons. First, focus groups indicate the collective views of a particular community of interest and permit analysis of the group processes behind particular interpretations and evaluations (Bloor, Frankland, Thomas, & Robson, 2001). Second, they tend to increase participants' sense of security, since no one individual is singled out or forced to respond to a specific question (Stewart, Shamdasani, & Rook, 2007). Hence, we conducted six focus groups with seventy-five community members in total. Two focus groups were conducted within each community, two years apart, with eight to twelve community members participating each time. NGO representatives used a snowball technique to recruit community members who had interacted with the voluntourists. Significantly, community members who chose not to engage with voluntourists during their stay did not form part of the sample. In order to facilitate participation by community members, local research assistants unconnected with the NGO conducted the focus groups in Tagalog, the official national language, or Cebuano, a dialect from the Visayas region, with the second author (not a Tagalog or Cebuano speaker) present during the first set of focus groups to strengthen network relationships. Sessions lasted between forty-five and seventy minutes. Questions were open and exploratory, enabling participants to talk about issues that were important to them. Broad themes included their experiences with the voluntourists and the financial and social impact of voluntourists on the community.

The second author and a research assistant also conducted semi-structured interviews with nine NGO representatives. On average, these interviews lasted one and a half hours and were conducted in English. Representatives were asked to evaluate the benefits and challenges of working with groups of voluntourists and to comment on the financial, social, political, and environmental impact of their visits on the community. Questions also included what types of persons they did not want to participate and behaviors that they would not want to see.

Data Analysis

We first engaged in emic coding of attributions that community members made about voluntourists' lifestyles, practices, and roles within the host community. We listed statements that documented how community members talked about what voluntourists did, the physical spaces they occupied, and the emotional connections that were negotiated. We generated a parallel list of statements from NGO representatives' interview transcripts about voluntourists' relationships with the community and their role with the NGO. We assigned thirty-two first-level codes to statements from both lists, including "novelty," "profile," "inviting to attend classes," "encouragement," "education," "travel," "interest," "entering homes," and "spending time."

As we began second-level coding to explore analytic relationships between these codes, we realized time was highly significant in both community members' and NGO representatives' accounts. We added a time marker to codes that indicated whether statements referred to voluntourists' arrival, their stay within the community, or their impact after departure. Second-level codes related to initial perceptions focused on *distance, difference,* and *attractiveness* (such as novelty, profile, and invitations), while relationships developed during voluntourists' stay led to codes of *time, equality, closeness,* and *willingness to interact* (including interest, entering homes, and spending time). Post-departure codes included *improvement* and *mobility* (such as education, encouragement, and travel).

As we were looking for the identities that these practices and qualities constructed, we applied three metaphors that succinctly expressed the essence of each second-order category: voluntourists were "exotic," "friends," and "role models." Focus groups discussed their relief that voluntourists were not dictatorial or domineering but because this metaphor was applied to imaginary rather than actual volunteers, we omitted this data from our analysis. Initially, the metaphors did not seem particularly original, perhaps because, as Oswick, Keenoy and Grant (2002) pointed out, metaphors tend to emphasize similarity between the target and source domains. Nonetheless, each metaphor was linked with a distinctive interpretive framework that structured who the voluntourists were to the community and who the community might be to them in quite distinctive ways. That is, figurative talk shapes behavior and has concrete and identifiable effects (Cornelissen, 2004). Hence, we coded for outcomes related to economic or material changes and cultural awareness that occurred in parallel with the invocation of particular metaphors/identity constructions.

We considered that the potential power imbalance between voluntourists and communities may have impacted the validity of our interpretations about the impact of voluntourists. That is, the NGOs' desire for voluntourists' visits to continue could have translated into an overly optimistic account of voluntourists' contribution to local communities. An NGO representative, for example, commented that she did not have any preference about the type of volunteer because "beggars cannot choose." In order to address this possibility, the second researcher's prolonged engagement with the community acted as a form of data triangulation, as did the gathering of data from community members across multiple sites, including the rural Visayas community that no longer received volutourists (Lindlof & Taylor, 2011). We also engaged in investigator triangulation, whereby we coded the focus group and interview data separately and compared coding schemes.

FINDINGS

In line with scholarship that views identity as fluid and context-driven, the data showed that identities were multiple and shifted over time (Ashforth, Harrison, & Corley, 2008; Holstein & Gubrium, 2000). The first identity ascribed to voluntourists by community members and NGO representatives was as "exotic" visitors.

An "Exotic" Identity

Community members focused on how voluntourists were *different* and *attractive*. Difference stemmed primarily from perceived socio-economic status, since all groups stayed in nearby accommodation with superior hygiene and living conditions. The female voluntourists were also framed as attractive: "They were so pretty—you just wanted to look at them." NGOs emphasized voluntourists' exotic status to encourage community members to participate in programs and projects and to "penetrate further into the community." NGO directors and workers constructed voluntourists as a magnet for local communities and a tool to "lift our profile." The executive director of one NGO elaborated that "foreign volunteers are a novelty…they are *story* in the local community, so they attract curiosity and interest." A woman from the Luzon region corroborated these NGO perspectives: "It was easy to get the women out of their homes." Another from the urban Visayas community commented:

> When they come, all of them, the Japanese, the Chinese [from Hong Kong], and the Australians, we all wanted to know what was happening. This was something new. The Filipino men and women from the NGOs are just one more Filipino face in the barrio. You listen, but "oh yeah," it's hard to get motivated, but these young people come with the NGO and they want to know you, they want to talk to you. You realize they are here to help the NGO and it made me more interested.

Consequently, NGOs strategically aligned voluntourists' exotic identity with their own organizational identity, sending them "out to all parts of the barrio to go into the homes to talk to the ladies and the men if they were home and not watching the cock fights and to invite them to the classes" or to "collect" children for medical checkups. NGOs considered that voluntourists' "personal [health promotion] messages were more effective than TV ads" because "they are foreigners so the local community listens more; they engage a personal relationship so there is trust and therefore what they tell them must be important because they are important."

Voluntourists, however, did not always seem aware of this exotic identity ascription or its implications. An influential community member in the Luzon region "tried to use the volunteers to get others motivated because they were so poor and their kids were not healthy, but the volunteers always said leave them free. These volunteers always talk about freedom." From her perspective, the volutourist could have taken advantage of her status and exotic identity to persuade other women to attend the classes, but did not do so, invoking instead her own cultural values of freedom. Interestingly, she concluded that, "here in the Philippines, you do what you are told, but some of those women did not come."

The Impact of Ascribing an Exotic Identity

The endorsement or rejection of voluntourists' exotic identity and their link with NGO programs created significant divisions within communities. Those who chose to participate tended to become closer to each other, whereas those who did not come to livelihood programs or nutrition classes were framed as less involved in the community than others:

> Who benefited? We all did. No—the ones who did not want to come, they didn't. Remember Pinki? She didn't want to come to the classes but she was the first in the queue with her kids for the doctor and the dentist. She is a funny lady. She always minds her own business (rural Luzon community).

Differences between the two groups got larger over time, with community members associating participation in programs with better employment opportunities, improved health outcomes, and opportunities to develop friendships with others. Even in the Luzon community that only hosted two groups in the late 1980s, a former *barangay* captain, an elected political official who represents 50 to 100 families in a village or suburb, insisted that if he could do it all over again, he would "make sure more people went to the classes. You can see how better off the people who went are after so many years. You see their kids, their houses. The ones who were too lazy, they are still no-hopers."

Those who took part gained access on occasion to "foreign" resources that were simply out of reach for other community members. An NGO representative explained:

> There was a story of a Japanese volunteer who sent money to pay for the hospitalization of a local girl who underwent surgery. When the girl survived, the family of the Japanese volunteer came to visit the girl to check how she was.

Participants from the two rural communities mentioned that those who had initially opted out later became jealous: "Some groups of women become friends because the foreign volunteers put them together for the classes. Some women felt jealous and left out but that is their fault because they did not want to come."

A "Friend" Identity

Whereas voluntourists were initially ascribed an exotic identity that focused on difference and status, interaction between voluntourists and community members who participated in programs led to the construction of a "friend" identity built on *physical closeness*, *time* spent together, and *mutual exchange*. All focus groups described the voluntourists as friends: they "became friends with us and our children" and "his wife made him go with her to the talks because he had no job when the Australians were here; she became friends with them." This identity ascription resulted from voluntourists' willingness to be physically close to families, to "come to our house and spend time with us" and to invest time "playing with our kids" and engaging in conversations about their lives and their culture (rural Visayas community). NGO representatives distinguished between the Filipino volunteers (doctors and nurses who ran free clinics) who "have a professional distance...and who are so busy" and task-focused and the voluntourists who dedicated considerable time to socializing. They described the voluntourists as being able to "reach the heart of the people" and make them "feel important in a non-patronizing way, because they...see the community as equals, as persons."

The friend identity was also premised on equality, sharing, and mutual exchange. The voluntourists offered the community their physical labor (construction of community infrastructure), their time, and their interest. Sharing these resources created a bond with the community: "The kids loved them. They made them feel important" (rural Luzon community). Adult community members also felt important when voluntourists asked questions, were culturally-curious, and told families "how we have many good things, our family, our faith, our cheerful happy lives even though we are poor" (urban Visayas commuinty). Community members reciprocated, by giving local crafts (that were sold to "*other* tourists") as presents, sharing food, preparing cultural performances, and discussing religion with voluntourists: "We shared with them, especially our religion. *We* taught the volunteers. We are very proud. Also they tell us we are very happy, all laugh. We teach them how we try and stay happy" (rural Luzon community). NGO representatives also framed voluntourists as benefiting from the intercultural exchange: "They learned a lot and gained a lot of insights about Filipino optimism and happiness which allow them to have a long threshold before crisis."

The Impact of Ascribing a Friend Identity

Community members reflected on how the voluntourists' interest in their lives and cultural uniqueness affirmed their cultural identity. Participants from the rural Visayas region explained that their community had not valued "being Filipino" and how many had tried to imitate American culture and Korean or Japanese fashion. They compared this with reinvigorated community participation in cultural festivals: "The barrio goes to the province festival so now we have a float, but we never used to." Moreover, festivals brought communities together, with "family members who are abroad or in the cities send us money or come back to help and join in." The urban Visayas community also focused on their pride that "our float in the Santo Niño parade is always one of the best and we make the most noise."

Community members commented that voluntourists' interest in them and their barrio created a desire to develop and sustain mutually-beneficial community relationships and show concern for shared physical environment. Communities got together to maintain infrastructure, painting halls and playgrounds, and caring for the community gardens. Focus groups in the rural Luzon community concluded:

The community…we are better friends [they all laugh]. They bring the community together and help make us proud, they help us clean up. We try and keep it clean now. Before we put rubbish outside the house: as long as the house is clean who cares about the outside? But not the foreign volunteers. They care and they teach us to care. Better for the kids; better for us.

Care for especially needy community members was continued after voluntourists' departure, as in the urban Visayas community where "we try and take care of the malnourished kids whose parents are bad, they gamble or take drugs, after the volunteers leave." Focus groups in the rural Visayas community also mentioned how they became more aware of needs, such as the woman whose "husband died when he was working in Abu Dhabi, and she had four young children. We helped her feed the children and fix her house." The rural Luzon community attributed the fact that the NGO had stopped coming to the fact that they had "more community spirit."

A "Role Model" Identity

Communities also constructed voluntourists as role models of *positive future change*, through education and opportunities for travel and intercultural contact, and *personal responsibility* for improved financial and social outcomes. As one focus group in the rural Luzon community pointed out, "We are better now, we have more money, and we tell the barangay captains what we think and what we want." This identity positioning began while voluntourists were working in communities but continued after they left through letter writing and, more recently, through social media. An NGO coordinator described how "most of the time, the community keeps the letters they receive and some of them even put the letters on their [family] altar–this manifests their high regard for that foreign volunteer." Voluntourists' educational level was framed as a passport for opportunity. Hence, not only did they "really help the children to like school [but] after they left, they wanted to know the children's school progress" (rural Visayas community). Several voluntourists sent money to sponsor children's education. Some children from all of the communities subsequently migrated to Manila, other large cities within the Philippines, or cities abroad, as a result of increased education and pursuit of better jobs. A mother from the rural Luzon community commented that "my Ruby went to Dubai because the foreign girls became her penpals and they encouraged her and gave her confidence. She met her husband in Dubai and now they have two kids. They send me money."

The Impact of Ascribing a Role Model Identity

Although older adult community members framed the role model identity positively, their children's imitation of voluntourists' upward aspirations and ability to be geographically mobile in order to better themselves economically created a clear generational difference within communities. As children's aspirations changed, they were no longer willing to live like their parents:

> All the children are leaving. We give them education, give them the best, but they do not want to stay. They do not want to raise pigs and chickens and grow vegetables. Besides this, the community is good. We have more money, a better health clinic, a nice school. We are happy. (rural Visayas community)

Changes in children's expectations led to migration: "All the kids are leaving. They do not want to live in the slums. They want to buy land" (rural Luzon community). Moreover, although children encouraged their parents to move away, the development of stronger community ties formed a strong connection with the status quo: "My children want me to leave the slum but I do not want to. I am happy with my friends." Another in the same focus group elaborated that "Manila is getting so big that we will have to move. In ten years, the houses will come and even factories, but we are happy. We are getting old. We want to stay here where we know everyone."

Nonetheless, the divide between children who had imitated voluntourists' educational and employment mobility and parents who refused to embrace change and clung tenaciously to tradition was more apparent than real. Statements, such as "we are happy" that seem at face value to indicate acceptance of the way things are, do not signify "resignation or withdrawal from an engagement or crisis or a shirking from personal responsibility" (Andres, 1994, p. 12). Instead, Filipino styles of interaction use these verbal markers to indicate determination to face obstacles and readiness for risk-taking (Pe-Pua & Protacio-Marcelino, 2000). Similarly to young people who carved out opportunities, older community members had proactively shifted houses prone to flooding to higher ground and lobbied local government officials to fight against the incursion of industrial development.

DISCUSSION: CONSTRUCTING "THEM" AND "US"

The findings indicated that host communities and NGO representatives ascribed multiple identities to voluntourists and that the temporal sequencing of the identity frames constructed for the "Other" mattered. Similarly to Dutton and Dukerich's (1991) early work on the temporal dimensions of collective organizational identity, present-moment choices constrained future decisions. The first, exotic, identity frame acted as a sine qua non for subsequent frames; without opportunities to relate, the identity construction of voluntourist as friend would have been unattainable. Similarly, the development of friendships during projects led to ongoing contact, role modeling, and encouragement after voluntourists returned to their own countries. These long-term friendships were based on mutual reciprocity, which required a free decision to contribute to the relationship.

From a community member

The foreign volunteers were fun. They were very nice and they wanted to know about you. They wanted to help us, they helped the NGOs with the classes and the medical clinics. They came to our house and spent time with us. They gave us little koalas and kangaroo stick-pins. We still have them. They became friends with us and our children. One still writes to me. Her children are getting big now. She sends me photos every year, like when the children were with Santa in the mall in Sydney. We were important to the volunteers. I wish they would come back. Jacinta and Alice did come back, and Anna the doctor also. She came for a conference three or four years ago and she came from Manila just to see us. Like we told you, we had fun, because of the friends we made and the gatherings we had.

A young mother, a squatter, living in very temporary housing, in a very poor rural barrio on the outskirts of a large metropolitan area when the volunteers came to the community

---

However, the underlying premise of agency, which was empowering for participants, was ironically what enabled other community members to opt out of the relationship completely. Agency, in this case, could be expressed through absence as well as presence; nonetheless, choosing absence led to a "peripheral trajectory" that did not lead to full participation in the community (Wenger, 2010). The contextual factors made it even more difficult for non-participants to retrace their steps, as the NGOs tended to leave specific barrios after two or three years of intensive work, to avoid the risk of creating dependence. Chances to connect and develop relationships with voluntourists were therefore no longer possible. Rather than overlapping and competing metaphors, frames were temporal: the acceptance of one metaphor indicated what kind of relationship one might be able to construct next. These sequenced identity constructions created particular pathways and visions of belonging and community.

Consequently, these findings allow us to interrogate in more depth the notion that volunteering, and voluntourism in particular, enables individuals to engage in actions for the good of another (United Nations Volunteers, 2011). We do so by teasing out who the actual beneficiaries of each voluntourist identity were. The "exotic" identity was reasonably short-lived but served as a bridge to initiate contact. Community members who subsequently engaged with voluntourists, and by extension participated in the NGO programs, reported considerable benefits that were simply not available to nonparticipants. In contrast, since the "friend" identity frame fostered the development of cultural pride and a broader interpretation of community, the spillover effects extended to the entire host community beyond those who had directly interacted with the voluntourists. In the case of the role model identity, which created community fragmentation through geographical relocation, community members who had not moved away received some benefit. For example, although Ruby's move to Dubai to earn more money seemed to situate the benefit outside the local community, Ruby's departure was still positive insofar as "Ruby and her husband send *us* money." Even in the case of apparent division, at least some of the beneficiaries continued to reside within the community.

Although othering is frequently framed as negative and alienating, in this case, the othering of the voluntourists led to far more ambiguous outcomes: the simultaneous enactment of unity and division within host communities. This implies that the voluntourism does not, in and of itself, lead to community empowerment and collaboration but can create new patterns of inclusion ("us" being those who did participate) and exclusion ("them" being those who chose not to participate). Interestingly, the voluntourists themselves were not blamed for the realignment of the lines between "them" and "us." The coordinator at one NGO insisted that "although I received complaints from the barrios, it was more related to different factions receiving more benefits from the volunteers. I could see no foundations, no problem, with the actual volunteers."

Given that this study did not include the voices, and hence the metaphors and counter-narratives, of those who chose not to engage with the voluntourists, the stories that were told about the voluntourists and their impact on the community are, in a sense, unfinished and open-ended. As Brown (2006) highlighted, stories are a "fabric [that] is both a patchwork quilt of narrative episodes stitched together through shared conversations, and rippled, with stories variously borrowing threads from each other, continuing and extending some, and seeking to unravel others" (p. 735). The stories that emerged from this study showed a sense of cohesion and strong commitment by participants to the particular version that was told, perhaps due to the connection between voluntourists and the local NGOs. The focus group methodology could have also encouraged individual participants to fold their individual memories into the collective story in an integrative way. We encourage exploration of discontinuities and loose threads, by examining differences within and among voluntourist groups and considering the impact of dissident voluntourists who did not engage with communities in ways that were expected.

CONCLUSION

This study has shown that host communities strategically positioned voluntourists as exotic to increase participation in NGOs' programs, took advantage of the more emergent friend identity to forge friendships within the barrio and foster broader community-level identification, and used the role model identity to encourage initiative and self-development. More significantly, the findings indicate that language, and specifically metaphor, is not "just talk" but acts to make things happen (Bencherki & Cooren, 2011). Effects of these ascribed identities were material in the form of better health outcomes, more job opportunities, and geographical relocation, as well as symbolic, such as the development of cultural pride, emotional connections with others, and a stronger sense of community.

The positive evaluation of voluntourists' identities by participating host community members was impacted by a host of contextual factors that make it difficult to offer sending agencies a single set of strategies for building successful voluntourist-community relationships or a guiding metaphor for voluntourists' identities. The voluntourists were perceived to be sincere and their interest in the community genuine, yet these traits may be difficult to replicate in a voluntourism market increasingly dominated by commercially-oriented sending agencies. The construction of identity would possibly be different in a culture that was not so responsive, and thus there is also a need to study host community relationships with voluntourists in a range of other intercultural settings. Since the majority of the community participants in this study were women, as were all of the voluntourists, future research could productively investigate how gender intersects with nationality, ethnicity, class, and culture in the construction of voluntourist identities.

The study confirms the importance of host communities' agency in attributing particular meanings to what voluntourists said and did. Voluntourists certainly contributed to host community constructions of their identity/ies. The transition from the exotic identity, which emphasized difference, to an ascription of a friend identity, for example, was influenced in part by voluntourists' decision to enter homes and relate to community members in a familiar way. However, community members' curiosity and interest in what voluntourists might have to offer initiated the process of identity construction and the decision to maintain contact with voluntourists and embrace values that could serve as positive resources for community development consolidated the role model identity. The study also underscores the interactive, dynamic, and indeterminate nature of identity construction. As the identities that community members gave to the voluntourists evolved, the community also changed, creating new ways of being "them" and "us."

REFERENCES

Andres, T. D. (1994). *Dictionary of Filipino culture and values.* Quezon City, Philippines: Giraffe Books.

Ashforth, B. E., Harrison, S. H., & Corley, K. G. (2008). Identification in organizations: An examination of four fundamental questions. *Journal of Management Studies, 34,* 325–374.

Barbieri, C., Santos, C. A., & Katsube, Y. (2012). Volunteer tourism: On-the-ground observations from Rwanda. *Tourism Management, 33,* 509–516.

Bencherki, N., & Cooren, F. (2011). Having to be: The possessive constitution of organization. *Human Relations, 64,* 1579–1607.

Bloor, M., Frankland, J., Thomas, M., & Robson, K. (2001). *Focus groups in social research.* London, United Kingdom: Sage.

Brown, A. D. (2006). A narrative approach to collective identities. *Journal of Management Studies, 43,* 731–753.

Burke, K. (1937). *Attitudes toward history* (3rd ed.). Berkeley, CA: University of California Press.

Burke, P. J. (1991). Identity processes and social stress. *American Sociological Review, 56,* 836–849.

Callanan, M., & Thomas, S. (2005). Volunteer tourism: Deconstructing volunteer activities within a dynamic environment. In M. Novelli (Ed.), *Niche tourism: Contemporary issues, trends and cases* (pp. 183–200). Oxford, England: Butterworth-Heinemann.

Cariño, L. V., & the PNSP Project Staff. (2001). Defining the nonprofit sector: The Philippines. *Working Papers of the Johns Hopkins Comparative Nonprofit Sector Project, no. 39.* Baltimore, MD: Johns Hopkins University Institute for Policy Studies, Center for Civil Society Studies.

Caton, K., & Santos, C. A. (2009). Images of the other: Study abroad in a postcolonial world. *Journal of Travel Research, 48,* 191–204.

Caucus of Development NGO Networks. (2009). CODE-NGO. Retrieved from http://code-ngo.org/home/

Cheney, G. (1983). On the various and changing meanings of organizational membership: A field study of organizational identification. *Communication Monographs, 50,* 342–362.

Collier, M. (2005). Theorizing about cultural identifications: Critical updates and continuing evolutions. In W. B. Gudykunst (Ed.), *Theorizing about intercultural communication* (pp. 235–256). Thousand Oaks, CA: Sage.

Collins, J., DeZerega, S., & Heckscher, Z. (2002). *How to live your dream of volunteering overseas.* New York, NY: Penguin.

Cornelissen, J. P. (2004). What are we playing at? Theatre, organization and the use of metaphor. *Organization Studies, 25,* 705–726.

Dutton, J. E., & Dukerich, J. M. (1991). Keeping an eye on the mirror: Image and identity in organizational adaptation. *Academy of Management Journal, 34,* 517–554.

Global Vision International. (2013). Work with local people on community development projects in the South Pacific. Retrieved from http://www.gviusa.com

Gonzalez, A. (2004). The social dimensions of Philippine English. *World Englishes, 23,* 7–16.

Grabowski, S. (2012). *Personal growth through volunteer tourism.* Paper presented at the CAUTHE 2012: The new golden age of tourism and hospitality. Melbourne, Australia. Retrieved from http://search.informit.com.au/documentSummary;dn=225206332831615;res=IELBUS

Guttentag, D. A. (2009). The possible negative impacts of volunteer tourism. *International Journal of Tourism Research, 11,* 537–551.

Heron, B. (2007). *Desire for development: Whiteness, gender, and the helping imperative.* Waterloo, Ontario, Canada: Wilfrid Laurier University Press.

Higgins-Desbiolles, F. (2003). Reconciliation tourism: Tourism healing divided societies! *Tourism Recreation Research, 28*(3), 35–44.

Holstein, J. A., & Gubrium, J. F. (2000). *The self we live by: Narrative identity in a postmodern world.* Oxford, UK: Oxford University Press.

Lindlof, T. R., & Taylor, B. C. (2011). *Qualitative communication research methods* (3rd ed.). Thousand Oaks, CA: Sage.

Lyons, K. D., & Wearing, S. (2008). Volunteer tourism as alternative tourism: Journeys beyond otherness. In K. D. Lyons & S. Wearing (Eds.), *Journeys of discovery in volunteer tourism: International case study perspectives* (pp. 3–12). London, UK: CABI.

McGehee, N., & Andereck, K. (2008). 'Pettin' the critters:' Exploring the complex relationship between volunteers and the voluntoured in McDowell County, West Virginia, USA, and Tijuana, Mexico. In K. Lyons & S. Wearing (Eds.), *Journeys of discovery in volunteer tourism* (pp. 12–24). London, UK: CABI Publishing.

McGehee, N.G., & Andereck, K. (2009). Volunteer tourism and the "voluntoured": The case of Tijuana, Mexico. *Journal of Sustainable Tourism, 17,* 39–51.

McGehee, N., & Santos, C. (2005). Social change, discourse, and volunteer tourism. *Annals of Tourism Research, 32,* 760–779.

McIntosh, A. J., & Zahra, A. (2007). A cultural encounter through volunteer tourism: Towards the ideals of sustainable tourism? *Journal of Sustainable Tourism, 15,* 541–556.

Mize Smith, J. (2013). Volunteer tourists: The identity and discourse of travelers combining largesse and leisure. In M. W. Kramer, L. K. Lewis, & L. M. Gossett (Eds.), *Volunteering and communication: Studies from multiple contexts* (pp. 189–209). New York, NY: Peter Lang.

Mostafanezhad, M. (2013). The geography of compassion in volunteer tourism. *Tourism Geographies, 15,* 318–337.

Ness, S. A. (2003). *Where Asia smiles: An ethnography of Philippine tourism.* Philadelphia, PA: University of Pennsylvania Press.

Osland, J. S., & Bird, A. (2000). Beyond sophisticated stereotyping: Cultural sensemaking in context. *Academy of Management Executive, 14,* 65–79.

Oswick, C., Keenoy, T., & Grant, D. (2002). Metaphor and analogical reasoning in organization theory: Beyond orthodoxy. *Academy of Management Review, 27,* 294–303.

Palacios, C.M. (2010). Volunteer tourism, development and education in a postcolonial world: Conceiving global connections beyond aid. *Journal of Sustainable Tourism, 18,* 861–878. doi: 10.1080/09669581003782739.

Pe-Pua, R., & Protacio-Marcelino, E. (2000). *Sikolohiyang Pilipino* (Filipino psychology): A legacy of Virgilio G. Enriquez. *Asian Journal of Social Psychology, 3,* 49–71.

Philippine National Volunteer Service Coordinating Agency. (2014). International volunteer programs. Retrieved from http://www.pnvsca.gov.ph/programs/programs_international.php

Raymond, E. M., & Hall, C. M. (2008). The development of cross-cultural (mis)understanding through volunteer tourism. *Journal of Sustainable Tourism, 16,* 530–543.

Rosaldo, R. (1988). Ideology, place, and people without culture. *Cultural Anthropology, 3*, 77–87.

Salazar, N. B. (2004). Developmental tourists vs. development tourism: A case study. In A. Raj (Ed.), *Tourist behaviour: A psychological perspective* (pp. 85–107). New Delhi, India: Kanishka.

Scott, C. R., Corman, S. R., & Cheney, G. (1998). Development of a structurational model of identification in the organization. *Communication Theory, 8*, 298–336.

Simpson, K. (2004). Doing development: The gap year, volunteer tourists, and popular practice of development. *Journal of International Development, 16*, 681–692.

Singh, T. V. (2002). Altruistic tourism: Another shade of sustainable tourism: The case of Kanda community. *Tourism: An International Interdisciplinary Journal, 50*, 371–381.

Stewart, D. W., Shamdasani, P. N., & Rook, D. W. (2007). *Focus groups: Theory and practice* (2nd ed.). Thousand Oaks, CA: Sage.

Stritch, R. L. (2011). *Be sugar in milk: Local perspectives on volunteer tourism in India and Uganda* (Unpublished master's thesis). Royal Roads University, British Columbia, Canada.

Tiessen, R., & Heron, B. (2012). Volunteering in the developing world: The perceived impacts of Canadian youth. *Development in Practice, 22*, 44–56.

Ting-Toomey, S. (2005). Identity negotiation theory: Crossing cultural boundaries. In W. B. Gudykunst (Ed.), *Theorizing about intercultural communication* (pp. 211–234). Thousand Oaks, CA: Sage.

Tomazos, K., & Butler, R. (2010). The volunteer tourist as "hero." *Current Issues in Tourism Recreation Research, 13*, 363–380.

United Nations Volunteers. (2011). *State of the world's volunteerism report: Universal values for global well-being*. New York, NY: Author.

Virola, R. A., Ilarina, V. R., Reyes, C. M., & Buenaventura, C. R. (2010). *Volunteerism in the Philippines: Dead or alive? On measuring the economic contribution of volunteer work*. Paper presented at the 11th National Convention on Statistics, Makatin City, Philippines, 4–5 October.

Wearing, S. (2001). *Volunteer tourism: Experiences that make a difference*. Wallingford, England: CABI Publishing.

Wearing, S., & McGehee, N. (2013). Volunteer tourism: A review. *Tourism Management, 38*, 120–130.

Weick, K.E. 1995. *Sense making in organizations*. Thousand Oaks, CA: Sage.

Wenger, E. (2010). Conceptual tools for CoPs as social learning systems: Boundaries, identity, trajectories and participation. In C. Blackmore (Ed.), *Social learning systems and communities of practice* (pp. 25–143). London, England: The Open University.

Wingham, T. (2013). Volunteering as a mechanism for starting over. *VolunTourist Newsletter*. Retrieved from http://www.voluntourism.org/news-feature192.htm

Zahra, A. (2006). The unexpected road to spirituality via volunteer tourism. *Tourism, 54*, 173–185.

Zahra, A., & McGehee, N. (2013). Volunteer tourism: A host community capital perspective. *Annals of Tourism Research, 42*, 22–45.

Zahra, A., & McIntosh, A. J. (2007). Volunteer tourism: Evidence of carthartic tourist experiences. *Tourism Recreation Research, 32*, 115–119.

Section 2:
US Volunteers Abroad

Voices from THE Peace Corps: An Intercultural Communication Study OF Blogs from Southern Africa

RICK MALLEUS
Seattle University

A Peace Corps volunteer serving in Mozambique wrote in her blog, "The adjustment from having 70 volunteers together to being completely alone in a site that has never had a volunteer living there before is pretty intense. I think the town just doesn't really know what to make of me right now…it's so much harder than I was anticipating." Living in a culture markedly different from her own, this volunteer's reflections illustrate the challenges international volunteers face adjusting to their host cultures. Established in March 1961, the Peace Corps has sent over 215,000 American volunteers around the world to serve in 139 different countries (Peace Corps, 2014). In 2013, the Peace Corps reported having 7,209 volunteers in 65 countries, with 46% of those volunteers being in an African country (Peace Corps, 2014).

The Peace Corps has been credited with playing a part in there being increased interest in how people "of diverse cultures could communicate more effectively" (Jandt, 2013, p. 35). Peace Corps volunteers live and work with host culture nationals, often being the only American in their living situation (Storti, 1997). Volunteers must "learn and conform to many of the norms and behaviors expected of people" (Storti, 1997, p. 152) in the host country. As Storti (1997) suggests, in order to be effective in their positions, volunteers "must become deeply immersed in the lives of the local people and must try to understand their view of the world" (p. 152). As a group of volunteers who spend years immersed in another culture, Peace Corps volunteers therefore are an interesting group to consider when thinking about real world intercultural interaction and intercultural communication. Insight into this group's experience can provide data by which to understand these intercultural experiences in more depth.

To that end, the overarching question that guides this research was "What is the nature of intercultural interaction that Peace Corps volunteers in Southern Africa experience as evidenced in blog posts?" This study analyzed the intercultural experiences of Peace Corps volunteers in four Southern African countries (Mozambique, Namibia, South Africa and Zambia). The voices of these international volunteers were heard through personal blogs kept during their international service sojourn. The study was interdisciplinary and applied theoretical frames from reflective writing and intercultural communication. The theoretical frames used in this study to explore the research question are discussed below. The study begins with a consideration of reflective writing found in blogs, followed by an examination of four intercultural communication constructs theorized as important to the experience of volunteers in an intercultural setting.

LITERATURE REVIEW

Reflective Writing and Blogs

With characteristics like the low barriers there are to their creation and maintenance, their ease of use, relatively easy interactivity and potential for wide distribution (Reese et al., 2007), blogs are growing in popularity and visibility (Burgess, 2006). Some Peace Corps volunteers are using this medium while on their intercultural sojourns in their host cultures.

Individual bloggers have different agendas, objectives, and motivations for maintaining blogs (Burgess, 2006; Gregg, 2006). It can be argued that blogs are a form of cultural production and a place for self-representation (Burgess, 2006). Peace Corps volunteers use personal blogs as a way to process their experiences and to communicate those experiences with family, friends, and others in the global audience who care to read their posts. As one Peace Corps volunteer in Southern Africa states in introducing her blog, "This blog is a way for me to share my Peace Corps experience, and archive my life...three years will be an adventure, and I invite you to follow along."

Generally blogs are associated with a single author, allowing an archival view into the blogger's world that is presented in reverse chronological order allowing a picture of the blogger's world to develop (Gregg, 2006; Dos & Demir, 2013). These qualities make blogs appropriate texts for content analysis. Further, blogs tend to have an intentional quality (Gregg, 2006). That bloggers use examples from their own lives in their posts, suggests blogs are constructivist in nature (Dos

& Demir, 2013). Social constructivism posits that meaning or truth comes from social interactions; therefore, language does not simply describe the world, "but creates the world" (Pavlik & McIntosh, 2011, p. 397). Symbols and signs therefore have "changeable meanings according to the context" in which they are sent (Pavlik & McIntosh, 2011, p. 397). Peace Corps blogs provide a window into the social interactions of the volunteers.

Bloggers represent themselves and their experiences rather than simply being represented by others (Pfister & Solitz, 2011). Real-world bloggers' writing is timely, frequent, and interest-driven (Freeman & Brett, 2012), and these are also important qualities when thinking about blog posts as potential texts for analysis. Bloggers think aloud, posting when they feel moved to write (Chong, 2010), which enables "critical refinement and thinking-in-process" (Gregg, 2006, p. 154).

Blogs can be reflective in nature, with blogging seen as a way to enhance and encourage reflective thinking (Chong, 2010; Dos & Demir, 2013; Gregg, 2006). Bloggers' posts are a personal "interpretation of their experiences, thereby revealing their interests and providing frequent insight into the communities in which they participate" (Freeman & Brett, 2012, p. 1033). Those insights are often arrived at through the reflective writing process, and it is those insights about Peace Corps volunteers' intercultural experiences that this study examined. Dos and Demir (2013) assert that blogs can amplify reflection, depth of learning, and knowledge bases, and it is this depth of critical reflection that may provide rich, specific detail about intercultural interactions to be revealed in blog posts from Peace Corps volunteers.

Intercultural Communication Frames

In addition to discussing reflective writing and blogs, it is necessary to briefly discuss four intercultural communication theoretical constructs. In this section of the study, the concepts of culture shock, intercultural communication challenges, cross-cultural comparison and intercultural adaptation are presented.

Culture shock. Ward, Bochner and Furnham (2001) effectively summarize some important ideas agreed upon in the field about culture shock: (1) People feel strain as they adapt to a host culture. (2) People experience loss as they feel deprived of things like friends, possessions, and a clear societal status. (3) People feel rejected or might reject others in the host culture. (4) People experience confused role expectations. (5) People feel anxious, surprised, and sometimes disgusted as they become aware of cultural differences between their culture and the host culture. (6) People feel helpless and not able to cope in the host culture. There is also agreement in the field that culture shock includes the ideas of "losing the power of easy communication" and of disrupting "self-identity, world views and indeed all systems of acting, feeling and thinking" (Furnham, 2010, pp. 87–88).

It is helpful to consider *signals* of culture shock (Abarbanel, 2009) because knowing the signals allows individuals to recognize that they may be experiencing culture shock. Some of the signals include "homesickness, boredom, withdrawal, need for excessive amounts of sleep, compulsive eating or drinking, stereotyping local people, reduced ability to work effectively and physical ailments" (Abarbanel, 2009, p. 136).

As Zhou et al. (2008) point out, much current thinking about culture shock frames the transition as "contact-induced stress accompanied by skill deficits that can be managed and ameliorated" (p. 65). Given this framing, it may be instructive to consider part of the transition during this period as a time of acculturation or adaptation (Zhou et al., 2008). When people are exposed to new cultures, their responses can be grouped into affective, behavioral and cognitive domains (Zhou et al., 2008).

Intercultural communication challenges. Communication challenges that volunteers may face as they cross cultures have a connection to culture shock, but deserve separate consideration because communication links sojourners to their new host environment (Gudykunst & Kim, 2003). Both verbal and nonverbal challenges can be found in intercultural interactions as sojourners encounter cultural variability in communication rules and behaviors (Gudykunst & Kim, 2003; Neuliep, 2012).

Effective intercultural communicators have message skills or "the ability to understand and use language and feedback" (Jandt, 2013, p. 36). The field has recognized four different verbal communication styles that reflect patterns of culture: direct-indirect, elaborate-succinct, personal-contextual, and instrumental-affective (Gudykunst & Ting-Toomey, 1988). Verbal styles pose multiple and different communication challenges for sojourners as dictated by the host culture's preferences and how those preferences agree or disagree with the sojourner's home culture preferences. It is noteworthy here to emphasize that language marks a person as belonging to an ingroup or being part of the outgroup because language is central to identity (Neuliep, 2012; Jandt, 2013; Lustig & Koester, 2013). In addition, idioms and different vocabularies might also be issues in intercultural communication related to language differences (Jandt, 2013).

In a host culture, sojourners may expect differences in verbal communication, but often do not expect differences in nonverbal communication (Albert & Ha, 2004). Not recognizing nonverbal communication cues or nonverbal misinterpretations have also been identified as barriers to effective intercultural communication (Jandt, 2013; Lustig & Koester, 2013). Misunderstandings due to cultural differences in nonverbal behavior are fairly common (Argyle, 1988). Nonverbal communication includes non-spoken symbolic communication, elements of the environment, which can be intentional or unintentional, conscious or unconscious, and can serve multiple functions (Jandt, 2013). For example in different contexts, a person may smile without planning to because they are happy (unconscious nonverbal behavior), or a person may smile to cover up embarrassment (conscious nonverbal behavior) or smile as response to a joke being told (intentional nonverbal behavior).

Nonverbal communication may be more trusted than verbal communication, especially if there is a conflict or contradiction between verbal and nonverbal messages (Ting-Toomey, 1999). Sojourners in a host culture may have difficulties making these distinctions in decoding nonverbal behavior and might make attributions about nonverbal behavior based on their home cultures, which makes it likely that different cultural groups may place differing interpretations on the same nonverbal behavior (Albert & Ha, 2004). For example, gestures are interpreted differently across cultures. Research has found that bringing "both hands together in the front and bowing had multiple meanings across cultures ('thank you,' 'hello,' 'goodbye'), as did bringing both hands to the sides of one's head and pointing the index finger ('the devil,' 'angry,' "horny')" (Matsumoto & Hwang, 2013, p. 8).

Cross-cultural comparison. One way volunteers in a host culture may try to develop their communication competence in trying to understand the host culture is by making comparisons to what they are familiar with because making those cross-cultural comparisons tends to be quite useful in helping sojourners understand cultural differences (Lustig & Koester, 2013). Sojourners can think about the implications that differences and similarities have for interpersonal communication by comparing and contrasting cultural patterns from different cultures (Lustig & Koester, 2013).

Reduction in uncertainty is an important reason for making cross-cultural comparisons. The "more we perceive another as similar to ourselves, the more we are able to reduce uncertainty about the person and to form accurate categories of him or her" (Neuliep, 2012, p. 327). It is worth remembering that tolerance "for ambiguity concerns a person's responses to new, uncertain, and unpredictable intercultural encounters" (Lustig & Koester, 2013, p. 71). By comparing and contrasting host and home country behaviors in specific situations, sojourners may be able to prepare themselves for higher levels of ambiguity than they are ordinarily comfortable with. One comparative tool intercultural communicators use is applying culture-general information about a culture to make sense of cultural practices (Lustig & Koester, 2013). For example, thinking about how someone from a host culture may be communicating from an ethnocentric position might allow a sojourner to consider how the host view might be different than the home culture perspective. Another tool that sojourners can use to help understand a particular culture is using culture-specific information (Lustig & Koester, 2013). For example, knowing where a host culture falls on a specific dimension of cultural variation, like power distance, allows sojourners to compare that host culture's position to their own culture's position as high, medium or low in power distance. Using culture general and culture-specific information in comparison may help reduce uncertainty about behavior in the host culture.

Intercultural adaptation. Communication lies at "the heart of the adaptation process" (Gudykunst & Kim, 2003, p. 373). As sojourners enter a host culture, their cultural identities may be marked by rigid cultural boundaries, but as they adapt over time, these boundaries may become less rigid (Reece & Palmgreen, 2000). Sojourners experience stress in host cultures and they adapt to help reduce stress, and this stress-adaptation-growth process is facilitated by interactions with people in the host culture (Kim, 1988).

Using information from making cross-cultural comparisons and also building up a store of knowledge about a host culture may over time result in changes in a sojourner's cultural identity (Reece & Palmgreen, 2000). Kim's theory of intercultural transformation suggests, in part, that adaptation is a process involving acculturation (new host culture learning) and deculturation (suspending and unlearning home culture) (Gudykunst & Kim, 2003). Adaptation is an outcome of acculturation (Berry & Sam, 1997) and can be defined as "a process by which individuals upon relocating into an unfamiliar cultural environment, establish (or reestablish) and maintain a relatively stable, reciprocal, and functional relationship with the environment" (Kim, 2008, p. 260).

Acculturation as a complex process includes many factors and involves behavioral and psychological changes that take place as a result of people from different cultures being in contact with each other (Berry & Sam, 1997). Further, it is important to remember that the sociocultural and psychological adaptation of a sojourner are both dependent on the degree to which the sojourner maintains home and host culture's values (Ward & Kennedy, 1994). Sojourners who travel often between multiple different cultures and who have meaningful host culture interactions during those sojourns in which acculturation and deculturation take place *might* undergo an intercultural evolution, achieving a global understanding allowing a universalized perspective (Kim, 2008).

RESEARCH QUESTIONS

Flowing from the literature discussed above, the overarching research question posed was "What is the nature of intercultural interaction that Peace Corps volunteers in Southern Africa experience as evidenced in blog posts?" To answer that question, four specific research questions were examined:

RQ1:   What insights into the experience of culture shock do Peace Corps volunteers' blog posts provide?

RQ2: What evidence of cross-cultural comparison do Peace Corps volunteers' blog posts provide?

RQ3: What reflections on intercultural communication challenges do Peace Corps volunteers' blog posts provide?

RQ4: What evidence of intercultural adaptation do Peace Corps volunteers' blog posts provide?

The methodology used to answer these questions is discussed in detail below.

METHOD

Text

Personal blogs of twelve American Peace Corps volunteers, who served in four Southern African countries (Mozambique, Namibia, South Africa and Zambia), were used as text for analysis. Peace Corps volunteers who were posted in Southern Africa and kept blogs were identified through an online search, and twelve were randomly selected to provide a variety of content and a substantial, yet manageable set of text for analysis. Three blog posts from each of the twelve Peace Corps volunteers were selected for analysis, with an entry being randomly selected from early in the volunteers' time in their host country, from the middle of their service and toward the end of their sojourn. The blog posts translated to forty typed pages of single-spaced text. These 36 blog posts served as the text for content analysis.

Instrument

To analyze the content of the Peace Corps volunteers' blog posts, a rubric was developed prior to reading the blogs. The rubric included four elements: culture shock, intercultural communication challenges (verbal and nonverbal), cross-cultural comparison, and intercultural adaptation. Each element of the rubric was operationalized based on the relevant literature discussed earlier in this study and are presented in Table 1.

Table 1. Coding Rubric.

Culture Shock	Cross-Cultural Comparison	Communication Challenge	Intercultural Adaptation
A sense of the loss of common cues that tell a person how to behave and how to communicate appropriately. Sense of disorientation.	Making comparisons between home and host cultures in ways of thinking, behaving, values, communication etc.	Expressed difficulty understanding verbal communication in the host culture.	Demonstrating the use of coping strategies or tactics that are appropriate in the host cultural context.
Loss of ability to accurately make sense of situations and environments due to cultural differences.	Making comparison between host and another culture in ways of thinking, behaving, values, communication etc.	Expressed difficulty making self understood verbally in the host culture.	Using language/ terms from host culture.
Losing the power of easy communication.	Making comparisons between home and host culture environment.	Expressed difficulty understanding nonverbal communication in the host culture.	Being able to explain different behavior in clear terms demonstrating understanding of cultural differences.
Feeling deprived of things a person is used to like friends, family, possessions, food, drink, ways of living etc.	Making comparisons between host and another culture's environment.	Expressed difficulty in knowing how to communicate nonverbally in the host culture.	Attempting/engaging in newly learned culturally appropriate behavior in the host culture.

Culture Shock	Cross-Cultural Comparison	Communication Challenge	Intercultural Adaptation
A sense of confusion about role expectations (for self and for others).		Explicit identification of nonverbal categories in the host culture.	
Feeling helpless and/or not able to cope normally in different situations.		Implicit identification of nonverbal categories in the host culture.	
Feeling surprised, anxious, worried, stressed by situations encountered in the host culture.			
Questioning identity (personal and cultural).			
Feeling homesick.			
Feeling bored.			
Withdrawal.			
Negative stereotyping of host culture and people			

Procedure

The rubric was applied to all the blog posts by two independent coders who marked blog text that provided evidence of the four different coding categories. Only coding elements that were coded as representing a specific intercultural communication element by *both coders* were included in this study. This decision was taken because this coder agreement represented the clearest, most unambiguous evidence in the blogs of the four coding categories. Text could be coded as belonging to more than one coding category. Only text that fell into one of the four categories was of interest and included in the results of this study.

FINDINGS

Reflections by the Peace Corps volunteers in all four coding categories were found in the text. Blog reflections on elements of culture shock and intercultural adaptation were found with higher frequency than those on communication challenges and cross-cultural comparison. Textual examples did not always fall neatly into one rubric category only and were therefore coded as evidence of multiple categories. For example the following paragraph was coded as both culture shock and communication challenges by both coders:

> As part of Damara tradition, my host family cooked goat head and feet two nights ago in preparation for a funeral. Caught slightly off guard, I questioned, "You eat the feet!?" My host grandmother and aunt, who speak only KKG, thought the words sounded so funny that they spent the remainder of the night laughing and saying over and over, "You eat the feet! You eat the feet!"

What follows are the common themes that emerged from analysis of the blog posts, beginning with culture shock.

Culture Shock

The insights into culture shock that the volunteers were experiencing were multifold and congruent with several well-established elements of culture shock reported in the previous research. To apply Gudykunst and Kim's (2003) idea, the *degree of strangeness* between the cultures in Mozambique, Namibia, South Africa and Zambia and the U.S. American culture is relatively high. This meant that Southern African cultures, when compared to U.S. American culture, were markedly different in several important respects. This volunteer's post illustrated her reactions to this strangeness:

> I haven't had a 'normal' week in my village in months....Who would have thought a Southern girl from the suburbs would be living this surreal life in another country. From one day to the next, I'm experiencing a variety of emotions: anger, elation, pain, frustration, excitement, mistrust, confusion....

Given this relatively high degree of strangeness, it is understandable that the Peace Corps volunteers would experience culture shock and that those normal manifestations of culture shock were reflected upon in their blogs. This study's findings provided insight into the volunteers' experiences that were consistent with both the literature on culture shock, as well as literature on Peace Corps volunteer experiences. A review of self-reported experiences of Peace Corps volunteers in Sub-Saharan Africa concluded that volunteers' reports realizing that "Ways of learning, thinking, behaving...taken to be universally and patently true" (del Mar, 2011, p. 358) were not.

From shock to adjustment. As a general pattern, the blog posts revealed more reflections on elements of culture shock in earlier posts and more reflections on adaptation in later posts. A volunteer's posts from Mozambique illustrated this adjustment process, with her earlier posts discussing feelings of isolation, needing to find courage to simply shop for food, and finding her expectations not being met, and her later posts discussing adjusting to seasonal availability of food in the market, conceptualizing technology as a luxury not a requirement for living, and accepting "bucket showers" as part of her Mozambican life. This finding is consistent with the way that culture shock and adaptation was conceptualized in the literature, with a gradual adjustment phase being usual for those immersed in a host culture (Kohls, 1996). This pattern would be expected as volunteers became immersed in the host culture, were shocked by the differences, and then slowly began to understand the host culture better. Over time, volunteers worked out how to communicate and behave in ways that were effective and culturally appropriate, slowly adapting to their host cultures. The blogs posts tended to demonstrate this adjustment trajectory.

Personal and professional. The blog posts also revealed that for the volunteers culture shock occurred both in their personal and professional lives while in Southern Africa. For example, on a professional level, a volunteer in Mozambique expressed dismay that a woman who she was visiting as part of her duties died soon after her visit: "...visiting a very young mother only to hear of her death 3 days later, August has been a very intense month." Having to deal with death, often, in her work was shocking to her. A Namibian volunteer pondered why at a center for orphans and vulnerable children she ran some "months it's like pulling teeth to get people to show up. June was a bad month but July is somehow booming. I have not yet deciphered the pattern of activity, it's completely random." This volunteer had not yet been able to work out the cultural reasons for why the center had such widely differing attendance month-to-month. A third example of culture shock in the professional realm can be seen in this volunteer's post about a home-based care program reaching a two-year milestone, celebrated by a work party: "It was unlike any party that I'm used to at home because there was a lot of eating and very little talking."

Being immersed in Southern African cultures also caused culture shock at the personal level. For example, a volunteer in Mozambique suggested: "Food becomes the center of your universe…not having the luxury of a supermarket down the street means that you think about food all the time." Another volunteer in Zambia commented on the personal experience of walking down a street:

I can't count the number of extended conversations I've had in the middle of the street with complete strangers. If I'm in a good mood, and not in a hurry, it's fine, but some days a 10 minute dialogue is just beyond me for some reason or another.

A volunteer in Namibia wondered at "an ENTIRE cut up cow was lying next to us on a tin plate they use for roofs just chillin right in my kitchen" and when a new well was about to be dug in her village, she was thankful at the prospect of "no more walking a long distance with heavy buckets" of water.

Surprise, stress, and anxiety. A major theme that emerged was blogged reflections on volunteers' surprise, stress, and anxiety about situations in the host culture. For example, here a volunteer reflected on her anxiety and stress related to a cockroach infestation in her Namibian house:

And all the time I was wondering why everyone was acting like I was a crazy person, everyone here has cockroaches, they just live with them! And here I am this strange American girl throwing money into a sinking ship.

Another example from a Peace Corps volunteer in South Africa reflected her surprise and stress: "I've tasted some of the most extreme foods ex. bugs, chicken intestines…smelled some of the most HORRIFIC body odor." A third example was from a volunteer in Mozambique traveling on a minibus: "As if I was not already uncomfortable enough, then she pulls out her breast to start nursing her baby right there in my seat."

Feeling deprived. Volunteers feeling deprived of things like friends, family, possessions, food, drink, and ways of living was another theme that emerged from the data. One volunteer listed things needed in Mozambique that were missing from her life: "…clean water & sewage systems, garbage removal & recycle systems, stable energy, reliable roads, building codes & enforcement of the codes." From a volunteer's Zambian sojourn came this reflection: "Our lives are so unstructured here that we yearn for people to tell us what to do…" as they miss the value of structure in their volunteer life in a rural village. A volunteer in Mozambique missed structure and certainty as she reacted to a bus not running on schedule and her reserved seat being given away: "I began an indignant rant in Portuguese about how I was there before and that he was lying and that they left early and now my seat was gone."

Disorientation. Another theme related to volunteers' experience of culture shock was feeling a sense of disorientation, not being able to make sense of the environment or situations due to cultural differences. For example, a volunteer reflected on field events at a school sports day: "Most of them were delayed for

1–2 hours because no one could find the equipment (e.g. javelin and discus), and just as important, no one had thought to bring any kind of measuring device to judge the distances. Sigh." Another volunteer wrote, "Now I just need to build up the courage to venture into the market so I can start cooking…it's so much harder than I was anticipating," as she felt disoriented, not yet able to make sense of her environment and new culture, and not yet feeling up to the relatively simple task of shopping for food.

Cross-Cultural Comparison

Compared to the blogged reflection on culture shock, there were fewer posts that made explicit cross-cultural comparisons. One reason for this finding may be that volunteers were not making *explicit* comparisons between cultures in their writing, but were rather *implicitly* comparing home (or other cultures) and host culture. For example, a volunteer in Namibia wrote of the stars in the night sky, "Africa showcases a different night sky." Implied in that text was the idea that something was being compared to the African sky (most likely the sky at home). Another example was from a volunteer in Zambia, "Life here is slow…but it is simple." Implied in this text was that the volunteer was comparing the pace of life in Zambia to the pace of life at home, and the complexity of daily life in Zambia to the complexity of daily life at home.

Two types of posts that did make explicit cross-cultural comparisons were found. One type of post compared host and home cultures. The second type of post compared host and home environments as volunteers tried to make sense of their intercultural experiences. Both types of cross-cultural comparison seemed to be used as a way to reduce uncertainty or ambiguity, a finding consistent with the literature (Neuliep, 2012; Lustig & Koester, 2013).

Additionally, cross-cultural comparison seemed to be used by volunteers as a way to make concrete what they are learning about themselves and their lives, providing a way for them to reflect on how their experiences in the host culture will have an impact on them in the future. For example, one volunteer wrote:

> Africa thickens your skin….I am going to be a much more laid-back person when I go home. And next time you are pulling your hair out while sitting in 405 traffic…just remember: you could be sharing your seat with a backpack, four picnic baskets, a woman and a baby who's pooping on you. Haha. I love Africa.

Her reflection implied that compared to the things that used to bother her at home, her experiences in the host culture will make her more relaxed, and less bothered by small annoyances that used to seem big back home. Another example compared Christmas in the U.S.A with the way the volunteer celebrated Christmas in Mozambique:

> The focus is on family, closer to how most of us celebrate Thanksgiving, the meal and the family....We stayed outside for most of the day and night, we played musica and just had a really nice peaceful and fun Christmas in Mozambique.

She seemed to express an appreciation for the family focus in the way Christmas was celebrated in her host culture.

Host and home culture. Examples of volunteers trying to make sense of ways of thinking, behaving, different values, and different communication styles by comparing home and host culture were found. One volunteer in Mozambique used a comparison to try and make sense of how she felt walking down the street in her host culture: "In the states, I never thought about how incredibly brave it is for someone who doesn't speak English well to navigate the busy streets, or to attend school." Another example can be seen in a volunteer who compared her life in her host country to her life at home: "I haven't had to worry about paying rent, or paying for health insurance, or existing in a world where I constantly 'need' a new wardrobe/car/phone." A third example can be seen in how a volunteer came to realize that in comparing what she has experienced in Mozambique, she can also see American culture more clearly:

> But perhaps you need to be removed from America to recognize what our culture is, both the good and the bad....Americans don't ask each other how they slept, or (often) ask about each others health and families each time they see each other."

This volunteer compared her experience in Mozambique to what she does and does not do when home in America, demonstrating she has made sense of parts of Mozambican culture and communication. These written reflections can be viewed as "thinking-in-process" as volunteers made sense of their experiences. This finding was consistent with the relevant blogging/reflective writing literature (Gregg, 2006).

Host and home environment. Reflections were also found where volunteers compared home and host environments. For example, a volunteer in Zambia wrote, "Yes, the bugs here are larger and more numerous than in America. This is probably the first stereotype of Africa that I've seen ring true." Her blogged reflection allowed her to think about her expectations prior to entering the host culture and compare those to the reality.

Volunteers also used environmental comparisons to help them describe their current experiences. For example, a volunteer in Namibia reflected on a "Hollywood-esque sign on the mountains welcoming visitors into town," while a volunteer in Mozambique suggested "I live in the beach site slash Las Vegas of Mozambique, so there will be a bevy of volunteers from all over Moz in my town (and my house) hanging out and enjoying some relaxation." These kind of comparative descriptions were helpful for both the volunteer and the readers of the blog in trying to understand the volunteer's experiences by taking what was familiar and applying it to the more unfamiliar. This type of blogging was consistent with descriptive reflection as described in the literature (Freeman & Brett, 2012).

Volunteers also made cross-cultural comparisons about parts of the environment connected to specific cultural traditions. Two examples were from volunteers in Mozambique:

> The sights, songs, and sounds of Christmas were very different here in my rural village in northern Mozambique that in North America. The fun commercialism of Christmas, like Santa toys, are just not present. There's no Christmas trees.

***

> Inyense are big-ass crickets, about which I have surmised three things….They must taste good, because the under-12 set treats them like the Holy Grail of foods, hunting them with the intensity and focus of chanterelle foragers or Black Friday shoppers.

The image of shoppers hustling to find bargains in a store in the U.S.A. on Black Friday was connected to the children intently searching for inyense in rural Mozambique; vastly different cultural settings and traditions, but the known image helps clarify the new experience for the volunteer.

Communication Challenges

Trying to be understood, and trying to understand the communication of host nationals were communication challenges about which volunteers blogged. Both verbal and nonverbal communication were reflected upon.

Being understood. Facing challenges in being understood was one theme to emerge. For example, a volunteer wrote, "When I speak in my 'funny' accent, some act like they can't understand me. It gets tiring to always be different, even when doing normal things." Another wrote, "Being an outsider sucks….When I don't know a word in Portuguese, people laugh." The volunteer recognized that her language skill (or lack thereof) marked her as an outsider, as not being part of the ingroup (Jandt, 2013), and this felt uncomfortable.

A volunteer in Zambia, Jaime, wrote, "So frequently I'll cause confusion when I introduce myself, and they think I've said 'Jimmy.' 'But that's a man's name!' is the most common response." Accent and unfamiliarity with the name caused confusion for the hosts in this instance. Vocabulary caused confusion for a volunteer in Namibia who related this communication episode:

> Napkins are called "serviettes" (napkins are feminine hygiene products) something my friend Chris and I found out the hard way when we went to the store and told the clerk we needed about 500 napkins for our party. She was a bit shocked.

Not only did language challenges concern not fitting in, but also volunteers reflected on how they tried to overcome those challenges so as to fit in and be successful in their communication. For example, a volunteer who often read to a child in the village wrote, "Then he began to ask me to re-read the page but to read it in Portuguese. So then I did my best translating Dr. Seuss into Portuguese."

Understanding others. Not being able to understand the hosts was also challenging. For example, a volunteer in Zambia's blog post recorded: "I sit outside with the men, sip my coffee and try to keep up with their conversation. I never can, they talk too fast and I inevitably end up zoning off and stare mesmerized at the red hot iron being skillfully molded by hands into axe heads." Or a volunteer in Mozambique wrote, "I get on a chapa and everyone is pointing and laughing and talking in Changana, of which I know none so I just sit there like an idiot." Once again, the feeling of being in the outgroup could be isolating, with language being central to identity (Neuliep, 2012)

Nonverbal communication. Different categories of nonverbal communication were discussed in volunteer's posts. One volunteer in Mozambique reflected on her experience of riding in a minibus with Mozambican passengers:

> Her hand might even be resting on my knee, because it is more comfortable there. Our skin is sticking together with sweat, and as much as I squirm away, I cannot even get half an inch of personal space...Can she not tell I am uncomfortable? Why is she keeping the window closed? My frustration builds and builds until I am almost ready to scream at this complete stranger.

Another volunteer in Namibia discussed riding in a "combi": "Your personal space is more than likely to be invaded." In these two examples, haptic (touching) and proxemic (space) behaviors were sources of discomfort. The interpretation and reactions to different nonverbal behavior may be culture-bound (Albert & Ha, 2004) as volunteers applied their own cultural standards in evaluation of the behavior.

Intercultural Adaptation

The blogs provided evidence of intercultural adaptation. Using language from the host culture, developing coping strategies, and trying out new, culturally appropriate behaviors were all themes that emerged from the data demonstrating how volunteers adapted to the host cultures.

Language use. Using language from the four Southern African host cultures was the most common way the volunteers demonstrated a form of adaptation. Evidence was found most frequently in volunteers' posts that showed adaptation of language to reflect host culture language in discussing life in Southern Africa. For example, in a detailed post reflecting language adaptation and consideration of that adaptation, a volunteer in Namibia wrote:

"Now" means in a little while, and "now-now" means right now. For example, "I'm eating lunch now-now, but I'm going to the store now." This can get a bit confusing, because say, "I'm coming just now," which could mean you are leaving now-now but coming back in a little while…now-now is one of my favorite Namibian phrases:)

Other examples of host language use demonstrating adaptation can be seen in a post from a volunteer in Mozambique who used multiple terms like, "Some part of me was terrified to set foot in her quintal…poking her head around the concrete barracca…wiping her hands on her capulana…." This host language use may be interpreted as being a form of language accommodation, that is, where communicators seek to accommodate those they are communicating with in the code they use (Gudykunst & Kim, 2003). In this case, the volunteers would be trying to accommodate those in the host culture by using language terms from Namibia, Mozambique, South Africa and Zambia.

This host language adaptation could also be interpreted as a demonstration by the volunteers of "testing out" a newly learned vocabulary, both for themselves and the audience for which they are writing their blogs. In a sense, they confirmed for themselves and their audience that they have learned something about the cultures they were living and working in. The volunteers demonstrated that learning by using language from those cultures even though they were all writing their blogs in English. This may be especially true for the volunteers who "translated" the host language terms for the audience. This can be seen for example, in the volunteer in Namibia who wrote, "French fries are called 'chips'…A grill is called a 'braai'…A large bus or van is called a 'combi.'"

Coping strategies. Volunteers' posts also provided evidence on adaptation through the use of coping strategies appropriate for the host culture. One example of this kind of practical adaptation was a volunteer in Namibia who blogged about moving cooking (as many other villagers did) outdoors to cope with cockroaches indoors in the kitchen. A second example of a practical coping strategy was a volunteer in Mozambique who now bought and ate expired foods saying "who cares if it expired last week??" All three volunteers found ways to manage in their new environments that were appropriate in those contexts.

Coping strategies can also be attitudinal. A volunteer in Mozambique provided a reflection about cultural differences that allowed her to cope more effectively:

And who is right? Who is wrong? No one is. And this is the immense beauty and overpowering frustration of cultural exchange. No matter what you do, no matter how much you learn, there will be things that bother you, things that seem rude or uncalled for when the simple fact of the matter is, they are just different.

By seeing the host experience through this attitudinal lens, the volunteer was able to manage the adaptation challenges more effectively. The way volunteers articulated those adaptations in writing and reflected on them with some specificity hinted at the effectiveness of those adaptations.

New behaviors. Evidence of a third type of adaptation by volunteers was also found, the theme of attempting newly learned culturally appropriate behavior. A volunteer in Zambia reported, "We sang traditional songs and danced traditional dances…." Another illustrative example can be seen in the volunteer in Mozambique who reported using a Mozambican recipe to make corn chowder that could be cooked "on a hot-plate, charcoal stove, or a fancy electric 4-burner!"

An example of descriptive reflection demonstrating personal interpretation (Freeman & Brett, 2012) was from a volunteer's blog from Zambia demonstrating new behavior adaptation that was informed by cultural understanding:

> After I finish up here, I'll buy some Blue Band and spaghetti at Charles Chaklika's shop. Although I can buy margarine and pasta at a number of food shops in town Mr. Chaklika has my loyalty being my host father's son and all.

The volunteer explained her actions (to record information about what they are doing) and provided the reasons why she was doing what she was doing (buying the food at a certain shop). The volunteer recognized the idea of community and loyalty in Zambian culture. Adaptation to host culture norms and practices has been found to be a characteristic of Peace Corps volunteers who are well adjusted to their host culture posts (Benson, 1978 cited in Brislin, 1981).

LIMITATIONS OF THE STUDY

The methodology limits the generalizability of this study's findings. Additional blogs from other Peace Corps volunteers serving in Southern African need to be examined for further evidence about their intercultural communication interactions in their host cultures before generalizable claims about the volunteers' intercultural communication experience can be made. A second limitation was that only the American volunteers' perspectives on the intercultural interactions were represented in the blog posts. The perspectives about the intercultural communication with the volunteers of those people from the host culture with whom the volunteers were interacting were therefore absent from this study's analysis.

From a volunteer:

Almost four years later, I find myself here, in Africa, trying (and failing) to find some way to say goodbye to this remarkable place that has been my home for the past three years...it has been a "tough assignment"...I would be lying if I said it hasn't. Though my good days certainly outnumbered my bad days, some of those low points were so low, it was hard to remember the good. Many days I wondered if anything I was doing was making any kind of positive impact on this country...But this experience has changed my life in ways I cannot articulate. What I gained professionally during my three years with the Peace Corps is definitely tangible, but what I experienced personally means far more to me...What has stood out the most for me and made the greatest impact on my life here have been the people. And that is what I will remember most about Africa. The people...Long ago I abandoned the noble ideals that I had joined the Peace Corps hoping to fulfil...And I hope when Namibians remember me, they will remember a person who did the best she could, where she was, with what she had...And so I dedicate this blog to them, my Namibian friends and family...who brought color and richness to my life...who helped me see myself, and the world, as they truly are...who challenged my spirit and broadened my horizons...who taught me the values of patience, strength and genuine humanity.

Peace Corps Volunteer, Namibia, 2005–2008

DISCUSSION

What is the nature of intercultural interaction that Peace Corp volunteers in Southern Africa experience as evidenced in blog posts? The results of this study indicated that Peace Corps volunteers were immersed in their host cultures, engaging in intercultural interactions at both professional and personal levels that were both successful and challenging, and that appeared to change over time, with volunteers making adjustments to their host cultures as their time in-country progresses.

This study provided support for the idea that these Peace Corps volunteers in Southern Africa struggled with cultural differences and culture shock, but also found effective ways to adapt to their host cultures in Mozambique, Namibia, South Africa and Zambia. This adaptation allowed them to do their work, appreciate elements of the cultures they were in and learn from their experiences.

It can be argued that Peace Corps volunteers "have, to varying degrees, left a tangible legacy in their respective countries of service" (Hall, 2007, p. 57). This study suggested that that an argument can also be made that the nature of intercultural interaction that Peace Corp volunteers in Southern Africa experienced, as evidenced in their blog posts, has left a mark on the volunteers, influencing their views of the countries, cultures, and communities to which they were posted, of the U.S.A. and themselves.

CONCLUSION

Volunteers who are considering joining the Peace Corps, and requesting a Southern African posting, would be well served to read blogs such as those examined in the study. Doing so may provide those volunteers an unfiltered, realistic sense of what a volunteer's day-to-day interaction with Southern Africans is like.

The findings also suggest that the Peace Corps may be well served to analyze blogs like those used in the study as the blogs could shed light on characteristics of successful (and unsuccessful) volunteers' intercultural interactions at both personal and professional levels. This data may be used to inform and improve intercultural communication training for volunteers, that is region specific and driven by qualitative data provided by using the blogs as texts for analysis. Training may be developed in stages to acknowledge and mitigate the cycle from culture shock to adjustment the data suggested volunteers experienced.

REFERENCES

Abarbanel, J. (2009). Moving with emotional resilience between and within cultures. *Intercultural Education, 20*, 133–141.

Albert, R.D., & Ha, I.A. (2004). Latino/Anglo-American differences in attributions to situations involving touch and silence. *International Journal of Intercultural Relations, 28*, 253–280.

Argyle, M. (1988). Intercultural communication. In L.A. Samovar & R.E. Porter (Eds.), *Intercultural communication: A reader* (pp. 31–44). Belmont, CA: Wadsworth.

Berry, J. W., & Sam, D. L. (1997). Acculturation and adaptation. In J. W. Berry, M. H. Segall, & C. Kagitcibasi (Eds.), *Handbook of cross-cultural psychology* (pp. 292–326). Boston, MA: Allyn & Bacon.

Brislin, R.W. (1981). *Cross-cultural encounters: Face-to-face interaction.* New York, NY: Pergamon.

Burgess, J. (2006). Hearing ordinary voices: Cultural studies, vernacular creativity and digital storytelling. *Continuum: Journal of Media and Cultural Studies, 20*, 201–214.

Chong, E. K. M. (2010). Blogging transforming music learning and teaching: Reflections of a teacher-researcher. *Journal of Music, Technology, and Education, 3*, 167–181.

del Mar, D.P. (2011). At the heart of things: Peace Corps volunteers in Sub-Saharan Africa. *African Identities, 9*, 349–361.

Dos, B., & Demir, S. (2013). The analysis of the blogs created in blended course through the reflective thinking perspective. *Educational Sciences: Theory & Practice, 13*, 1335–1344.

Freeman, W., & Brett, C. (2012). Prompting authentic blogging practice in an online graduate course. *Computers and Education, 59*, 1032–1041.

Furnham, A. (2010). Literature review, personal statement and relevance for the South Pacific. *Journal of Pacific Rim Psychology, 4*, 87–94.

Gregg, M. (2006). Feeling ordinary: Blogging as conversational scholarship. *Continuum: Journal of Media and Cultural Studies, 20*, 147–160.

Gudykunst W.B., & Kim, Y.Y. (2003). *Communicating with strangers: An approach to intercultural communication.* 4th edition. Boston, MA: McGraw-Hill.

Gudykunst, W.B., & Ting-Toomey, S. (1988). Verbal communication styles. In W.B. Gudykunst & S. Ting-Toomey (Eds.), *Culture and interpersonal communication* (pp. 99–115). Newbury Park, CA: Sage.

Hall, M.R. (2007). The impact of the U.S. Peace Corps at home and abroad. *Journal of Third World Studies, 24*, 53–57.

Jandt, F.E. (2013). *An introduction to intercultural communication: Identities in a global community.* Los Angeles, CA: Sage.

Kim, Y.Y. (2008). Intercultural personhood: Globalization and a way of being. *International Journal of Intercultural Relations, 32*, 359–368.

Kim, Y.Y. (1988). *Communication and cross-cultural adaptation: An integrative theory.* Philadelphia, PA: Multilingual Matters Limited.

Kohls, L.R. (1996). *Survival kit for overseas living: For Americans planning to live and work abroad.* Yarmouth, ME: Intercultural Press.

Lustig, M.W., & Koester, J. (2013). *Intercultural competence: Interpersonal communication across cultures.* Boston, MA: Pearson.

Matsumoto, D., & Hwang, H.C. (2013). Cultural similarities and differences in emblematic gestures. *Journal of Nonverbal Behavior, 37*, 1–27.

Neuliep, J.W. (2012). *Intercultural communication: A contextual approach.* Los Angeles, CA: Sage.

Pavlik, J.V., & McIntosh, S. (2011). *Converging media: A new introduction to mass communication.* New York, NY: Oxford University Press.

Peace Corps. (2014). Retrieved from http://www.peacecorps.gov

Pfister, D.S., & Soliz, J. (2011). (Re)conceptualizing intercultural communication in a networked society. *Journal of International and Intercultural Communication, 4*, 246–251.

Reece, D., & Palmgreen, P. (2000). Coming to America: Need for acculturation and media use motives among Indian sojourners in the US. *International Journal of Intercultural Relations, 24*, 807–824.

Reese, S.D., Rutigliano L., Hyun K. & Jeong, J. (2007). Mapping the blogosphere: Professional and citizen-based media in the global news arena. *Journalism, 8*, 235–261.

Storti, C. (1997). *The art of coming home.* Yarmouth, ME: Intercultural Press.

Ting-Toomey, S. (1999). *Communicating across cultures.* New York, NY: Guiford.

Ward, C., Bochner, S., & Furnham, A. (2001). *The psychology of culture shock.* London, UK: Routledge.

Ward, C., & Kennedy, A. (1994). Acculturation strategies, psychological adjustment, and socio-cultural competence during cross-cultural transitions. *International Journal of Intercultural Relations, 18*, 329–343.

Zhou, Y., Jindal-Snape, D., Toppings, K., and Todman J. (2008). Theoretical models of culture shock and adaptation in international students in higher education. *Studies in Higher Education, 33*, 63–75.

CHAPTER EIGHT

How Was Your *"Trip?"* Long-Term International Volunteering AND THE Discourses of Meaningful/less Work

LACY G. McNAMEE
Baylor University

BRITTANY L. PETERSON
Ohio University

KELLY K. GOULD
Baylor University

I think one of the things that people don't realize is the language when you talk to some-one who has come back from an experience like that. One of the most hurtful things that someone could have said to me after that two years was, "How was your trip?"...How was your *trip*? Well, I don't know, how was your "trip" to college? You know, being there for four years? It's not a trip. That was my *life*.
                                                – Cynthia, Life Learners missionary in Egypt for two years[1]

***

Volunteers confront assorted, even conflicting discourses regarding the purpose and value of their service (Ganesh & McAllum, 2009; McAllum, 2014). More so, long-term international volunteers are even further exposed to divergent dis-courses regarding the very nature of work and legitimacy of volunteer efforts due to their cross-cultural immersion (see Callahan & Hess, 2012; Fee & Gray, 2011;

McWha, 2011). Communication scholarship on work meaning/fulness suggests that these volunteers, such as religious missionaries and humanitarian aid providers, draw upon these myriad "identity-shaping discursive resources" to guide their interpretations of their experiences and shape their sense of self-worth (Kuhn et al., 2008, p. 163; Zorn & Townsley, 2008). Likewise, Ganesh and McAllum (2009) argued that discourses of volunteering and volunteerism "enable the creation of particular forms of identity-centered performance" for volunteers (p. 364).

Presently, there is little research centered specifically on the ways and extent to which long-term international volunteers draw upon cross-cultural discourses of volunteering and work at large to make sense of the meaning/fulness of their service. In an effort to shed light in this vein, this study examined the experiences of 24 American volunteers who served for periods ranging from three months to six years at a time in global south regions across Eastern Europe, Asia, North and West Africa, South America, and the Pacific Islands. To contextualize this study, communication-centered views on work meaning/fulness and the extant scholarly attention to cross-cultural discourses of work and volunteering are summarized in turn.

Cross-Cultural Discourses of (Volunteer) Work Meaning/fullness

Communication scholars have increasingly called for inquiry into the various meanings tied to work and the extent to which various forms of work are considered meaningful (see Cheney, Zorn, Planap, & Lair, 2008; Zorn & Townsley, 2008). While this has been examined in other fields including psychology, sociology, and economics, a communication-centered approach uniquely reflects on the intersubjective processes whereby these meanings arise, as well as the value-laden discourses that inform those meaning-making processes. Along these lines, Cheney and his colleagues (2008) argued that to truly examine the notion of "meaningful work," which "encompasses central life interest, job satisfaction, work-life balance, life satisfaction, perspectives on the career, spirituality, and the meaning of leisure," is to "call the very nature and goals of work into question" (p. 140). Further, Lair, Shenoy, McClellan, and McGuire (2008) emphasized that "the meanings we attach to work as well as our definitions of what we consider meaningful work reflect the norms, expectations, and priorities of the particular society we live in" (p. 176; see also, Dempsey & Sanders, 2010). Thus, Americans who serve for extended periods in the global south represent a particularly unique case for examining individuals' construction of work meaning/fulness in that they are dually confronted with home and host country discourses concerning the very essence and value of (volunteer) work.

American Discourses of (Volunteer) Work

Cheney et al. (2008) synopsized scholars' overlapping historical-cultural depictions of work in Western societies as follows: *work as labor*, evident in work-rest dichotomies (e.g., work-life balance), *work as personal growth* (e.g., providing skill development), *work as intrinsically valuable* (e.g., creating a sense of self-worth), *work as instrumental* (e.g., providing income), *work as means for status* (e.g., professions prototypically revered by society), and *work as calling* (e.g., pursuit of some transcendent goal). They further stated that previous Euro-American-centered scholarship has suggested that work is considered meaningful when it is freely done, affords autonomy, facilitates worker's minds and morality, provides fair wage for physical welfare exhibited, and does not inhibit one's ability to pursue happiness. Nonetheless, Kuhn et al. (2008) has asserted that contemporary capitalistic discourses of "impermanence" (stemming from telecommuting, temporary work, etc.) and "difference" (e.g., as demonstrated by generational shifts in understandings of work-life balance) have "disrupt[ed] simple determinations of who belongs, has opportunities, and succeeds" in the accomplishment of meaningful work in American society, thus, suggesting that there is no monolithic understanding of what constitutes work and meaningful work activities (p. 167).

With that said, Kuhn et al. (2008) also acknowledged that particular organizations and occupational subcultures provide discursive resources for informing our understandings of work meaning/fulness. Notably, they pointed out that the American nonprofit sector, for which organizational volunteering is ubiquitous, often frames work as spiritual calling, altruistic sacrifice, and important advocacy, which helps members to "mak[e] sense of their work and infus[e] it with value" (p. 164). However, Dempsey and Sanders (2010) argued that these discourses have also normalized long hours and low wages as intrinsic to meaningful nonprofit work. Further, they and others have contended that the entrepreneurial facet of contemporary nonprofit discourse privileges market logics of hierarchy, formalization, and efficiency as vital to the accomplishment of this line of work (see also, Ganesh & McAllum, 2012; Sanders, 2012). Yet even as volunteer roles increasingly emulate norms of employment-based work, scholars have suggested that American discourses still position volunteering as "an inferior variant of paid work" (Ganesh & McAllum, 2009, p. 367) or, as Clair (1996) found in her analysis of college students' narratives, as antithetical to a "real job" (see also, Broadfoot et al., 2008).

Global South Discourses of (Volunteer) Work

Given the prevailing Euro-American bias in scholarship literature at large (Broadfoot & Munshi, 2007), there has been comparatively little attention to discourses of (volunteer) work meaning/fulness rooted in global south contexts. Communication scholars have suggested that non-Western discourses may position work broadly as a web of relationships and problematize binaries like volunteer/employee, individualism/collectivism, and organizational/non-organizational volunteering (Cheney et al., 2008; Ganesh & McAllum, 2009), but there is scant empirical inquiry in this vein. As such, Ganesh and McAllum (2009) argued that "researchers at the very least ought to avoid attributing definitive status or reifying an operational cross-cultural definition of volunteering" until further exploring how "contexts without a history of charity-based volunteerism make sense of what volunteers do" (p. 365).

As one of few studies in this vein, McAllum (2014) recently examined the ways in which New Zealand natives assigned meaning to their domestic volunteer efforts, and she ultimately interpreted two "pathways of meaning" described as *freedom–reciprocity*, a deliberate and free choice of self-development whereby community service is offered in exchange for personal development and relationships, and *giving–obligation*, an act of much-needed service that requires time and energy commitments as well as financial stability. Given these distinct meanings, it follows that non-American contexts seemingly advance diverse discourses concerning the meaning/fulness of volunteer work, as well.

Past theses and dissertations on Peace Corps volunteers have offered some insight into the specific nature of these discourses, describing volunteers as struggling to adjust to host nationals' rejection of individualism, planning, and formalization (e.g., Hanchey, 2012; Lombas, 2011). Additionally, interdisciplinary research on various long-term international volunteers has presented findings alluding to the idea that host country nationals, paid expatriates, and even the volunteers themselves perpetuate discourses that position such volunteers as lacking the requisite knowledge, skills, and cultural awareness to accomplish valuable work (e.g., Devereux, 2008; McWha, 2011). Nonetheless, most of these studies have not principally examined volunteers' sensemaking of their work meaning/fulness in light of these cultural discourses. This gap in scholarly insight prompted the particular questions and methods that guided this research.

RESEARCH QUESTIONS AND METHODOLOGY

Theories of intercultural communication offer mixed views of the ways in which long-term international volunteers draw from home or host country discourses of work and volunteering to make sense of their experiences. On one hand, Kim's (1988, 2001) cross-cultural adaptation theory suggests that these volunteers may experience deculturation, or the loss or abandonment of one culture over time. However, Kramer's (2003) notion of intercultural fusion and plus-mutation alternatively implies that multiple cultural influences have an additive effect on volunteers' future thinking and experiences, a position that is supported by recent studies of long-term international volunteers (e.g., Callahan & Hess, 2012; Fee & Gray, 2011). Assuming support for this position, long-term international volunteers are then confronted with myriad discursive resources to make sense of the meaning/fulness of their time and efforts abroad.

Thus, while Cheney and his colleagues (2008) declared that volunteer activities should be considered in the wider range of "work" activities and argued that, "for many people, such secondary or even largely invisible activities may be far more meaningful than their paid employment," the scholarship on (volunteer) work meaning/fulness and long-term international volunteers suggests that these individuals' views of their service are likely far more complex given their unique positionality (p. 142). To shed insight in this vein, the study examined the following research questions:

RQ1:   What meanings do long-term international volunteers assign to their service, and to what extent do they make sense of these experiences as meaningful work?

RQ2:   How do volunteers draw upon home and/or host community discourses in these meaning-making processes?

To explore these questions, we examined 24 Americans' retrospective narratives of their experiences as long-term volunteers in global south regions across Eastern Europe, Asia, North and West Africa, South America, and the Pacific Islands. According to Sherraden, Stringham, Sow, and McBride's (2006) classifications of international volunteers, we included participants who served medium (3–6 months) and long (6+ months) terms, resided in group- and individually-based arrangements under significant international exposure, and were sent by their organizations to promote international understanding, citizenship, and peace as well as provide development aid and humanitarian relief. The specific facets of this participant sample and the sources and forms of data we collected are detailed in turn.

Sampling and Data

Among the 24 participants in this study, three individuals completed what Sherraden et al. (2006) deemed medium terms of service (3–6 months); however, two of them, a married couple, also served multiple terms totaling 14 years abroad. The remaining participants served longer terms (six or more months), with two of those participants completing the most extensive single term of six years apiece. The majority of participants who volunteered for longer periods of time lived abroad for only one term, but three of them completed several terms, with one person even serving four terms of five years each (20 years total). All volunteers were extensively immersed in their host countries' cultures and interacted daily with nationals. After initial periods of group training, roughly half of the volunteers carried out their service in relative isolation from other Americans (i.e., as lone individuals or married couples) while the other volunteers worked and/or lived in teams with fellow volunteers.

Participants were sponsored by seven different international voluntary service organizations which promote global peace and education as well as provide humanitarian aid/relief (Sherraden et al., 2006). Five of these organizations (Challengers, Missions of Mercy, Soul Searchers, Church Growers, and Life Learners), which sponsored 16 participants, are religiously affiliated and focus on Christian evangelism in addition to education and aid/relief efforts (e.g., teaching English). Such organizations were expressly included as they support a considerable segment of long-term international volunteers, yet they have been seldom examined in academic research to date (for an exception, see Diekhoff, Holder, Colee, & Wigginton, 1991). The remaining two organizations (Peace Corps and Medical Outreach), which sponsored eight participants, have no religious affiliation. Participants were recruited through professional networks formed from previous research projects, personal networks formed from our own volunteer experiences (e.g., the third author's experience as an overseas missionary), and subsequent snowball sampling. After early phases of analysis, maximum variation sampling of underrepresented volunteer types (e.g., non-religious medical service providers) was additionally implemented to assess the degree of overlap in different volunteers' experiences (see Tracy, 2013).

Each author conducted in-depth, narrative-style interviews in an effort to evoke participants' sensemaking processes from their retrospective stories. These semi-structured interviews focused on volunteers' experiences prior to, during, and after their service, and open-ended questions like "Tell me about your early experiences?" and "What stood out in your relationships and interactions with the local people?" invited participants to direct the conversation to areas they viewed with significance. Interviews ranged from 50 minutes to two hours in length with most interviews lasting approximately one hour. These conversations yielded approximately 26 hours of audio-recorded data that was subsequently transcribed for analysis.

Analytic Processes

We engaged in grounded, thematic analysis of the data and coded using Owen's (1984) interpretive guidelines of *recurrence, repetition,* and *forcefulness.* Recurrence was achieved when participant narratives "had the same thread of meaning" even when the exact phrasing differed (p. 275); for example, volunteers variously emphasized how they grew professionally or personally during their service. Repetition focused on specific words, phrases, and sentences that recurred verbatim throughout the data (e.g., "my whole life," "it was my life"). Finally, the concept of forcefulness, or participants' passion for particular issues and ideas, guided our interpretation of volunteers' meanings/meaningfulness of their service and the discursive resources that informed their constructions (e.g., friends' and family members' trivialization of their service as an exotic trip or adventure). The web-based collaborative office suite Google Docs facilitated our analytic process by enabling us to code concurrently, add analytic memos using the notes function, and even "chat" about emergent codes in real time using the instant messaging interface.

In the initial coding process, the first and second authors divided the transcripts and read through them individually to "spark [our] thinking and allow new ideas to emerge" (Charmaz, 2006, p. 48). Afterward, we collaboratively crafted a focused coding strategy to analyze our research questions, a process which "requires decisions about which initial codes make the most analytic sense to categorize your data incisively and completely" (p. 57). Our primary codes focused on the meanings participants assigned to their service. Then, analytic memos were generated about the discourses that informed participants' constructions of each meaning and the ways in which participants engaged discourses to discern the meaningfulness of their service. As these primary codes and memos were created, we began to systematically code the data for the degree to which participants viewed each meaning as affording them a sense of value, worth, satisfaction, and success (i.e., meaningfulness). Analytic memos were particularly helpful in scrutinizing our interpretations in this vein.

Midway through this coding process and after collapsing several codes (e.g., calling), we established four overarching codes which are detailed in the findings. Throughout this process, several strategies were implemented to ensure rigor and credibility in our work. In addition to interviewing different types of long-term international volunteers who served in various countries, we drew on supplemental data sources such as expert interviews (e.g., international social workers, representatives of sponsoring organizations), literature produced by and about the sponsoring organizations, and personal accounts of former volunteers (e.g., weblogs) to inform our analytic interpretations. Further, we enhanced the credibility of our work by drawing upon the third author's member reflections of her own year-long experience as a missionary in China (Tracy, 2010). Our interpretation and discussion of the data is presented in turn.

THE MEANINGS OF LONG-TERM INTERNATIONAL VOLUNTEERS' SERVICE

Participants assigned four core meanings to their long-term volunteer experiences: as analogous to *employment/career*; means of *personal development*; a form of *philanthropy/humanitarianism*; and an encompassing *whole life* endeavor. In our interpretation, they vacillated between these meanings in efforts to arrive at meaningful understandings of their experiences, though the enduring struggle toward significance was still apparent in several participants' narratives. Consistent with Kuhn and colleagues' (2008) argument concerning the identity-shaping power of work discourses, volunteers' individual espousal/rejection of American and host country discourses concerning (volunteer) work elucidated the sense of meaningfulness they ultimately acquired from their perceived "employment," "developmental," "philanthropic," and "life" experiences. Thus, volunteers who constructed the same service meaning but were uniquely influenced by various (volunteer) work discourses often divergently made sense of their service as meaningful/less. We discuss each of these meanings and their meaningful/less sensemaking dynamics in turn.

Service Experience as…Employment/Career

Multiple volunteers equated their service with that of a traditional employment contract, a meaning that was fundamentally evident in participants' labeling of their roles as "jobs" and their recurrent references to "job descriptions," "personnel issues," "getting hired," and so forth. Additionally, volunteers spoke of their roles as analogous to career-advancing internships or professional development opportunities. Rachel, for example, even persuaded a friend who was denied admittance to graduate school to get a "job" with the Peace Corps to fill the "gap years" after college graduation:

> It was 2008 and the economy had not crashed just yet. All my friends thought they were going to find jobs, too, but they hadn't found them yet…I felt like I was in the best position because I knew no matter what I had a job and it was going to be exciting.

Similarly, Phyllis referred to her Peace Corps service as, "Professionally, it gave me the 'in' that I needed with the Fish and Wildlife Service…I was like the second female hired as a fishery biologist in the southeast…. You get the same benefits that a veteran gets for hiring." Other medical aid providers and missionaries likewise spoke of their experiences as opportunities to develop skills and credentials to further their careers in speech pathology, physician work, and vocational ministry.

Beyond this labeling, though, volunteers' overall construction of their service as employment/career was readily evident in their assessments of their organizations' socialization of them from *prospective* to *established* to *former volunteers* (see Kramer, 2011). For example, in reflecting on their time prior to becoming established volunteers, participants critiqued their organizations' screening processes according to the extent to which they were clear, organized, and rigorous. Many volunteers clung to the employment-based notion of job matching, and given that many of their organizations appeared to heavily scrutinize prospective volunteers' skills and qualifications, these participants were often subsequently shocked when their ultimate country and role assignment did not complement their technical expertise and/or language proficiencies.

As new volunteers, participants who held an employment/career frame focused on the perceived professionalism of the organization's orientation, training, and transitioning processes. For example, missionary couple Lilian and Edwin spoke about the comprehensive training programs implemented by Challengers and how adequately that training prepared them for their new life abroad. Other volunteers also commented on the overall "legitimacy" and "backing" of the organizations, deeming them credible when they maintained standards of efficiency, formalization, and perceived productivity.

As these examples intimate, volunteers were often prominently influenced by American discourses of marketization, professionalization, and technical rationality. Thus, participants whose experiences lived up to the prototypical American standards of full-time employment contracts gained a sense of meaningfulness from viewing their service in this way. Conversely, volunteers who clung to these American work discourses yet experienced chaos, inefficiency, and few if any measurable results from their service struggled to interpret their time spent as valuable. It was in this vein that missionary Kelly questioned her sense of purpose, given the absence of concrete, tangible outcomes from her efforts in China:

> I'm a doer…if I'm not achieving something, then what's going on? So for me not to have something measurable that I could literally say, "Okay, this is what I did," then…a lot of my frustration was my time was spent over coffee and tea with people…there was nothing to bring home. Nothing to say, "Okay, here's what we did."

Learning to embrace global south discourses of flexibility and fluidity as well as recasting one's service in terms of other meanings helped some of these frustrated volunteers eventually attain meaningfulness from their time abroad. For example, Church Growers missionary Wes explained, "We did have goals, and even towards the end…we would ask each other…'Hey, how many people did you share with this week?,'" but then he went on to admit, "I would never do this today" because he had learned to conceptualize productivity and success in more than just quantifiable terms during his time.

Service Experience as…Personal Development

Diverging from the previous meaning, personal development centers on the life enrichment that occurs outside of employment-based contexts and accentuates volunteers' yearnings toward self-actualization. Volunteers who privileged this meaning viewed their time abroad as a journey to discover or enhance emotional maturity, cultural awareness, spiritual growth, and adventure. Accordingly, these participants focused on their own growth and change as central to the experience and, thus, referenced "I" and "me" prominently throughout their reflections. For example, Jennie, a Peace Corps volunteer, described her decision to serve with her husband Adam in Fiji as:

> For me, I enjoy living in different places and meeting new people and trying different things.... When my husband and I got married in 2008, we were talking a little bit about what to do, how to move forward, and I was like, "Oh it would be kind of fun to live somewhere else for a little while before we have a house or kid." And he suggested, "Well, why don't we just do the Peace Corps? If we're going to do it, let's go do it." I was just interested in going really anywhere, doing anything....

Like Adam and Jennie, many volunteers spoke of the excitement that came with moving to an exotic, unfamiliar location. Others underscored the means of escape that the lengthy term of service afforded them. Hannah, a Church Growers missionary, was one of several who envisioned her time abroad in this way, saying, "For me, it was the complete kind of freedom of I don't have to mess with my family issues."

As these excerpts demonstrate, volunteers who gained a sense of meaningfulness from their personal development frame often rejected or remained unaffected by American discourses that privilege paid work over volunteering. Still, several volunteers struggled to view their experiences as meaningful in light of these discourses. According to participants' narratives, family members and friends often stressed such discourses and therefore indicted the volunteers' endeavors as frivolous, selfish, and irresponsible. For example, Nathaniel recalled the following about his decision to serve in China for four years with Missions of Mercy:

> Both my sisters were really supportive. However my mom was less supportive. You know, she wanted me to stay and kind of live the American dream and prepare for my retirement—which is all valid. A parent wants their child to be [successful]...but I kind of had a different plan. So it was a little bit harder for my mom.

In order to maintain a sense of meaningfulness, volunteers like Nathaniel conversely embraced somewhat of a "you only live once" mentality and envisioned careers and other commitments (e.g., house mortgage, children) as future endeavors. In this way, they drew upon American discourses of self-actualization as an important dimension of work, and, thus, when they benefitted and grew from their experiences, they naturally made sense of them as valuable. However, volunteers who were heavily influenced by American acclaim of paid work and/or failed to gain considerable emotional, spiritual, or social benefit from their time abroad struggled to see their experiences as meaningful. For example, participants who regretfully abided by the largely paternalistic cultures of their host countries (e.g., African tribes, Middle East regions) often wrestled with a personal sense of failure for perpetuating narrow gender roles and expressed longing for richer, more inclusive relationships with nationals.

Service Experience as…Philanthropy/Humanitarianism

Consistent with prevalent cross-cultural discourses of volunteering, participants also made sense of their experiences as philanthropic or humanitarian service. While all volunteers who interpreted their experiences in this way similarly focused on making a difference or affecting beneficial change, they also divergently envisioned their efforts in two distinct ways that we refer to as *charity* versus *equipping*. Those who made sense of their humanitarian efforts as charity typified a more paternalistic stance of helping impoverished, ignorant people who cannot or will not help themselves. In this vein, Peace Corps volunteer Phyllis spoke of how much "they loved us" and that "those people in that country [Central African Republic]…could not believe that a white woman would leave America and come over to help them."

But while many volunteers initially made sense of their service in this way, several volunteers eventually uncoupled themselves from this charitable view and alternatively adopted an equipping stance as they became further immersed in the global south culture. Thus, rather than envisioning their "aid" as the panacea to nationals' problems, those who constructed the equipping meaning favored a more social work-based interpretation of their role as empowering and collaborating with locals to define and address community needs over time. Life Learners missionary Cynthia illustrated this brand of sensemaking in her philosophy of working with locals in Thailand and Egypt, stressing that she had to first learn from them before suggesting alternatives. She emphasized the importance of adopting their aphorisms and abiding by their practices, even those that she did not personally espouse, so that nationals would acknowledge "Oh, she's one of us." For example, while working in an orphanage, she followed local philosophies of childcare before ultimately suggesting that additional nurturing would improve the children's behavior and adjustment over time.

Initially, volunteers whose service took on a philanthropic/humanitarian meaning were often influenced by American discourses linking professionalized standards with volunteer success, albeit such quantifiable accomplishments based on strategic planning and implementation rarely came to fruition. As such, few volunteers acquired a sense of meaningfulness solely from the charity-focused philanthropic/humanitarian frame. Conversely, volunteers who moved toward an equipping-centered view in lieu of charity-based understandings often ultimately made sense of their efforts as meaningful. In doing so, they spoke of learning to defy Americanized notions of work that privilege market logics of formalization, efficiency, and quantifiable outcomes, as well as embrace global south discourses that emphasize the fluid, relational, and improvisational dimensions of work. While serving in Guinea-Bissau, Africa, Peace Corps volunteer Leslie pivoted from a charitable to equipping view of her efforts in this way:

> I really wanted to help, but there was a time of the year when they literally didn't have any food. So whatever kind of help I could give them was not the kind of help that they needed...I was like, "Well we can apply for these grants, and we can build a well and get new varieties of seed that could be higher yield." And they were like, "No, I don't have food for my baby today...that's all fine, but I really just need cash." So...there was a lot of conflict between what *I* thought I was there to do and what *they* thought I was there to do."

Thus, by breaking out of the "American mindset," as several participants referred to it, volunteers like Leslie managed to redefine their success. For example, Nathaniel reflected on his four years as a missionary in China as: "I did not go in there and rock their worlds or change their lives forever but some good things happened, some good projects happened, some good people happened, so that's what the *success* of it was."

Nonetheless, even among volunteers who viewed their efforts as humanitarian equipping, their sense of meaningfulness was intermittently shaken by family members who propagated American discourses positioning volunteering as subordinate to employment-based work. One of the most poignant illustrations of this came from Eddie, whose father couldn't understand why he would leave his "stable job" in the oil and gas industry to become a missionary: "My dad said if I'm going to the [Missions of Mercy] school, he's not going to call me his son anymore, and I cannot come back home." His father was true to his word, and for a period of years after Eddie devoted his life to missions, his father effectively disowned him before eventually reestablishing contact. Still, Eddie and others ultimately rejected these types of discourses and, hence, came to understand their service efforts as valuable and worthy.

Service Experience as...Whole Life

Unlike the aforementioned meanings constructed by volunteers, the final meaning of participants' service experiences makes no delineation of volunteering from other roles and activities during one's time abroad. That is, volunteers additionally made sense of their service experience as all-encompassing or, as many participants labeled it, their "whole life." Consistent with global south discourses which do not as clearly demarcate work/life and public/private binaries, in the eyes of many long-term volunteers there was no prominent bifurcation of volunteering from socializing, leisure, and other life spheres. As Church Growers missionary Wes explained:

> I see it more as a part of—it wasn't just a mission, and maybe that's where mission gets a little bit distorted. It was more like my life. I basically chose to move my life overseas. I didn't just go to do a mission trip. I went to live there, so I lived there, and I loved and I prayed and I think a lot of that stuff, you can't take that away.

Participants who constructed meaning in this way stressed the interpersonal dimensions of volunteering, both in terms of relationships with fellow volunteers and host country nationals. Accordingly, the line between being in one's role versus not being in it was continually blurred because, as one volunteer said, "You're literally living life with them." Many volunteers spoke fondly of the pervasive presence of fellow volunteers, like Eddie's wife Camilla, who served alongside him with Missions of Mercy:

> There's something that you get in a relationship when you travel with people and you experience these total out-of-the-box experiences where you might be somewhere and you don't know that person that well, but we need to go get water or we need to find a way to eat. You become really close.

Likewise, volunteers celebrated the bonds they developed with those in their communities. In this vein, Leslie explained that her Peace Corps host family gave her their last name as a sign of inclusion, and even after she moved out after completing her training, she kept the name because she "really did feel like they were [her] family there."

However, volunteers also expressed frustration, anger, and anxiety regarding the encompassing nature of their volunteer identity and the seemingly inability to escape it. For volunteers like Jennie, this often stemmed in part from living with a host family: "You're staying in someone's house, eating whatever foods they prepare and sharing this bathroom...it was just kind of overwhelming...[the Peace Corps host family] wanted to make sure we were comfortable, but I think that sometimes it was a little bit overbearing." For others, this sense of institutionalization stemmed from interactions with fellow volunteers, as was the case for Olivia with her team of Church Growers missionaries:

> It was like fighting for a day off. That was something that was huge. I'm kind of drowning [doing] six days a week on and one day off.... [I] had to get permission to say I wanted to go to a triathlon...they [team leaders] were always reluctant to let us go.

Participants who made sense of their service simply as life in totality, for better or worse, resigned themselves to remain somewhat undecided as to whether their time was meaningful. In short, they interpreted the experience as "it just is." However, some volunteers clearly were more peacefully resolved to this indecision than others. Those who seemed more content often had unconventional upbringings (e.g., military families, extensive global travelling) and, thus, were more insulated from American discourses that privileged traditional employment contracts. Still, as Camilla's story illustrates, returning home often evoked mixed emotions as they attempted to reconcile their life abroad with their life back in the United States:

> We don't own a house. We're just now having children because we never were on that time-line, that trajectory. But now we are...so we are a little bit back of the trajectory of most people our age, but we feel like we're behind. We kind of don't care, but then you kind of do care, you know?

Other volunteers struggled to respond to Americans who wittingly and un-wittingly belittled the significance of this time in their lives. Church Growers missionary Evie, for example, experienced this with family members:

> They were sweet, but they also couldn't understand what was going on with me. You don't talk a lot about the experiences because it's hard to convey it, and there were emotions I was feeling really strongly that I couldn't even understand myself, much less try to explain to someone else.

Evie captured the sentiments of many others who often recalled feeling particu-larly dejected when family or friends depicted their experience as an exotic adven-ture/trip or as a phase that is/was disconnected from and/or irrelevant to the rest of their "real" life. Wes, for example, lamented, "There's nothing worse than starting to tell a story and someone says, 'Okay, I've got to go.' I think when you realize that not everybody has the capacity to [express genuine concern]...you've got few people you can actually really share with." Thus, volunteers who maintained a sense of meaningfulness from their whole life experience often withdrew from relationships with these friends and family, thus somewhat insulating themselves from American discourses that trivialize the importance and value of volunteering.

STUDY IMPLICATIONS

In line with calls for scholars to "consider the discursive forces that determine what kinds of work/worker becomes 'meaningful/meaningless,'" this study considered how long-term volunteers themselves draw upon cross-cultural discourses of vol-unteers, volunteering, and work at large to make sense of their service experiences (Broadfoot et al., 2008, p. 157). The findings demonstrate that volunteers vacillated between four meanings (employment/career, personal development, philanthropy/ humanitarianism, whole life) in attempts to assign value to their time abroad and maintain a sense of contentment and self-worth when reflecting on their time as a volunteer.

From a volunteer:

When I told my dad I was going to China he was like, "I don't think this is a good idea. What are you going to do for your future? What about retirement? Why do you want to go overseas when we have people that you can help here?" I felt so guarded and misunderstood, like I had to defend myself, but all those practical things did actually kick in. I honestly didn't have any answers for him because, at that time, I was still wrestling with it, too. I felt so drawn to China, but I didn't know why. I thought, "Asian languages intimidate me. It's dirty, and there are too many people." And then after I came back, it was worse. I kept thinking, "What am I doing with my life? Now what? Ok, I just gave my life to this organization and now I feel like...abandoned." You know, you're just realizing who you are, your identity, and then you come home. And then there's my dad again, saying, "*Now* what are you going to do? What job are you going to get?"

Kelly (third author), missionary in China for one year

In summation, volunteers who were heavily influenced by American market-based discourses of work seldom found meaningfulness in defining their experiences as employment/career and charity-based philanthropy/humanitarianism, given that their efforts typically fell short of professionalized standards of success; alternatively, volunteers gained a sense of meaningfulness by drawing upon global south discourses to redefine their experiences as opportunities for personal development and philanthropic/humanitarian equipping. Additionally, volunteers made sense of their experiences, not just as a job, adventure, or act of service, but as an all-encompassing whole life endeavor that was more or less meaningful depending upon the relationships and interactions they had with their American friends/family, fellow volunteers, and host country nationals. Several scholarly and practical implications of these findings are highlighted in turn.

Considerations for Theory Development and Research

At the broadest level, this study affirms the scholarly position that examinations of the very meanings of work and meaningfulness that individuals assign to it should take into account the biases that come from the particular cultural contexts in which we are situated (Dempsey & Sanders, 2010; Lair et al., 2008). Notably, this study's insights into the experiences of long-term international volunteers disrupt several Euro-American understandings of volunteer work and volunteers' sensemaking of their work as presented in the scholarly literature to date. For one, our participants' experiences of volunteering as "whole life" run counter to the implicit assumption that volunteering is bracketed separately from other aspects of life and, therefore, volunteers intermittently extricate themselves from their volunteer identity to embody other roles such as colleague, neighbor, family member, and friend. Thus, these findings support Ganesh and McAllum's (2009) position that international constructions of volunteering "hold the potential to change our understandings of the discursive boundaries dividing help, home, and work that mainstream perspectives on volunteerism construct" (p. 366).

Second, these findings contest the enduring depiction of volunteers as chiefly motivated by a desire to engage in altruistic service. Specifically, this analysis disputes views advanced in some interdisciplinary studies that long-term international volunteers are distinct from other development workers in the sense that they are "generally motivated by humanitarian rather than financial concerns" (Devereux, 2008, p. 359). Conversely, this study found that several volunteers prominently viewed their service as a means to develop professional credentials/experience to advance their paid careers. Also, many participants principally engaged in service to escape challenging or undesirable life circumstances or to grow spiritually and emotionally, whereas philanthropic/humanitarian concerns were more ancillary in their decision-making processes.

Third, while we agree that "a great deal of meaningful work occurs outside of paid work" and that, as scholars, we "must expand our vision to consider many types of work not ordinarily recognized as 'productive' or as having official status in society," the findings of this study suggest that volunteers themselves may actually struggle to view their work as meaningful (Cheney et al., 2008, p. 144). While many of the long-term international volunteers who participated in this study were able to shift between meanings to ultimately arrive at an interpretation of their experience as worthwhile and valuable, several still struggled, even months and years after their service, to make sense of their efforts and time as meaningful in the end. Just as we critique societal discourses which perpetuate narrow understandings of volunteers, as researchers, we must also take care not to assume that our participants view themselves or their roles in the same ways that we envision them.

Lastly, these findings support recent communication-based studies of international volunteers and theories of cross-cultural communication that envisage the influence of multiple cultures on individuals' sensemaking as additive and synthesizing rather than substitutionary and supplanting (e.g., Callahan & Hess, 2012; Kramer, 2003). That is, as participants in this study found themselves positioned amidst divergent views of what constitutes work meaning/fulness, they drew upon both American and global south discourses to make sense of the nature and purpose of their volunteer experiences.

Insight for Volunteers and Organizations

In a practical sense, this study illuminates several potential insights for both long-term international volunteers and the international voluntary service organizations (IVSOs) that sponsor them. First, given that one of participants' chief frustrations was the poor fit or match between their skills/experience and their ultimate service placements, IVSOs should consider how they might more transparently communicate with prospective volunteers. Specifically, we recommend that during the screening process organizations clarify that while prospective volunteers' relevant skills and experience may be extensively scrutinized, they may not ultimately be matched according to these credentials due to other factors such as an immediate need for volunteers in other roles and/or regions. This type of realistic messaging will help volunteers to establish their expectations accordingly.

Second, while many volunteers expressed satisfaction with the comprehensive training processes they underwent prior to embarking on their journeys, many voiced stories about the isolation and confusion they endured throughout their time abroad. In light of this, we suggest that IVSOs devote increased attention and resources to continued support and development for their volunteers throughout their service commitment. Though some of the organizations our participants were affiliated with already engage in these types of activities, other IVSOs might benefit from providing volunteers with host country sponsors and offering (semi) annual debriefing sessions for volunteers in the same geographic area.

Third, as family and friends were cited as often perpetuating American discourses of work, which stifled some volunteers' abilities to construct meaningful experiences, IVSOs might thoughtfully consider the role they can play in equipping volunteers to talk with family and friends about this well-intentioned yet stress-inducing and hurtful communication. Organizational strategies in this vein might be as simple as reminding volunteers that their loved ones lack the cross-cultural perspectives they've adopted or as elaborate as initiating formal programs to educate family and friends about the consequentiality of their communication with those who serve internationally (as Peace Corps and some other organizations have explored).

Finally, the findings of this study suggest that volunteers would benefit from simply gaining a broad knowledge of the varied meanings they will likely construct from their experiences and the ways in which cross-cultural discourses of (volunteer) work may potentially shape their understandings of the purpose and value of their time abroad. Toward this end, IVSOs could establish mentorship programs that pair new volunteers with tenured former or current volunteers. Seasoned volunteers' advice might better equip novice volunteers to constructively reconcile the discourses they'll likely confront before, during, and after their service so that they may ultimately retain a sense of meaningfulness from their experiences.

CONCLUSION

American volunteers who serve for months and years at a time in the global south are concomitantly faced with home and host country discourses concerning the very essence and value of their work. This study suggests that these discursive resources spur long-term volunteers to assign four meanings to their service (as analogous to employment/career, means of personal development, a form of philanthropy/humanitarianism, and as an encompassing whole life endeavor) and that by oscillating between these meanings, volunteers often construct meaningful, self-edifying understandings of their experiences. Nonetheless, this research also demonstrates that heavy influences of American market-based discourses of work all too often impede volunteers' capacities to recast their purpose and success in alternative ways. As was the case with our participants, many long-term international volunteers come to understand their experience, not just as a resume-builder, voyage, or philanthropic commitment, but as all-encompassing—in essence, as one's entire life. Thus, scholars, organizational practitioners, friends, and family should carefully heed their words when referring to these individuals' endeavors, as even the smallest label or phrase may redefine a volunteer's own understandings of his or experience.

NOTE

1. With the exception of Peace Corps and the third author's name, all organizations and participants have been assigned pseudonyms. Given its distinctiveness as a large U.S. governmental organization, the Peace Corps is a fundamentally identifiable organization and, hence, no anonymous designation was created.

REFERENCES

Broadfoot, K. J., & Munshi, D. (2007). Diverse voices and alternative rationalities: Imagining forms of postcolonial organizational communication. *Management Communication Quarterly, 21,* 249–267.

Broadfoot, K. J., Carlone, D., Medved, C. E., Aakhus, M., Gabor, E., & Taylor, K. (2008). Meaningful work and organizational communication: Questioning boundaries, positionalities, and engagements. *Management Communication Quarterly, 22,* 152–161.

Callahan, C., & Hess, J. (2012). Experiences of deculturation among United States Peace Corps volunteers. *Journal of International Communication, 18,* 49–62.

Charmaz, K. (2006). *Constructing grounded theory: A practical guide through qualitative analysis.* Thousand Oaks, CA: Sage.

Cheney, G., Zorn, T. E., Planap, S., & Lair, D. J. (2008). Meaningful work and personal/social well-being: Organizational communication engages the meanings of work. In C. Beck (Ed.),

Communication Yearbook 32 (pp. 136–185). Washington, DC: International Communication Association.

Clair, R. P. (1996). The political nature of the colloquialism, "a real job": Implications for organizational socialization. *Communications Monographs, 63,* 249–267.

Dempsey, S. E., & Sanders, M. L. (2010). Meaningful work? Nonprofit marketization and work/life imbalance in popular autobiographies of social entrepreneurship. *Organization, 17,* 437–459.

Devereux, P. (2008). International volunteering for development and sustainability: Outdated paternalism or a radical response to globalisation? *Development in Practice, 18,* 357–370.

Diekhoff, G. M., Holder, B. A., Colee, P., & Wigginton, P. (1991). The ideal overseas missionary: A cross-cultural comparison. *Journal of Psychology and Theology, 19,* 178–185.

Fee, A., & Gray, S. J. (2011). Fast-tracking expatriate development: The unique learning environments of international volunteer placements. *The International Journal of Human Resource Management, 22,* 530–552.

Ganesh, S., & McAllum, K. (2009). Discourses of volunteerism. In C. S. Beck (Ed.), *Communication Yearbook 33* (pp. 342–383). New York, NY: International Communication Association.

Ganesh, S., & McAllum, K. (2012). Volunteering and professionalization: Trends in tension? *Management Communication Quarterly, 26,* 152–158.

Hanchey, J. (2012). *A postcolonial analysis of Peace Corps volunteer narratives: The political construction of the volunteer, her work, and her relationship to the "host country national"* (Master's thesis). Retrieved from ProQuest Dissertations and Theses. (1519560)

Kim, Y. Y. (1988). *Communication and cross-cultural adaptation: An integrative theory.* Clevedon, United Kingdom: Multilingual Matters.

Kim, Y. Y. (2001). *Becoming intercultural: An integrative theory of communication and cross-cultural adaptation.* Thousand Oaks, CA: Sage.

Kramer, E. M. (2003). Cosmopoly: Occidentalism and the new world order. In E. M. Kramer (Ed.), *The emerging monoculture: Assimilation and the "model minority"* (pp. 234–291). Westport, CT: Praeger Publishers.

Kramer, M. W. (2011). Toward a communication model for the socialization of voluntary members. *Communication Monographs, 78,* 233–255.

Kuhn, T., Golden, A. G., Jorgenson, J., Buzzanell, P. M., Berkelaar, B. L., Kisselburgh, L. G., Kleinman, S., & Cruz, D. (2008). Cultural discourses and discursive resources for meaning/ful work: Constructing and disrupting identities in contemporary capitalism. *Management Communication Quarterly, 22,* 162–171.

Lair, D. J., Shenoy, S., McClellan, J. G., & McGuire, T. (2008). The politics of meaning/ful work: Navigating the tensions of narcissism and condescension while finding meaning in work. *Management Communication Quarterly, 22,* 172–180.

Lombas, L. L. (2011). *Individualism in action: An investigation into the lived experiences of Peace Corps volunteers* (Doctoral dissertation). Retrieved from ProQuest Dissertations and Theses. (3491145)

McAllum, K. (2014). Meanings of organizational volunteering: Diverse volunteer pathways. *Management Communication Quarterly, 28,* 84–110.

McNamee, L. G., & Peterson, B. L. (2014). Reconciling "third space/place:" Toward a complementary dialectical understanding of volunteer management. *Management Communication Quarterly, 28,* 214–243.

McWha, I. (2011). The roles of, and relationships between, expatriates, volunteers, and local development workers. *Development in Practice, 21,* 29–40.

Owen, W. F. (1984). Interpretive themes in relational communication. *Quarterly Journal of Speech, 70*, 274–287.

Sanders, M. L. (2012). Theorizing nonprofit organizations as contradictory enterprises: Understanding the inherent tensions of nonprofit marketization. *Management Communication Quarterly, 26*, 179–185.

Sherraden, M. S., Stringham, J., Sow, S. C., & McBride, A. M. (2006). The forms and structure of international voluntary service. *Voluntas: International Journal of Voluntary and Nonprofit Organizations, 17*, 163–180.

Tracy, S. J. (2010). Qualitative quality: Eight "big-tent" criteria for excellent qualitative research. *Qualitative Inquiry, 16*, 837–851.

Tracy, S. J. (2013). Interview planning and design. *Qualitative research methods* (pp. 130–156). Malden, MA: Wiley-Blackwell.

Zorn, T. E., & Townsley, N. (2008). Introduction to the forum on meaning/ful work: Studies in organizational communication setting an agenda. *Management Communication Quarterly, 22*, 147–151.

CHAPTER NINE

Bridging Cultural Gaps: U.S. Voluntourists Teaching English IN China

JANICE HUA XU
Holy Family University

Cultural shock can be related to a stressful transitional period when individuals move from a familiar environment into an unfamiliar one. It is the sense of dislocation and the problems that result from the stress of trying to make all sorts of adjustments necessary for living in a foreign culture, including both psychological and even physical symptoms (Beamer & Varner, 2008). Scholars believe there are common experiences encountered by all individuals engaged in cross-cultural travel. Although the motivations, level of commitment, and lengths of travel might be different, "all individuals crossing cultures face some common challenges as they pioneer lives of uprootedness and gradually establish working relationships with their new milieus" (Kim, 2001, p. 4). As newcomers, they are compelled to make adjustments in their habitual ways of carrying out their life activities. Meanwhile, the cross-cultural contact experiences of individuals can be determined by situational factors such as time span, purpose, and types of involvement. Sojourners who travel to another country for a specific purpose and a limited amount of time have experiences very different from immigrants or refugees, due to their different expectations and whether the travel is voluntary and prepared (Beamer & Varner, 2008). Also, the level of culture shock could be more intense if there is a great cultural distance between the host and home countries, defined as differences between the home culture and the new culture in such factors as cultural values, language, verbal styles and nonverbal gestures, as well as religious and economic systems (Ting-Toomey, 2012).

This study examines the issue of cultural shock for short-term volunteers travelling abroad, in particular, volunteers who teach English as a second language in a foreign country where they also travel nearby for sightseeing. "Voluntourists" are travellers who combine service activities with leisure while exploring a new culture, who represent a growing trend in international volunteering and service learning (Crabtree, 2008; Ooi & Laing, 2010; Stebbins & Graham, 2004). While their activities abroad can benefit the local community as well as providing valuable personal experiences to themselves, their journeys could be challenging due to the demands of their tasks and the cultural adjustments needed. Whereas many volunteers possess the qualities of diligence, patience, and common sense, which are important for teaching non-native speakers, the work can involve considerable emotional wear and tear on both volunteer teachers and their students if done by trial and error (Snow, 1996). In addition to the work demands of classroom teaching, culture shock could be also affecting the level of satisfaction and quality of service of the volunteer teachers while abroad.

As cross-cultural travellers, voluntourists from developed countries could face a unique combination of factors, making their adjustment experience abroad different from tourists, business travellers, immigrants, or study abroad students. Their travel is short-term, voluntary, usually in temporary groups, hosted by foreign institutions, and comes with work responsibilities often unfamiliar to them. The current literature on culture shock experiences rarely addresses the experiences of voluntourists teaching English abroad. This study examines the experiences of U.S. volunteers from the Minnesota-based non-profit organization Global Volunteers (GV) working in two Chinese cities—Xi'an and Kunming—and how they manage and overcome culture shock to fulfill their roles as temporary teachers. While the organization has worldwide activities, this study focuses on its short-term volunteers in China teaching school children, college students, or rural teachers in English language training programs, and touring local sights between class assignments.

Through the individual journals from different volunteer teams from 2007 to 2012 posted on GV's website (http://chinateamjournal.blogspot.com/) from the field, this study explored how different dimensions of culture shock (Bochner, 2003) were manifested in the experiences of the blog writers. It identified coping strategies used by team members at various stages of their trips, to enable themselves and each other to perform professionally in a challenging setting, and turn the encounter with a new environment into a culture learning experience.

Managing Cultural Shock for Sojourners

There are three components of the process of ABC culture shock: affect, behavior, and cognitions; that is, "how people feel, behave, think and perceive when exposed to second-culture influences" (Bochner, 2003, p. 7). According to this ABC model of cultural contact, the response to unfamiliar cultural settings is not a passive, largely negative reaction, as early literature on cultural shock suggests, but rather an active process of dealing with change (Ting-Toomey, 2012). The affect dimension may include both anxiety and excitement because culture shock involves a variety of feelings over time and in different intensities. The behavior dimension refers to the coping activities of the traveler, for instance, taking actions to follow new rules and conventions in interpersonal interactions, which could be adaptive responses to increase self-efficacy. Examples of behavior adaptation include using chopsticks in restaurants or bowing in social situations in Asia. The cognition dimension focuses on culture as a system of shared meanings, manifested in physical, interpersonal, institutional, existential and spiritual events. Individual responses in this dimension can be evaluated through their interest in other cultures, tolerance for cultural differences, and positive attitudes toward new or unusual cultural environments (Bochner, 2003). For instance, the traveller to a low time-sensitive culture learns not to be frustrated when the foreign friend is 15 minutes late for an appointment, as punctuality is not so important in that culture and the transportation system may not be so reliable. The ABC model has implications for interventions aimed at decreasing culture shock and increasing the likelihood of achieving positive culture-contact outcomes. For instance, a survey of young British volunteers working in 27 countries found that cultural distance was the strongest predictor of culture shock, followed by problems at work. Higher culture shock scores for volunteers at three weeks after arrival predicted a greater risk of early return home and lower satisfaction with their time abroad (Mumford, 2000). Thus, for volunteers working abroad, understanding the causes and consequences of culture shock could be helpful to both the individuals and the volunteer organizations.

In general, those with realistic, accurate and positive expectations of their cross-cultural experiences have less difficulty than those with unrealistic expectations. Attributes such as mindfulness, culture-sensitive knowledge, and tolerance for ambiguity can also help the adaptation process (Ting-Toomey, 2012). Another factor in sojourner adjustment is the extent to which they have host-culture friends, who act as informal culture-skills mentors. Ward, Bochner, and Furnham (2001) observed that visitors who socialized only with members of their own cultures did not perform as well on a variety of measures as sojourners who had established non-trivial links with their hosts. Meanwhile, support from fellow travellers could be powerful during adjustment to unfamiliar roles in a different culture. In a study of teachers in cultural exchange programs, Gleeson and Tait (2012) found sojourner groups teaching abroad could form a transitory community in the host country to support their academic and social learning, and share resources to achieve their common goal, even though the community disbanded upon their return to the home country.

Although the term "culture shock" is often associated with negative psychological reactions, in recent years some scholars argue that in many circumstances culture contact can be a satisfying experience (Bochner, 2003). Effective management of culture shock can bring a sense of positive well-being, self-esteem, and personal growth. For volunteers who venture abroad to provide services to others, the contact with people in a new culture, though challenging, can enrich a sense of achievement through fulfilling personal and professional goals. As Kim (2001) found from the experiences of Peace Corps volunteers, each adaptive challenge in the new environment can make the travellers feel "awakened from their taken-for-granted assumptions with a heightened sense of self, offering an opportunity to grow beyond the perimeters of the original culture (p. 6)."

Challenges During Short-term Teaching Abroad

Promoters of voluntourism claim it can offer transformational experiences for the participants and valuable output for the destination locations (Tomazos & Cooper, 2012). A voluntourist team often includes individuals from a wide range of backgrounds and professional experiences, which could benefit the developing country host communities. Meanwhile, some educators believe that for the hosting schools, the subjects, pedagogy, and concepts that volunteers teach will not make as much difference as the mere presence of the outsiders (Bularzik, 2011).

Voluntourists teaching English abroad may go through not only culture shock typically experienced by tourists (Furnham, 1984; Hottola, 2004), but also face challenges in professional settings similar to student teachers going abroad on short-term assignments. Most voluntourists, like student teachers, lack experience in professional teaching.

Similar to voluntourists, many American student teachers travel abroad to teach English-based lessons to promote cultural exchange (Ferry & Konza, 2001) and introduce overseas children to student teachers' home cultures (Davcheva, 2002), while gaining experiences in a range of pedagogical activities. Student teachers from the U.S. have found that children in host countries address their teachers with more respect, and the experience of cultural learning gave them new perspectives on their own cultures (Cushner & Brislin, 1996). They also realized that some aspects are universal, such as classroom management and administrative procedures, so those with teaching experiences in their home countries can benefit from their past classroom practices. Meanwhile, as material resources in the host country might be very limited, the visiting teacher, who might find the education facilities and teaching materials inadequate, needs to be creative in curriculum preparation and delivery of instruction (Quezada, 2004).

Due to the differences in education systems between Western and Asian countries, one source of culture shock can be the different expectations about the teacher's role in class. For instance, a survey of Chinese college students found that teachers are expected to give the right answers and to be good moral examples (Zhang & Watkins, 2007). The same researchers also found that Chinese teachers and foreign teachers in China have different notions about what makes for a good English teacher. The foreign teachers considered diversity in activities and adaptability to change the most important, while Chinese teachers valued proper teaching techniques and teachers' knowledge most.

Santoro and Major (2012) found that Australian pre-service teachers attending short-term study programs in Korea and India felt challenged to move beyond their comfort zone into new and unfamiliar territory, and into states of dissonance and discomfort. The teachers identified dissonance resulting from physical discomfort, dissonance resulting from culturally different communication styles and expectations about appropriate behavior and interaction, as well as dissonance resulting from incidents/events that challenged their views of themselves and their own cultures.

According to Tang and Choi (2004), the teachers' personal-professional development during the international field experience takes place in the action context, the socio-professional context, and the supervisory context. The action context refers to classroom teaching activities. The socio-professional context is the interactions with various agents, including teachers, fellow student teachers or peers and other personnel in the wider school life. The supervisory context involves interactions with their local and home organization supervisors, as well as assessment of their teaching performances. Though voluntourists might face a looser supervision and evaluation process than student teachers, and different Chinese schools have different practices overseeing classes taught by foreign volunteers, these contexts could be relevant when examining their roles in their assigned teaching posts.

Through a close look at the experiences of ESL voluntourists in China, this study examined various sources of culture shock in the action context of their classroom teaching, in the socio-professional context of interacting with others outside the classroom, and in the supervisory context of interacting with their host institutions and team leaders. By analyzing the written self-accounts of the individuals, it studied how the process of culture shock is manifested in the three components of affect, behavior, and cognitions. Specifically, the study addressed voluntourists' emotional coping processes, behavior adjustments, and sense of cultural learning while assigned to different teaching posts in China. This includes their intercultural communication activities as individual travellers and as voluntourist groups.

METHOD

To address this research topic, the author analyzed 270 journal entries of GV volunteers' experiences teaching in China, posted by individuals in teams from 2007 to 2012 on the organization website, some accompanied by photos. There were four entries posted in 2007, each including journal contents from different members of a whole team. There were 38 entries posted in 2008, 29 entries in 2009, 120 in 2010, 22 in 2011, and 57 in 2012, all posted by individual members while in the field.

The organization uses blogs by its volunteers serving in different countries to promote its mission, stating these are "real life global volunteering stories about volunteering abroad, volunteering internationally, notes from the field, lifelong friendships, reflections, and tales of how each person makes a world of difference" (http://globalvolunteers.blogspot.com). According to the author's correspondence with GV administrative staff, the blogs are written from the volunteers' personal point of view as part of a team journaling exercise, intended to help the team process the experience together, and was a foundational element of GV's team management from the very first program in 1984. Initially compiled for internal use, the journals written in recent years were edited and posted on the organization website to provide a way for family members, friends, and potential volunteers to "experience" the service program with the volunteers. Though not all individuals chose to write the journals, each team usually elected/appointed an individual in charge of the team journal with the advice of the country manager/team leader, and most GV volunteers shared their journals with team members in the field and contributed writings to the blogs (personal communication, April 4, 2014). Although the blogs were somewhat edited, they include detailed accounts of both positive and negative parts of the volunteers' experiences, and therefore can be considered a useful data source.

Journal writing is a way of gaining feedback from the self and experiencing our lives in a way that provides meaning through reflection (Progoff, 1992). An open blog site enables volunteers to made sense of their own experiences through telling stories to others about their service. As research data these blogs provide first-hand materials of the affective, behavior, and cognition dimensions of the cultural contact process of the GV volunteers in China.

The author analyzed each team's blogs from their arrival in China to their final day of field service and departure. By using the affect, behavior, and cognition dimensions of culture shock, the author attempted to find common themes in the blogs about how the volunteers felt, how they acted, and how they made sense of what happens in the new environment, throughout the phases of orientation/settling down, cultural adjustment and adaptation, cultural learning, and departure. In analyzing these dimensions, the author examined the volunteers' contact with others in the action context as well as the socio-professional context, namely, their interactions with the Chinese students/teachers they teach, with the hosts and staff, and with fellow volunteers.

The author first identified the themes of each blog by putting them into different categories based on types of their behavior/activities, such as arrival/orientation, first day teaching, classroom strategies, facility problem, socializing with hosts, and discussions with fellow volunteers, followed by analyses of the affect/emotional experiences of the volunteer related to these activities. For the cognition dimension of the volunteers, the author searched for the bloggers' reflections of what they have learned from their experiences.

The analysis results section presents themes that appeared frequently, such as getting used to a new environment, meeting strangers, and finding solutions to solve a problem, as well as some themes that appeared less frequently but were reported by some volunteers, such as feelings of doubt about the significance of their work. These themes are included because they were repeated in different volunteer blogs, representing a part of the volunteer experience as a whole instead of isolated and unusual occurrences, though some were described in detail and some were briefly touched upon.

Context: GV Volunteer Teams in China

GV started its program in China service in 1996. The volunteers work through local partner organizations to "teach conversational English to students of all ages; demonstrate English skills and resources to teachers; care for mentally challenged children; (and) promote girls' education" (www.globalvolunteers.org/china). The durations of their stays range usually from two weeks to three weeks, paid for by themselves, and some volunteers who were highly satisfied with their journeys return multiple times.

Each team consists of 6 to 20 volunteers led by international staff and volunteer team leaders. The volunteers come from different professional background and age groups, from teenagers to retirees. For instance, among the 13 volunteers of GV Team 149, Martin Choy posted to their blog June 23 and 24, 2007, "The age group ranges from the twenties to the eighties." GV has been collaborating for years with their key partners in China–Kunming Normal University, Xi'an Biomedical Technical College, Xi'an University of Science and Technology, Xi'an Normal University, and La La Shou school for autistic children. Kunming, the capital of Yunnan province in Southwest China with warm weather, is home to many minority groups. Xi'an is an ancient capital of China in the northwest, with well-known tourist attractions, including the terra cotta soldiers at the tomb site of the First Emperor.

The volunteers have built a good reputation for the organization, and each year the project coordinators in China work with newly-arrived team members to match them with suitable teaching assignments. The teaching placements are usually assigned after their arrival, and members of one team can be assigned to different schools. Occasionally the volunteers were doing team teaching, meaning two volunteers teaching one class at the same time, and sometimes they rotated assignments among team members.

In Kunming, most of the GV volunteers were teaching at Kunming Normal University which trains local teachers. The teachers were sent by the elementary and middle schools in the region, with varying years of teaching experience. For many of them the conversations they have with GV volunteers were their first extended experience with native speakers of English. Some volunteers were also teaching school children, with assistance from their regular teachers. For instance, Team 162 reported in a blog on October 5, 2008, that during their trip "Eight volunteers provided 210 hours of conversational English language instruction to 45 teachers and 72 secondary school students." In Xi'an, while some GV volunteers taught children with autism in a private school, most were teaching English to university students.

The volunteers of a team stayed in the same hotel, had breakfast together, took a shuttle bus to their assigned teaching locations, and returned to the hotel in the evenings. They often took short sightseeing trips together to nearby tourist attractions, sometimes with their hosts. They might also have dinner together, share stories of the day, and read journals written by each team member. Among the team members, each took on specific coordinating roles and responsibilities. For instance, different individuals in Team 161 to Kunming were assigned as journal managers, health and safety coordinators, free time activity coordinators, final celebration coordinators, and official photographers.

FINDINGS

Cultural Shock When Settling Down

Each volunteer team's blogs starts with their arrival in China. The volunteers wrote about how they got settled in their new environment, as the blogs noted different aspects of their everyday life, including food, shelter, transportation, weather, and daily schedules. Upon their arrival, the volunteers would gather for a self-introduction and orientation session with their team leaders, who would review GV's policies and guidelines. Each team member was usually asked to list their personal goals during the trip, in categories such as to build positive relationships, to serve, to learn, to have fun, and to grow. The local team leader would also offer health and safety tips to the volunteers, for instance, going out with at least two other travellers. Team 173, which taught in Xi'an in summer 2009, was given a health alert to be extra vigilant—wash hands, cover mouths after sneezing, avoid touching eyes, and drink lots of water due to an outbreak of H1N1 flu. While still dealing with jet lag, the volunteers would learn about their teaching assignments and meet with representatives from their host institutions, sometimes the presidents and deans of the colleges who would express welcome and introduce the schools to them.

While many volunteers had previous international service and ESL teaching experiences, some individuals found the initial adjustment demanding, because of the immense cultural difference between China and U.S., ranging from food and living accommodations to cultural customs and expectations, or behaviors of local people in public places like elevators. One teen volunteer named Alex wrote that in her team's ride through the city traffic on July 18, 2008, "the many near collisions are not what I notice most about these bus rides." Instead, it was the stares of pedestrians on the street, as the locals rarely met any Westerners. Volunteers might find their hotel air conditioner not working in the summer humidity, or the daily rush hour shuttle ride from their hotel to the schools a hair-raising experience, but they usually got settled in their new physical environment after a few days and started to engage in their teaching duties.

For a young volunteer unfamiliar with the socio-professional setting of a Chinese school, being the center of attention among foreigners while unable to understand the language or anticipate what is coming could be a stressful psychological experience. Katrina Beattie wrote about the day she and another volunteer were introduced to Chinese teachers at a private school for autistic children in Xi'an (posted on May 14, 2011):

> There was a room full of teachers, speaking in Chinese all at once. I could feel the panic rising up from my feet and sweat dripping down my back! How is this going to work? The room was very humid and everyone was looking at Peace and myself. Baoli, my team leader, began translating in English. I began to relax and a sense of well-being came over me. I knew this is where I was meant to be, here and now, at this moment.

The affect dimension of culture shock is demonstrated here through the initial feelings of helplessness, puzzlement, and "panic," due to language barrier, humid weather, and the unfamiliar people. With the translation of the team leader, the volunteer was able to communicate with the local professionals and get a sense of order and calm, and therefore play her role of the newcomer being introduced to the school teachers.

The volunteers were expected to engage in social activities with their hosts from time to time. They might also take arranged tours with their hosts, who were still strangers to them. The volunteers would try to act politely and properly to leave a good impression on their hosts in the new country. In a blog posted October 24, 2010, a volunteer, Judith, described a tour of Xi'an with a few team members and a Chinese host: "And a lovely day it was, though shot through with the nervous cultural dance of Chinese politeness and American unfamiliarity with Chinese social custom." Apparently the interactions during the tour involved the affect dimension of cultural shock, with some level of caution and nervousness from both sides trying to get to know each other.

One behavior adjustment for volunteers was that they were frequently the center of attention in entertainment occasions, including occasional English speech festivals held by the students, or English Corners where local students engaged in English conversations in a park. Some volunteers also described kara-oke events at local bars or dinners at the homes of the staff/teachers of their host institutions. The blogs expressed appreciations of the opportunity to see the real lives of Chinese people, while noting the large amount of food served, which could be too spicy, with multiple courses of dishes and various unfamiliar drinks, teas, and soups. Among the volunteers, some preferred to have more private times to themselves and participated in less social activities.

Challenge of Teaching Chinese Students

After the initial days of settling down in their work routines and getting used to their fellow team members, the blog contents focus more on the teaching expe-riences and interactions with the Chinese students. Many GV volunteers used words such as "rewarding" and "wonderful" to describe their classroom experience, and reported their students were eager to learn. They found that many students considered lessons with the volunteers a desirable alternative to their routine class-room experiences, with a sense of novelty. Leon Ablon wrote about his experi-ence with students of Xi'an University of Science and Technology in a blog on October 8, 2007:

> I was assigned to a group of 11 students, nine boys and two girls, all about 17 years old and studying numerically-controlled machines. They were eager, bright and, after some encouragement, not at all shy. We each told our life stories and, in every case, something came up that was a take-off point for learning a new word or phrase or a chance to work on some fine point of pronunciation. After a lot of laughter and what felt like the passage of only ten minutes, our hour and a half was up and it was time for us volunteers to go back to our hotel for lunch. I eagerly anticipate our next meeting tomorrow morning when we will have our next encounters with these marvelous students.

The volunteers wrote that some students had poor English language skills and low confidence in speaking in class. Though eager with smiles, they had little to say in class. One volunteer indicated that usually only half of her class was inter-ested in practicing their English. A few volunteers found their students silent in the first class, in which they tried to break the ice by doing self-introduction and showing family pictures, though they started to respond to questions more in the second class. Some volunteers who attempted to address the students individually found it difficult to pronounce their Chinese names. Volunteer Jane Stein wrote in a blog on October 9, 2007:

> For most, their English skills are poor and confidence in speaking it quite low. Initially, only a few students shyly but willingly responded to answering questions such as "what do you like to do." A round of head-shoulder-knees-toes loosened them up, and by the end of the morning every student was responding actively to questions.

The volunteers used various classroom strategies to keep the learning process lively and interesting, including musical chairs and singing English songs—such as "You Are My Sunshine and Rain, Rain, Go Away." They also used maps and magazine pictures to engage the students in discussions. Some taught a baseball session in a gym class, while others practiced ballet exercises and balloon volleyball games with students during class breaks. In one case the reason for the classroom activities were really practical—the classroom was freezing, so the two volunteers co-teaching the class asked students to push the desks back to play musical chairs to students' singing, then taught ballroom dance and yoga to warm up everyone.

Occasionally, a volunteer could be unprepared for the specific classes assigned due to an unfortunate combination of factors, such as miscommunication about student levels, unavailable teaching materials, and inconvenience of classroom readiness due to facility problems. This could be very stressful for someone without a teaching background. Volunteer Peace Gardiner wrote in a blog on May 18, 2011, four days after her arrival in Xi'an:

> My classes were supposed to be held in the library, but there was no power so they asked if I minded walking up to the fifth floor for class. I asked where the materials were, the ones left by other volunteers, but Della said there were none. I had a rough outline and a few materials, so I went with what I had. My class was about 25 people, but only 2 boys!... Everybody kept telling me these kids were low level, but several of them have studied English 5 or more years and knew a lot. All the stuff I had for reviewing numbers, time, all way too easy for them. In fact we blew through everything I had in the first hour, with 2 more to go....

To get through the rest of class, the Chinese English teacher observing the class helped out by assigning written exercises, and the GV volunteer assisted the students in their writing. Occasionally volunteers were surprised by the specialized English vocabularies of the university students. For example, volunteers teaching at Xi'an Biomedical Technical College in September 2010 discussed topics of wave energy, wave length, amplitude, various meters, and oscilloscopes in English with medical instrument majors. They also acted out dialogues the students wrote about toothaches, cavities, and teeth that got knocked out with dental students.

The volunteers then worked on pronunciation problems—the students wanted to drop the "g" in "ing" and add an "e" to the final "d" in a word.

Young volunteers similar in age with their Chinese students found that the students felt less nervous in classrooms with them, and to their surprise, the students could even share common music interests with them. Volunteer Peace Gardiner found that her Xi'an students knew of Justin Bieber and Lady Gaga, but gave blank stares when Frank Sinatra and Elvis Presley were mentioned. In class she was surprised to find that students came to her, one after another, to ask her to write her name on their textbooks, probably because she was the first native English speaker coming from afar to teach them English. Occasionally the enthusiasm of the students in the volunteers themselves could be overwhelming. One teen volunteer realized that during class breaks there were always students taking his photo, probably because he was the first Westerner they encountered, so he hid in the restroom.

The demands on the volunteers to adapt to unexpected situations requires more than behavioral coping responses. One volunteer, Kerri, noted in a poem in a blog in July 31, 2007: "As with most things in China, It didn't go quite according to plan." For instance, to show the TV program *Seinfeld* in the university auditorium, they tried one computer after another until they finally found one that worked. The volunteers demonstrated qualities of patience, flexibility, and endurance in an environment where technology facilities are not always reliable.

As time went by, volunteers often found that they had established bonds with their students after the short-term teaching period, and felt sentimental when departing from them. Katrina, who taught at the private school for autistic children, found that she had become emotionally attached to the school:

> My last day was sad for me. In just two weeks, I had become attached to the sixth grade boys and all the teachers and students at that beautiful little school with little room and little money.

Cultural Learning: Interaction with Chinese English Teachers in Training

Many volunteers were able to learn about Chinese culture and reflected on the cultural differences through discussions with the Chinese English teachers in the training programs, for instance, on current affairs, their views on happiness, their favorite book or movie characters, and so forth. Some volunteers had in-depth discussions with these teachers on the differences between American and Chinese education systems, and the pros and cons of the strict parenting style of "Tiger Mom" described in a popular book. Getting to know the work requirements and daily struggles of some of the Chinese school teachers also made the volunteers reflect upon their own lives and appreciate their own situations. Sabrina in Team 162 wrote on October 5, 2008: "My troubles at home are almost meaningless when compared to the struggles the people of China have faced this year—to think that I thought I was having a rough year." Realizing the school teachers' lack of material possessions, one team used hotel room giveaways, such as emory boards, combs, and shower caps, as prizes for class exercises.

The blogs indicates that the volunteers and the Chinese teachers have demonstrated a lot of professional respect toward each other, and could often built rapport quickly due to some common values and shared interests. Greg, a volunteer, noted in a blog on October 15, 2010, that he particularly enjoyed teaching the English teachers:

> I've been enjoying teaching, but even more I've enjoyed talking to the English teachers. This is partly because their English level is higher, and partly because I know that as much as I am helping their students, I'm also helping them in their jobs. Seeing their teachers talking in English to foreigners must build respect in the students for their teacher's ability.

Many volunteers felt appreciative of the gestures of friendship from the Chinese teachers. The sense of cultural learning and personal growth could come from both sides. Team 162 in Kunming posted a blog on October 5, 2008:

> We learn much more of the challenges they face in their packed classrooms, of the disparate salaries and working conditions for the private school teachers Kerri and Natalie talked to on Tuesday afternoon. One asked, "Can you tell me how to get the government to change things?" Across town at Kunming Teacher's Training College, another wrote to us "How do we change the world?" We stand in awe. We are humbled.

Evidently these volunteers were seen by the local teachers as not only instructors of English language, but people who could listen to and advise on their issues of concern. This is probably because the volunteers were seen as knowledgeable, well-intentioned, and impartial outsiders capable of providing valuable perspectives different from people around them.

The frequent raining in Kunming during summertime was an issue many volunteers noted in their blogs. This sometimes caused inconvenience to their teaching and sightseeing plans. They also indicated admirations to their students who accepted their circumstances without whining or complaint. Team 161, with 13 members, was one of the teams affected by the rainstorms. One volunteer named Leon was particularly touched by the efforts of their students to arrive in class in a flood about two feet deep on the street on July 2, 2008:

> During the morning all but one of our missing students straggled in. The most interesting story was told by Eileen who arrived two hours late to class: her children had to row her across the flood so she could reach transportation to the school. I later heard stories from other volunteers of students who walked in the rain for two hours in order to catch at least

the last half hour of class. What amazing behavior! It is no wonder China's economy is growing so quickly.

Support and Encouragement

Some blog writers detailed their emotional journeys in their service trips, including the ups and downs of teaching for the first time, as well as the support they received. GV volunteers found they had to have patience and endurance to help students improve their English pronunciations, especially when some students themselves seemed not so motivated. On a hot and humid day in Xi'an, Marcella described in a blog (September 17, 2010) that after teaching a satisfying morning class, the afternoon class turned out to be a big challenge to her patience:

> However, my afternoon class was truly a test of my endurance in teaching. It was hot to begin with plus there were students I guess were in the class by command. This was not an ideal situation for a non-professional teacher like me, without a great deal of self control, who was tempted to scream and run out of the room. What saved me in this afternoon class was to see some improvements in 5 students from my last week's class. I guess I did make a difference. On our drive back to the hotel from the school I was wondering whether our teaching in this school is a waste of time. Claudia and Maggie were trying to convince me it wasn't. And that we do make a difference because there is a cumulative effect.

Later that day, when touring the Han Tomb Museum, the blog writer was convinced that their work indeed could make a difference, when one of their team members complimented the English of a shop girl, who told them she had GV teachers in 1997, and said with a smile: "I'll never forget them!" With the encouragement and support from fellow volunteers, as well as the local shop girl's fond memory, the volunteer who had an urge to "scream and run out of the room" in a stressful class felt reassured that their efforts were eventually worthwhile.

The volunteers of each team often had to work together to brainstorm for ideas on group events and activities, as they were expected to represent the "exotic" American culture to their hosting schools. Since ceremonies are very important in Chinese culture, and the presence of Westerners a rare spectacle, the volunteers were always invited to contribute to the entertainment activities of their welcoming and farewell parties, a showcase of songs and dances from both cultures. The volunteers, with little anticipation of this aspect of their service trip, planned for performances collaboratively to meet the hosts' expectations, which might pose short-noticed challenges. Marcella in Team 187 wrote in Xi'an on September 23, 2010:

> Teaching hundreds of students ballroom dancing is an unimaginable task. Hmmmm! There seemed to be a communication problem between our team and the school. However,

Maggie is a fast thinker having been a teacher for over 20 years: she has learned how to compensate when the chips are down. Maggie suggested we teach the students Swing and the Twist if we have to. After solving the dancing lesson problems we had to solve our second challenge for the Friday afternoon program. The students expect us to sing and dance…

Among the GV volunteers, a small number were returnees with previous teaching experience in China, and have established some level of friendship with the local teachers. For volunteers who return to China after some years, reuniting with their Chinese friends could feel very rewarding. In Xi'an, volunteer Ginny was excited to get a visit from a Chinese English teacher Tara she met 5 years ago, who was single then but now married and had a baby. Ginny wrote on October 11, 2010 about her personal friendship with Tara:

> An interesting story to me, and hopefully for those either reading or listening to this journal was when Tara asked my advice about buying a new to-be-built apartment five years ago. Her colleagues told her to wait for the man to buy the apartment. I told her that I would buy the apartment and when the man came along, I would let him buy the apartment and rent out her apartment. She did this too.

The volunteer appreciates Chinese teacher Tara's trust in seeking advice on important personal matters, and was able to offer perspectives different from her Chinese colleagues. The fact that Tara took her advice indicates the level of their intercultural friendship, as the decision involved different perspectives of women's financial independence. The same volunteer also noted that she maintained contact with a few other Chinese university teachers, and helped them when they visited the U.S. for academic exchange programs.

Accomplishment and Impact

Cross-cultural contact not only entails adjustment and cultural learning for the travellers, but could also have an effect on the host community. The impact made by the volunteers on their students went far beyond that of language teaching. The exposure to representatives of another culture was an eye-opening experience for many Chinese young people. One Chinese English teacher in Kunming wrote that the volunteers' altruistic actions and professional enthusiasm gave her a "shock" and a fresh sense of direction in her repetitive teaching work in a primary school:

> Now after being an English teacher for ten years, I feel bored of the routine work. Sometimes I even imagine me like a farmer and my students like the plants. My work is just like farmers planting crops in the fields every year. This feeling makes me very uneasy. But my mind has been changed by the Global Volunteers teachers who have come to teach us. I

am shocked by their action. Many of them have retired, but they still fill every student with great enthusiasm. Everyday my dear teacher Danielle and Aleatha greet us with the most beautiful smiles.

The essay, posted on GV website on December 22, 2009, expressed sincere thanks to the volunteers for their service. Though the sense of personal growth by the Chinese students/trainees might vary, they gained a real sense of motivation for foreign language learning, which previously was only a course requirement without any tangible application opportunity.

When the 2008 economic crisis brought a decline in the number of GV volunteers to China, a plea written by an English teacher and the Director of Foreign Affairs Office at Xi'an Biomedical Technical College posted at the GV website in December 2008 expressed their appreciation on behalf of teachers and students for GV volunteers and a sincere wish for their continuous service. The plea explained how volunteers were "like a fresh spring stream" that gave enthusiasm to the students to learn English. The plea further elaborates:

> Not merely because of their fresh appearance and their interactive way of teaching. Their patience, patience and encouragement also gave the students courage, which is likely to influence not only their English learning but even their whole life. Moreover, their sincerity, respect, frankness, honesty, dedication and good sense of humor are all life lessons for us.

While some volunteers might question the impact one could make abroad in the local community in a couple of weeks, the plea indicates that the mere encounter could make a long-lasting difference. The service of the volunteers has been in high demand by the Chinese institutions. According to the GV website, the organization responds to the requests of over 70 educational institutions in Yunnan and Shaanxi Provinces for native English speakers to teach conversational skills. Globally, the organization sends up to 2,500 volunteers a year, mostly Americans and Canadians, to more than 100 communities in 20 countries. Among them the fastest growing demographic for Global Volunteers are those under 20. This may be because more and more parents and grandparents take their offspring with them (Kohl, 2003). This can be seen as evidence that the voluntourist experience can be a self-regenerating practice with potential for further growth.

From a volunteer:

Being the only male student in the class is difficult enough but after all the girls described their names a "sweet flower", "beautiful girl", and "lovely lotus", when asked to define his Chinese name it was apparent that no definition was forthcoming. And so he became known as William. After several girls had introduced themselves with information about their villages, etc I gave William a smile and a nod. After much hesitation he arose. In quite good English, he spoke a sentence. The teacher who was assisting me whispered to me, "Those are first English words I have ever heard him speak." She was his regular English teacher and William was one of 62 students. For me this was a heart warming moment and I imagine William must have had his own unique feelings as well. Just about that time the teacher figured out what the translation of William's Chinese name is "King Dragon" and thus William became King Dragon—a well deserved name. I await my next meeting with King Dragon this morning.

–By GV volunteer Gail, posted in a blog on May 20, 2009, while teaching at Xi'an Biomedical Technology College

CONCLUSION

Though the GV volunteers are generally prepared psychologically for challenges of a different culture, and interact daily with co-volunteers of the same team, they still experience various types of stress or culture shock. Most volunteers managed to find a sense of purpose and contribution from their students, many of whom demonstrated obvious progress in their English language speaking and communication abilities. As time goes by, the individual journal accounts typically turn from initial bewilderment to the teaching methods, classroom activities, and friendship with the Chinese students, and for some, the differences between American and Chinese education systems. The volunteers' interactions inside and outside the classrooms with the Chinese people impacted their understanding and sensitivity towards the culture of China and its social issues, as seen in some blogs discussing child protection laws among other topics. The cognitive dimension of cultural learning is evident as the volunteers reflect on the differences they observed between China and their own culture, often with fellow volunteers. These learning moments might occur under inconvenient circumstances, such as the rainstorm that disrupted normal teaching, revealing inadequate infrastructure, but which showcased the personal strengths of the students getting to classes on foot.

The blogs also provided detailed narrations of sightseeing tours and street adventures, and the accounts of some volunteers helping villagers build houses and visiting earthquake victims in hospitals, though this study did not focus on those entries. It is evident that the engagements with the host culture outside classrooms were also instrumental in facilitating the adjustment process in the host culture, enabling them to refresh themselves after the daily teaching task and build a sense of empathy in the society to which their students belong. These activities could bring increasingly sophisticated understanding of cultural difference through active and multi-level participation in cross-cultural engagement.

Though the limited data reported in this study cannot be generalized to short-term volunteer teachers' experiences in other international contexts, which might vary in goals, duration, timing, and professional learning opportunities, it sheds light on the meaning of cross-cultural experiences of voluntourists and their roles in professional settings abroad. It demonstrates that for volunteer teams who overcome the vast cultural distance between U.S. and China and contribute to the education of students who have a lot of differences and similarities with them at the same time, a short trip can make a long-lasting impact.

REFERENCES

Beamer, L., & Varner, I. I. (2008). *Intercultural communication in the global workplace* (4th ed.). Boston, MA: McGraw-Hill.

Bochner, S. (2003). Culture shock due to contact with unfamiliar cultures. *Online readings in psychology and culture, 8*(1), 7. http://scholarworks.gvsu.edu/orpc/vol8/iss1/7/

Bularzik, S. B. (2011). *Social justice in action: Learning through foreign volunteers in Chinese schools.* (Doctoral dissertation, University of Pittsburgh).

Crabtree, R. D. (2008). Theoretical foundations for international service-learning. *Michigan Journal of Community Service Learning, 15*, 18–36.

Cushner, K., & Brislin, R. W. (1996). *Intercultural interactions: A practical guide* (vol. 9). Thousand Oaks, CA: Sage.

Davcheva, L. (2002). Learning to be intercultural. In G. Alred, M. Byram, & M. Fleming (Eds.), *Intercultural experience and education* (pp. 67–86). Clevedon, United Kingdom: Multilingual Matters Ltd.

Ferry, B., & Konza, D. (2001). Supporting cross-cultural adaptation during practice teaching in China: Reflections on a decade of experience. *Educational Practice and Theory, 23*, 79–96.

Furnham, A. (1984). Tourism and culture shock. *Annals of Tourism Research, 11*, 41–57.

Gleeson, M., & Tait, C. (2012). Teachers as sojourners: Transitory communities in short study-abroad programmes. *Teaching and Teacher Education, 28*, 1144–1151.

Hottola, P. (2004). Culture confusion: Intercultural adaptation in tourism. *Annals of Tourism Research, 31*, 447–466.

Kim, Y. Y. (2001). *Becoming intercultural: An integrative theory of communication and cross-cultural adaptation.* Thousand Oaks, CA: Sage.

Kohl, J. (2003). Links of a chain: Waves of Global Volunteers seek high impact in needy communities. http://www.globalvolunteers.org/media/Links_of_a_Chain.pdf.

Mumford, D. B. (2000). Culture shock among young British volunteers working abroad: Predictors, risk factors and outcome. *Transcultural Psychiatry, 37*, 73–87.

Ooi, N., & Laing, J. (2010). Backpacker tourism: Sustainable and purposeful? Investigating the overlap between backpacker tourism and volunteer tourism motivations. *Journal of Sustainable Tourism, 18*, 191–206.

Progoff, I. (1992). *At a journal workshop: Writing to access the power of the unconscious and evoke creative ability.* Los Angeles, CA: J. P. Tarcher.

Quezada, Reyes L. (2004). Beyond educational tourism: Lessons learned while student teaching abroad. *International Education Journal, 5*, 458–465.

Santoro, N., & Major, J. (2012). Learning to be a culturally responsive teacher through international study trips: Transformation or tourism? *Teaching Education, 23*, 309–322.

Snow, D. (1996). *More than a native speaker: An introduction for volunteers teaching English abroad.* Alexandria, VA: Teachers of English to Speakers of Other Languages, Incorporated.

Stebbins, R. A., & Graham, M. (Eds.). (2004). *Volunteering as leisure/leisure as volunteering: An international assessment.* Cambridge, MA: CABI.

Tang, S. Y. F., & Choi, P. L. (2004). The development of personal, intercultural and professional competence in international field experience in initial teacher education. *Asia Pacific Education Review 5*, 50–63.

Ting-Toomey, S. (2012). *Communicating across cultures.* New York, NY: Guilford Press.

Tomazos, K., & Cooper, W. (2012). Volunteer tourism: At the crossroads of commercialisation and service. *Current Issues in Tourism, 15*, 405–423.

Ward, C. A., Bochner, S., & Furnham, A. F. (2001). *The psychology of culture shock.* New York, NY: Routledge.

Zhang, Q., & Watkins, D. (2007). Conceptions of a good tertiary EFL teacher in China. *TESOL Quarterly, 41*, 781–790.

CHAPTER TEN

Making Good: The Identity AND Sensemaking OF International Mission Trip Volunteers

KATELIN FREDERICK
JENNIFER MIZE SMITH
Western Kentucky University

More than 1.5 million individuals in America participate in mission trips each year, a considerable increase from around 500 mission trip volunteers in 1965 (Horton, 2011). Mission trips range anywhere from one week to year-long commitments and are often affiliated with religious organizations. "Being called or volunteering to go on a mission trip can be one of the most satisfying experiences for a person of faith," explained Bruscke (2013), because "you get to visit a different community or culture and become directly involved in a project or in teaching tenets of your religion" (p. 1). Mission trips cost approximately $2 billion annually, paid by volunteers, their sponsors, or fundraising efforts (Horton, 2011).

The growing, global phenomenon of short-term missions (STM) has increasingly attracted scholars' attention, particularly in the last decade (Priest & Howell, 2013). Research has examined volunteer preparation (e.g., Dearborn, 2003; Howell & Dorr, 2007), local effectiveness (e.g., Ver Beek, 2006), and benefits (e.g., Campbell et al., 2009) of STM trips. Other studies have focused on volunteer experiences, particularly the relationship between mission trip participation and post-trip behaviors, such as increased giving, volunteering, prayer, and civic engagement. Although participants report having experienced life changes, the translation into increased charitable behaviors has been met with both confirming (e.g., Beyerlein, Trinitapoli, & Adler, 2011) and disconfirming evidence (e.g., Probasco, 2013; Ver Beek, 2006). Some scholars have integrated identity into their discussions of volunteer experiences, but few have explicitly explored identity. One exception is Walling et al.'s (2006) study that focused on the cultural identity of students who participated in short-term international mission trips. Findings revealed that students' experiences contributed to negative reactions toward their home culture.

Collectively, extant research suggests that STM volunteers enact multiple identities (e.g., faith-based, charitable, cultural), but scholars have yet to adopt a communicative perspective of mission volunteer identity. Therefore, the purpose of this research was to explore how mission volunteers construct and perform identity(ies) during service. Furthermore, since identity is an ongoing, discursive process, it also examined the implications for identity as mission volunteers made sense of and gave meaning to their experiences. While contributing broadly to identity literature, this study specifically enhanced our understanding of volunteer identity in international service and faith-based contexts.

LITERATURE REVIEW

Identity and sensemaking have been explored in a variety of contexts. However, few scholars have examined organizational contexts such as churches or organizational members who volunteer their time, money, and other resources to service projects abroad. The next section briefly reviews extant literature relevant to mission trip volunteers, particularly how they communicate and negotiate identity during service and how they retrospectively make sense of their experiences upon returning home.

Identity Construction

Identity is the sense of self (i.e., self-concept) gained through talking and interacting with others (Mead, 1970). Our discourse and interactions shape the way we see ourselves, how we project ourselves to others, and how others see us. Identity, then, is always in flux as we continually construct and reconstruct a multiplicity of possible selves (Gergen, 1991). Our multiple identities are influenced by an unlimited number of sources, including social categories (as suggested by Social Identity Theory; Turner, 1991), roles (as suggested by Identity Theory; Stryker, 1980), organizations (Collinson, 2003; Hogg & Terry, 2000), and values (Hitlin, 2003).

As a particular identity becomes salient, we seek ways to enact that identity, engaging in activities and organizations that are reflective of that "self" (Ashforth & Mael, 1989). For example, if we identify with a particular role, we will engage in behaviors that are consistent with that role (Burke & Reitzes, 1981; Charng, Piliavin, & Callero, 1988). Depending upon the role and context, we may have to "shift" among various "selves." According to Weick (1995):

Identities are constituted out of the process of interaction. To shift among interactions is to shift among definitions of self. Thus the sensemaker is himself or herself an ongoing puzzle undergoing continual redefinition, coincident with presenting some self to others and trying to decide which self is appropriate. (p. 20)

Identity shifts will occur as we categorize ourselves as the same as or different from others.

Jung and Hecht (2004) synthesized these notions in their Communication Theory of Identity (CTI). They situated identity in four layers: (a) personal, (b) enacted, (c) relational, and (d) communal. The *personal layer* refers to one's self-concept or self-image; the locus of identity is the individual. The *enacted layer* refers to the performed or expressed self, where the locus of identity is communication. In the *relational layer*, the locus of identity is relationship. Identity is produced in social interaction with others, shaped by others' perceptions, and influenced by social roles and the relationships themselves. Finally, the *communal layer* places the locus of identity in groups, such that group members share collective group characteristics. In short, "Identity resides in a person, communication, a relationship, and/or a group" (Hecht, Warren, Jung, & Krieger, 2005, p. 262). The four layers are "interpenetrated" and work together, though they may sometimes be contradictory. For example, a female may have a salient personal identity as a mother but is not allowed to enact that identity in her workplace.

Jung and Hecht (2004) emphasized not only how communication produces identity, but also how identity *is* communication. The meanings we internalize from our interactions with others, as well as the way we communicate about ourselves and others in interaction, all contribute to our sense of identity.

Other scholars have similarly emphasized the communicative nature of identity. Scott, Corman, and Cheney (1998) claimed identity is "revealed through discourse" (p. 304). Our narratives are guided by our self-perceptions (Gilbert, 2002). The stories we construct about our self and others enable us to sustain "a satisfying self-concept" (Horrocks & Callahan, 2006, p. 69). Therefore, communication is an integral part of constructing who we are, and identity is continually reconstructed through interactions and discourse.

Sensemaking

Because individuals need a sense of identity, they try to make sense of their beliefs and actions, with the goal of "maintaining a consistent, positive self-conception" (Weick, 1995, p. 23). The process of sensemaking "structures the unknown" (Waterman, 1990, p. 41) and helps us assign meaning to what has occurred. Individuals recount various events, people, places, and things that led to a decision or course of action and then try to make the outcomes seem sensible. The meanings ascribed, however, are shaped by one's identity because "what the situation will have meant to me is dictated by the identity I adopt in dealing with it" (Weick, 1995, pp. 23–24). The more potential selves there are from which to draw, the more possible meanings to extract. Therefore, according to Weick (1995), sensemaking is "grounded in identity" (p. 23).

Sensemaking requires reflection; therefore, it can only occur in retrospect (Louis, 1980; Weick, 1995). Weick (1995) and others have argued that "the reality [is] that people can know what they are doing only after they have done it" (p. 24). Although Weick admitted that hindsight may be inherently biased, he argued for the importance of learning from history and creating a *feeling* [italics in original] of order, clarity, and rationality" (p. 29).

Individuals, however, are not simply onlookers to what occurs. Rather, they are active participants in producing much of their own environment—a process that Weick (1995) called enactment. Individuals extract particular cues from what has occurred and embellish them in ways that create plausible, though not necessarily accurate, explanations. Those stories are shared with and tested on others. The "accounts that are socially acceptable and credible" (Weick, 1995, p. 61) are then retained for the future.

Summary

In summary, extant literature posits that one's identity is comprised of many multiple selves (Gergen, 1991), residing in different layers (Jung & Hecht, 2004), and constructed and communicated through discourse (Scott et al., 1998). In the context of the current study, short-term mission trip volunteers may embrace multiple identities, including those reflective of their religious affiliation (e.g., Christian, Catholic, Baptist), their profession (e.g., doctor, dentist, teacher), or other roles (e.g., parent, caregiver). Mission volunteers may also enact other, less attractive/positive identities, such as ethnocentric tourist. We can gain a better understanding of mission volunteers' identity by observing their talk and interactions.

Past research also suggests that individuals make sense of decisions and behaviors only in retrospect (Weick, 1995). For mission trip volunteers, their acts of service may become increasingly meaningful after they return home and can reflect on and discuss their trip with others. Therefore, it is important to allow mission volunteers the opportunity to assign meaning to their own interactions and experiences. To that end, we pose the following research questions:

RQ1:   What identities do short-term mission volunteers appear to enact during a mission trip?

RQ2:   How do short-term mission volunteers make sense of their experiences after re-
        turning home from a mission trip?

This study may further our understanding of STM volunteers, their self-perceptions, and the meaning made of their experiences. It may also contribute to a broader understanding of volunteer identities in general.

METHODOLOGY

This research employed a case study approach and ethnographic methods to explore the identity and sensemaking of STM volunteers. Specifically, qualitative inquiry "locates the observer in the world" (Denzin & Lincoln, 2000, p. 3) and enabled the first author to become a participant observer.

Process and Participants

After receiving Institutional Review Board approval, subjects were recruited from two volunteer mission groups, each preparing for a week-long trip to a foreign country. The first author was a member of both groups and gained permission from group leaders to email volunteers about participating in this study. Of the 36 total mission volunteers, 34 agreed to participate. Participants ranged in age from 14–60. Fifteen were 18 and under, and the median age was 37. Nine participants were male, 25 were female, and all were American and Caucasian.

Mission Trip Context

Heredia, Costa Rica. Heredia, Costa Rica is located 30 miles northeast of the capitol city of San José. The Spanish-speaking natives were warm and hospitable, anxious to learn about American culture and values. This mission group included 13 teenagers and 5 adults. Volunteers led crafts, recreation, music, and other activities in a local school of approximately 100 preschool and elementary students. They also assisted with some construction, such as pouring a concrete floor for a local church.

Port-au-Prince, Haiti. The Caribbean city of Port-au-Prince, Haiti is home to nearly 900,000 people. The Haitians reflect both French and African cultures and speak a blended language called Creole. The mission group included 16 adults and 2 minors. Participants assisted in a medical clinic and facilitated children's activities in a vacation bible school (VBS) type setting. Work was also done in an orphanage funded by several of the churches whose members volunteered on this trip.

Data Collection Procedures

Interviews. Fourteen participants participated in pre- and/or post-trip semi-structured interviews. Pre-trip interview questions asked about participants' interactions with other mission volunteers and their perceptions of a mission trip. Post-trip interview questions asked how mission volunteers reflected on their experiences and how they talked to others after returning home. Interviews ranged from 8 ½–46 minutes and averaged 13–14 minutes. Although post-trip interviews ran longer than pre-trip interviews, younger participants generally offered brief responses with little elaboration when probed. Thus the average interview length is a reflection of participant age and experience. All interviews were audio recorded and transcribed verbatim, yielding 96 pages of typed, double-spaced text.

Journals. All participants were asked to keep journals during their trips. Journal writing elicits feedback from the self and provides meaning through reflection (Progoff, 1992). Participants were given guiding questions exploring their roles on the trip, any conflict of roles, communication of beliefs/values, and their thoughts on the different cultures. Following each trip, journals were collected and typed verbatim. Twenty-four of the 34 total participants completed journals, yielding 55 pages of typed, double-spaced text.

Participant Observation. Finally, data were collected by participant observation. Participant observation often uncovers more in-depth information about participants and the context in which they are situated. The first author logged a total of 112 hours working alongside volunteers in both locations. Activities included working with youth, conducting VBS activities at a local school, pouring a concrete floor for a local church, and doing door-to-door evangelism.

Although participants were aware of the research project, they appeared to behave naturally. The first author was treated as a group member rather than an outsider collecting data. Following activities, field notes were recorded to capture participants' expressions of feelings after encountering the local people, their discussions of those encounters with others, and the different roles/identities that participants appeared to enact. Field notes were typed verbatim and yielded 20 pages of double-spaced text.

Data Analysis

Data were analyzed using thematic analysis consisting of open, axial, and selective coding (Strauss & Corbin, 1998). Open coding generated 310 codes and 24 larger categories. Next, two rounds of axial coding examined the relationships among categories. While working back and forth between the categories and the data, four overarching themes emerged to address the research questions of interest. Repetition, recurrence, and forcefulness were used to constitute a theme (Owen,

1984), and each theme was supported by at least half of the participants. The data were then reexamined for any outliers that did not fit within a theme. Finally, data clips were chosen that best reflected each theme, and participants were given pseudonyms.

A variety of verification procedures were used to ensure rigor in the analytic process and to establish trustworthiness in the interpretations of the data. First, both authors reviewed and agreed upon the themes. Second, peer examination probed for potential researcher biases and better understanding of codes and analysis (Lincoln & Guba, 1985). Three peers agreed that the findings seemed coherent and well supported by the data. Third, member checking, "the most crucial technique for establishing credibility" (Lincoln & Guba, 1985, p. 314), was employed. Six participants (three from each volunteer group) all agreed that the findings were accurate representations of their experiences and the interpretations coincided with their own. Finally, thick, rich, descriptions were used to create "deep, dense, detailed accounts" (Denzin, 1989, p. 83) that help bring readers into the research scene, enabling them to evaluate the findings and interpretations themselves to determine plausibility and coherence.

FINDINGS

Mission trip volunteers appeared to enact multiple identities during their service in a foreign land. Specifically, the majority of volunteers agreed upon enacting a Christian identity, shifting among role identities, and negotiating their American cultural identity. As they attempted to make sense of these identities and their volunteer experiences, many seemed to internalize meanings that may have long-term effects on their self-perceptions.

Multiple Identities of Mission Trip Volunteers

Enacting a Christian identity. Participants' discourse and actions first and foremost reflected a Christian identity. Nearly all of the volunteers described a Christian self and the kind of Christian beliefs that should be part of mission service. For example, 35-year-old Richard, a lineman for a utility company, said, "Obviously being a Christian is a big belief on this trip, but more than that, believing that you can serve God by serving others." In addition, 18-year-old Kyla noted, "First and foremost, I believe you have to be a Christian. Mission work is very tedious and tiring, so you need a good, giving, Christian heart to truly experience the process completely."

Others were equally adamant about the importance of Christian values but also emphasized actions. Kelly, a 43-year-old teacher, claimed, "We all share a common goal and belief; we came to share the Gospel message to the people of Haiti and to help them any way we could." High school senior Hannah agreed and wanted others to see her as a Christian. "I've, of course, been Hannah on this trip," she explained, "but I pray I've been a little Jesus, too. I pray that others have been able to see His light shine through me in the way that I have acted this week." In short, simply identifying one's self as a Christian was not enough; it was important to demonstrate a Christian self for others to see as well.

For many, Christian identities were communicated through both words and deeds. Ella, a 38-year-old massage therapist, demonstrated her Christian beliefs daily, "mostly through my actions, but also verbally," she explained. Deidre, a 55-year-old retired teacher, said, "One way I have communicated my beliefs is by example. Another is by telling others about them." Additionally, Rebecca, a 20-year-old college student, admitted, "By teaching VBS and growing relationships with the locals, we have shown love the way Jesus commanded us to do." Similarly, Jenna, a 48-year-old human resource administrator, said, "Hopefully, I have communicated [my beliefs] through my actions and my words." In pre- and post-trip interviews, participants acknowledged that sharing their faith with others had been a motivating factor to participate in mission work.

Participants' reflections were supported by the first author's on-site observations. Christian values were evident in both talk and behaviors as participants witnessed to others in the marketplaces and town squares and interacted with the native people during worship services. Mission volunteers constructed emotion-filled narratives to share their faith, both with those they came to serve and with trip leaders and fellow team members. Many participants recounted the comfort God had provided in difficult situations. Numerous stories and conversations centered on their Christian principles and spiritual challenges—all pointing to an overarching identity that seemed to be a foundation for other multiple selves.

Shifting role identities. In addition to a Christian identity, participants also shifted among particular role identities throughout their service. More specifically, participants viewed themselves and each other as construction workers, teachers, mother-figures, and servants.

Participants noticed that they adopted different identities at different times, depending upon the context and task at hand. For example, 15-year-old high school junior Sheila explained, "At church, I have been a helper. I have helped paint, clean, and other small jobs, but when it is time for VBS, my role has switched to music leader." Fourteen-year-old Betsy had also worn multiple hats as "a server, listener, and observer" and admitted, "Each of these jobs has helped me to learn new things and have a new perspective." Participants appeared willing to shift their service roles as needed to get the job done, such as Shawn, a 38-year-old chiropractor, who described his experience this way:

> I played the roles of servant, doctor, leader, friend, brother, kid, dad, and security guard. I relished in each role, enjoying each one, and very much enjoying switching from role to role, giving me a break from each role. I shifted between these many roles each day, depending on where we were, what we were doing, and who was with me.

Although some roles were temporary, related to a given task at a given time, other roles were perhaps more enduring. For instance, Ella described feeling like a "mother-figure, role model, and messenger of God" saying she had "served the Haitian people in different ways." She further explained:

> I feel like I serve as a mother-figure at the orphanage because these children's mothers aren't in their lives. I have been a messenger of God by sharing His word with and praying with the people in the clinic….I have tried to serve as a positive Christian role model in both the orphanage and the clinic, as well as in our mission team.

It was noted in the first author's field notes that a group of female volunteers often visited the Haitian orphanage to take snacks, play games, make crafts, and tell Bible stories. While many of the women were mothers, others were not. Regardless, each woman assumed a motherly role, performing activities that traditionally a mother might do, such as feeding and playing with the children.

Participants also constructed and shared stories about their role identities. One participant was overheard telling another how good it felt to be a leader on the trip and how she was reaffirmed by others who said she set a good example. In short, many participants adopted multiple role identities, some spawned by particular service tasks and some cultivated by the perceptions of others.

Negotiating an American cultural identity. In addition to a Christian self and other role identities, participants also enacted, and sometimes negotiated, a cultural identity. Participants had to manage their American self to adapt to various situations in a foreign mission field. For example, Alissa, an 18-year-old high school senior, admitted the culture was very different from America. "I think it was very important to stay open-minded on this trip, to the food, people, customs, etc. I've reminded myself and others on my team…not to judge too quickly," she confided. Ella described other cultural and environmental differences, particularly "tolerating the heat and dealing with the language barrier." Richard admitted his "biggest adjustment" was getting used to the slow Caribbean pace where, unlike America, "Time doesn't matter."

Perhaps the most interesting quote came from Hannah:

> I personally thought the difference in the cultures was beautiful. I adopted some [differences] while there and hope to take some back, but I, of course, kept some mannerisms from home. I figured the people there would enjoy meeting a gringo rather than a wannabe "Tico."

In other words, Hannah thought the Costa Rican people would want to meet a genuine American, rather than someone just trying to emulate the local customs and behaviors.

Not everyone, however, adjusted as easily to a culture that was very different from their American upbringing. Rebecca's adjustments were "hard and quick." As she explained, "The first day we were there, it was everything from what they ate, to how they drove, and how they acted. It was definitely something to get used to." Rebecca seemed to have experienced what many would call "culture shock." Although she, like the others, had heard stories about the cultural differences, she was not quite prepared. Jenna was similarly surprised by her new surroundings, saying:

> We had none of the luxuries from home, no air conditioning, walking almost everywhere instead of riding/driving, two meals a day instead of three. We were the minority, not the majority ethnic group, language barrier, not treated fairly (overcharged, taken advantage of, etc.). The city we stayed in was not as safe as at home, and the government and police were unfair.

Nonetheless, participants learned to adjust, in large part by negotiating some of their taken-for-granted American expectations and behaviors. Many Costa Rica volunteers reminded themselves of T.I.N.A., an acronym for "This is not America," which they had been given in a pre-trip informational meeting. When volunteers found themselves in situations where they wanted to complain about unfamiliar foods, the hot weather, or uncomfortable living conditions, they were encouraged to remember, "This is not America."

The trip leader had anticipated that participants might have a difficult time being respectful of and sensitive to cultural differences, particularly since many of the Costa Rica volunteers were teenagers. As he explained:

> I know how it can be when you get into a new environment and almost everything is totally different from home, especially when you have a bunch of teenagers who are away from their parents and families, some for the first time. They are going to be pretty shocked at some of the things they see and experience on this trip. Letting them know up front is helpful, but you can never truly understand until you're there.

Just as the trip leader had anticipated, the acronym became useful for several participants. Hannah, for example, admitted:

I had to keep reminding myself of T.I.N.A. the whole time. I'm usually pretty open-minded to new things, but it was hard sometimes having to be courteous when we didn't like the food or we couldn't understand what they were saying.

Although some missed the comforts of America, volunteers wanted to leave the locals with a favorable impression and tried to "fit in" as much as possible. Deidre nicely summarized the sentiments of most volunteers, saying, "It's just a simple fact that we adjust to what is around us, so the heat and the people become part of who and what we are."

In summary, participants had to adapt quickly to the different cultures in which they were immersed. Whether it was the heat, lack of punctuality, getting around on foot, or other differences, volunteers adjusted so they could perform the services they went to provide. Participants often compromised or set aside the values and norms of their American identities in an effort to be compatible with local cultures and to be accepted by the natives.

MAKING SENSE OF MISSION TRIP EXPERIENCES

The second research question explored how mission trip volunteers made sense of their experiences. By and large, participants emphasized the personal changes they felt and the likelihood of those changes enduring upon their return to their everyday lives in the U.S.

Making good for good. The theme, *making good for good*, illustrates the ways in which participants had begun to reflect on, interpret, and give meaning to their mission experiences abroad. Some participants expressed their beliefs in having created meaningful change for those they served. For instance, Kent, a 46-year-old respiratory therapist, said, "I thank God for how He has placed Haiti on my heart. I know I can't change this place, but I can make it better for a week at a time." Most, however, focused on changes that had occurred in themselves. In participants' journals, 22 reported personal changes, such as becoming more humble, grateful, and loving. For example, Tara, a high school senior, shared:

At the end of the week, I gave almost everyone [the kids] a ball. If you gave a kid in America that, they couldn't possibly be as thankful as these kids. It really humbled me. I'm so blessed. I just need to enjoy life and be as thankful as them....This trip has impacted my life so much.... I've been so humbled by everything I've seen and experienced on this trip.

Fifteen-year-old Sarah also felt changed, saying, "I realized how attached I had become to the kids and that I had impacted their lives. I think it has shown me that loving on people can change your own heart as well."

Furthermore, most all expected the personal changes to last upon their return home. Kyla explained:

> I believe the changes I experienced on this trip are lasting. It touched my heart way too deeply not to be, and I know that God will lead me back to Haiti to continue to do His work and share His love.

Kendra, a 17-year-old high school senior, agreed, saying:

> I believe this change is forever. No matter where I am at in life, I can always look back at this trip and be thankful. It has taught me the importance of loving on everyone and unity of your church family. I know that every time I look back at my Costa Rica trip, I can smile and know that I have learned so much, and I can't wait to take my love back home.

Several others expressed similar sentiments, including Deidre who said, "This mission trip experience is definitely going to be a change to last a lifetime for me. I am already forever changed and will never forget what I've seen, tasted, smelled, and lived this week in Haiti." Judy, a 32-year-old teacher, added, "I feel this is a permanent change. I don't feel like I will become less compassionate when I get back home because this experience will always be a part of who I am." Jenna, in her post-trip interview said, she, too, had been "forever changed," but admitted to "still processing the events of this trip" and would be "for months to come." As these comments suggested, several participants felt an immediate change of heart that they expected to endure for a long time. They expressed intentions of living differently upon their return home, but as Jenna pointed out, the sensemaking process had really only begun.

Both journal entries and post-trip interviews also revealed that participants wanted to share their experiences and perceived "change" with others. Many recalled having told numerous mission trip stories to friends and family, often in an effort to encourage others to consider mission service.

In contrast, two participants expected any personal change to be relatively short lived. Bob, a 15-year-old high school junior, admitted, "I just think once I get back home, everything will go back to normal. I'm not going to have to worry about being mannerly and accommodating to differences;" he added, "so things will be just like before we left." Matthew, a 17-year-old high school senior, also thought change was less likely for him. "I have been on a foreign mission trip before, and I made a lot of change then," he explained, "but I don't think I'll be making those changes again based on this trip because it had already been done before."

Despite the different feelings of these two teen participants, the overwhelming majority of participants described their experiences as life changing in terms of faith, love, and perceptions of others. As they made sense of their volunteer experiences, they seemed to view themselves differently, having constructed a new identity that was more compassionate and loving, and most were eager to communicate this change to others upon returning home.

DISCUSSION

This study employed identity and sensemaking as conceptual frameworks for exploring the experiences of STM volunteers. The first research question explored the various identities that appeared to emerge through conversation and interaction of mission volunteers as they served. The findings can be interpreted through Jung and Hecht's (2004) four identity layers: personal, enacted, relational, and communal.

Not surprising, given the faith-based context of mission trips, participants overwhelmingly defined themselves as Christians. Although mission volunteers or missionaries may be members of any religious group, the terms are often used in Christian denominations. At the *personal* layer of identity, participants clearly viewed themselves as having particular Christian beliefs and values. To these volunteers, being a Christian was essential to their self-concept. Explained another way, applying Giddens' notion of structuration and regionalization to identity, as did Scott et al. (1998), the Christian self occupied a large, front, and centrally positioned identity region, indicating positive identifications of great importance to participants' self-definition.

A Christian identity was not only self-perceived; it was enacted. The *enactment* layer, according to Jung and Hecht (2004), is about performance and expression. Individuals' discourse and narratives, as posited by Scott et al. (1998) and Horrocks and Callahan (2006), offer particular insight into the identity being performed. In this case, participants constructed stories and testimonies that clearly communicated a Christian self, having noted that one of the primary reasons they participated in a mission trip was to share their faith with others.

From a volunteer

A year and a half after my experience in Costa Rica, I can't say I still think about it as much as I should. It's not something I reminisce on every day and maybe not even every week. It's so easy to get back into your day-to-day routine and forget the life changing things you learned. But sometimes…sometimes God will show me something. He'll lead me to an old photo, a song, a name, a memory, and it's as if I have just returned. I've found that I don't have to think specifically of my trip to change my thoughts and actions but that my mindset has been completely transformed. I definitely still fall short in many ways but contentment and thankfulness have become so much easier.

I would trade my trip for nothing in this world. It was an experience unparalleled to any other, and I cherish it as one of my dearest memories. I will never forget how loved, humbled, and cherished I felt. The love God showed me through the people of Costa Rica was unlike any other. I think you agree to do mission work under the premise that you will be helping other people, and you do. But the person who's really changed is you.

Hannah, a 17-year-old high school senior

Participants performed and expressed their Christian values both to those they were serving and to each other. From the very practical acts of teaching and providing medical assistance, to the heartfelt testimonies and confessions shared with locals and fellow team members, participants communicated their Christian selves in both words and deeds. Although Hecht et al. (2005) acknowledged the potential for a "personal-enacted identity gap" when "one's expressed self in communication can be different from one's self-concepts" (p. 269), the nature of the faith-based volunteer context clearly allowed congruence between the personal and enacted layers of these participants' identities.

Participants also assumed other identities as they formed relationships with others, which Jung and Hecht (2004) described as the *relational* layer of identity. In some cases, volunteers' identities shaped their work and interactions, such as those who were doctors and dentists at home fulfilled those same roles abroad. In other cases, interactions shaped participants' identities by creating roles in which others perceived them (e.g., mother-figure to orphans in Haiti). So while participants' own self-images contributed to their role identities, participants also internalized how others viewed them and responded in ways that were expected of them.

Many participants identified with more than one role, for example, construction worker in the mornings and teacher in the afternoons. While working in shifts, participants interacted with different volunteers and locals in different settings, and they shifted among their role identities depending upon the context. As Weick (1995) explained, "To shift among interactions is to shift among definitions of self" (p. 20). Therefore, it is not unusual for individuals to simultaneously identify themselves as members of multiple groups (Kuhn & Nelson, 2002). The key, according to Jung and Hecht (2004), is relationship. Identities are both constructed by the self and "ascribed to the self by others" (p. 264).

Lastly, participants offered evidence of negotiating their cultural identity as Americans, which reflects Jung and Hecht's (2004) *communal* layer of identity. As the authors explained, "Identities emerge out of groups and networks" (p. 264) where members share common characteristics, memories, and history. The all-American volunteer groups were quickly reminded of their American-*ness* when they came face-to-face with a perceived "Other." Participants' cultural identity would likely have been less salient had the volunteers served in a mission field at home or in a culture more closely aligned with American customs. Although these participants did not appear to respond negatively toward their home culture as student missionaries did in Walling et al.'s (2006) study, they did seem to have an increased cultural awareness. The international contexts illuminated taken-for-granted assumptions and forced participants to confront and respond to differences in food, customs, and language. As a result, several participants found themselves compromising their American norms so they could better adapt to a foreign culture and be more accepted among the locals they wanted to serve.

While their adaptations may have been only context dependent and thus short-lived, they provide a glimpse of what Jung and Hecht (2004) described as the interplay of identity layers. Clearly, the cultural identity of these participants, though present, took a backseat to their personal identity as a Christian. These findings contradict Linhart (2006) where youth mission volunteers' perceptions and experiences were greatly shaped by their own culture. In this study, participants' Christian selves were most salient and provided the lens through which all other identities were filtered. If there were any contradictions between identity layers, it would be a communal-enacted gap wherein participants' expressed self did not necessarily reflect their communal (i.e., American) self. Any dissonance that might have occurred, however, was rectified by the Christian self-concept (i.e., their personal identity) that seemed to ground and frame all other layers of identity.

The second research question explored how mission trip volunteers made sense of their experiences. Findings revealed that participants' sensemaking was indeed tied to their identity, just as Weick (1995) described. Through the process of journaling (often completed on the plane and bus rides returning home) and post-trip interviews (conducted 2–3 weeks later), mission volunteers reflected on what had occurred. As Weick proposed, participants attempted to make sense of all that had happened "by asking, what implications do these events have for who I will be?" (pp. 24–25). In response, the majority of participants believed they had experienced lasting personal changes due to their service. Although they did not necessarily articulate any anticipated change in specific behaviors, they perceived themselves as more thankful, more humble, and more loving due to their experiences abroad.

At first glance, two participants seemed to be outliers, as they both refuted the idea of any long-term personal change. The first participant felt that his life would simply return to normal after the trip and the T.I.N.A. ("This is not America") mentality would be forgotten. The second, who had been on a previous mission trip, believed he was less affected by this one and would not make any new changes. Although these two volunteers did not agree with other participants, they seemed to engage in the same sensemaking process—all asked themselves what the situation had meant to them. As Weick (1995) argued, sensemaking foregrounds the "activity rather than the outcome" (p. 13); so while two participants may have reached a different conclusion, their retrospective process of reflection was actually quite similar to that of the other volunteers.

While reflecting, the majority of participants focused on internal change within their own lives versus any external factors (e.g., food, weather, language) they had found difficult. Weick (1995) referred to specific contextual elements as "cues" and the process of recalling certain events or experiences as "selection." He also discussed the process of retention, which relates to what events, facts, or aspects of an experience that an individual chooses to remember over time. Throughout the sensemaking process, mission trip volunteers selected and focused on the events they felt were most important. The two outliers may have simply selected, embellished, and retained different cues than others and then proceeded to make sense of those in relation to the self. Most, however, seemed to have selected and retained similar memorable moments in which they felt their self-perceptions had been changed in meaningful and lasting ways.

Furthermore, participants shared their stories with others, which demonstrated the communicative aspect of sensemaking. According to Weick (1995), "People discover what they think by looking at what they say...." (p. 182). Therefore, sensemaking is not just an internal processing of one's own experiences; sense is made through interacting and conversing with others about past events. According to Weick, depending on the perceptions we feel others have toward our behaviors, we then justify or rationalize why we acted in a certain way. For these participants, sharing stories about their mission trips likely helped them work out their own understanding of their experiences as they continued to reflect on what had happened in conversation with others.

According to Probasco (2013), storytelling is an important process for travelers because "the construction of a coherent and consistent story about the meaning of a trip and repetition of this story over time may operate as a reinforcement of a particular moral identity" (Allahyari, 2000, p. 221). So while extant research has provided little evidence of long-term behavioral change following short-term mission trips, Probasco reminded us that the stories and other "discrete events of travel" are important in and of themselves, as they may become "meaningful markers of personal identity" (p. 221). In this case, participants' stories about love and faith seemed to reflect and reaffirm their already salient Christian self.

It is also interesting to note that participants' sensemaking seemed to center on the self as opposed to those they had encountered. Participants could have tried to make sense of the host country and how they perceived the mission volunteers, perhaps even wondering if their short-term service had made a difference or worrying that those served may have felt abandoned by their departure. One might also expect participants to express sentiments of guilt after seeing such poverty in relation to their own American circumstances, similar to Mize Smith's (2013) study where the majority of volunteer tourists "employed a discourse of guilt about what they had and what they could not provide" (p. 203).

In contrast, participants in this study did not question the benefits of their service or the inequity in their circumstances. Rather, they framed their work in terms of having accomplished important tasks, including having established relationships that would enable future volunteers to return to those communities. Their glass-half-full attitude may be a reflection of their religious identities or may be indicative of individuals' need to pursue positive social identities that will enhance their self-esteem (see Hogg & Terry, 2000). Rather than evaluating the material circumstances of those they served, participants seemed to evaluate the internal self—what they experienced and how they had been affected. Wearing, Deville, and Lyons (2008) suggested that volunteer tourism may be "as much a journey of the self as it is a journey to help others." These findings suggest the same may be true of mission voluntarism.

Pragmatically, STM trip organizers might benefit from including more identity discussions in pre-trip preparation meetings. While getting prepared for cultural differences and service tasks, mission volunteers should also get prepared for the identity work that will naturally occur as they enact and reflect on their beliefs and self-perceptions. Trip leaders might also want to integrate some form of self-reflection both during and following the trip to help volunteers better understand and benefit from the sensemaking process. This could be in the form of journaling, as requested in this study, post-trip debriefing meetings, or other opportunities in which volunteers could begin constructing and sharing their stories. Perhaps researchers would find more long-term behavioral changes among STM volunteers if their feelings of having been "changed" were talked about, supported, and encouraged upon returning home.

LIMITATIONS AND FUTURE RESEARCH

While participant observation added to both the rigor of inquiry and insightfulness of interpretations, this study was limited by the small number of participants relative to those who serve as STM volunteers each year. The sample was also limited to one ethic group and one religious denomination. Future studies should include larger, more diverse mission volunteer samples. The application of the CTI can also be extended, particularly as a frame through which to compare and contrast the layers of identity between international and domestic mission volunteers, as well as between secular and faith-based volunteer groups. More broadly, CTI may prove useful to understanding other kinds of service-oriented volunteers. While a Christian identity was most salient among these participants, a more general service identity may be similarly enacted by volunteers in other non-religious contexts. Finally, these data may have been influenced by potential issues of social desirability. Participants may have knowingly or unknowingly engaged in deception of self and others by saying what they thought they were "supposed to say," particularly about any life changes resulting from their mission experience. Longitudinal studies exploring STM volunteers' talk and behaviors following their mission trips could offer better interpretations of the long-term changes they initially described.

CONCLUSION

In conclusion, this study employed ethnographic methods to explore the identity and sensemaking of short-term mission volunteers. Findings revealed that mission volunteers shifted among multiple identities during service abroad and appeared to enact all four of Jung and Hecht's (2004) layers of identity: personal, enacted, relational, and communal. Their personal Christian identity seemed to be the most salient, most stable, and most important to enact. Relational identities were more temporary and often tied to particular volunteer tasks. Their communal identity as Americans was perhaps most negotiated and most influenced by the international context in which volunteers served. The differences in culture illuminated the American self in ways that get taken for granted and are made invisible when one is among others who share common characteristics and beliefs. By and large, participants connected their identity with sensemaking, as they made sense of their experiences in terms of self-change and reported stories as an important sensemaking tool employed to create meaning and reaffirm identity.

REFERENCES

Allahyari, R. (2000). *Visions of charity: Volunteer workers and moral community*. Berkeley, CA: University of California Press.

Ashforth, B. E., & Mael, F. (1989). Social identity theory and the organization. *Academy of Management Review, 14*, 20–39.

Beyerlein, K., Trinitapoli, J., & Adler, G. (2011). The effect of religious short-term mission trips on youth civic engagement. *Journal for the Scientific Study of Religion, 50*, 780–795.

Bruscke, K. (2013, January). *How to dress on a mission trip*. Retrieved from http://traveltips.usatoday.com/dress-mission-trip-1488.html

Burke, P. J., & Reitzes, D. C. (1981). The link between identity and role performance. *Social Psychology Quarterly, 44*, 83–92.

Campbell, C., Campbell, D., Krier, D., Kuehlthau, R., Hilmes, T., & Stromberger, M. (2009). Reduction in burnout may be a benefit for short-term medical mission volunteers. *Mental Health, Religion and Culture, 12*, 627–637.

Charng, H. W., Piliavin, J. A., & Callero, P. L. (1988). Role identity and reasoned action in the prediction of repeated behavior. *Social Psychology Quarterly, 51*, 303–317.

Collinson, D. L. (2003). Identities and insecurities: Selves at work. *Organization, 10*, 527–547.

Dearborn, T. (2003). *Short-term missions workbook: From mission tourists to global citizens*. Downers Grove, IL: InterVarsity Press.

Denzin, N. K. (1989). *The research act* (3rd ed.). Englewood Cliffs, NJ: Prentice Hall.

Denzin, N. K., & Lincoln, Y. S. (2000). *The discipline and practice of qualitative research*. Thousand Oaks, CA: Sage.

Gergen, K. J. (1991). *The saturated self: Dilemmas of identity in contemporary life*. New York, NY: Basic Books.

Gilbert, K. R. (2002). Taking a narrative approach to grief research: Finding meaning in stories. *Death Studies, 26*, 223–239.

Hecht, M. L., Warren, J. R., Jung, E., Krieger, J. L. (2005). A communication theory of identity: Development, theoretical perspective, and future directions. In W. Gudykunst (Ed.), *Theorizing about intercultural communication* (pp. 257–278). Thousand Oaks, CA: Sage.

Hitlin, S. (2003). Values as the core of personal identity: Drawing links between two theories of self. *Social Psychology Quarterly, 66*, 118–137.

Hogg, M. A., & Terry, D. J. (2000). Social identity and self-categorization processes in organizational contexts. *Academy of Management Review, 25*, 121–140.

Horrocks, A., & Callahan, J. L. (2006). The role of emotion and narrative in the reciprocal construction of identity. *Human Resource Development International, 9*, 69–83.

Horton, D. J. (2011, May 24). *Short-term mission trips: Are they worth it?* [Web log post]. Retrieved from http://www.huffingtonpost.com/dennis-jhortonphd/shortterm-missiontrips-a_b_866197.html

Howell, B., & Dorr, R. (2007). Evangelical pilgrimage: The language of short-term missions. *Journal of Communication & Religion, 30*, 236–265.

Jung, E., & Hecht, M. L. (2004). Elaborating the communication theory of identity: Identity gaps and communication outcomes. *Communication Quarterly, 52,* 265–283.

Kuhn, T., & Nelson, N. (2002). Reengineering identity: A case study of multiplicity and duality in organizational identification. *Management Communication Quarterly, 16,* 5–38.

Lincoln, Y. S., & Guba, E. G. (1985). *Naturalistic inquiry.* Newbury Park, CA: Sage.

Linhart, T. D. (2006). They were so alive! The spectacle self and youth group short-term mission trips. *Missiology: An International Review, 34,* 451–462.

Louis, M. R. (1980). Surprise and sense making: What newcomers experience in entering unfamiliar organizational settings. *Administrative Science Quarterly, 25,* 226–251.

Mead, M. (1970). *Culture and commitment: A study of the generation gap.* Garden City, NY: Natural History Press.

Mize Smith, J. (2013). Volunteer tourists: The identity and discourse of travelers combining largesse and leisure. In M. W. Kramer, L. K. Lewis, & L. M. Gossett (Eds.), *Volunteering and communication: Studies from multiple contexts* (pp. 189–209). New York, NY: Peter Lang.

Owen, W. F. (1984). Relational themes in interpersonal communication. *Quarterly Journal of Speech, 70,* 274–287.

Priest, R. J., & Howell, B. M. (2013). Introduction: Theme issue on short-term missions. *Missiology: An International Review, 41,* 124–129.

Probasco, L. (2013). Giving time, not money: Long-term impacts of short-term mission trips. *Missiology: An International Review, 41,* 202–224.

Progoff, I. (1992). *At a journal workshop: Writing to access the power of the unconscious and evoke creative ability.* Los Angeles, CA: J. P. Tarcher.

Scott, C. R., Corman, S. R., & Cheney, G. (1998). Development of a structurational model of identification in the organization. *Communication Theory, 8,* 298–336.

Strauss, A., & Corbin, J. (1998). *Basics of qualitative research: Techniques and procedures for developing grounded theory* (2nd ed.). Thousand Oaks, CA: Sage.

Stryker, S. (1980). *Symbolic interactionism: A social structural version.* Menlo Park, CA: Benjamin/ Cummings.

Turner, J. C. (1991). *Social influence.* Milton Keynes, UK: Open University Press.

Ver Beek, K. A. (2006). The impact of short-term missions: A case study of house construction in Honduras after Hurricane Mitch. *Missiology: An International Review, 34,* 477–495.

Walling, S. M., Eriksson, C. B., Meese, K. J., Clovica, A., Gorton, D., & Foy, D. W. (2006). Cultural identity and reentry in short-term student missionaries. *Journal of Psychology & Theology, 34,* 153–164.

Waterman, R. H., Jr. (1990). *Adhocracy: The power to change.* Memphis, TN: Whittle Direct Books.

Wearing, S., Deville, A. & Lyons, K. D. (2008). The volunteer's journey through leisure into the self. In K. D. Lyons & S. Wearing (Eds.), *Journeys of discovery in volunteer tourism* (pp. 65–71). Wallingford, England: CABI Publishing.

Weick, K. E. (1995). *Sensemaking in organizations.* Thousand Oaks, CA: Sage.

CHAPTER ELEVEN

Implications FOR Constructing THE "Serviceable Other": Desired vs. Actual Outcomes IN Rotary's International Service Projects[1]

BRETT J. CRAIG
Nazarbayev University

TRACY RUSSO
University of Kansas

Organizations involved in international service make choices regarding target recipients and project design in working towards desired outcomes. In making these choices and in interacting with people of different societies, cultures, and classes around the world, beliefs about themselves and about the recipients, the "Serviceable Other" of the developing world (Sampson, 1993), inform volunteers and organizations. Beliefs about the *self* and the *other* influence choices in approaches to service which can be not only ineffective but potentially harmful for recipients.

Though admitting failure is generally not done publicly, many volunteers involved in international service are disappointed by outcomes that fall short of the desired long-term change in the developing world and express such disappointment in various ways (Maugh, 2013). Billions of dollars from public, non-governmental donations are spent each year through Non-Governmental Organizations (NGOs) with needs still increasing (Development Initiatives, 2009). The lasting change many hope for and even expect as a result of the volunteering hours given, money spent, and projects implemented often never materializes (Holmen, 2009; Swidler & Watkins, 2009). An examination of the talk of volunteers in one such organization revealed one reason desired outcomes of what poor people can become are not achieved. The volunteers in this study envision service as creating a lasting change for the better in people's lives by helping them become more self-sufficient. By comparing this envisioned service with these volunteers' reports of enacted service, this study explored possible inconsistencies between the volunteers' theory and practice.

Examining how volunteers involved in international service discursively construct themselves and the recipients of service as they perceive needs and then design projects to address those needs leads to an understanding of how accounts and beliefs of the *other* and the *self* influence practice. The context of international service is one where the discursive construction of the *self* and the *other* is particularly salient. In constructing the *other*, in this case the recipients of service, volunteers are indirectly constructing themselves. Their constructions of the other reveal how they describe the needs of recipients of service as those who need to be served by the assets of the volunteers.

The implications of construction and categorization of groups involved in international service are significant in that categories and descriptions, when fixed and unchanging, influence perceptions of the context and roles groups play. This study provides a review of relevant literature regarding social identity and constructing the other in international service followed by a method section describing the semi-structured qualitative interviews used to address the research questions. This is followed by the analysis and interpretation of the data with implications and suggestions for practice.

THE INTERNATIONAL "SERVICEABLE OTHER"

Social Identity and Othering

The intercultural scene where international service projects are carried out can be understood from a social identity perspective. Tajfel and Turner (1986) explained that individuals can relate to others in an interaction on a continuum, from individual identity on one end to social group identity on the other. Turner, Hogg, Oakes, Reicher, and Wetherell's (1987) contribution to the social identity perspective, Self-Categorization Theory (SCT), adds the importance of process and context. People create and select social categories that support their self-concepts.

Depending on the context, people select categories that are accessible to them and that fit the situation.

An important aspect of categorization is that categories are defined in relation to other categories (McGarty, 1999). It is through this type of social categorization that individuals identify things in their social context, but it also provides an orientation to self-reference, to create and define the individual's own place in that context relative to the other elements of the context. Understanding oneself in a social context "always depends upon social categorization" (Oakes, 2001, p. 3). In other words, "there is no 'us' without 'them'" (Reid, Giles, & Harwood, 2005, p. 244).

A critical perspective on interactions and perceptions of groups in an international context has produced a body of scholarship regarding how the cultural, racial, or national *other* is constructed strategically to serve the purposes of a dominant group's desired self-image. A perspective of othering frames the practice of constructing the *other* by a dominant group as justification for intervention and even domination from a constructed superior status. The differences perceived between groups that serve to justify relational dynamics are not objective but are "a social mapping of the human world" (Sampson, 1993, p. 160). The constant construction of this "social map" involves the issue of power in discursive constructions of social groups. As Sampson (1993) has argued, "it is nevertheless useful to suggest that every construction has a dominant group—the constructors—and its others, those who are constructed" (p. 4). The communication about the *self* and about the *other* is an important place to examine how constructions of the *other* serve to construct the *self*.

This dialectic is referred to as *the serviceable other* by Sampson (1993), a term he borrows from author Toni Morrison who used it to explain how many white authors constructed African Americans. Sampson takes Morrison's example of a *serviceable other* and applies it to a larger context in which dominant groups define themselves by constructing an Other that is in contrast to what they desire to be their own self-image. That dominant group indirectly describes themselves through their descriptions of an outgroup. By negatively characterizing a different social group, an *other*, the *self* is claiming what it is by what it is not.

Constructing the International "Serviceable Other"

The poor are considered, by both themselves and others, as a social category (Appadurai, 2004). While often thought of in strictly economic terms, the poor see themselves and are seen in dynamic ways. They are more than "just the human bearers of the condition of poverty. They are a social group, partly defined by official measures but also conscious of themselves as a group, in the real languages of many societies" (pp. 64–65). Categorizing the *other* in terms of a social construction such as poverty allows for the labeling of the condition of the *other* as a social problem that then justifies intervention and action (Escobar, 2002). Escobar (2002) addresses the categorizing of the *other* as discursive. The groups involved in development and service are constructed discursively and in relation to one another. As a discourse, problems can be identified and categories created to design and implement particular projects. The development discourse identified categories of people in need of assistance such as the illiterate or the marginalized. These categories and characterizations serve not only to justify intervention but also to maintain the perception of superiority and the need for continuous international development and service projects.

The difference between desired and actual outcomes in international service warrants an examination into how perceptions of the *other* in international service are influential in project design and implementation. This study sought to identify the beliefs and perceptions held by volunteers in a particular organization and how such perceptions may be influencing the design and implementation of international service projects. It further sought to learn how volunteers construct themselves and what this says about the *other* and about service. To address these issues, the study was conducted in an organization where some volunteers are actively involved in the design and implementation of international service projects aimed at particular groups of recipients.

Rotary International

Rotary International is by some measures the largest NGO in the world. Its members are involved in a variety of service projects, both locally and internationally. Their motto, "Service Above Self," (Rotary International, n.d.a) states their desired self-image and purpose. The organization self-identifies as non-partisan and non-sectarian, and its membership is open to business and professional leaders. However, membership in Rotary is controlled and guided as it can only be gained by invitation or sponsorship by an existing member. Most clubs also require professional diversity among their members by even limiting the percentage of members that can be from the same profession. Rotary's membership requirements reveal how salient social categories are from their perspective in establishing organizational identity.

The requirements of active membership also reveal the commitment Rotarians have to their organization and to service. Attendance is required at weekly meetings, but Rotarians involved in service generally dedicate more time, energy, and money than the minimum requirement.

Rotary International service projects vary in purpose and location, from installing water filters in rural Panama to building schoolhouses in India. Funding for these projects comes from the Rotarians themselves, either through club-level donation or through additional assistance from the Rotary Foundation, which is funded by membership dues (Rotary International, n.d.b). Because of autonomy at the club level, Rotarians are able to influence the design of service projects. Though Rotary International provides guidelines and recommendations for international service, the actual projects are planned, proposed, and implemented at the local club and district levels. Rotary's rule, however, is that an international project must have the cooperation of a local club in order for the funds raised by the sponsoring club to be matched by the Foundation. Official publications state that international service is best performed when it includes the abilities of recipients and empowers people and communities (Rotary International, n.d.c).

Volunteers in organizations such as Rotary, who are involved in international service, travel to far-off places in order to address problems faced by the poor of the developing world. Often their projects target specific problems such as water and sanitation, preventable and treatable diseases, or primary education in areas where they feel the state has neglected or not been able to address these needs. The choices made by volunteers like these Rotarians reflect their values and purpose, but they also reflect their beliefs and assumptions about the people they choose to serve with their projects.

Based on the literature regarding the *self* and *other* in the international service context, this study addressed the following research questions:

RQ1: How do Rotarian accounts of their international service work reveal their constructions of *self* and *other*?

RQ2: How do these discursive constructions influence their international service choices?

METHODS

We chose the semi-structured qualitative interview (Lindlof & Taylor, 2002) and used an interview protocol (available from first author) that addressed the participant's volunteering experience from a past, present and future perspective. While some questions addressed the division between the Rotarian and the recipient of service (e.g., How do you think they see you as a foreigner or outsider?), most questions focused on the Rotarian's perspective on the purpose of service and what good service looks like. The goal was to analyze how Rotarians talked about themselves and those they serve by allowing them to share their service experience. Qualitative interviewing is an effective research method when the goal of the researcher is to highlight subjective human experience (Taylor & Bogdan, 1984), in this case the accounts of Rotarians regarding themselves as volunteers and the recipients of service.

Participants

The participants for this project were 32 Rotarians (M_{age} = 62.00, SD = 11.81, 18 males, 14 females) who have recent experience with and may still be involved in international service projects through their local club membership with Rotary International. Male participants ranged in age from 42–79, with a mean age of 64.06 years (SD = 11.83). Female participants ranged in age from 37–78, with a mean age of 59.36 years (SD = 11.69). Participants identified themselves as white (30 or 94%), Asian (1 or 3%), and Hispanic (1 or 3%). For purposes of identity privacy, the names of participants have been replaced with pseudonyms.

An initial contact through an acquaintance with a member of Rotary who had recently returned from an international service trip led to an invitation to attend a Rotary district conference in the area in the spring of 2011. Contacts were made at this conference with potential participants. More contacts were made through these initial contacts using snowball sampling methods.

Interview Procedures

Interviews took place face-to-face in the location of preference for the participant (e.g., coffee shops, workplaces, and residences). Interviews lasted from 23 to 83 minutes, with an average length of 43 minutes. Because two couples were interviewed simultaneously, a total of 30 interviews totaling more than 21 hours of recorded talk were conducted resulting in 500 pages of double-spaced verbatim transcription.

Data Analysis

We used an open and axial coding technique (Lindlof & Taylor, 2002; Miles & Huberman, 1994) to analyze the data. Strauss and Corbin (1998) describe the process of open coding as when "data are broken down into discrete parts, closely examined, and compared for similarities and differences" (p. 102). In this stage of the analysis we assigned codes to establish connections across interviews and to focus on participants' explicit meanings. Some examples of these codes are "work ethic," "commitment to service," and "appreciated." From the data, 45 open codes were generated.

We then analyzed the codes with axial coding in which codes were compared with other codes and refined in focus (Lindlof & Taylor, 2002) according to the research questions. Codes were refined by eliminating redundancy and by categorizing them into codes about the *self* and codes about the *other*. We created a third category for codes which included both the *self* and *other*. The most prevalent example was the commonly referenced proverb of "teaching a man to fish" as a description of the ideal approach to service. The purpose of axial coding is to move beyond open coding by integrating categories and forming initial interpretations of the data. We paid special attention to outliers or counterexamples in order to make sense of them in relation to other comments from participants and as a check against possible premature conclusions. We also showed a description of themes to two participants to serve as member checks. The member checks reported agreement with the themes, but they urged the themes be presented within the context of Rotary's mission and purpose.

ANALYSIS AND INTERPRETATION

The analysis showed that these Rotarians' accounts of their experiences in international service serve to position themselves and recipients of service in a relationship where in talking about one of these groups (themselves or those they wished to serve), an implied understanding of the other group is revealed. The emergent themes from their talk describe recipients of service projects in ways that serve to affirm the self-image the Rotarians desire for themselves.

Furthermore, in this study, the relationship established in describing the *self* and *other* revealed an inconsistency between expressed values and actual practices. These Rotarians gave accounts of what they valued as the desired outcome to international service while their accounts of themselves and recipients as well as the projects actually carried out generally contradicted their expressions of how they wanted to be serving others. This demonstrates how, in international service, Othering can lead to practices that contradict expressed values of how to do service. Their projects in general are not having the lasting impact they desire, and they are in need of changing their approaches to international service projects.

Rotarians Are the Solution

From their reports regarding why they choose to be involved in international service, Rotarians described themselves as being a solution to the recipients' problems. This solution involved being the right type of volunteer, willing to do what international service requires, exemplifying the very purpose of Rotary, "Service Above Self." Specifically, the Rotarians described themselves as being the expert in the situation and having the required work ethic to solve these problems that no one else has apparently solved. These descriptions serve to position Rotarians as not only willing but capable of solving the problems so apparent in their perceptions of the recipients.

These Rotarians frequently referenced their expertise in a field or knowledge of technology as what they bring to international service. Those who have educational and career training and skills specific to identified needs were especially eager to put those to use through these projects. As Carla, a nurse practitioner, said, "They don't want to go see what's being done, or oversee a project; they want to provide their expertise, and their personal capabilities, which is where I was at." Having expertise that they perceived recipients lacked was a motivator for these Rotarians to see themselves as having much to contribute.

The difference Rotarians saw themselves as making was possible because they saw the situation of the recipient as being somewhat easily solved—from not only an expertise standpoint but a financial one as well. Rotarians described themselves as being capable of fixing problems because of multiple assets and abilities. As Justin, a financial analyst and business owner, said, "I think I have a lot to contribute. I think I have an exceptionally lot to contribute, both financial and experience, time and energy and that kind of stuff." Even those who did not have related expertise still found ways of justifying what experience they did have to the success of carrying out the project. Steven mentioned his life experience of growing up on a farm as something that helped him contribute to the project because he knew he could "do some things."

This again demonstrates the perceived simplicity of the problem which attracted Rotarians to it in the first place. They reported one of the main reasons to do international service was that overseas they could get "more bang for your buck." This reference was made not only to making grant money stretch farther but also in using expertise and knowledge they deemed absent from the situation of the recipient. It was obvious to these Rotarians that because recipients lacked so much in not only material resources but also knowledge and expertise that Rotarians' efforts would drastically improve recipients' conditions.

Rotarians Can Get It Done

Rotarians described themselves as being able to get projects done and make a difference because of both their strong work ethic and an efficiency mindset. The participants of this study presented themselves and other Rotarians who went on these trips as "workers" (Sam, a store owner who now also makes volunteer trips on his own). Many expressed dissatisfaction with trips that involved much more observation and fact-finding than those trips that involved hands-on work. As Kendra, a real estate agent, commented, "I'm a hard worker. If you give me a shovel I will mix cement by hand just like I did in Jamaica, just like I did in Guatemala. Just tell me what to do." Having hands-on experience for a feeling of satisfaction and achievement was important for Rotarians on these trips.

The desire to work hard and feel that they had accomplished something was reported to sometimes cause problems with recipients. An example is Carla's comments on how she perceived recipients not wanting to see her and the other

Rotarians work so hard because the recipients saw them as not being used to it. "They're extremely hospitable people," she said, "and they don't, in any way, want to put—have you put out, or work beyond your means." This made it difficult, she said, because "we're ready to sweat it out. We're ready to go without a cold shower where we stay. We're okay with that." The experience of doing the hands-on work themselves demonstrates a focus on Rotarians and projects rather than on recipients.

Similar to a work ethic, Rotarians talked about themselves as having an efficiency mindset, how to plan and manage tasks. This description was used commonly to contrast themselves with recipients and why they were not able to accomplish much on their own. As Barbara, a bank manager, put it, "a lot of people from other countries work on a different timeline than we do. They have a different sense of timing and attention to time. I don't know how to describe it." Many used this difference as evidence for why Rotarians were needed to get projects done. Chiara, a news reporter with volunteer experience from several countries, said that Americans "have such a straightforward way of this is what I can do, this is how I'm going to do it and this is what I need to get done, and we plow ahead on any project we do." Rotarians saw what they could accomplish in a short service trip and compared it to their perception of how little recipients had ever done for themselves.

Dependent on Outside Help

Recipients were consistently described as needing help because they cannot improve their situation on their own. The recipient simply does not know how. This emphasis is most clear in the description of recipients of water filtration projects. The behavior of recipients was a demonstration to the Rotarian that the recipients do not know how to avoid the harmful effects of poor sanitation. "I think they don't understand all the environmental issues and the science," Katie, a project manager, said. "I mean, it's like you go to a creek and someone will be washing the baby here and then this here someone is washing their laundry, and then here is the person getting water for tonight's stew."

Barbara's perception of the need to inform or educate the people about this problem demonstrated a link between poverty and their ignorance. She said, "You know, they are impoverished, they don't understand…they don't have good drinking water, they don't have good sanitation systems, they don't know about the benefits of simply washing one's hands to help cure so many—prevent diseases."

According to these Rotarians, if recipients do not know how to prevent these problems, they must be shown how by someone outside their community. As Matt, a radiologist who volunteers on medical trips, commented, "Well, I mean, if you've been there 600 years and nobody's ever showed you how to wash your hands, it's a little difficult." Because they haven't known for so long, as Steven states, it would need to start with "just education. That would be–probably it would be a start for these people." However, even when they are perceived to have some knowledge regarding sanitation, they are still seen as incompetent. James, a financial advisor, says, "You know, they have their dirty water and clean water and the next thing you know they're mixing them. It's just an accident that can happen. A splash, a kid doing something stupid."

Not only were recipients reported to lack knowledge to improve their circumstances, but they also did not have access to vital assistance such as healthcare and environmental resources. According to these Rotarians, it was obvious enough just by looking at the recipients what they needed. As James put it, "these people are sick from a million things. When you walk up to these people, when you see them from that far away, they just look like people, and when you're this close you realize how sick everybody is." Such accounts of recipients not only described them as needing medical care but as having not received it locally.

From the local to the national level, Rotarians reported recipients to be stuck in a situation that does not provide adequate opportunity for improvement. The lack of basic assistance or resources provided by the local environment was commonly discussed by Rotarians as a reason for their poverty. Grant, a facilities manager who recently went on his first trip, observed that the people on the Comarcas (the reservations for indigenous people in Panama) are "just barely above camping out, their living situation. Access even to contaminated water was not that easy in some cases." An understanding of the environment not providing for the needs of the people was not restricted to these reservations, however. Rotarians often described the local environments of people in developing nations as "destitute" or "decimated," "having no firewood to cook with" (Dehn). As Dawn, an event coordinator, described the successes of her efforts in serving recipients, she said, "We've kept them fed." Rotarians viewed the recipients as dependent on the service, and there was no end in sight. Not only is the environment no longer providing adequate resources for the people, but any solution provided by Rotarians is reported to come from outside the local or even national context as well.

Static Understanding of Server and Served

How Rotarians see themselves and those they mean to serve in this context is important because it influences how they communicate with recipients and enact service. The Rotarians in this study described the context of international service as involving themselves and recipients in a static relationship, the Rotarian as the source of answers for the recipient. They saw themselves in this context as the ones who serve or provide service while the recipients are always the ones needing to be served. In describing this context, the Rotarians demonstrated what Harre and

Moghaddam (2003) refer to as *indirect positioning*. Rotarians positioned themselves indirectly by talking about recipients as in need of assistance, implying that their actions towards the recipients positioned them in the moral high ground, as the ones responding to the need.

Reports of their service, specifically in who performed the labor in projects, did not reveal involvement of or contribution from recipients in any meaningful way. Many Rotarians actually described service as needing to be performed solely by Rotarians to fulfill the satisfaction and purpose they desired. As Carla explained it, to "contract the labor out, I think, somewhat defeats the purpose of some of these volunteer projects." Rotarians generally presented themselves as not only having the work ethic but also expecting to do all of the work the project entailed. For the most part, recipients were not considered able to or even wanting to do the work. Carrying out projects was often described as rushed and tightly organized in order to accomplish as much as possible and for Rotarians to feel that the trip was worth it because of how much they got done. A focus on themselves as the workers and contributors, however, has restricted the Rotarian's perception of recipients by not seeing what the local people can contribute or even accomplish on their own. The Rotarian will always be the one to serve while the recipient will always need the service. The Rotarian and recipient, in the accounts of these Rotarians, are fixed as members of social groups, categorized by a permanent relationship of helper and helped, server and served, developed and undeveloped.

A clear example of this description is Justin's categorization of countries involved in this context.

> There are certain countries that are prosperous. There are certain countries that are educated. There are certain countries that have the financial resources and the desire to make a difference and help other countries, be it political or a show of power or just they intrinsically want to help people. There's a boatload of countries that need the help.

Which specific countries belong in which categories were obviously not made explicit in Justin's comments or in the comments of other Rotarians. It was clear by their experiences and countries to which they have travelled to do international service, however, that there is a common understanding among these Rotarians which countries belong in which categories.

Sampson's (1993) definition of the serviceable other is useful in understanding how Rotarians construct themselves and recipients of service in the international service context. As this study shows, the recipient is constructed in ways that set up a need for intervention coming from the outside, and the Rotarian is constructed as being capable and resourceful enough to be the answer to the recipient's problems. The discourse demonstrates that in order for these Rotarians to be capable of doing so much good, there must be much need and much good not being done by others. In order for Rotarians to be constructed as a solution to the problems of recipients, they must be experts, which means the recipients must be lacking in knowledge. For the Rotarians to be hard-working, the recipient must not have a good work ethic. If the Rotarian has a strong desire to serve those in need of help, the recipient must be in need of help.

The idea that these positions are unchanging is important because it undermines the very purpose of service as expressed by these Rotarians.

Service Should Encourage Self-sufficiency

Rotarians reported the best way to serve recipients was doing sustainable projects that empower people to help themselves. A sustainable project, according to these Rotarians, is one that not only delivers benefits to the recipients over the long term but also can be maintained by the recipients themselves. A reference to the well-known Eastern proverb about teaching a man to fish was referenced by many of the Rotarians interviewed. It says, "Give a man a fish and you feed him for a day. Teach a man to fish and you feed him for a lifetime." Rotarians referenced this proverb when talking about the most desirable and effective approach to serving recipients. As Andre, a retired professor of entomology, put it, if he "could help those people make a living," he could help them "for their livelihood and their kids and future generations."

This proverb was also referenced when talking about organizations that are doing too much for people in need and not allowing them to do for themselves, thus giving the perspective that it does harm to give the fish instead of teaching to fish. Jake, a commercial broker and developer, said, "You know, Haiti is a classic example of a place that has been milking off the tit for so long that they're almost at the point of destroying their infrastructure and their skill sets." He said too many service and humanitarian groups are "going there and do for them instead of teach them to fish kind of idea. ...from a sustainability perspective, I mean, they need to be taught to fish instead of handed a fish." Dehn, a family physician who has volunteered extensively in Haiti, illustrated a similar perspective of encouraging participation and self-sufficiency. "One of the biggest things is you don't do what they can do for themselves," he said.

This evaluation of how service should be done was prevalent in the discourse of these Rotarians; however, these same Rotarians focused heavily on their own contributions and assets as being the solution to the recipients' problems. They described themselves as the workers and contributors, and the projects, like installing water filters or building schools, were described as being carried out with little to no involvement of the recipients. Projects are generally designed to allow Rotarians to accomplish tasks and solve problems rather than support efforts in self-sufficiency and strengthen capabilities.

While clean water and education projects can be considered as means to a sustainable end, the more important issue is in the implementation of projects and transfer of responsibility. Because these Rotarians focus on problems for which they feel they have solutions, their solutions do not include recipients and therefore are not generally maintained over the long term. Though these projects address immediate needs, the assets and contributions of these Rotarians, which they desire to donate for tangible satisfaction, are not transferred to an increase in recipient contribution and maintenance.

Dissatisfaction with Outcomes

These Rotarians, though confident in their abilities to help recipients and dedicated to the work they were doing, were not necessarily content with their experiences of serving the international recipients. Some raised questions about project design and even their roles in projects. Matt asked the question, "What's our endpoint?" He said he wanted sustainable missions where it "becomes more and more the people that you're trying to help become involved and take ownership and take over." He did not see that happening in his experiences. Neither did Carla, who admitted she didn't see local people taking over her projects anytime in the near future. Although these Rotarians wanted to do sustainable service that would encourage self-sufficiency among recipients, they did not seem to recognize why their projects were not creating those outcomes and did not know how to address this problem.

Steven, a retired public official, challenged his own thinking with regards to his contribution to the water filtration project. As he considered his role of "grunt labor," he questioned why it was necessary for someone like himself to be in Panama, installing water filters. "I don't know why people from here go all that way to do it when there are Rotarians there, come to think of it," he said.

Like Steven, other Rotarians commented on the difference they saw between themselves and the Rotarians of the partnering club in the country where the service was being carried out. These Rotarians were often described as being good hosts and interpreters, but not as wanting to be directly involved in carrying projects. Such reports further strengthened these Rotarians' constructions of themselves as the workers, affirming the need for their presence and participation. However, these reports were often accompanied by dissatisfaction as differences in involvement between the two clubs were reported to be a negative aspect of the projects. Even when it was noted that locals could be participating in the service project, those locals were generally Rotarians and not recipients of the service.

One Rotarian did challenge the description of recipients as being unable to do anything for themselves in this regard. While Josie, an art specialist who recently returned from her first trip, admitted she observed many needs in her trip to Panama, she commented that the people "are not starving and wearing rags. They are better off than is sort of—I don't know how to put that. It's not like they are well-off but they are doing okay. They are managing." Josie said it seemed like there was much to be improved in recipients' living conditions, but that recipients were actually meeting many of their own basic needs and improving their conditions through their own efforts.

One other Rotarian expressed the perspective that his service could be one of supporting existing local efforts instead of strictly bringing support and service to the recipient. Dehn, in speaking of local organizations in Haiti to address malnutrition in children, said he "found that they were actually doing some remarkable work. They'd had a tremendous impact on malnutrition in the area through educating the mothers."

Not all projects Rotary clubs sponsor are designed and implemented in this same fashion. Some create long lasting relationships with other clubs and recipient communities. Other projects are significantly larger and involve other very prominent organizations as can be seen with the success of the PolioPlus program. Most of the Rotarians in this study, however, described themselves and recipients as belonging to categories or roles in terms of who serves and who needs help, without changes to this relationship in the foreseeable future. Such reports deserve closer attention in understanding the relationship between volunteer constructions of themselves and those they serve and how such constructions influence choices made in international service.

DISCUSSION

The Rotarians who participated in this study demonstrated a genuine and sincere desire to provide service to people they reported to be less fortunate and even suffering throughout the developing world. Their desire to do good for others at their own expense is admirable, and, contrary to Miller's (2007) assertion that NGOs generally underinvest in learning, these Rotarians are actively involved in seeking answers to problems and improvements in methods and approaches. Because of such a sincere interest to not only do more to serve others but to do it better, it is important to point out to these Rotarians, and other volunteers doing similar work, how the construction of recipients in self-serving ways constrains them from knowing recipients from other perspectives. Further, it causes volunteers to contradict expressed beliefs about how service should help people help themselves by empowering those people to be more independent from outside assistance through self-sufficiency.

> *From a volunteer:*
>
> I think everybody has a purpose in their life that they may or may not have clearly defined. I have mine clearly defined. I can tell you without reservation that the purpose for my life is to be a gentle, loving, caring, giving man who helps other people. Period. I apply it in my business; I apply it with my family, my children, my grandchildren. I apply it in Rotary; I apply it at church; I apply it in every contact that I have with everybody in every situation. That's just who I am. Not everybody's like me, but Rotary does attract—at least the people that are particularly involved and passionate—that kind of people. Some people join Rotary for the wrong reason, and they stay for the right reason. It's the way it is; it's the way of the world. But most people, they'd like to help other people. They'd like to make a difference. They'd like to know that what they did was significant. It's a significance thing. We're making a difference in people's lives. It's rewarding. Makes me feel good.
>
> A financial services manager involved with Rotary International.

Rotary's own member guidelines for service strongly encourage sustainability and participation of local communities. However, these Rotarians demonstrated seeing themselves as having all the required solutions and expertise, which leaves no reason to consult recipients on needs and projects. This denies recipients the opportunity to take part in decision-making about needs and the implementation of projects. Because of the construction of the *self* as the expert and worker, these Rotarians struggle to balance their contributions with the participation and involvement of the recipient of service, the *other*. This may be especially problematic for volunteers of any organization who are drawn to service because of their perceived ability to do some good.

This of course is not a general criticism of volunteers who want to contribute their assets and abilities to the benefit of someone in need, but rather it does highlight the potential harm in categorizing the volunteer and recipient in this context. Categorization can lead to the perceived homogeneity of categories, particularly of the other category or outgroup (Haslam et al., 1996). These categories influence practices in carrying out projects and frustrate volunteers when sustainability and transfer of ownership is not fulfilled. Perhaps even worse, projects carried out in this manner send the message to recipients that they are neither a part of nor responsible for their own development, leaving them to see themselves as dependent on the developed world (Bilgrami, 1995). The consequence, as Ferguson (2006) put it, is that the recipients of service performed in this manner come to see themselves not only as less developed but as less capable of developing than the outsiders bringing proposed solutions. The construction of such categories has its advantages for volunteers like these Rotarians. Not only are volunteers affirmed in their self-image as being able to bring expertise and work ethic to a situation that is lacking in both, but they are ensured to always be needed. Problems can only temporarily be fixed if no one is there to maintain the solution brought in from the outside. Therefore, there will always be projects, and there will always be people in need. Though their constructions of themselves and the recipients of their projects create this relationship, the Rotarians in this study have given ample evidence that this is not their conscious desire.

Implications and Recommendations for the Practice of International Service

The categorization of the *self* and *other* and the approaches to service projects, as demonstrated by this group of Rotarians, is also likely to be found in other volunteering organizations involved in international service. If volunteers like these Rotarians want to serve recipients in ways that support self-sufficiency and encourage sustainable change, a place to begin is in reconceptualizing international service to include the perspectives and participation of the recipients of service and not just their own abilities to solve problems.

Rotary's official guidelines to service include the recommendation to begin by analyzing a community's assets before determining solutions to problems. Instead of beginning the planning of projects by focusing on an observed need, Rotarians are encouraged to examine the capacities and assets available to and being utilized by recipients. An understanding of service that includes recipients as people with assets, that aims to assist recipients towards an empowered position, stays true to the core purpose of service while expanding it to include the greater long-term benefits Rotarians desire. The idea that recipient communities also possess assets and can make contributions is also found in the popular press in such books as *When Helping Hurts* by Corbett and Fikkert (2009). However, such ideas, while encouraging the inclusion of recipients in service, do not challenge the categorization volunteers are constructing through their Othering.

Beyond the popularized notion of needs assessments and participation from local communities, a de-categorization of the volunteer and recipient is the next step in establishing cooperative relationships and sustainable projects. While a localized capacity assessment can help volunteers learn what people are already doing for themselves, a de-categorization of the volunteer and recipient will challenge the homogenized perception that volunteers are superior by being volunteers and that recipients are still in fact only recipients. When recipients become involved in service projects, they too become volunteers. Volunteers can then work with these recipients, or rather "more volunteers," in supporting and encouraging their resilience, innovation, and expertise in local matters by working towards local solutions. Organizations such as Rotary can address this disconnect between objectives and outcomes by addressing the rigid categories of volunteers and recipients. Providing examples of volunteers from all communities, not just those from the developed world, participating together and incorporating multiple perspectives, efforts, and assets can help deconstruct these rigid categories of volunteer and recipient.

In the case of Rotary International, projects are planned at club levels and funded in part by the Rotarians themselves. At club, district, regional, and even international levels, Rotarians regularly meet together and share their projects through presentations. As evidenced in this study, some if not many Rotarians involved in international service strongly self-identify as the workers, the contributors, the ones to get it done. Suggesting this identity should be altered will likely be resisted and even seem contradictory to their purposes. Instead, helping volunteers such as these Rotarians to see their assets as additions to the service effort rather than as a contrast to the recipient's state may be more effective. Communication channels are already a part of Rotary's operations, and such channels can be utilized to change the current perspective of service as "doing for" into a standard of "doing with."

The practical implications for how we think about ourselves and others, how we talk about ourselves and others, and how those perceptions influence our approach to our interactions with others can significantly change the approach to international volunteering in the developing world. Volunteers should challenge themselves, and challenge each other, on the proposal and design of projects by asking questions regarding categorical assumptions of involvement and expected outcomes. Is the project to fix a problem with strictly imported assets or to work with people in sharing assets and discovering collaborative solutions? Hopefully the findings of this study encourage volunteers to examine their perspective and continue using their skills, expertise, and resources to improve the situations of their fellow human beings around the world in an even more effective and empowering manner.

Limitations and Future Research

This study used Rotarians involved in international service from a particular region in the United States. The participants in this study may not be representative of American Rotarians as a whole; however, they are likely to be similar to volunteers in other organizations. The effects Othering has shown to have on approaches and subsequent outcomes to international service are likely to be found in other organizations using employees or volunteers. However, the specific characterizations and categorizations of the *self* and *other* of each group should be examined in order to determine the possible effects on the practices in each particular context.

CONCLUSION

This study provides a starting place for a discussion regarding these issues, and much more research needs to be done to further the understanding of the complex context of international service and volunteers, recipients of aid and development, and nongovernmental organizations. Future research should address the perspectives of recipients of projects and their own discursive constructions of the *self* and *other* from their standpoints. As the findings in this study suggest, an understanding of perceptions of the *self* and *other* in this context can be of value to volunteers who assess needs, design, and implement service projects based on their constructions of themselves and the recipients of these projects. These findings also support the importance of critically examining the choices made in practice with regard to the goals and values of organizations and individuals in this context.

NOTE

1. Material drawn from first author's dissertation, Department of Communication Studies, University of Kansas.

REFERENCES

Appadurai, A.(2004). The capacity to aspire: Culture and the terms of recognition. In V. Rao & M. Walton (Eds.), *Culture and Public Action* (pp. 59–84). Stanford, CA: Stanford University Press.

Bilgrami, A. (1995). What is a Muslim? In A. Appiah & H. L. Gates (Eds.), *Identities* (pp. 198–219). Chicago, IL: University of Chicago Press.

Corbett, S. & Fikkert, B. (2009). *When helping hurts: How to alleviate poverty without hurting the poor...and yourself.* Chicago, IL: Moody.

Development Initiatives. (2009). *Public support for humanitarian crises through NGOs.* Wells, UK.

Escobar, A. (2002). The problematization of poverty: The tale of three worlds and development. In S. Schech & J. Haggis (Eds.), *Development: A cultural studies reader* (pp. 79–92). Oxford, UK: Blackwell.

Ferguson, J. (2006). *Global Shadows: Africa in the neoliberal world order.* Durham, NC: Duke University Press.

Harre, R. & Moghaddam, F. (2003). Introduction. In R. Harre & F. Moghaddam (Eds.), *The self and others: Positioning individuals and groups in personal, political, and cultural contexts* (pp. 1–11). Westport, CT: Praeger.

Haslam, S. A., Oakes, P., Turner, J., & McGarty, C. (1996). Social identity, self-categorization, and the perceived homogeneity of ingroups and outgroups: The interaction between social motivation and cognition. In R. Sorrentino & E. Higgins (Eds.), *Handbook of motivation and cognition: The interpersonal context* (pp. 182–222). New York, NY: Guilford Press.

Holmen, H. (2009). *Snakes in paradise.* Sterling, VA: Kumarian Press.

Lindlof, T., & Taylor, B. (2002). *Qualitative communication research methods* (2nd ed.). Thousand Oaks, CA: Sage.

Maugh, C. M. (2013). Blogging for peace: Realistic job preview strategies from the 21st century Peace Corps volunteer. In M. W. Kramer, L. K. Lewis, & L. M. Gossett (Eds.), *Volunteering and communication: Studies from multiple contexts* (pp. 25–44). New York: Peter Lang.

McGarty, C. (1999). *Categorization in social psychology.* Thousand Oaks, CA: Sage.

Miles, M. B., & Huberman, A. M. (1994). *Qualitative data analysis: An expanded sourcebook* (2nd ed.). Thousand Oaks, CA: Sage.

Miller, J. (2007). Neither state nor market: NGOs and the international third sector. *Global Media and Communication, 3,* 352–355.

Oakes, P. (2001). The root of all evil in intergroup relations? Unearthing the categorization process. In R. Brown & S. Gaertner (Eds.), *Blackwell handbook of social psychology: Intergroup processes* (pp. 3–21). Malden, MA: Blackwell.

Reid, S. A., Giles, H., & Harwood, J. (2005). A self-categorization perspective on communication and intergroup relations. In J. Harwood & H. Giles (Eds.), *Intergroup communication: Multiple perspectives* (pp. 241–263). New York, NY: Peter Lang.

Rotary International. (n.d.a). About Rotary. Retrieved December 12, 2013, from https://www.rotary.org/en/about-rotary.

Rotary International. (n.d.b). Our structure. Retrieved December 12, 2013, from https://www.rotary.org/en/our-structure.

Rotary International. (n.d.c). *Communities in action: A guide to effective projects.* Retrieved July 26, 2012, from https://www.rotary.org/en/document/577

Sampson, E.E. (1993). Identity politics: Challenges to psychology's understanding. *American Psychologist, 48,* 1219–1230.

Strauss, A., & Corbin, J. (1998). *Basics of qualitative research: Techniques and procedures for developing grounded theory.* Thousand Oaks, CA: Sage.

Swidler, A., & Watkins, S.C. (2009). Teach a man to fish: The sustainability doctrine and its social consequences. *World Development, 37,* 1182–1196.

Tajfel, H., & Turner, J. C. (1986). The social identity theory of intergroup behavior. In S. Worchel & W. G. Austin (Eds.), *Psychology of intergroup relations* (7–24). Chicago, IL: Nelson-Hall.

Taylor, S., & Bogdan, R. (1984). *Introduction to qualitative research methods: The search for meanings* (2nd ed.). New York, NY: Wiley.

Turner, J. C., Hogg, M. A., Oakes, P. J., Reicher, S. D., & Wetherell, M. S. (1987). *Rediscovering the social group: A self-categorization theory.* New York: Blackwell.

CHAPTER TWELVE

Constructing "American Exceptionalism": Peace Corps Volunteer Discourses OF Race, Gender, AND Empowerment

JENNA N. HANCHEY
The University of Texas at Austin

Many scholars consider American exceptionalism to be "one of the most, if not *the* most, important narratives that pervade contemporary American culture" (Edwards, 2012, p. 366). However, it is often only considered in relation to a small range of topics: American foreign policies that lead to war, military build-up, or invasive action (Motter, 2010; Patman, 2006; Rojecki, 2008). The importance of this narrative is beginning to be analyzed in media culture as well (Rojecki, 2008; Söderlind, 2011), but there remain large sectors of U.S. American[1] life where the impact of American exceptionalism[2] is under-theorized. This study analyzes the way that American exceptionalism is reinforced and reconstructed in the discourse of returned Peace Corps volunteers (RPCVs).[3]

The idea that U.S. Americans are somehow "exceptional" is both an assumption guiding the mission of the Peace Corps and a point of fundamental tension for volunteers (Fischer, 1998). Cobbs Hoffman (1998) describes how the Peace Corps was started at a time when there was a "widespread belief that American norms represented the pinnacle of progress and were self-evidently good" (p. 25). This belief in U.S. exceptionality allows for it to empower other countries—to help others develop—underlies the U.S. Peace Corps to some extent, even today

(Cobbs Hoffman, 1998), and acts as a common thread running throughout RPCV descriptions of their experience living and working for two years in host countries. However, when discursively (re)constructed in conversation, the myth of American exceptionalism becomes a point of struggle. When RPCVs encounter challenges to American exceptionalism, they face contradictions through the hidden assumptions within its use: whiteness, masculinity, and national superiority.

In narrating their experiences, "[p]eople draw on gendered, heteronormative, classed, raced and colonial discourses to...justify their action or inaction and make sense of the things that happen to them in organizational life" (Baines, 2010, p. 120). RPCVs are no exception. In their descriptions of time spent abroad, Peace Corps volunteers draw on these discourses as a sensemaking aid. This study examined how discursive access to U.S. American exceptionalism often requires reinscriptions of whiteness, masculinity, and an imperial attitude toward the host country.

AMERICAN EXCEPTIONALISM AND ITS INTERSECTIONS

American exceptionalism is an ideological myth that underlies much of U.S. American discourse and public life. It "evokes attitudes of national autonomy and superiority" (Ivie & Giner, 2009, p. 360) by construing the "United States [as] unique among, if not superior to, other nation-states" (Edwards, 2012). Based in "a pervasive faith in the uniqueness, immutability and superiority of the country's founding liberal principles" (Patman, 2006, p. 964), American exceptionalism provides a "conviction that the USA has a special destiny among nations" (Patman, 2006, p. 964), particularly because of its purportedly superior morality.

The sense of the U.S. as a "morally elevated" nation (Ivie & Giner, 2009, p. 361) gives rise to a logic allowing for intervention in other countries. The idea of the U.S. as a "shining city on a hill" has pervaded public discourse for centuries, leaving "little doubt that the USA has continued to think of itself as a special nation...with a moral and religious mission to the world" (Patman, 2006, p. 965). This legitimizes foreign intervention, as the U.S. sees itself as coming from a higher moral position, one that grants the right to arbitrate international disputes, fix other nations' problems, and invade and attack other peoples. The invocation of U.S. moral superiority constructs the national other as morally bereft in comparison, and allows for the U.S. to rationalize its intervention as necessary and just.

American exceptionalism also allows for an unquestioningly positive construction of humanitarian aid. Patman (2006) notes that "a sense of exceptionalism inspired the USA...to embark on a quest to improve the world" (p. 965), a quest that often includes humanitarian projects. Although many U.S. humanitarian interventions have positive implications, others promote military goals under the guise of aid. As Motter (2010) examines, the possibility for "humanitarian militarism emerges from an exceptionalist rhetoric of compassionate generosity" (p. 509). Relying on a similar sense of elevated morality, the discursive underpinnings of U.S. militarism and humanitarianism are quite similar. As Söderlind (2011) argues, American exceptionalism "inflects every discourse involving relations between the United States and its—internal as well as external—others" (p. 9).

However, at the moment, most studies have only focused on U.S. *public* discourse regarding American exceptionalism, and have ignored how it is negotiated and constructed through everyday discourse. As the face of the U.S. to many people around the world, Peace Corps volunteers discursively display how American exceptionalist ideas play out in practical interactions with national others. Although scholars have examined the way that explicit or implicit appeals to American exceptionalism are used in order to garner public support for foreign policies or action, few have examined how those foreign policies are enacted. This study provides insight into the negotiation of American exceptionalist ideologies in practice by examining how the ideological pillars of American exceptionalism are reinforced on a day-to-day basis in Peace Corps volunteer discourse.

The Peace Corps Volunteer: Where Exceptionalism Meets Humanitarian Aid

Patman (2006) argues that "soft power" is more important than ever in maintaining a hegemonic idea of American exceptionalism, and "soft power" in foreign policy is something with which the Peace Corps has often been associated (Cobbs Hoffman, 1998). The Peace Corps is an independent U.S. government organization that has sent over 215,000 volunteers to 139 countries in the past 50 years to serve for two-and-a-half years (Peace Corps, 2014). Begun in 1961 by John F. Kennedy, the institution of the Peace Corps responded to exigencies of the Cold War, the rise of the so-called Third World, and unflattering portrayals of U.S. Americans abroad (Cobbs Hoffman, 1998; Fischer, 1998). Volunteers "and their altruism put a positive face on global interventionism" (Cobbs Hoffman, 1998, p. 7), with the hope of making international friends for the nation (Fischer, 1998).

However, the Peace Corps has just as big of an influence on the U.S. national imaginary as it does any other nation (Cobbs Hoffman, 1998). As such, "the Peace Corps is perhaps one of our clearest windows onto the abiding tension in the United States between a foreign policy of self-aggrandizement and a foreign policy that promotes the values of democracy and peace" (Cobbs Hoffman, 1998, p. 4). Examining Peace Corps volunteer discourse provides a particularly interesting perspective on the contradictions inherent in an enactment of American exceptionalism for the benefit of other nations. Volunteer discourse also reveals an oft-missed part of American exceptionalism: "[H]ow exceptionalist rhetorics function as a motive for American global hegemony when no evil enemy is in sight" (Motter, 2010, p. 509).

Postcolonial Perspectives

The nationalistic discourse underlying American exceptionalism can be examined using postcolonial theory. Postcolonial theory is an interdisciplinary field of study which is "committed to theorizing the problematics of colonization and decolonization" (Shome & Hegde, 2002, p. 250), with an explicit commitment to "a radical critique of colonialism/imperialism and neocolonialism" (A. Prasad, 2003, p. 7). A large percentage of postcolonial theory is focused on interrogating and deconstructing Western practice and thought in order to reveal the (neo)colonial dynamics therein (A. Prasad, 2003).

There is a dearth of postcolonial studies in communication (Shome & Hegde, 2002), and qualitative communication research in postcolonial theory is especially underrepresented. In fact, only a few postcolonial ethnographies (Supriya, 2002; Supriya, 2004) or qualitative studies (Norander & Harter, 2012; Pal & Buzzanell, 2013) exist. This may stem from the West's historical use of ethnography to support (neo)colonial mindsets (Prasad, P., 2003). However, this project used ethnographic methods to critically analyze the construction of Western narratives *regarding the West itself*, and how such narratives affect relationships with other peoples. By turning the gaze back on the West (though being careful not simply to re-center the West), ethnographic and other qualitative research methods can be appropriated for postcolonial use.

Intersectional Concerns

A postcolonial theoretical position often leads to an emphasis on intersectionality. Intersectionality emphasizes the impossibility of extricating one individual facet of power from others; that is, neocolonialism cannot be analyzed thoroughly without concurrently examining gender, race/ethnicity, and class (Acker, 2006; McCall, 2001; West & Fenstermaker, 2002). Although it is difficult to keep a focus on these continually interweaving power dynamics in the moment of participant observation or interview conduction, the process of revealing U.S.-centric thought underlying constructions of others requires continual interrogation of *all* aspects of representation, including gender, race, and nation. Intersectional perspectives thus formed the basis for this project, and set it apart from other analyses of American exceptionalism. In analyzing with an eye towards intersectionality, this study found that the negotiation of U.S. American exceptionalism often assumed certain perspectives on, and discourses of, race, gender, and nation. The following section briefly describes the research methods before moving into analysis.

METHODS

This research draws from both participant observation and interviews. Over the course of six months, I attended formal Peace Corps information sessions (15–20 people in attendance), special recruitment events (100–200 people in attendance), and classroom announcements (4–30 people in attendance) at a large university in the western U.S. Each event included 2–20 RPCVs describing their experiences to prospective volunteers. As a RPCV who served in Tanzania from 2007–2009, I was truly a *participant* observer, and took field notes detailing not only information and experiences presented by recruiters and returned volunteers, and questions and comments from prospective applicants, but also my own contributions and responses. My experiences in Tanzania were woven throughout my field notes as well, when salient to the happenings at hand. As a participant observer in Peace Corps recruitment events, I was often asked by prospective volunteers if they could hear about my experiences over coffee at a later date. Such meetings functioned as both participant interactions and interviews, so I wrote field notes in addition to recording the dialogue. In a way, these meetings may be conceptualized as ethnographic interviews (Lindlof & Taylor, 2011). They were organic and emergent from the scene. Though they did not occur in that very moment in time, they were still an "*informal, conversational interview*" (p. 176, emphasis in original), as the prospective volunteers were able to ask me just as many questions as I asked them. In total, I collected 20 hours of participant observation and 57 pages of single-spaced field notes.

Additionally, I conducted in-depth interviews with 11 recently returned (i.e., in the past five years) Peace Corps volunteers. I found initial interview subjects by sending out a call on the local RPCV listserv, and continued by soliciting further subjects through snowball sampling (Lindlof & Taylor, 2011). I used an interview guide as a basic structure, but often added questions based on the unique experiences of the interviewees. All of the interviewees lived in the surrounding metropolitan area, self-identified as white, and were between 25 and 35 years old. The interviews were audio-recorded and transcribed, totaling 200 pages of single-spaced transcriptions. In order to protect the identity of the people I interviewed, I have not only changed their names, but also removed the name of the country of service.

Drawing from these field notes and interview transcripts, this study links my own personal experience as a RPCV and field researcher with the narratives of other returned volunteers. To find the themes that create the basis for this study, I focused first on an emic approach to the data (Lindlof & Taylor, 2011), using open coding to find salient themes. During the process of axial coding, I allowed my postcolonial and intersectional theoretical positions to guide the analysis, looking etically for connections to race, gender, and nation. Although I specifically asked interview participants what it was like being of their race and gender in their countries of service, I was surprised to find that what it meant to be "American" came up unsolicited in every interview. The argument of this study emerged by looking for the connections and disjunctures between these facets of identity throughout the data.

Although the textual fragments that I choose to use in this piece come more often from interviews than participant observation, the same themes appear throughout my fieldwork. The interview format made it easier for participants to delve in-depth into themes that were present in less detail in participant observation events. Thus, these quotations were chosen as they gave a more detailed account of the phenomenon, but they are also representative of narratives found in other ethnographic contexts.

EXCEPTIONAL CONSTRUCTIONS: WHITENESS, MASCULINITY, AND THE ABILITY TO EMPOWER

The (White) Exceptional American

After a large recruitment session, a prospective volunteer voiced interest in meeting for coffee to talk about my experiences in the Peace Corps. She asked me a few questions, and noted in one of my responses that I had shifted from studying physics as an undergraduate to completing graduate work in communication. She asked me why my life plan had changed so drastically.

As I reflect on the conversation, I remember having difficulty thinking of how to explain the complicated situations which had first drawn my attention to structures of inequality. So, I began by describing the gendered dynamics at work in my school in Sub-Saharan Africa. Conscious of the risk that my narrative could be read as villainizing men of my host country, I attempted to render a narrative that rather implicated U.S. Americans as perpetrators. I said:

> I got more interested in what are those dynamics, the social structures that keep people from being equal in different situations. A lot of it wasn't just gender too, but also racial-nation inequalities that I saw happening. Like, volunteers at some point, some volunteers, not everyone, would begin to say things like, "Well, I deserve to sit at the head table at the banquet, because I'm white." And it's kind of a mindset that you get in to some extent, because you're constantly being treated differently. Not just because—cuz not all volunteers

are white, obviously, that one was—but being an American, being different, being from the place where they would all like to go live, you get treated differently. And if you let that go to your head, I don't know, people started saying things where I'm like, "I don't think that's ok." But when you're just treated that way day after day after day after day after day, you start thinking about yourself differently.

In my attempt to side-step around construing systemic power issues as the problem solely of my host country, I ironically end up reinforcing a racialized view of U.S. Americans as normatively white.

In referring to this as a "racial-nation" inequality, I am assuming two things: that my host country is generally populated with black people, and that the U.S. is generally populated with white people. I catch myself in the middle of my statement and realize my mistake, but the remainder of the explanation rings a bit hollow. I don't really know—as I claim I do—if this is actually a phenomenon based on being U.S. American; the volunteers that I was referring to who began thinking that they all deserved their place at the head table were all white. I assumed the experience that I had as a white volunteer, and the experience of the white volunteers that I knew, was generalizable to any U.S. volunteer in the Sub-Saharan African country where I lived.

In other words, though I knew volunteers of color and would never consciously claim their experience to be the same as mine, being unconscious of my own racial privilege led me to generalize my experience. Unfortunately, when reviewing my field notes and interview transcripts, I realized that the excerpt above is not an isolated instance of color-blind racism (Bonilla-Silva, 2010); rather, it is indicative of a theme found throughout white volunteer narratives. All the volunteers that I interviewed self-identified as white,[4] and all of the volunteers I spoke with at recruiting events had light-toned skin. On multiple occasions, they revealed a similar assumption to my own. Though these racist assumptions are clearly a problem in and of themselves, they also connect to the discourse of American exceptionalism.

The assumption in the narratives of white volunteers that their experience is representative of volunteers in general ties into both the idea that being U.S. American is special or exceptional, and the invisibility of whiteness (Nakayama & Krizek, 1995; Shome, 2000). The assumption of American exceptionalism implies whiteness in RPCV narratives, and is brought out most strongly when the implied whiteness is challenged. When American exceptionalism is challenged because the volunteer in question is not white, the contradictions inherent in American exceptionalism are revealed, and the white volunteer does not know how to make sense of the situation.

The following interview excerpt is an excellent example. Linda, a RPCV who served in a Sub-Saharan African country, describes her experience hitchhiking home one night with friends, on an evening when they had a particularly difficult time finding a ride:

I was traveling with two other Peace Corps volunteers, another white person like myself, and then an African American. And when I pulled over a car, it was an Afrikaner, and he said, "I don't take black people." And I said—I mean, I should have—this is how I look back on it. I should've just said, "Okay. See you later." You know? I don't want to be with someone who says comments like that. But instead I was like, "Well, he's *American!*" And, you know, tried to, I don't know, reason with him that way. And so he said yes, but then the whole car ride he kept trying to be almost apologetic and say things like, "I'm not racist, but…" and go on with his stories of how he saw differences between whites and blacks. And it was really uncomfortable for all three of the American volunteers, but especially for the African American volunteer. …It felt bad, felt wrong. It felt wrong even for me to say—I don't know why I get so stuck on this—but why would I reason with him, "But he's an American"? You know? I mean, I know I was appealing to him and making him maybe think about it, but I just don't feel like that should be even an argument, you know? It shouldn't be part of the fundamental reason why he should take us, because he's an American. Yeah, he's black, but he's American. I felt really bad about that, but at the moment I just wanted to get home. And, I mean, I told my African American volunteer friend, I told him what he said. I was like, "Do you want to get in the car with someone who just said that?" And he hesitated, but he was like, "Let's go." So he also had the same feeling of just wanting to get down the road.

Importantly, Linda's attempt to reason with the driver by labeling her Black friend "American" is narrated not only with guilt, but with confusion. First, her guilt over the comment was deflected: she focused on how difficult it was to get a ride that night and long they were waiting, and she added at the end that the African American volunteer said it was fine and wanted to take the car, too. This functions similarly to diminutives in color-blind race talk (Bonilla-Silva, 2010), which attempt to qualify the racial significance of a comment or phrase. Obviously, this is something that Linda has often reflected on. However, it still bothered and confused her. She asked rhetorically, "why would I reason with him?" and explained that she doesn't "feel like that should be even an argument" at all. Linda cannot quite figure out *why* it shouldn't be an argument, and why it bothered her so much that she tried to reason with the driver in that manner.

Fundamentally, it reveals a contradiction. In the narrative seen throughout white RPCV discourse there is an assumption that U.S. Americans are special simply by virtue of being *American*, regardless of race—a universalization of whiteness (Shome, 2000). But here is a U.S. American who is not being recognized as special. Linda has come face-to-face in this circumstance with both her privilege as U.S. American and her privilege as white, but as the combination contradicts the dominant construction of American exceptionalism, she is at an impasse. What Linda cannot quite put into words is that underlying an idea of American exceptionalism is an assumption that the exceptional American is white. The myth of American exceptionalism is a racialized myth.

The (Masculine) Exceptional American

Whiteness is not the only hidden facet of American exceptionalist discourse in RPCV speech. Additionally, there is a negotiation of masculinity in the stories of both male and female volunteers. This section focuses on female volunteer masculinity and how it allows access to American exceptionalism. Although this female struggle for masculinity disrupts some dominant power relations, it reinforces others.

When Anita, a RPCV who served in South America, was asked what her experience was like being a woman in her country of service, she replied:

> Yeah, I guess that I didn't face a lot of adversity, because I think that they [the men of her village] just saw me as a foreigner. And somehow that gave me some respect, even though I was a woman.

Here, Anita's position as U.S. American gave her access to respect. This was contrasted with the way in which Anita spoke in the interview about the host country national women that she knew. Anita was respected "even though" she is a woman; however, women of her South American village were not allowed out of the house without their husband's permission, were not aware of their husband's affairs with other women, and were cat-called in the street.

Anita gained respect because they just saw her as a foreigner, and not a foreign *woman*. This begs the question: as what kind of foreigner did they see her? Certainly whiteness ties into this example, but Anita's comment also implies that her position as U.S. American gave her access to a type of masculinity. Rather than having to deal with the gender roles of that particular South American village's culture, she gets to trade her status as a white U.S. American for masculine clout: the positionality of U.S. American is automatically considered a masculine positionality.

Yet, the U.S. female volunteer was only allowed access to American exceptionalism up to a point: where the performance of masculinity fails, so did the female volunteer's ability to access American exceptionalism. Thus, the exceptional American was assumed to be masculine. In the following excerpt from an interview, Tiffany described what it was like being a woman in the Sub-Saharan African country in which she served. In this story, the assumed masculinity and respect that "should" come with being U.S. American was challenged:

> I'll never forget this government official [who] said something to me that…was crass and it was inappropriate, and it was presumptuous, like something having to do with sexuality. And I called his ass out on the spot, in front of a bunch of government people. And I'm like, "What did you say to me? It is inappropriate for you to talk to me or any other woman in that manner, especially an American, on top of everything. We don't abide for this, I won't stand for this! I represent all the women in Peace Corps, I represent any other woman in

the same position as me, I represent women from your country who you should treat with better respect." I laid into him in front of all these people....Cuz it's like, I've always felt like when people were rude to you in a degrading-gender way, I wasn't just responding for me, it wasn't my personal response, it was for all women. Because I felt like I was really standing up against huge boundaries for women. And what type of woman would I be to not stand up against this shit right now? What type of—how would I be helping anyone if I just backed down? And I would never back down.

After the government official makes an inappropriate comment about her, Tiffany's initial response implied that it was especially inappropriate for him to have said that to her because she's "American." Tiffany seemed to say that he should have known better than to say that to an American, because *Americans* won't stand for it. Tiffany's response assumed a certain masculine privilege that goes along with being U.S. American, and when that privilege is challenged by the host country national, she lashed out. Consider the way she ended her story: that she will never back down. Underlying American exceptionalism is an inherent assumption of masculinity.

My field notes display similar assumptions of U.S. female masculinity in other interactions with RPCVs. One prospective volunteer at a recruitment event described how she became interested in the Peace Corps after meeting a RPCV who had shared that during service she "had been sexually assaulted and people followed her everywhere" and was sick for almost the maximum amount of days that Peace Corps allows before being sent home, but despite these challenges the volunteer said she "wouldn't change a thing" and would "definitely," "100%" choose to do it again. This narrative made the prospective volunteer so interested in the Peace Corps that she was looking into the possibility of changing her citizenship from Canadian to U.S. American simply to be able to join. What drew this prospective volunteer was certainly not the possibility of victimization, violence, or illness, but the strength, resilience and power she saw displayed in the RPCV: A masculinity that allowed the RPCV to transcend the circumstances and implicitly placed her on a superior level of morality when compared with the host country nationals.

A second facet of Tiffany's story was how she saw it as her duty to stand up to the official on the behalf of all women of the world. She stated that she represents all women, everywhere. The idea of American exceptionalism underlay her ability to act as hero of the women of the world. Tiffany saw it as her responsibility to stand up to that comment because it represented a "boundary" to all women, and not all women in the world can or will stand up for themselves, so she must do it for them. Thus, an inherent U.S. American masculinity was assumed in the implication that females of *other* nations were not so empowered. As Mohanty (1991) describes, the discursive idea that the Western woman can and should stand up for the "Third World" functions imperialistically and constructs a monolithic "Third

World woman" who needs saving. U.S. American females are able to stand up for other (female) people of the world because they're U.S. American, and that implies masculinity—and power. By preserving the requirement of masculinity, Tiffany and other female volunteers were able to access U.S. American exceptionalism.

The (Disempowered) International Other

In RPCV discourse, whiteness and masculinity often constitute American exceptionalism. This section suggests that this exceptionalism also allows volunteers to "empower" host country nationals. Empowerment is a development discourse that is often taken for granted (Kapoor, 2008), but this study displays why it needs to be interrogated: The discourse of empowerment is based on assumptions of U.S. American exceptionalism.

During participant observation at a Peace Corps classroom announcement, one recruiter claimed, "Peace Corps is all about empowerment." This statement may seem straight-forward, yet empowerment is not a neutral concept. The construction of who can empower and who needs empowerment in these narratives is politically constructed, and often conflicts with normative volunteer values. As Fischer (1998) notes, "The volunteer was supposed to enter the third world with an open mind about how, in the end, humanity is all the same" (p. 162); however, this typical volunteer belief in universal equality conflicts with the fact that "[j]ust by being there, volunteers were a living implication that they knew how to do things and they were there to teach the locals, who did not" (p. 181).

Volunteers often spoke of "obvious" issues in their countries of service: gender equality, self-esteem, lack of resources, and racial tensions. These "obvious" problems were construed as things that U.S. Americans have the ability to help fix through empowerment. As an exemplar, one of the obvious problems that Linda saw in her Sub-Saharan African community was her students' lack of self-esteem. They often used an Arabic phrase meaning "If God wills," implying to Linda that they didn't believe they had control over their own lives, which to her was "really sad." She explained:

> They weren't empowered to believe that they had control because of the death that they had seen, and because of the years of apartheid. That was really tough for me. Just the phrase, "But we can't, cuz we're black." And I did my best to, you know, fight those myths, but I'm just one person.

In Linda's story, there were multiple factors contributing to the students' belief—which she sees as a "myth"—that they do not have control over their lives. The first factor is that her students are black, and second that they or their parents lived through apartheid. The coupling of black skin with the experience of apartheid implies that for many years, black people were extremely oppressed, and to a large extent, did not have control over their lives. However, now that apartheid was over, Linda saw the barriers to black students' control of their lives as also having ended. Third, she believed that the prevalence of HIV/AIDS and other fatal diseases contributed to this feeling as well.

The veiled narrative in Linda's comment is that she, as an U.S. American volunteer, knew better than the students: she knew that they *can* take control of their lives. However, for some reason they didn't believe that. This knowledge led Linda to feel an imperative to help; her students clearly needed her assistance in order for them to have a better way of life. Again, this functions in an imperialistic manner that dismisses the host country national experience of the world. In Linda's narrative, believing in the "myth" that they did not have control was negatively valenced, leading to issues of self-esteem. She did not recognize this as a different way of experiencing and being in the world, but rather a mistaken view of the world based on the experiences they have that *people aren't meant to have.* The implicit assumption in this narrative is that a white, middle-class, U.S. American experience was normative, and experiences that differed—such as living under a racially oppressive regime or experiencing death as a normal, regular occurrence—caused these Sub-Saharan African students to see the world in *the wrong way.*

This constructs a need for U.S. American assistance. Similar to Cloud's (2004) study of the Western presumption that Afghan women need rescuing from their culture, here the African students need to be rescued by the (white) American from their cultural mindset. It is ironic that this serves to reinforce the Western ability to save, given that this mindset was constructed partially by white colonists (Fanon, 1963/2004; Ngũgĩ, 1986). Interestingly, this narrative of racial inability manifests differently in regard to different nations. Balaji (2011) describes how pity for the Black population of New Orleans after Hurricane Katrina quickly turned to anger because of the "inherent (white) American ideal that individuals can 'pull themselves up' from adversity" (p. 59). However, U.S. Americans responded to victims of the Haitian earthquake with pity at the (racially and nationally) backwards state. The ability to "pull yourself up by your bootstraps" is assumed for U.S. Americans, even U.S. Americans of color, but it is *not* thought to apply to people of "developing" countries. Yet, this emotional response of pity is not neutral, but "implicitly selfish and rooted in our desire to assert power over our Others" (Balaji, 2011, p. 64).

The discourse of empowerment is further dependent on the construction of host country national culture as monolithic and unchanging. Volunteers, in both interviews and at recruitment events, often describe the culture of their host country in a singular way. One prospective volunteer said that he applied for Peace Corps because he wanted to eventually travel the whole world, and it would be very easy to get to more developed places later on in life, so he should "knock out" the "backwater" places first. In both field notes and interviews, multiple RPCVs referred to "the culture" of their host country as "patriarchal" or "very patriarchal." A few avoid the generalization inherent in these statements by speaking only of their own community, or the school environment in which they taught; however, there is still an assumption that patriarchy is something that exists *over there*, and not in the United States.

Volunteer narratives, in order to reconcile the perceived "need" host country nationals have to be empowered with the assumption that host country culture is static and cannot change, related current host country culture to U.S. American culture in the past. However, in their depictions, this telos of development was dependent upon U.S. American interference and assistance. Unless there was U.S. American assistance in human empowerment, the host country culture would remain static, and they would not fulfill their developmental potential and promise. This logic allowed for Peace Corps volunteers to mitigate the contradiction between a belief in national egalitarianism and American exceptionalism (Fischer, 1998).

The idea that host country cultures are simply "behind the times," and will eventually catch up to the pinnacle that has been reached by U.S. American culture was voiced by many volunteers. In an interview, Carl explained his view of gender equality issues in the developing world by saying, "You know, and in America, we've come a long way in terms of, like gender equality, and whereas in a developing country, it's like a hundred years ago." This statement problematically portrayed the U.S. as the standard for development, and revealed a U.S.-centric worldview.

The U.S.-centrism of the narrative that "developing" countries are temporally behind the United States on a linear path of development created the basis for U.S. American intervention and the enactment of empowerment. Otherwise, the host country cultures would remain stuck in the same monolithic form indefinitely. Anita, when describing her moral struggle with the way in which (heterosexual) romantic relationships worked culturally in the South American village she lived in, said:

> I feel like a lot of developing countries are, if I could relate it back to U.S. history, like fifty years ago, and how they just have to progress from that. And it's almost like they're just behind the times. Then I feel like there's at least hope that things are going to change. And it's more—let's focus on the bigger picture, and getting the infrastructure there, so that they could eventually move towards thinking in a different way and more progressive way. Because if I just started there without all of the other infrastructure existing, it didn't make sense to them, and they didn't value that at all.

Anita explains what she feels like her place was in assisting a cultural shift in gender roles. She attempted to "focus on the bigger picture" and on "getting the infrastructure there," because if she immediately attempted to get the men in her village to marry only one woman, or allow their wives a voice, "they didn't value that at all." In her view, they were too far behind. U.S. Americans needed to help by getting the correct infrastructure in place; in other words, the culture was not going to be able to develop unless there was some structure provided to help them develop in the correct manner.

Here, unless something U.S. American was brought in, unless U.S. Americans used their exceptionality to empower the host country, the culture would remain static. Anita described this idea as providing hope that things can change. This, of course, implied that the most hoped-for situation should be the realization of the same type of development that exists in the U.S. Relegating the host country national culture to the realm of U.S.'s past allowed the volunteer to avoid having to make sense of the contradictions between the cultures, moralities, and ethics to which s/he has been exposed.

"You Just Don't Have That Same Ability": Returning American Exceptionalism Home

In an interview with a female volunteer named Robyn, who served in a South American country, she mentioned that there was something extremely special to her about her Peace Corps experience.

> I have a lot of pride in what I did. Which I had never really, you know, I've always done well in school, and really excelled at what I was doing, but I don't think that was ever something that I was super proud about, just because it wasn't—because I didn't take ownership for it. But I have so much ownership towards the community I was in, and the projects that I did, relationships that I still have with the town. I'm really proud of that. And I think sometimes I wonder if that, like, I'll never feel that again. Or if, at least, I'll always be looking for that, and if that's changed my perception on what I can accomplish....Meaning like, I wonder if I'll always be feeling a lack of—like, I'm not doing enough because you just don't have that same ability. It's such a unique experience, that you're never going to find that in anything else. Right? So, it's something that I feel really proud about having achieved, but never being able to find that again. Does that make sense?

Robyn, in summing up her experience, explained that her perception of what she has the ability to accomplish has been changed, and implied now that she has returned to the United States, she will never have the chance to accomplish so much again. She does not have "that same ability" in the U.S. Robyn believed she was able to facilitate a special kind of change with her projects in South America that she may never be able to enact in her life (that is, in the United States) again.

Connected with the discourses discussed so far, Robyn implied that she will not be able to have such amazing accomplishments in the U.S. because *there is not enough to change*. The massive impact, the accomplishments that Robyn was so proud of, could only be made in a country that is "behind," as Anita put it. When host country cultures are construed as developmentally backward, there are a variety of large changes that ostensibly need to be made before they can reach the U.S.'s level of development. Robyn can never enact that kind of change again in the U.S. because there is an assumption that the U.S. is the pinnacle of global life: in a word, exceptional.

From a volunteer

I thought long and hard about my students' problems with responsibility, choices, and goals. Perhaps, it came to me, they have such problems because they don't understand that there are decisions to be made. The answer to all things, the answer they've heard since birth, is "Mungu akipenda." If God wills. In an agrarian society, how much do you truly have control over? So much is dependent upon the rain, the soil, the sun. Will we have enough food? Mungu akipenda. Will we be able to walk to the other village today to sell vegetables? Mungu akipenda. ...Where does the ability to make decisions come to play?

...How can I dare to be frustrated when I cannot encourage them to be self-motivated? I am attempting to push them into a way of thought that runs counter to the way they've seen the world for their entire lives. I cannot change the core of their worldview. ...My words must sound like foolish noise. Their world has different rules. And how could you imagine that the world could possibly look different if you've never been outside of a single valley for your entire life? Landscape is always mountainous. Large boulders always dot the hills. It never rains from June to September. Everyone eats cassava. Everyone has black skin.

Except her...

Excerpt from an email of the author's to friends and family during Peace Corps service

---

CONCLUSION

This study examined the ways in which RPCV discourses are based in an idea of American exceptionalism. Unlike past studies that have shown how American exceptionalism is deployed to gain support for U.S. foreign policy in public discourse, this study investigated how American exceptionalism imbues day-to-day discourse. Using an intersectional lens, it demonstrates that American exception-alism is not simply a nationalist discourse, but also one that centers whiteness and masculinity through the way it is negotiated in conversation.

However, the particular experience of being a Peace Corps volunteer is also one that opens up possibilities for challenging American exceptionalism. Just as the volunteers cited throughout this piece have struggled with how to understand and express their experiences, the act of international volunteering is one that allows for meeting contradiction head-on, and challenging normative views. As Fischer (1998) describes,

> Volunteers' experiences overseas [force] them to break down the bars of the cultural prison. Their relationship with the Peace Corps leadership, their living conditions, their work, and their relationship with the people they [work] with all [convince] them to reevaluate many previously held cultural assumptions. (p. 3)

RPCV discourse can work to (re)constitute, shift, and even deconstruct the myth of American exceptionalism. The experience of living and working day-to-day for multiple years with people from a different country and culture creates opportu-nities for intense reflection on cultural presuppositions, opportunities that are not readily available to international travelers or visitors. As this study demonstrates, these opportunities often arise when facing challenges to strongly-held beliefs and assumptions. By discursively renegotiating fundamental assumptions about what relationships between the U.S. and host countries should look like, RPCV dis-course has the ability to shift conceptualizations of what it means to volunteer. If RPCV discourse truly took the contradictions inherent in American exceptionalist discourse into account, how might the relationships between volunteers and host country nationals change? What might these new partnerships look like? What could be achieved with a worldview that recognizes and privileges host country national ability and knowledge?

Such challenges and contradictions offer rich opportunities to scholars, as well. The Peace Corps is an organization based on U.S. privilege, yet it can also act to challenge privilege. Moments and spaces that display this contradiction allow scholars to investigate both the problematics and possibilities created by interna-tional volunteering.

NOTES

1. Many critical scholars consider the use of "American" as conflated with the U.S. to be problem-atic, and indicative of a U.S.-centric worldview that obscures other North American and South American populations. As this phenomenon is often related to American exceptionalist thought, I use the designation "U.S. Americans" throughout this study for consistency, sensitivity, and clarity.

2. I use "American exceptionalism" to figure U.S.–specific attitudes and ideologies in this paper. Although I am careful in other places to denote the U.S. as something which cannot be conflated with America-in-general, the phrase "American exceptionalism" is used ubiquitously in both scholarly literature and public discourse, and will be used in an unqualified manner in this study.

3. "Returned Peace Corps volunteer" or "RPCV" is the official title given by the U.S. Peace Corps to volunteers who have completed their service. Peace Corps uses "returned" instead of "former" in order to highlight the continuing work that returned volunteers do in the U.S., educating U.S. Americans about other nations and peoples.

4. It was not my intent to interview only white returned volunteers when I began this study. Rather, it happened that no volunteers of color responded to my calls for interviews.

REFERENCES

Acker, J. (2006). Inequality regimes: Gender, class, and race in organizations. *Gender & Society, 20,* 441–464.

Baines, D. (2010). Gender mainstreaming in a development project: Intersectionality in a post-colonial un-doing? *Gender, Work and Organization, 17,* 119–149.

Balaji, M. (2011). Racializing pity: The Haiti earthquake and the plight of "others." *Critical Studies in Media Communication, 28,* 50–67.

Bonilla-Silva, E. (2010). *Racism without racists: Color-blind racism & racial inequality in contemporary America.* Lanham, MD: Rowman & Littlefield.

Cloud, D. (2004). "To veil the threat of terror": Afghan women and the <clash of civilizations> in the imagery of the U.S. war on terrorism. *Quarterly Journal of Speech, 90,* 285–306.

Cobbs Hoffman, E. (1998). *All you need is love: The Peace Corps and the spirit of the 1960s.* Cambridge, MA: Harvard University Press.

Edwards, J. A. (2012). An exceptional debate: The championing of and challenge to American exceptionalism. *Rhetoric & Public Affairs, 15,* 351–367.

Fanon, F. (2004). *Wretched of the earth.* (R. Philcox, Trans.). New York, NY: Grove Press. (Original work published in 1963).

Fischer, F. (1998). *Making them like us: Peace Corps volunteers in the 1960s.* Washington, DC: Smithsonian Institute Press.

Ivie, R. L., & Giner, O. (2009). American exceptionalism in a democratic idiom: Transacting the mythos of change in the 2008 presidential campaign. *Communication Studies, 60,* 359–375.

Kapoor, I. (2008). Hyper-self-reflexive development? Spivak on representing the Third World 'Other.' *The postcolonial politics of development* (pp. 41–59). New York, NY: Routledge.

Lindlof, T. R., & Taylor, B. C. (2011). *Qualitative communication research methods.* Los Angeles, CA: Sage.

McCall, L. (2001). *Complex inequality: Gender, class, and race in the new economy.* New York, NY: Routledge.

Mohanty, C. T. (1991). Under western eyes: Feminist scholarship and colonial discourses. In C. T. Mohanty, A. Russo, & L. Torres (Eds.), *Third world women and the politics of feminism* (pp. 51–80). Bloomington, IN: Indiana University Press.

Motter, J. (2010). American exceptionalism and the rhetoric of humanitarian militarism: The case of the 2004 Indian Ocean tsunami relief effort. *Communication Studies, 61,* 507–525.

Nakayama, T. K., & Krizek, R. (1995). Whiteness: A strategic rhetoric. *Quarterly Journal of Speech, 81*, 291–309.

Ngũgĩ, W. T. (1986). *Decolonizing the mind: The politics of language in African literature.* Portsmouth, NH: Heinemann.

Norander, S., & Harter, L. M. (2012). Reflexivity in practice: Challenges and potentials of transnational organizing. *Management Communication Quarterly, 26*, 74–105.

Pal, M., & Buzzanell, P. M. (2013). Breaking the myth of Indian call centers: A postcolonial analysis of resistance. *Communication Monographs, 80*, 199–219.

Patman, R. G. (2006). Globalisation, the new US exceptionalism and the war on terror. *Third World Quarterly, 27*, 963–986.

Peace Corps. (2014). Life is calling. How far will you go? Fact sheet. *Peace Corps.* Retrieved from http://files.peacecorps.gov/multimedia/pdf/about/pc_facts.pdf

Prasad, A. (2003). The gaze of the other: Postcolonial theory and organizational analysis. In Prasad, A. (Ed.), *Postcolonial theory and organizational analysis: A critical engagement* (pp. 3–43). New York, NY: Palgrave Macmillan.

Prasad, P. (2003). The return of the native: Organizational discourses and the legacy of the ethnographic imagination. In Prasad, A. (Ed.), *Postcolonial theory and organizational analysis: A critical engagement* (pp. 149–170). New York, NY: Palgrave Macmillan.

Rojecki, A. (2008). Rhetorical alchemy: American exeptionalism and the war on terror. *Political Communication, 25*, 67–88.

Shome, R. (2000). Outing whiteness. *Critical Studies in Media Communication, 17*, 366–371.

Shome, R., & Hegde, R. S. (2002). Postcolonial approaches to communication: Charting the terrain, engaging the intersections. *Communication Theory, 12*, 249–270.

Söderlind, S. (2011). Introduction: The shining of America. In S. Söderlind & J. T. Carson (Eds.), *American exceptionalisms: From Winthrop to Winfrey* (pp. 1–14). Albany, NY: State University of New York Press.

Supriya, K. E. (2002). *Shame and recovery: Mapping identity in an Asian women's shelter.* New York, NY: Peter Lang.

Supriya, K. E. (2004). *Remembering empire: Power, memory, & place in postcolonial India.* New York, NY: Peter Lang.

West, C., & Fenstermaker, S. (2002). Doing difference. In S. Fenstermaker & C. West. (Eds.), *Doing gender, doing difference: Inequality, power, and institutional change.* New York, NY: Routledge.

Section 3:
Cross-cultural Volunteering at Home

On Equal Terms? Desired Equality AND Concealed Hierarchy IN A German-Turkish Mentoring Project

ANNA SARAH PFEIFFER
Lund University

Volunteering has often been conceptualized as an activity carried out to help or assist individuals who are considered less privileged and needy (e.g., Clary & Snyder, 1999; Van Till, 1988). Over the past three decades, however, the ideal of creating *partnership* relations has come to outshine the rhetoric of *helping* (Impey & Overton, 2013; Lewis, 1998). A partnership perspective recognizes that individuals or communities who are to be helped have assets of their own (Brett, 2003). It rejects paternalism, and instead promotes egalitarian, and participative approaches to volunteering (Baaz, 2005; Impey & Overton, 2013). Both practitioners and academics broadly support this turn to partnership, but little research explores this ideal empirically.

Against this background, this study explored the individual experiences of volunteers who were expected to facilitate such a partnership approach in an intercultural German-Turkish mentoring project. Mentoring projects are widely established in voluntary work to support young people who are deemed socially or economically marginalized (Piper & Piper, 2000; Rose & Jones, 2007). In the studied project, approximately 100 German volunteers engaged as mentors for a child with a Turkish migration background. The mentor tandems usually met once a week to pursue common activities. The German volunteers were urged to meet the Turkish children and their families on "equal terms" (in German: "auf gleicher Augenhöhe") and as "partners."

The present study explored how the ideal of creating partnership relations and equality between those who *help* (i.e., German volunteers) and those who *are helped* (i.e., Turkish immigrants) was realized in practice. It focused in particular on the challenges of achieving such an ideal. These challenges were related to an inherent paradox when partnership is suggested as an ideal state for a relationship that tends to be hierarchical in practice. That is to say, relations between a party who helps and another who is helped (i.e., a knowing mentor and learning mentee) already implies the unequal power exercise.

The study showed that even though volunteers broadly embrace the rhetoric of equality, their accounts of the volunteering experience show more complexity. Drawing on postcolonial insights, the study found that the prevailing rhetoric of partnership often concealed existing hierarchies. Hierarchical relationships are based upon deeply rooted cultural assumptions about the West brought into being essentially through communication (Grimes & Parker, 2009). The study's overall contribution was to outline challenges and encourage reflection when working with socially desirable ideals in intercultural voluntary work.

PARTNERSHIP: TOO GOOD TO BE TRUE?

Partnership approaches to human development have enjoyed growing popularity in volunteer settings (Impey & Overton, 2013; Lewis, 1998). Voluntary organizations approach various social problems (e.g., poverty, gender inequality) with the proclaimed recognition that those who are to be helped have their own capabilities (Brett, 2003). Volunteering has thus—at least rhetorically—moved gradually away from paternalistic modernist approaches to aid, which tended to have a passive and inferior view of the recipients (Impey & Overton, 2013). Instead volunteers are now supposed to enable target groups rather than educate, and to promote local involvement. Thus, the partnership era that has impacted voluntary work claims to be a participatory and egalitarian one (Contu & Girei, 2014).

There are, however, critical voices (especially in development assistance) that point to the complex dynamics when helpers engage within a partnership paradigm (e.g., Cooke & Kothari, 2001; Gomez, Corradi, Goulart, & Namara, 2010). A central point of critique is that the rhetoric of partnership does not match the practice of volunteering/development assistance where uneven power relations prevail. A prominent example is the case of mass-marketed *voluntourism*. This is a form of episodic volunteering (Lewis, 2013) where Western agencies send volunteers to African, Latin American, and Asian countries to improve local living. Even though these arrangements are often promoted as encounters on equal terms, they tend to be driven by "supply-side factors," such as the search for self-development, rather than local demand and need (Impey & Overton, 2013, p. 111; see also Mize Smith, 2013).

Critical authors argue that partnership and participation have been degraded to mere "buzzwords" (Contu & Girei, 2014, p. 205), and turned into a mainstream idea (Lewis, 1998). Donors apparently drive claims for partnership in order to legitimate the projects they designed (Brett, 2003; Impey & Overton, 2013). Moreover, while the discourse of partnership suggests mutuality, partnership arrangements may permit paternalistic helpers to push forward their interest (Baaz, 2005), create new dependencies (Cooke & Kothari, 2001), and underestimate the difficulties marginalized individuals have to access deliberative processes (Brett, 2003). Some authors go as far as to propose that partnership and participation are not neutral concepts, but managerial tools that facilitate a subtle tyranny (Cooke & Kothari, 2001) of the so-called developed world. Partnership discourses from this perspective reinforce inequality by "co-opting dissent" (Contu & Girei, 2014, p. 205).

Whether one agrees with this radical critique or not, it points to an important aspect. That is, the ability to participate on equal terms is unevenly distributed between cultural groups. Arguably, it is the "product of long historical processes" (Brett, 2003, p. 14), often involving a colonial history. The rhetoric of partnership applied in relationships where one party *helps* another may indeed smooth over long existing inequalities (Kapoor, 2008). Inequalities manifest themselves not in direct, but subtle ways, with both sides being trapped in their own past and cultural context. This study shows, for example, how German volunteers discursively reproduced established ideas about themselves (e.g., as modern civilized Westerners) and Turks (e.g. as backwards), despite the intention to meet on equal terms. To explain such a paradox, we need to understand how the communication of certain vocabulary—such as partnership, mentoring, Turkish immigrants—defines "key realities of the situation" (Ashcraft, Kuhn, & Cooren, 2009, p. 4). As shown in the next section, postcolonial thinkers bring important aspects of communication to the fore by highlighting the impact of colonial discourses, even after the end of direct colonialism.

POSTCOLONIALISM AS THEORETICAL LENS

Postcolonial theory provides a helpful lens to analyze the reproduction of stereotypes despite the prevalent partnership rhetoric. Postcolonialism is understood as a theoretical perspective that explores the continuing discriminating effects of long established "representations, reading practices, and values" nurtured by the West (McLeod, 2000, p. 5). A central argument from a postcolonial stance is that colonial discourse created certain hierarchical truths about the colonized, which continues to powerfully shape social relations (Muhr & Salem, 2013). A prominent writer who developed this argument is Edward Said (2003). He showed how an unequal dichotomy between the Orient and the Occident has been established through the representations of North Africa and the Middle East by Western colonial powers. According to Said (2003), the following distinction became taken for granted:

> On the one hand there are Westerners, and on the other there are Arab-Orientals; the former are (in no particular order) rational, peaceful, liberal, logical, capable of holding real values, without natural suspicion; the latter are none of these things. (p. 49)

In line with the above distinction, the Orient-Occident-relationship came to be seen as that "between a strong and a weak partner" (Said, 2003, p. 40). What's more, with the help of this uneven discourse, the West arguably produced the Orient as an inferior entity that needed to be civilized (Said, 2003). Hence, colonial powers continued to exert discursive power over former colonies, even after direct colonialization ended.

In voluntary sector studies, a postcolonial perspective has mostly been applied to understand volunteering in development assistance (Palacios 2010; Perold et al., 2012). It has been shown how volunteering establishes in subtle ways colonial ideas about the locals as inferior, passive and unreliable, and the Western volunteers as superior, active and reliable (Baaz, 2005). Another study revealed how Western volunteers were perceived as "being of higher economic status," and "often as a superior race" (Perold et al., 2012, p. 186). In that sense, both Westerners as well as individuals considered non-Western incorporated "the [continuously repeated] Western fantasy of the Orient" into their self-view (Bhabha, 1994, p. 95). In so doing, colonial hierarchies are kept, despite the goal of overcoming power-imbalances.

Baaz (2005) explains this paradox by showing how the boundaries between the colonizer and the colonized traditionally served to legitimize the presence of the former as the one who civilizes. Today, boundaries between the development worker and the alleged "partner" are often maintained in a similar fashion (Baaz, 2005). Thereby the presence of an expert is justified. The maintenance of boundaries, however, is not necessarily deliberate, and Baaz (2005) warns to assume that "that partnership was never intended" (p. 8). Boundaries are not created to discriminate, but they help individual volunteers constructing a meaningful identity as the omniscient who assists and advises (Baaz, 2005; Palacios 2010). Such all-knowing individual depends on the construction of unknowledgeable others. Baaz (2005) and Palacios (2010) thus point to the paradox identity dimensions in aid relations.

Discussing identity dimensions, Banerjee and Linstead (2001) also highlight the West's desire to consume the "other"–that which is strange and exotic. Take the example of Westerners going on organized hiking tours where they are promised to meet local cultures and learn about herbal medicine. In such cases often a romanticized, exoticized "other," rooted in simplistic and traditional imagery, helps

Western individuals to assume identities as superior, modern, industrialized individuals with more complex ways of life–even if the assumed characteristics may be a fantasy (Banerjee & Linstead, 2001).

Overall, postcolonial theorizing sets out to analyze and challenge established beliefs about the differing worth of human beings rooted in a colonial mindset. Postcolonial theory was used in this study of a German-Turkish mentoring project to investigate relations that are penetrated by such subtle hierarchical thinking. It assisted in examining and challenging how hierarchies are discursively maintained in contemporary society that promotes equality (Muhr & Salem, 2013). By reading the data through a post-colonial lens, this study's overall purpose was to investigate how relationships between a *helping* and a *helped* party–common in voluntary work–are vulnerable to the subtle exercise of power despite the desire for equality.

CASE DESCRIPTION: THE MENTORING PROJECT

The present investigation is based upon a three-month ethnographic study (Hammersley & Atkinson, 2007) of a German volunteer organization. The intercultural mentoring project was the organization's flagship program. It matched a German adult with a child (aged between 6 and 12 years) of Turkish decent in so-called "mentoring tandems." The project philosophy was to create partnership relations on "equal terms" between the two parties. The activities of the mentoring-tandems were intended to reflect a partnership philosophy. Common activities where both parties could explore the city, exchange their cultural practices (e.g., cooking); "play" and be with each other in trusting ways were promoted. Thus, mutuality, and activities that would boost the mentee's self-confidence were encouraged.

At the same time "integration" of the "socially disadvantaged" children was promoted. The terms related to Germany's migration history. The country experienced large scale Turkish guest worker migration in the 1960/70s during a period of economic boom (Faist, 1993). Most guest workers and their families stayed on. Even though many have found their place in a material, cultural, and political sense in German society, Turkish immigrants have still limited access to resources (e.g. language skills, social networks, capital, etc.). The term "disadvantaged" described that the children selected for the project came from poor, often traditionally oriented, religious families who were educationally disadvantaged.

Project coordinators used the terms "integration" and "disadvantaged" with care in a non-totalizing way where the capabilities of the disadvantaged were emphasized, and Germans as members of the mainstream society were reminded to open up to intercultural learning. These terms were nevertheless at odds with the project's partnership philosophy. The idea that integration could be achieved by the help of a German mentor was not easily compatible with a partnership ideal, as it constructed one way of living (i.e., German) as superior to another (i.e., Turkish). The way in which the project was explained and promoted was therefore already imbued with tensions.

METHODS

As an ethnography, the research was exploratory and interpretative in nature (Silverman, 2013). I conducted the study as part of my doctoral project focused on volunteers' experiences of recognition. I volunteered in the above-described mentoring project. This is in line with the ethnographer's goal to have prolonged contact in the field in order to account for local meanings (Prasad, 2005). I became the assistant of the project leader, and worked on project-related issues (e.g., volunteer recruitment). My engagement had the character of a full-time job. This helped me to gain a deep understanding of the project's philosophy (i.e., partnership), the project's administration, and its people. In addition to participant observations, the fieldwork included: twelve interviews with voluntary mentors, three interviews with project facilitators (all interviews were open-ended and lasted between 50 and 200 minutes), one focus group with mentors on intercultural challenges, and the study of various organizational documents (e.g., brochures, e-mails). All interviews—the study's main data-source—were transcribed and consequently translated from German to English.

A first analysis of the collected data by constant comparison method (Glasser & Strauss, 1967) drew my attention to the tension between the project's prominently repeated objective to create partnership relations and the volunteers' stories that revealed existing inequalities. Being attentive to sameness and difference in my data, I developed broad themes that reflected this tension in the mentors' accounts. Those themes were for instance: "assuming/rejecting a superior identity position," "reproducing/rejecting stereotypical representations of the Turkish immigrant population in Germany," and "promoting/rejecting integration as a project goal."

Based upon the inductive, grounded-theory like development of broad themes (Glaser & Strauss, 1967), the guiding research questions for this study materialized. Namely: How are relationships between a *helping* and a *helped* party—common in voluntary work—vulnerable to the subtle exercise of power despite the desire for equality? Further processing my data in light of this question, I refined my analysis by deductively applying a postcolonial framework. Following the hypothesis that the mentors' approaches to volunteering are potentially shaped by hierarchical colonial discourses, I further analyzed their accounts with the help of the following questions:

- How did German volunteers talk about their mentoring role? Did they attempt to educate, integrate, or civilize their Turkish counterpart?
- How did German volunteers talk about the Turkish side? Which common stereotypes about the Turkish immigrants in Germany were discursively reproduced or resisted?
- How did German mentors talk about partnership and equality? What notions of superiority and inferiority were discursively evoked?

Given space limitations and my goal to provide in-depth empirical insights, I focus upon the stories of three key volunteers. Their stories are presented as vignettes that encapsulate contrasting answers to the above questions present in my entire data. The individuals selected thus reflect the broad spectrum of volunteers' approaches to partnership in intercultural voluntary work.

Finally, I want to add that my representation of the volunteers may create a somewhat distorted picture because both vignette number one and two focus on how easily volunteers fall into the trap of reproducing stereotypes. It is important to emphasize that the danger to fall into the trap, as well as the active battling of this trap (as shown in vignette number three) were equally present in my data, perhaps the active battling even more. As I am interested in bringing the challenges of partnership to the fore, I decided to emphasize the morally problematic cases.

FINDINGS

To highlight how volunteers grapple with the partnership ideal, three vignettes were chosen as vivid examples of how partnership, even when explicitly embraced, is endangered by efforts to "educate," "coach," and "integrate" (terms used by mentors) the assumingly needy party. However, the vignettes are also examples of how partnership can be practiced to some extent based upon curiosity and self-reflection.

Idealistic Partnership: "We Enrich One Another Equally"

Claire is a successful career-woman who decided to participate in the project as "it was based on equality." She and her own family wanted to "learn about Turkish facets," and Claire was eager to highlight the close connection between both families:

> This relation with the [Turkish] is not only about me giving something, but I believe that you get something back....We enrich one another equally, and in the meantime this has resulted in a friendship.

Here she embraces the project's philosophy of equality and mutuality. Claire accentuated how much she learned from her mentee Leila and from Ayse (Leila's mother), such as "caring for four children" and "cooking for the whole group plus six guests." However, Claire also clarified that in her daily life—packed with job/ family obligations and engagements in various social, sporty, and charitable activities—she did not have the time to be a housewife.

Despite the rhetoric of mutuality, some one-sidedness became noticeable in Claire's story. This was connected to the theme of integration. Claire said that she liked the project as it was "about children who are to be integrated into German everyday life." She saw the task of integration to be primarily that of the Germans, saying that "ultimately it is *us* [Claire's emphasis] who need to open doors." Claire enjoyed "teaching children" and portrayed herself as a legitimate representative of a German society into which the *others* were to be integrated. Claire described her efforts:

> They [the Turkish family] were all born and raised here, went to German kindergartens, German schools and so on. But they have mostly contact amongst each other, cause there's nieces, nephews, cousins, and whatnot! For them it is the best thing in the world to sit together and eat....My mentee girl Leyla does therefore not have many insights into German families. So when we started to meet...I wanted to get her out of there....It was important to me that Leyla goes with us to the theatre, the museum...that she does things that we do with our family. Like baking Christmas cookies and so on.

The quote highlights how Claire took on the role of a cultural coach. Claire added that one of her "biggest achievements" was to facilitate a sports camp for Leyla during the summer vacations. She saw the need for encouraging this "since Leyla is a bit sweet-loving." At her Turkish home, there was arguably too much food, and too little care for the body. As the Turkish family had "quite different priorities with respect to child education," Claire did not only coach Leyla, but also her mother, for example, by advising her to not let the television run constantly in the background.

Claire's coaching stories highlight a stark contrast between her life and that of the Turkish family. Implicitly, she represented her own lifestyle as more desirable. That is, the lifestyle as a busy, emancipated, educated, culturally interested, both family- and career-oriented, healthy, and socially engaged woman. Claire assigned to herself a broad range of attributes associated with so-called modern, capitalist, and complex Western societies. She presented a counterpart to the Turkish family, which she depicted in terms of established clichés (e.g., they eat and cook a lot, they are living in big patriarchic family clans), and arguably as members of backward/inferior cultural group, despite the rhetoric of equality.

Having gotten to know Claire during my fieldwork, I had the impression that she had a genuine interest in establishing equal relationships with the Turkish family. She was passionate about her work, and did not seem aware of how she implicitly belittled the other party. I also believe that there was a relationship of mutual care with the Turkish family. Yet, it proved difficult in the interview to extract what precisely Claire was learning and/or getting back from the Turkish family. Even though she emphasized to gain "extremely valuable insights" into Turkish culture, she did not give examples that would specify that value. This made the talk of mutuality and equality sound empty at times. For instance, the value of learning to "cook" and "host people" becomes problematic, as those examples suggest (Turkish) backwardness in terms of gender relations.

Overall, Claire's vignette illustrates how volunteers–despite demonstrating goodwill to help others–may fall into the trap of reproducing stereotypes that imply Western superiority. It also raises the question how or whether at all equal partnership relations and the goal of integration are compatible within a mentoring framework. Claire's partnership account is labeled "idealistic" because she aimed at fulfilling a popular ideal of volunteering. Yet, in striving for a very ambitious–perhaps overly ambitious–partnership ideal that would *also* facilitate the mentee's integration, she seemed to have lost sense of true equality.

Simulated Partnership: "Of Course This Is Not At Eye Level"

Herbert depicted himself as an achiever and a doer. A successful career at a multinational corporation helped him to leave his working class background behind. Herbert repeatedly mentioned his present upper-class lifestyle that included a fancy suburban villa and a "cool car." Overall, Herbert told the narrative of a happy, active, hard-working, self-made man, who was in the position to help another party through his voluntary engagement. About his motivation to volunteer he said:

> I found this charming, the fact that it is possible to do something here *to promote integration*. I have to say that *I have really gotten some insights into a completely different class*: so this is a family that receives social aid…, and getting an in-depth impression of how they live is quite an experience. (emphasis added)

Like Claire, Herbert embraced the goal of integration. He also saw himself as a legitimate German representative and presented his own lifestyle in stark contrast to that of the Turkish family. Not only above, where he suggests a "completely different" class belonging, but also several other stories revealed the contrasts Herbert saw. Where Herbert described himself as someone who "has a great life" and a "great career," he described the mentee's father as "a relatively weak person" who is "ill a lot, who also does not have a permanent job and [pauses] who is not in the position to educate his child." The mother of Ahmed (his mentee-boy) was described as tougher, "even though she cannot read and write." Herbert admitted that both Turkish parents were "good willing." Yet he did not see them as capable to give his mentee boy the "assistance to make it in [German] society."

To help Ahmed "make it" was therefore the central goal of Herbert's engagement. In his "coach role," Herbert taught Ahmed upper-class jargon as well as table manners, which Ahmed arguably did not have:

> Ahmed now fully mastered to eat spaghetti. I teach this by saying for example, "my children always have to do this, and now you have to do this too." And then, of course, he gets back home, and when he sits at the table, his parents will probably say: "How come you now eat so weird, so finicky." I believe that this... might also be helpful, because after all, at your university, you will also sometimes see people–depending, of course, on the educational level–who eat like this [leans forward, simulates bad table manners]. If you behave like that in certain professions, you have no chance.

Herbert appeared to enjoy his role as a benevolent advisor who transmitted superior cultural knowledge, not only to Ahmed but also his parents. He advised them in educational matters, concerning "pocket money, breakfast rituals." or about "reading books at night" to the children. Herbert elaborated:

> Every once in a while I ask the family to have a cup of tea. I say, "Well your wife makes such a good tea, let's have a cup again." So we sit together, chit-chat a bit while the boy is present.... We talk about this and that, like the school-grades. The man is the one who mostly speaks with me. The wife sits silently there, sometimes also a bit lower than the man.

Herbert's depiction of his relation to Ahmed and his family are problematic from a partnership perspective. Other than Claire, who claimed equality at least rhetorically, Herbert depicted the other side fairly straightforwardly as culturally backwards (i.e., the silent wife), uncultivated (i.e., no eating manners), uneducated (i.e., analphabetic), weak and unmotivated (i.e., unemployed). In so doing, Herbert established an obvious hierarchy, as these negatively connoted attributes were diametrically opposed to his self-presentation.

In a later stage of the interview, Herbert admitted openly that due to the extreme differences, he tried to "maintain distance" between him and the family, for example by keeping up the German formal address. He added:

> ...well, how can I say that, *of course this is not at eye level, and I try to cover this up as best as possible.* So, it is like this: if you now have a professor, you don't talk to him at eye level. (emphasis added)

Thus, according to Herbert, an equal relationship could never be achieved between the Turkish family and himself who–just like a professor–was in a higher position.

The vignette of Herbert illustrates a similar but more explicit tension with the partnership ideal as Claire's case. His partnership account is labeled "simulated" as Herbert covered up for the admitted lack of equality. Nevertheless, Herbert emphasized a mutual learning process. He mentioned how getting in contact with "a family that is part of a level of society with which you never have contact" was "quite instructive." He emphasized that he "learned a lot" in this relation. Thus, even though Herbert emphasized the intricacies of partnership (i.e., that equality is unrealistic), he held on to the ideal in some ways (i.e., "I learn so much"). What Herbert described as "learning" seemed, however, to be more of a confirmation of his own superior status based on "experiencing" the "other" world. This raises questions such as: What does the "learning" that most mentees referred to actually consists of? What function does the emphasis on learning serve if it does not materialize in practice? These questions will be addressed in the discussion, following the third vignette.

Reflexive Partnership: "I Don't Have This Helpers' Syndrome"

Laura, director of a sheltered workshop, described her lifestyle as very "privileged." She was thrilled by the project's philosophy of equality, and described this as the reason for choosing the mentoring project:

> I thought: yes, that's it!…Away from this picture, "oh there are some poor people and you have to support them." And instead: yeah, just be there for other people. And just do something with them together, in a normal way. And thereby break barriers that exist between different groups.

Laura wanted to connect to people who lived under less privileged circumstances. Similarly to Herbert and Claire, Laura described her affluent background during the interview. But she presented this as a matter of "having been lucky" rather than the result of working harder or leading a better life than others. Accordingly, she did not see herself as being in the position to facilitate integration (in fact, she did not use that term at all), or to be a "helper" and "role model." She added, "I don't have this helper's syndrome, that I feel I need to help someone. I simply wanted to do something I haven't done before." The quote suggests that Laura saw the project as an opportunity to extend her own horizon. Thus, the notion of learning entered the picture. Laura emphasized "learning from the other" as crucial for "breaking open cultural barriers."

She described various encounters in her voluntary engagement that fostered mutual learning, partly by experiencing culture shocks. A vivid example is Laura's description of her first meeting with the Turkish family:

> Laura: At this first encounter, all the stereotypes of mine where I was convinced I did not have them came through! [Laughs out loud] I mean most of us think we're very liberal and enlightened… no? And when I came into this family…I sat opposite to a woman with a headscarf, she was pretty veiled [Laura makes scared noise] and a

man–the dad–who looked at me in such a mean way. I thought immediately "Oh god…I wanna get out of here!" This was somehow my defence reaction, against the head-scarf. …But already during the talk this broke open. Anna: How did this "break open"? Laura: Well, I did not feel comfortable…and there was a lot of resistance inside me. But…I was also very interested in them….I have always many questions. And I approached these three…in an open way, just being myself and curious as usual. And yeah, then I realized how this situation opened up somehow. Especially with the mother who is a very amazing person. Anna: What changed? How did you realize this? Laura: The looks changed. Yeah, the way that the mother looked at me all of a sudden. She is an open woman. All of a sudden, also this headscarf seemed different; it was gone all of a sudden. I did not see it anymore, but I saw her beautiful eyes and her beautiful hair shining through beneath the headscarf.…The dad sat there in the same fashion throughout. Later I learned that he was very much against this project, it was an initiative from his wife.

In the description of their first encounter, Laura admitted negative feelings towards attributes she associated with male domination and backwardness of the other culture (e.g., angry-looking man, headscarf). However, by remaining "curious" and "open," and learning about the other (e.g., that the allegedly suppressed veiled mother was the one who did the talking, and who initiated the encounter), these cultural symbols took on a different meaning. Arguably, self-reflection about how deeply stereotypes were embedded in her thinking helped her to overcome these to a certain extent.

Laura reflexively approached the project's goal of building up a partnership relation on equal terms. In her first meetings with Umut (her mentee boy), she let him determine their activities, and made the conscious decision to stay in his environment, rather than taking him to "her" world. She spent the first meetings in his room:

His room is a mini-room. There is a bed, and then there's his desk, and on top of that is his Wii [the Nintendo computer game]. Our first activity was to play Wii. I asked him: "What do you play there? Show this to me. And I will later also show you what is important to me." And then I really played Wii for 3 hours. I was knocked out afterwards.

Even though playing computer games was not Laura's number one choice of pedagogic activity, she immersed herself into the game. In that sense, Laura did not launch a cultural education initiative (e.g., reading educative books, going to the museum), but tried as she said "to simply be there" for her mentee and learn from him–in that case how to play computer games.

She said that in this simple way of being with each other, conversations about "important things in life" took place. For example, Laura described how she discovered what Umut learned in the Koran school, that it was "not that indoctrinated as one would expect." Laura also engaged in discussions about religion with Umut's mother, who had become a "friend" of hers, and who had changed her "view about what religion meant." Laura expressed several times a deep respect for the worldview and way of being of Umut's mother, demonstrating good knowledge about the mother's personal background.

Laura's initial explicit recognition of the other party's value, which turned established ideas about her role as the superior, knowledgeable mentor upside-down, seemed to form an important precondition for her version of equality and mutuality-based partnership. That is to say, only by lowering her own status first, and positively discriminating the other party, she felt ready to engage in a relation of mutual give and take. Eventually Laura also "gave" explanations about her German life-style, her relation to religion, her view on the importance of learning at school, and so on—and in that sense became a mentor to Umut in a conventionally understood way.

Overall, Laura's vignette sketches how relations on equal terms may be practiced. It seems that by reflexively encountering her own stereotypes, and by taking a more humble position towards intercultural encounters, a partnership between the involved parties developed. Also the notion of learning is more explicit in Laura's case—as in "learning to play a new game," and "learning about religion." This last, arguably successful, partnership relation is labelled "reflexive" as self-reflection was arguably a key aspect for its development.

DISCUSSION

All three vignettes show how the partnership-ideal is commonly drawn upon. The vignettes, however, also indicate how volunteers of the same project conceptualize partnership differently. Claire's "idealistic" and ambitious account of partnership seemed to essentially encompass three notions. Namely, *equality* (i.e., Claire embracing the philosophy of "equal terms"), *mutual learning* (i.e., gaining "extremely valuable insights" into Turkish culture), and *integration* (i.e., Claire wanting to "open doors"). Herbert emphasized only two of those notions when admitting to "simulate" equality. Thus, his account of *mutual learning* (i.e., learning through experiencing contrasting worlds), and *integration* (i.e., helping his mentee "to make it") was his way of realizing the project's partnership ideal. Lastly, Laura strived for *equality* (i.e., letting Umut determine their activities), and *mutual learning* (i.e., about religion). However, *integration* was not part of her "reflexive" partnership concept.

From a volunteer:

I was a bit afraid of Christmas. I did not feel comfortable about this topic, as it is not a Muslim feast. So I always tried to avoid talking about Christmas. And then we had the 23rd of December. I got a call from my mentee, asking me to come over. I told them, well it's the 23rd. I was actually quite busy before Christmas... I had literally no time. "You MUST come" they insisted. So I said, OK, then I'll come over now. I got there and the Turkish family had this little present prepared for me. I had to sit down and he [the mentee] said to me "I want to give you something for Christmas." When I opened the package I saw a cup with a picture of my favorite music band. I was deeply touched. What followed was a very intense conversation about the meaning of these festivities. I asked them: "But for you Christmas does not mean anything, no? Why are you doing this?" And they answered: "But for YOU it has a meaning!" I felt a deep recognition of my person in this moment.

Laura about her voluntary engagement as a mentor

The vignettes thus highlight how the meaning of the prominent partnership ideal is far from straightforward in the practice of volunteering. It is understood and practiced differently. The different meanings that partnership takes on are shaped and negotiated in joint communication processes (see Ashcraft, Kuhn & Cooren, 2009), which cannot be controlled by the respective voluntary organization. The diverse attributes assigned to the partnership ideal opens tensions through which the mentors manoeuvred with partly paradoxical consequences.

Integration Versus Equality/Mutual Learning

The described relationships between mentors and Turkish families revealed a major tension between mutual learning and equality on the one hand, and the goal of integration on the other. Arguably, mutuality and equality were impaired when volunteers explicitly aimed at the integration of their mentees, and vice versa. Vignette three shows this quite nicely. Laura did not attempt to integrate her mentee into her world. Her way of being with Umut and his family came closest to a participatory and egalitarian ideal of partnership (Brett, 2003; Impey & Overton, 2013). As opposed to Claire, Laura did not attempt to take Umut *out* of his environment, but rather immersed herself *into* his life, his religion, etc. Thereby she signalled that his and his family's way of being was of equal worth to hers.

Claire and Herbert's vignettes showed how both intended to combine relations of mutuality and (in Claire's case) equality with the goal of integration. However, the former aspects were partly sacrificed in the name of the latter. Herbert and Claire's vignettes suggest that their mentees lost their voice to a certain extent, as they were pressed into an allegedly enlightened Western society in which children learned proper table manners and engaged in sports. The proclaimed partnership relations became asymmetrical in practice (Baaz, 2005; Cooke & Kothari, 2001; Contu & Girei, 2014) as both Claire and Herbert promoted their Western lifestyle as the superior blueprint for a fulfilled, advanced, successful, worthy life. Despite the good intent to establish mutuality in terms of letting themselves be shaped and challenged by the other, such reciprocal imprinting rarely took place. Both could not give concrete examples of how they learned from their counterpart. Instead, established stereotypical representations in German society of "the Turks" as a migrant group were reproduced. Namely as a group that is backwards in terms of gender relations *(the woman makes tea, but does not speak)*, eating manners *(they eat a lot, perhaps too much)*, family bonds *(they're just hanging out in big family clans)*, body-care *(they don't do sports)*, or literacy and education *(they don't go to the museum or read good books)*.

Interestingly, even though there was considerable rhetorical difference in terms of how Claire and Herbert reflected upon equality, they both seemed to practice a similar version of integration-based partnership that left little room for an encounter on equal terms. Those two cases that rhetorically are so contrasting thus highlight how the subtle stereotypical thinking in Claire's case can result in similar power-inequalities like a direct embracement of hierarchy by Herbert. Post-colonial thought, where the more implicit and often unknowing power-relations are brought to the fore, supports this observation.

A postcolonial reading of the data suggests that partnership lost its original egalitarian meaning when the volunteers portrayed individuals of Turkish descent as an entity that needed to be integrated into German society—or in other words be "civilized" (Said, 2003, p. 3). It can be argued that false hierarchical truths of Western superiority impacted how voluntary helpers of the mentoring project saw themselves, their task, as well as the oriental Turkish other (Muhr & Salem, 2013). The mentoring framework of the project seemed to enhance inequality between both parties against the intention of the project facilitators. It brought an assumingly knowing and an ignorant party who needed to be helped into being (Baaz, 2005; Perold et al., 2010).

Overall, it could be argued that the goal of partnership-based integration (as promoted by Herbert and Claire) is unachievable in practice. Even when a careful version of integration is promoted, and when integration is officially seen as subordinated to partnership, this may be turned around in practice with partnership becoming subordinated to the goal of integration, and hence turning into empty rhetoric. This leads to the conclusion that partnership relations and the goal of integration are hardly compatible within a mentoring framework.

Identity Dimensions of a Partnership Discourse

If we agree that at times partnership is empty rhetoric, the question emerges why it was so prominently emphasized by volunteers in relation to their engagement. As highlighted earlier, the notion of *mutual learning* is of particular interest here. Even though Herbert and Claire continuously stressed that they learned so much from the Turkish families, this alleged learning rarely had an admiring undertone. What Herbert and Claire described as "learning" (e.g. to cook and host many people, learning about life in a lower social class) seemed to be mainly the insight that their life without poverty, or big family clans was somehow preferable. It can therefore be argued that the rhetoric of partnership and mutual learning also served the function of securing their own identities, as is explained next.

One could ask, what motivated volunteers to stress learning aspects of their engagement in terms of experiencing the Turkish families through attributes opposed to their self-view (e.g., unemployment, poverty, pre-modern family bonds, patriarchic gender relations)? Or differently put: What is "quite instructive" about getting in touch with people from another "level of society" (Herbert)? One answer is that volunteers' interest in learning about the other in an intercultural project can be alternatively conceptualized as a desire to "consume an exotic pre-industrial otherness" through their voluntary engagement (Banerjee & Linstead, 2001, p. 700). The cases of Herbert and Claire have shown how volunteers received a peculiar satisfaction from experiencing Turkish otherness in predetermined, and exoticized forms (e.g., the servant woman who prepares tea). This is not to say that intercultural learning was completely absent. The point is that in following the discourse of learning—as an important element of partnership—and applying it to their volunteering experiences, individuals *also* constructed their identities as modern individuals. These identities, arguably, were based on romanticized and partly simplified imaginaries of the Turkish families (see Banerjee & Linstead, 2001; Bhabha, 1994).

Arguably, the satisfaction individuals derived from encountering predetermined images does not align with a proclaimed desire for partnership. It prevented an encounter on "equal terms" as self-worth was derived from subtly depicting the other as inferior. Herbert's vignette exemplifies this. Comparing his own affluent life to that of the Turkish family, and becoming their coach, showed him even more how he has "made it," and how potent he was as opposed to the assumingly impotent other. Thus, rather than learning concretely with or about the Turkish other (as in Laura's case), the discourse of mutual learning fostered the maintenance of boundaries between both parties. These boundaries served partly as a justification for the mentors' presence. Arguably, they assisted them in constructing meaningful identities of themselves as the all-knowing whose advice is needed (Baaz, 2005; Palacios, 2010).

Nothing but an Empty Buzzword?

It could be argued that the partnership discourse in volunteering runs the danger of reproducing unequal relationships by smoothing over subtle stereotyping that are not in line with the very idea of partnership (Cooke & Kothari, 2001; Contu & Girei, 2014). Arguably, the way in which volunteering becomes essentially a project of the self, delimits openness and curiosity towards the other–an important precondition to meet on equal terms. In that sense, one could align with the critics of the partnership discourse dismissing it as an empty "buzzword" (Contu & Girei, 2014).

However, in pointing out the subtle exercise of power, the argument made here is not that partnership was never intended (Baaz, 2005). Generally, the mentors did not purposefully maintain boundaries and hierarchies (Herbert's case presents an extreme case). Claire's commitment to partnership, which was reflected in the great majority of the interviews, was arguably honest or true to the extent that one can say this about interview statements. Thus, the argument is not that the emptiness of partnership served the conscious goal of concealing a Western civilization project, or that of identity boosting. Instead, it seemed that hierarchy slipped in as volunteers grappled with the paradox of being the knowing mentor, who was expected to facilitate partnership relations, and in some way to contribute to integration. The problem, perhaps, is that a mentoring framework by definition places more responsibility on the mentors' shoulders, and neglects the stake the counterpart (i.e., the mentees, their families) has in creating encounters on equal terms.

It is therefore too simple to accuse the volunteers of exerting power over the Turkish families. Instead, it is important to keep the complex and often paradoxical constellations in mind under which volunteers engage in projects aimed at enhancing intercultural dialogue and understanding. Those constellations are never free of historically established uneven power-relations. As shown, these power relations are brought into being through language, which means, however, that they can, like in Laura's case, also be communicatively re-negotiated (Ashcraft, Kuhn, & Cooren, 2009). In the present study, inequality was partly rooted in a general notion of Western superiority, and the specific German-Turkish history of guest worker migration. Yet, as the vignette of Laura has shown, relations of equality can be established to a certain extent if one's own stereotypes are actively encountered, and when an interest in the other prevails.

CONCLUSION

By an in-depth discussion of volunteers' accounts of their experiences, the study has drawn attention to common challenges experienced in intercultural voluntary work settings, such as the challenge to live up to the ideal of equality and partnership while assisting another person. The study has shown how volunteers' efforts to establish self-worth through volunteering may partly run against the establishment of partnership relations and intercultural learning. These challenges were, however, not discussed to personally critique volunteers or the limits of their voluntary goodwill. Rather, the empirical descriptions aimed to highlight how easy it is to fall into commonly established notions of the enlightened "West" versus the backwards "non-West".

By focusing on the communicative aspect of volunteering, the study has shown how discourses of mentoring create tensions, which in turn may impair collaborative relationships. A communication lens thus helps us to make sense of how subtle stereotyping occurs and its powerful consequences. It also raises the question if and how communication can help to deal with the paradoxes of voluntary work in general and those of mentoring in specific. That is to say, by shifting the discourses of volunteering to acknowledge and embrace tensions as an "everyday experience" (Ashcraft & Trethewey, 2004, p. 174), voluntary organizations may be better prepared to assist volunteers maneuver through possible paradoxes. In line with this, the study has hopefully shed more light on the paradoxes of grand ideals (such as the one of partnership) in volunteering, as well as on how relations on equal terms can be achieved–if only momentarily–in voluntary work.

REFERENCES

Ashcraft, K. L., Kuhn, T.R., & Cooren, F. (2009). Constitutional amendments: "Materializing" organizational communication. *The Academy of Management Annals, 3*, 1–64.

Ashcraft, K. L., & Trethewey, A. (2004). Developing tension: An agenda for applied research on the organization of irrationality. *Journal of Applied Communication Research, 32*, 171–181.

Baaz, M. (2005). *The paternalism of partnership: A postcolonial reading of identity in development aid.* London: Zed Books.

Banerjee, S. B., & Linstead, S. (2001). Globalization, multiculturalism and other fictions: Colonialism for the new millennium? *Organization, 8*, 683–722.

Bhabha, H. K. (1994). *The location of culture.* London: Routledge.

Brett, E. A. (2003). Participation and accountability in development management. *The Journal of Development Studies, 40*, 1–29.

Clary, E. G., & Snyder, M. (1999). The motivations to volunteer: Theoretical and practical considerations. *Current Directions in Psychological Science, 8*, 156–159.

Contu, A., & Girei, E. (2014). NGOs management and the value of 'partnerships' for equality in international development: What's in a name? *Human Relations, 67*, 205–232.

Cooke, B., & Kothari, U. (Eds.). (2001). *Participation: The new tyranny?* London: Zed Books.

Faist, T. (1993). From school to work: Public policy and underclass formation among young Turks in Germany during the 1980s. *International Migration Review, 27*, 306–331.

Glaser, B. G., & Strauss, A. (1967). *The discovery of grounded theory: Strategies for qualitative research.* Chicago: Aldine.

Grimes, D. S., & Parker, P. S. (2009). Imagining organizational communication as a decolonizing project: In conversation with Broadfoot, Munshi, Mumby, and Stohl. *Management Communication Quarterly, 22*, 502–511.

Hammersley, M., & Atkinson, P. (2007). *Ethnography: Principles in practice.* New York: Routledge.

Impey, K., & Overton, J. (2013). Developing partnerships: The assertion of local control of international development volunteers in South Africa. *Community Development Journal, 49*, 111–128.

Kapoor, I. (2008). *The postcolonial politics of development.* New York: Routledge.

Lewis, D. J. (1998). Interagency partnerships in aid-recipient countries: Lessons from an aquaculture project in Bangladesh. *Nonprofit and Voluntary Sector Quarterly, 27*, 323–338.

Lewis, L. K. (2013). An introduction to volunteers. In Kramer, M.W. Kramer, L.K. Lewis, & L.M. Gossett (Eds.), *Volunteering and communication: Studies from multiple contexts*, (pp. 1–22). New York: Peter Lang.

McLeod, J. (2000). *Beginning postcolonialism.* Manchester: Manchester University Press.

Mize Smith, J. (2013). Volunteer tourists: The identity and discourse of travelers combining largesse and leisure. In M. W. Kramer, L. K. Lewis, & L. M. Gossett, (Eds.), *Volunteering and communication: Studies from multiple contexts*, (pp. 189–209). New York: Peter Lang.

Muhr, S. L., & Salem, A. (2013). Specters of colonialism—illusionary equality and the forgetting of history in a Swedish organization. *Management & Organizational History, 8*, 62–76.

Palacios, C. M. (2010). Volunteer tourism, development and education in a postcolonial world: Conceiving global connections beyond aid. *Journal of Sustainable Tourism, 18*, 861–878.

Perold, H., Graham, L. A., Mavungu, E. M., Cronin, K., Muchemwa, L., & Lough, B. J. (2013). The colonial legacy of international voluntary service. *Community Development Journal, 48*, 179–196.

Piper, H., & Piper, J. (2000). Disaffected young people as the problem. Mentoring as the solution. Education and work as the goal. *Journal of Education and Work, 13*, 77–94.

Prasad, P. (2005). *Crafting qualitative research: Working in the postpositivist traditions.* New York: M. E. Sharpe.

Rose, R., & Jones, K. (2007). The efficacy of a volunteer mentoring scheme in supporting young people at risk. *Emotional and Behavioural Difficulties, 12*, 3–14.

Said, E. (2003). *Orientalism.* London: Penguin.

Silverman, D. (2013). *Doing qualitative research: A practical handbook.* Thousand Oaks, CA: Sage.

Van Til, J. (1988). *Mapping the third sector: Voluntarism in a changing social economy.* New York: Foundation Center.

CHAPTER FOURTEEN

Organizing FOR Social Justice: Serving THE Needs OF Bhutanese Refugees IN Atlanta, Georgia

RATI KUMAR
Central Connecticut State University

MOHAN J. DUTTA
National University of Singapore

A major humanitarian crisis of this decade, the Syrian refugee exodus in the wake of civil war, escalated to over 2 million people in 2013 (CNN, 2013), refocusing the dire need for refugee assistance. Additionally, United Nations statistics at the end of 2012 show 15.4 million refugees worldwide, ranging from countries in South Asia, the Middle East as well as Africa (UNHCR, 2013), demonstrating the spectrum of refugee needs, not isolated to a single population.

Stepping into the role of humanitarian assistant, various UN signatory countries have continually participated in the process of refugee resettlement—which now forms one of the pillars of the international refugee protection system. Within this gamut of support, "two-thirds of all resettled refugees are taken in by the United States" (United Nations, 2013). Recognizing the UN definition of refugees as persons who have crossed national borders due to a "well-founded fear of being persecuted for reasons of race, religion, nationality, membership in a particular social group, or political opinion" (UN General Assembly, 1950, Article 1), the United States has played an active role in refugee resettlement. With the arrival of almost 75,000 refugees (of which about 14,000 were from Bhutan) in 2009 alone (Office of Refugee Resettlement, 2011), the United States has since 1975 resettled approximately 2.6 million refugees, after the enactment of the Refugee Act of 1980. A vast network of voluntary agencies and non-governmental organizations are catering to this huge refugee population, sometimes supplementing, and often times leading, the rehabilitation initiatives for these refugees (Office of Refugee Resettlement, 2013).

A majority of this support is provided through volunteer members of aforementioned agencies (Catholic Charities, 2013; International Rescue Committee, 2013; Church World Service, 2013; U.S. Committee for Refugees and Immigrants, 2013) who, despite their laudatory participation in the resettlement assistance structure, beginning in the 1970's (Office of Refugee Resettlement, 2013), are part of a network, now considered "ripe for reform" (Bruno, 2011). In addition to the logistical issues of this program such as taking a "one size fits all" approach to varied refugees populations (Migration Policy Institute, 2011, p. 7), many scholars question the nature of the capacity building enterprise being carried out extensively by non-governmental agencies. Korten (1990), Eade (2007), Dutta and Pal (2010), and Hulme and Edwards (1997) critique the nature of NGO operations as being inherently designed to retain power themselves by espousing a neoliberal[1] agenda, thus undermining the true nature of voluntary assistance to vulnerable communities. Furthermore, there is an undeniably intimate relationship between NGOs, market, and state forces, particularly when NGOs operate as government subcontractors for tasks such as refugee resettlement (Wood, 1997). Scholars like Spivak (1998), position the role of such neoliberal enterprises as fundamentally imperial entities, reinforcing colonial logic, denying the possibility of discourse with the subaltern—which in this context are represented by the voices of marginalized populations such as refugees. In volunteer micro-practices, this translates to an emphasis on contractual obligations in the workplace, to the exclusion of other social values (Harvey, 2005), leading to the othering of refugees by situating them as clients and volunteers as caseworkers, and engaging in top-down communicative practices.

Thus, while these volunteer resources unquestionably provide support to the resettlement process, there is a need to be circumspect and critically analyze the discourse within these support structures, in an attempt to better aid the refugees through volunteer services, which closely meet the community's needs, and also safeguard volunteer practices from becoming co-opted by a neoliberal agenda. During such inquiry, questions at the forefront should be: What are the interplays of power and control in the organizing processes of nongovernmental organizations that position themselves as serving refugees? What are the discourses through which the staff and volunteers of such organizations construct the recipients of their services and their relationships with these recipients? In the articulation of such issues, there is a need to critically analyze the major network of volunteers and their agencies, which often provide the primary support structure for these resettled refugees.

In doing so, this study used a predominantly critical lens, focusing on the issue of marginalization through imperial colonization, particularly as it relates to understanding volunteers' and staff members' negotiations about the recipients of their services, and their communicative framing about the needs of these recipients. The backdrop of this inquiry is the Bhutanese refugee community, which was primarily resettled in the Metropolitan Atlanta area in the southern state of Georgia in the United States. Using the culture-centered approach (CCA) as the theoretical framework, this analysis emphasizes the chasms in communication during voluntary assistance, resulting from traditionally expertise based volunteer services (Dutta & Pal, 2007). In utilizing CCA, the scholar's primary interest is to "engage the margins with the goal of creating spaces for listening to the margins, as well as for creating possibilities for transforming the globalization processes that continually participate in the creation of the margins, and in the enactment of violence on the margins" (Dutta, 2008, p. 2) by engaging the tenets of culture, structure and agency.

The next section explains the backdrop of the study, from the Bhutanese exodus to resettlement in the United States, specifically examining the results of the interviews with volunteers working at the grassroots level of the resettlement initiative. This is followed by the critical analysis and discussion of the implications of the findings for bridging miscommunication gaps between the volunteer services and the refugee needs, suggesting improvements to the volunteering process in the resettlement community.

From Bhutan to the United States

Bhutan is one of the smallest countries of the Indian subcontinent, though thinly populated, has great ethnic diversity, with as many as four main ethnic categories: Ngalong in the west, the central Bhutanese, the Sharchop in the east, and the Lhotshampa or "Nepali Bhutanese" in the south. A commonly made distinction in the country is that between the Buddhist "Drukpas" of northern Bhutan and the often Hindu, Nepali-speaking, "Lhotshampas" or southern Bhutanese (Hutt, 2005), who migrated from Nepal and India to Bhutan between 1865 and 1930 (Hutt, 2003, p. 24).

Traditionally an absolute monarchy, Bhutan began its transformation to a constitutional monarchy during the 1950s (Hutt, 2005), when King Jigme Dorji Wangchuck initiated participatory politics by establishing the country's legislature (Rose, 1977). In 1972, when 16-year-old Jigme Singye Wangchuck ascended the throne upon his father's death, there arose fears of a plot to create a "Greater Nepal." This led the Bhutanese government to push for a "one nation, one people" national identity reflecting the culture of the country's prevailing ethnic groups (Evans, 2010). By the end of the 1980s, there was a marginalization of the southern Bhutanese, mandating an adoption of the northern Bhutanese dress and language in the south, including elimination of the Nepali language from school curricula (Hutt, 2003; Rose, 1994). Beyond this, Nepali-speaking families were separated when all members were unable to prove their ancestral Bhutanese nationality under the seven categories of citizenship devised by the government (Hutt, 2005; Amnesty International, 1992). In the 1990s, the government began initiating military action, after demonstrations erupted, protesting the arrest of a Lhotshampa member of the Royal Advisory Council, Tek Nath Rizal. To justify their actions, they declared the presence of over 100,000 illegal Nepali immigrants (Royal Government of Bhutan, 1991), leading to an exodus of Lhotshampas to the India–Nepal border, where recognizing the need, the United Nations High Commission for Refugees made provisions for their refuge in five camps.

Resettlement in the United States

After the failure of numerous bilateral talks between Nepal and Bhutan regarding the repatriation of the refugees, the international community provided resolution in the form of humanitarian aid through refugee resettlement agreements in 2008 in countries of the North, such as the United States, Norway, Canada, Denmark and New Zealand (Lawoti, 2010). It was in accordance with this agreement that the greater Atlanta area of Georgia was selected as a location for resettlement of this refugee population. The Bhutanese families are primarily resettled in the Clarkston, Decatur, and Stone Mountain areas, in low-rent apartments, which were assigned to them by refugee relief agencies, with the Bhutanese tending to be clustered in apartment complexes with other refugees from Bhutan (Centers for Disease Control, 2009). While agencies provided each family with three months' rent and utilities, $100 in cash, a ride to the Social Security office to apply for a card, and a tour of Atlanta to familiarize them with MARTA and the basics of getting around (CDC, 2009), volunteers from resettlement agencies and independent agencies provided a strong support network, which filled in the bureaucratic gaps left by the official channels of resettlement.

Both the organizations from which we drew volunteer participants, Drishti and OneWorld, have chapters in various cities across the United States, also offering refugee resettlement assistance. It is noteworthy, that both of these organizations play a major role in the resettlement services offered in the greater Atlanta area, and also that Drishti is a Hindu faith-based, humanitarian nonprofit, while OneWorld is a Christian faith-based, humanitarian nonprofit with a missionary focus. Lastly, OneWorld is one of the federally designated resettlement agencies in the area, which is also responsible for the distribution of resources allotted by the government, in addition to rendering volunteer services locally.

Overall, both organizations offered financial help, material help in the form of clothing and essentials such as food, employment assistance, vocational training, mobility, cultural acclimatization support, and also spiritual support. In helping families adapt to their new environment, the volunteers drove the refugees to medical appointments, helped them acquire driving licenses, donated used cars to them, offered English as a Secondary Language classes, offered rides to the refugees' preferred places of worship, and some have also established mentoring relationships with families that they have been working with for extended periods of time.

METHOD

The primary goal of this study was to analyze discursive practices between the mediating volunteers and refugees; the agenda of knowing the how and the why of these practices prompted us to adopt a qualitative research method approach (Lindlof & Taylor, 1998). Initially what began as a key informant based sampling strategy seamlessly led into a snowballing strategy as the interviews progressed. Additionally, Bhutan's isolationist policies altered only a decade ago rendered this population significantly culturally different from their host community in the United States, making them an appropriate group for a culture-centered analysis.

Creswell's (2007) opportunistic sampling strategies were adopted to develop as well rounded of a sample as possible through flexibility and openness to opportunities arising in the field, regarding both sampling strategies and methods used (Lincoln & Guba, 1985).

Data gathering was primarily done through fifteen, one to two hour in-depth interviews with volunteers drawn from two organizations, Drishti and OneWorld, discussed in detail below. Due to our key informant's connection with Drishti, twelve of our interviews were conducted with Drishti volunteers, while three were conducted with three OneWorld members (one staff member and two volunteers).

Also, while ten interviews were individual, five of our participants chose to be interviewed in the field with partner volunteers, in the process of offering assistance. Since each of these group interviews had one predominant participant, we selected the data for that participant for analysis. In summary, our data set, for the purpose of analysis, consisted of twelve interviews; ten from Drishti, and two from OneWorld. All volunteer excerpts are from Drishti participants, unless noted as OneWorld volunteers.

Except for the five interviews noted above, the interviews were conducted in a private setting (either at community centers, the homes of refugees, or offices of volunteers) at a mutually agreed upon date, time, prioritizing the privacy and comfort of the participants.

At the beginning of the interviews, participants were reminded of their voluntary participation and the right to discontinue at any time, in which event, their interview records would be destroyed promptly. All interviews were audio recorded digitally after getting permission from the participants. A reflexive journal of notes and audio recordings of researcher reflections were also maintained. The audio recordings were transcribed and both researchers cross-checked the transcriptions. To ensure internal data validity (Creswell, 1994), the researchers engaged in member checking during the data gathering process, providing participants the opportunity to confirm the researchers' summary of their own interviews. All participants provided consensus on the data gathering, and only one requested a copy of the transcript. A grounded theory constant comparison method was used for analysis, extracting and identifying the dominant themes (Strauss & Corbin, 1990) in the interview transcripts. The identification and analysis of dominant themes was done in conjunction by both researchers, and also took into account the field notes and informal interactions with the participants. To further ensure analytical rigor, ten of the participants were provided with, and approved of, an overview of the initial data analysis themes. Two of the participants were not reachable for this part of the process. A set of "probability statements about the relationship between concepts, or an integrated set of conceptual hypotheses developed from empirical data" (Glaser, 1998) were then developed co-constructively by the researchers through the analysis process.

RESULTS

The three main interconnected threads that were found to run throughout the data are: (1) articulation of need in volunteer-refugee relationships, (2) from material services to pedagogy, and (3) networks of communication. These three threads together point toward an interconnected web of organizing processes among the volunteer workers and service staff that is directed toward meeting the needs of the Bhutanese refugee community in Atlanta, Georgia. At the heart of these threads is the interplay of communicative processes in addressing the needs of the refugees, framed under the broader understanding among the volunteers and staff members of the needs of the community.

Articulation of Need in Volunteer-refugee Relationship

The initial needs and expectations of the community were intertwined with the communication of these needs to the organizations that were providing the support. As our conversations explored the gaps between community understandings and organizational understandings, participants continually pointed toward the communicative needs of the community and the relevance of donors and volunteers in understanding the local needs of communities, framed often in terms of top-down information delivery from the organization to community members. Note the articulations of a volunteer, Arnav:

> The initial goal was simply; they had a culture shock. So one of the very first families never saw a highway, so the moment they walked the Lawrenceville highway they were scared. They had never seen a highway before they came here. You know they had no exposure to English, they had no exposure to health care or the school system. Everything is complicated here. So our initial goal was to be there for them, help them along, and facilitate their integration at that time. And there was a lot of excitement. We used to take weekends off and take the families to apply for jobs, to look for starting positions for them. It turned out very quickly that they would not show up for work and would not want to be housekeeping and so they would simply not show up. And so what happened, the employers very quickly said "We don't want to hire Bhutanese."

What we saw in Arnav's articulation was the juxtaposition of the initial excitement among volunteers amidst the frustration when after assisting the Bhutanese families with applying for and securing jobs, the families would simply not show up for work. This led to the reluctance of the employers in the area to hire Bhutanese workers. Embedded in this narrative was the taken-for-granted assumption of the gratefulness on the part of the refugees, irrespective of the commensurability of their skills with the opportunities offered. This was further corroborated in the field by the researchers in numerous encounters where refugees trained as doctors, educators, and administrators were required to work as grocery baggers and warehouse labor, due to certification issues.

Also ensconced in the above narrative were pejorative assumptions about the backwardness of the refugees, who had no exposure to the amenities of modernity such as roads, hospitals, and school systems. The simplistic backwardness of Bhutan was juxtaposed in the backdrop of the complexity of the life in the US. In their participatory terminology and articulations of "being there" for the refugees, volunteers such as Arnav displayed their internal colonial logics of altruism based on taken-for-granted assumptions of superiority. The hard work of the volunteers was juxtaposed against the laziness of the Bhutanese refugees who would simply not show up for work, thus reiterating the opposition of employers to hiring Bhutanese.

It is also in this domain of articulating local needs that volunteers discussed the importance of communicating their resources and resource allocation processes with the community members in the backdrop of their local needs and their inability to meet these local needs, pointing to spaces of misunderstandings and dissatisfaction. Another volunteer, Bharat, learned that despite making announcements and distributing fliers in the community with information about donors and volunteers, it did not clarify the charitable nature of the refugee-volunteer relationship for refugees. He said for example:

> The time we had...when we could not meet their demands, like when we gave [them] the rice cookers; we bought like 120 of them and we ran out of them, we didn't realize. So, there was a long list of people who had signed up. And then we made money and bought those rice cookers and went to deliver them and we had a big commotion there. And people started telling us "You are not distributing it fairly" and we had no idea who was complaining. And then it turns out that they all thought that it was some kind of mismanagement going on and people who were responsible were not doing their job and we said, "Look, these are volunteers and they will disappear if we don't act properly to the donors."

In this instance, Bharat discussed the inability of the volunteer agencies to meet the demands of the refugee community, positioned amidst the lack of understanding among the recipients who were not "acting properly." In the absence of this ability to meet the local demands, community members became frustrated and questioned the ways in which resources were being distributed, suggesting that the volunteers and donors were not doing their jobs responsibly. In making sense of this incident when the volunteers ran out of the rice cookers to donate, Bharat noted the importance of communicating the relief processes and the ways in which resources were secured and distributed to recipient community members. Inherent in Bharat's articulation was the assumption that the recipients would act properly if they were well-informed about the nature of volunteering. The notion of misunderstanding was constituted within an information-based framework where he positioned the role of the organizations in providing adequate information to the recipients.

In this miscommunication, he noted a fundamental gap between the interpretive frame of refugee community members about the nature of volunteering and the interpretive frames of donors and volunteers working in the field. In spite of top-down information strategies such as announcements and fliers, the interpretive frame of the community was not engaged as community members did not really understand the volunteering processes. Noting this gap between the localized understanding among the Bhutanese community members and the understanding of the donors and volunteers, Bharat suggested that volunteers and donors learn about the lived experiences and local interpretive frames among refugee community members so that community members could be better educated about the nature of volunteering and that it was a volunteer force which was helping them out.

Delving deeper, this demonstrated the inability of volunteers to recognize that their perceptions of appropriate volunteer-recipient relationships may not be the touchstone of such interactions. According to Choden (2003), at the Centre for Bhutan Studies, while the concept of voluntary acts through informal networks in Bhutan was well recognized, there were not many formal voluntary and non-government organizations in the country. Complicating this further was the interaction of the refugees for the past two decades with formalized international NGOs in camps (PhotoVoice, 2006) with a focused dedication to the Bhutanese issue, as opposed to the discretionary nature of assistance offered through voluntary organizations in the United States. This may have resulted in the expectations of the community for formal accountability from the local volunteers, as opposed to "treating them properly" as suggested by Bharat. Eisha, another volunteer, said she felt that the refugees were not "thankful" for the unusual "initial cushion" of rent and food stamps provided by volunteers and were unable to grasp the gravity of the need for self-sufficiency. Drishti's attempts at communicating the relevance of education as a step towards self-sufficiency were unsuccessful. She states:

> We spent a whole summer...we had volunteers come together and take them for SAT classes for free. We waived all the tuition fees, we provided them with books, we provided them with scientific calculators. But they wouldn't show up because they didn't want to wake up and go on a Saturday morning when the volunteers would come to take them and bring them back and so we kind of gave up on that experiment. This year, the first year we had like 6 or 8 students in one subdivision that we were in for. It was only 4 of them that attended all of the classes.

In her articulation, Eisha pointed out that the misunderstanding among Bhutanese refugee members, who received food stamps and had their rents paid, led to the development of classes to address these communicative needs. Furthermore then, Eisha discussed how the classes, developed to help the community members and the children in the community develop academically, failed because of this absence of an understanding that connected the volunteers with the Bhutanese refugee community, and like Arnav, juxtaposing the volunteers as participatory and supportive versus the refugees as uncooperative and lazy. She finally added that "the cultural understandings of work" among refugee community members, were different considering many of them had well paid jobs in Nepal before they were displaced, and may not be accustomed to "lower level" work.

A One World volunteer, Chris, also believed that for the Bhutanese, being on welfare support provided by international agencies in camps for over two decades, there was a different understanding about the extent of support provided by volunteers in the United States. He noted that they may conflate the role of volunteers here with that of volunteers they encountered in refugee camps, or assumed these volunteers were government agents distributing resources promised to the community upon resettlement in the United States. He noted:

> They were told they were going to whatever country, and then they were picked up there, brought here and settled in their apartments, so some of them thought that this would go on forever....They really thought the government will take care of that....In fact, when we did the bazaar in December 2008 I didn't realize they really thought that was all pub-

lic money, that it was government money. They didn't realize that it was volunteers had organized the whole thing. It only became obvious to me when I started talking to them. They had no clue where all this came from. When we were talking to individuals and groups, saying that we had spent $50,000 putting it all together and giving it to them, they thought it was government money.

Further, speaking about the demoralizing effect of this disconnect between the expectation and reality of assistance, including volunteer support, Don, another OneWorld staff member notes:

I think the challenges are always expectations…and some of those expectations come from just what the person thinks they're going to get when they come here, others' expectations come from what people either here or there have told them and just generally not completely correct ideas of what to expect here as far as their agency and volunteers. What to expect as far as American [volunteer] help, how Americans treat them, how soon will I be to get a job, when they're expected to start paying things on their own, just expectations like that and that's always hard for a family or an individual when they come here…and there's a real dip in just overall happiness or thoughts for the future. People just get discouraged and they think I'm not sure if I should of come here to begin with.

It is through this realization that the local cultural context and the world of meanings of the refugee community needs to be taken into account that Fateh points out:

The last 6–9 months what we have done is when people ask for help we kind of see what it is and then provide that particular area of help rather than trying to get all the community together and make it like an ongoing educational venture. We have the manpower to do it but we don't have the reciprocal interest for us to be able to do that.

Worth noting here was the centrality of understanding the communicative needs of the community. Instead of turning the support services into an educational venture, the process of engaging in volunteer work and trying out different top-down services has led volunteers like Fateh to realize that these top-down services were not likely to work unless they were aligned with the needs of the community. Therefore, the notion of providing assistance has shifted to the framework of listening to specific needs that emerge from within the community and then responding to those needs so that resources were aligned with the specific needs of the community.

As noted throughout this section, the articulation of local needs of the Bhutanese refugee community was vital to developing a support system that was responsive to these needs. Through the complex processes of experiences in offering services to the Bhutanese refugee community, the volunteers discussed the importance of finding a common framework that connected the local understandings of needs with the understandings of needs among volunteers and donor staff.

The discursive space around offering services to the refugee community was constituted around the framing of the community as one in need. In the in-depth interviews with the project volunteers, the gaps in the articulated needs of communities and the services that the agencies were able to offer become evident. Also worth noting in the articulations of the volunteers were the differential perceptions of the services offered and the expectations of the refugees before they come to the US. Absent from the discursive constructions of needs was participation of community members from the refugee communities in the articulations of these needs; also absent were articulations that seek to understand the roots of these gaps in the perceptions of community members. Therefore, the frames constituted around needs primarily reflect the understandings of problem configurations as guided by the interpretive frames superimposed by the staff and volunteers on their relationships with the Bhutanese refugee community in Atlanta, homogenizing the population through the primary descriptor of its needs.

From Material Services to Pedagogy

Participants in this project often communicated their roles and the roles of their organizations as providing services in meeting the needs of the refugee community members. These services ranged from engaging materially with the structural inequities faced by the Bhutanese refugees in Atlanta to providing resources for securing access to jobs to creating opportunities for learning information that would help the refugee community members negotiate the broader political and economic structures in Atlanta as well as in the US.

Note for instance the provision of transportation services that is coordinated by Drishti in the community. Given the lack of adequate transportation facilities among the Bhutanese refugees, Drishti has created a provision for car donations that addresses the transportation needs of community members. Here was what Gaurav had to say:

> With the vehicle donation program, we were able to get cars also with Drishti. Because Drishti not only takes donations, it then reconditions the cars, and makes them safe before it actually donates to a family. They do all the paperwork. They take the family to the department of motor vehicles' registration, give them the title, then follow up with the family. You know making sure that they are being safe about it. What they have done is incredible in terms of humanitarian work for this community.

In this example then, the work of Drishti not only centers on the creation of the structural resources through the donation of cars, reconditioning them and making them safe, but also in taking the family to the bureau of motor vehicles, getting them the title of the car, and following up with the family to make sure that the car is safe. The work of the organizing efforts of Drishti therefore moved from creating material resources to working through the bureaucratic structures to ensuring that the transition to using the cars was smoothly accomplished.

In addition to the creation of material frameworks for offering services that were directly tied to the material needs of community members, the volunteers as well as donor staff also discussed the creation of educational opportunities. Hiten noted that at the local Hindu temple (a Drishti collaborator) professors reduced the overall cost for SAT training for refugee students, volunteered tutoring time, and provided transportation. Despite this, only four students completed the eight-week training, following which, he said:

> This year we had a lower goal and lowered it to three students, taking promises from them that they would actually come. Only one student came all the way and did well. So what we see is the reality of their life is such that this kind of tutoring, intense academic tutoring is not something that they can handle...because their refugee life was a lot less structured and a lot less demanding of them. So, then we had classes on a regular basis to help them with math, history, chemistry. We had trained teachers and volunteers, trained educated volunteers but that also petered off because the kids started dropping off. So, the initial goals kind of changed.

In their understanding of providing support, volunteers such as Hiten talked about the importance of academic support to create opportunities for advancement. In the above excerpt, Hiten discussed how the volunteers came together to pool resources, volunteering times of professors, waiving the tutoring fees, and providing transportation for the 8-week intensive course. However, similar to what was noted earlier, the likelihood of the utilization of such pedagogic services among Bhutanese refugee students was low. In seeking to understand this low utilization, Hiten pointed toward the different frameworks of localized understandings of life and more specifically, of academic tutoring. He noted that the structured nature of intense tutoring did not fit with the much less structured and less demanding life of children in refugee camps.

On a similar note, Indraneel, a volunteer with the Art of Living Foundation, and subsequently Drishti shares:

> ...so we are running a project; it's called RISE...which is Refugee Integration and Self Empowerment Project, and as part of RISE we conduct programs for them which are basically trauma relief programs, where we use Yoga and other Yogic techniques to help them release stress because they have been living in these camps for a very long time and a significant amount of mental trauma and stress associated with them moving to a new country and getting acclimatized to a new culture and environment over here.

Worth noting here was the development and delivery of services such as Yoga techniques to address the stress and trauma associated with the movement of the refugees to a new country, the process of getting acclimatized to a new culture, and the challenges of starting a new life in a new country. Therefore the RISE program specifically worked on developing techniques for releasing tension and developing an attitude for releasing stress and trauma. The processes of yoga here were seen as means for internal empowerment for bringing about changes in the internal conditions of trauma and for preparing refugee community members to manage their transitions with a more peaceful and relaxed perspective. Once again, the emphasis here was on the top-down delivery of pedagogic programs deemed relevant by the volunteering organization, couched in participatory terminology such as "helping refugees deal with stress," and as constituted within the traditional scope of services typically offered by the organization. The programming offered by the Art of Living Program Foundation here was an existing program that was widely circulated globally, and delivered in specific contexts.

Networks of Communication

The initial organizing for delivering services for the refugee community started as individually-based service work that was directed at meeting the needs of the community. Therefore, the engagement of organizations in offering services to the refugee community often originated with the individual-level work of an organizational member who volunteered with the community. This individual commitment then moved toward the commitment of a broader collective in addressing the specific needs of the community; it is through communication that the collective-base of offering support to the Bhutanese refugee community was created. Here was an articulation of Jatin, who served as an independent volunteer for the project:

> So, my initial involvement was as an individual helping someone who needed help. At that point as I realized that there was a lot more that was involved and so at that point I started contacting people and expanding the volunteer base of work for the community, for the Bhutanese families.

He went on to elaborate how, as the President of the Hindu Temple of Atlanta at the time, he got that organization involved with the cause, organizing both the first reception for the community and then a bazaar, in collaboration with Drishti, who made this a "priority project" for their organization. In Jatin's reference to the initial years of organizing, he pointed out the role of initial contacts in creating a space for solidarity. Contacting people and communicating with them created the volunteer base and expanded it in order to meet the needs of the Bhutanese families. Narayan pointed out that as the number of refugee families started growing, there was greater need for organized collective efforts and this was done through personal contacts and through communication with various stakeholders. Also, he referred to the frame of humanitarian aid that played a key role in bringing different organizations together under one roof. The scope of community services expanded through the involvement of organizations such as Drishti. The various organizations that were involved in addressing the needs of the refugee community served a wide variety of roles. Individuals played key roles in the development of networks, in the assessment of needs, and in the delivery of appropriate services by connecting supplementary organizations based on needs such as health or spiritual needs, with the central volunteer organization. This point was elucidated by Dr. Kamesh who said:

> We requested help from the Georgia Association of Indian Physicians (GAAPI), then I had recruited VIBHA to help, then I had recruited the Satyasai to help, and I'm part of all these organizations depending on the type of help that we are trying to provide....but if you say what would be the primary...as far as I can tell the only organization that has the refugee welfare as primary goal is Drishti and therefore I consider that to be the primary organization.

Here, Dr. Kamesh individually worked with a variety of organizations, seeking their assistance in serving the needs of the community. His membership in these organizations gave him the knowledge base to seek out support from the organizations; furthermore, his knowledge of the internal workings of the organizations as well as the specific needs they met allowed him to coordinate his communication efforts with the organizations. The concept of inter-agency coordination was highlighted by Lokesh, another Art of Living Foundation volunteer, who met a Drishti volunteer socially, resulting in his consequent involvement with Drishti. He said:

> Because somebody who was working for Drishti contacted me, asking me if I could help and then I went and met people from the community, I understood what their problem was and I thought it's an interesting project to take up....In this case the community itself was receptive to doing something like this; rather than me having to go and convince them that this is our program and this will be good for you.

In this case, having networks in other organizations was an entry point into the community and to understanding its needs. The need was initially articulated by Drishti and then communicated to him, and he responded to this call for help. Lokesh had come to know about the needs of the Bhutanese community through his networks with Drishti, and also viewed Drishti's outreach positively, in juxtaposition to what he stated as "the need to take a lot of permissions in the US" before offering their services. Salient in the voices of the participants in this project was the coordination between the different agencies in order to meet the needs of local refugee communities.

Worth noting in this frame of inter-organizational networks was the absence of community voices and community participation amidst the processes of the delivery of services. As the volunteers who participated in the project discuss the communicative strategies through which they fostered the delivery of services for the Bhutanese refugees, critically absent from the discourses were references to networking with the refugee community members themselves as participants in the processes of co-creating service delivery points. The descriptions of the processes of organizing presented a top-down framework through which the services are delivered.

DISCUSSION

This project was situated within the context of exploring the narratives of civil society staff members and volunteers offering services to refugees within a neoliberal landscape, connecting the language of assistance and social justice with a broader agenda of global movements and neoliberal reform (Dutta & Pal, 2010). The postcolonial lens adopted engaged with the processes of organizing among civil society organizations serving the Bhutanese refugee community. The tensions that emerged in the postcolonial frames of civil society organizing in the context of offering services to the Bhutanese refugee community drew attention to the structural and contextual gaps that were present in the interfaces between the organizations and their community stakeholders, depicting the top-down framework of neoliberal governance in spite of its usage of participatory terminology. These gaps were situated amidst the cultural differences and the structural contexts within which the volunteers and their Bhutanese refugee clients were located, and were also tied to the divergent agendas of NGOs and volunteers, and communities receiving their services. In the in-depth interviews with volunteers and staff members serving the Bhutanese refugee communities, the stories of offering services to the community continually pointed to the relevance of listening to the voices of the local communities through a culture-centered approach, and simultaneously demonstrated the consequences of not engaging community members from marginalized contexts in the processes of decision-making (Dutta, 2008).

From a volunteer

As volunteers, I personally feel that we do a better job while we interact with these people on a weekly daily basis, and we have befriended
them, instead of agencies waiting for these people to come and report
problems to them. We don't treat them as something, as customers or
projects. We treat them as people and we are friendly with them. There
are so many families that I visit just like that. Just like it's my own family. I go to their house; like so many times they call me asking, "Where
are you? I haven't seen you in a while." So we have that kind of personal
interaction, so we know what their problems are. So, we know, because
they express it, in their own way they express it; we understand what
their problems are. Not to say that I have complete grasp of all their
problems. I don't. But, they do, I feel they express to us much more
easily than they would to the agencies. Because for them going to the
agencies is like getting an appointment, meeting that person and that's
just a very restricted amount of time that he can talk, understandably
so, because there are so many other things to take care of. So, as an informal network, we are able to understand their problems much more
easily.

A Drishti volunteer, speaking about the benefits of informal versus formal communicative practices when serving the refugee community

The articulations of local needs were central to the political economy of the
NGO and volunteer work. However, the framing of the needs of Bhutanese refugees were largely different from the ways in which the community organizations
serving them understood these needs, and these departures created spaces of misunderstanding and divergence between the volunteers and the refugees. The gaps
between the two parallel worlds in the contexts of needs then shaped the interpretations and misunderstandings between the organizations and their clients, often
framed by volunteers and staff members in terms of the lack of awareness among
refugee community members. Therefore, salient in the narratives of offering services to refugee community members were articulations of localized needs and the
framing of these needs within the frameworks of the community organizations
that were delivering the services. However, missing from the discursive spaces that
foregrounded the needs of community members was the demonstrations of processes that engaged the participatory capacities of community members in meaningful ways. Once again, along the lines of the culture-centered approach that
foregrounds the participatory capacity of subaltern sectors in the articulations of

local needs, the in-depth interviews continually pointed toward the importance of locally grounding the problem frames and the corresponding solutions, and the importance of moving beyond an information deficit framework to a framework of co-construction that engaged community participants.

The articulation of the gap between the locally shared needs of the community members and the understandings of these needs among the community organizations' volunteers who were delivering these services points to a greater need for postcolonial reflexivity of organizational practices, especially as they relate to the development and delivery of services to refugee community members. While recognizing the difference between the formal NGOs (often government subcontractors) and volunteer organizations, there were similar discursive constructions by volunteers from both types of agencies, positioning themselves as experts assisting the refugees.

Postcolonial deconstructions of organizational practices draw attention to the communicative gaps that exist as a result between the organizational structures where services are configured and the localized constructions of refugee community members. Continually narrated through the interviews of the volunteers was the discovery of the local needs of Bhutanese refugee community members, and the situation of these needs within the organizational capacity to understand. The delivery of services to the refugee community members was situated within an organizational environment that was far removed from the experiences of Bhutanese refugees displaced from their homes. It was on the basis of this observation then that we note the importance of culture-centered communication scholarship that is fundamentally driven by the emphasis on listening to the voices at the margins and is committed to the creation of dialogic spaces for subaltern participation (Dutta, 2008; Dutta & Pal, 2010).

In referring to the range of services their organizations provide, organizational members and volunteers discussed a wide range of services, from meeting basic material needs of community members to the development of pedagogical programs and training opportunities for community members. Once again, in the stories that articulated the delivery of this range of services, worth noting, were the glimpses of the lessons learned by volunteers, emphasizing the foregrounding of community voices in figuring out the goals of the organization. Also, the interview narratives highlighted the roles of inter-organizational networks in the delivery of services. Therefore, the delivery of services was not only constituted within the figuring out of local needs but also in the figuring out of communication strategies for communicating among the various organizations serving the needs of the Bhutanese refugee community. Ultimately, this project points toward the importance of culturally-centered communication projects that continually connect the local-global actors in the development of services to the broader framework of social justice.

NOTE

1. Neoliberalism is "a theory of political economic practices that proposes that well-being can best be advanced by liberating individual entrepreneurial freedoms and skills within an institutional framework characterized by strong private property rights, free markets, and free trade" (Harvey, 2005, p. 2)

REFERENCES

Amnesty International. (1992). Bhutan: Human rights violations against the Nepali-speaking population in the south. Retrieved March 20, 2011, from http://www.amnesty.org/en/library/info/ASA14/004/1992/en

Bruno, A. (2011). Congressional Research Service Report for Congress: US refugee resettlement assistance. Retrieved December 15, 2013, from https://www.fas.org/sgp/crs/row/R41570.pdf

CNN (2013). Number of Syrian refugees rises above 2 million, U.N. agency says. Retrieved November 18, 2013, from http://edition.cnn.com/2013/09/03/world/meast/syria-refugees-unhcr/

Cable News Network. (2013). Number of Syrian refugees rises above 2 million, U.N. agency says. Retrieved November 18, 2013, from http://edition.cnn.com/2013/09/03/world/meast/syria-refugees-unhcr/

Catholic Charities. (2013). Catholic Refugee Resettlement Volunteer Program. Retrieved December 10, 2013, from http://www.ccoc.us/volunteer/refugee-resettlement-volunteer-program

Centers for Disease Control. (2009). CDC Volunteers Aid Bhutanese Refugees. Retrieved December 10, 2013, from http://www.cdc.gov/news/2009/04/bhutanese_refugees/

Choden, T. (2003). Traditional forms of volunteerism in Bhutan. The Centre for Bhutan Studies. Retrieved 16 March, 2013, from http://www.bhutanstudies.org.bt/wp-content/uploads/monograph/monoVolunteerism.pdf

Church World Service. (2013). Refugee resettlement. Retrieved September 18, 2013, from http://www.cwsglobal.org/what-we-do/refugees/us-programs/refugee-resettlement.html

Creswell, J. W. (2007). Qualitative inquiry and research design: Choosing among five traditions (2nd Ed). Thousand Oaks, CA: Sage.

Creswell, John W. (1994). Research design: Qualitative and quantitative approaches. Thousand Oaks, CA: Sage.

Dutta, M. (2008). Communicating health: A culture-centered approach. London, UK: Polity Press.

Dutta, M., & Pal, M. (2007). The internet as a site of resistance: The case of the Narmada Bachao Andolan. In S. Duhe, New media and public relations (pp. 203–215). New York, NY: Peter Lang.

Dutta, M., & Pal, M. (2010). Dialogue theory in marginalized settings: A subaltern studies approach. Communication Theory, 20, 363–386.

Eade, D. (2007). Capacity building: Who builds whose capacity? Development in Practice, 17, 630–639.

Evans, R. (2010). Bhutan. Contemporary South Asia, 18, 25–42.

Glaser, B. G. (1998). Doing grounded theory: Issues and discussions. Mill Valley, CA: Sociology Press.

Harvey, D. (2005). A brief history of neoliberalism. New York, NY: Oxford University Press.

Hulme, D., & Edwards, M. (Eds.). (1997). NGOs, states and donors: Too close for comfort? New York, NY: St. Martin's.

Hutt, M. (2003). Unbecoming citizens. Oxford, UK: Oxford University Press.

Hutt, M. (2005). The Bhutanese refugees: Between verification, repatriation and royal realpolitik. *Peace and Democracy in South Asia, 1,* 44–56.

International Rescue Committee. (2013). Resettling refugees. Retrieved September 15, 2013, from http://www.rescue.org/our-work/resettling-refugees

Korten, D. (1990). *Getting to the 21st century: Voluntary action and the global agenda.* West Hartford, CT: Kumarian.

Lawoti, M. (2010). Nepal and Bhutan in 2009. *Asian Survey, 50,* 164–172.

Lincoln Y., & Guba, E. G. (1985). *Naturalist inquiry.* Newbury Park, CA.: Sage.

Lindlof, T. R., & Taylor, B. C. (1998). *Qualitative communication research methods.* Thousand Oaks, CA: Sage.

Migration Policy Institute. (2011). The faltering US refugee protection system: Legal and policy responses to refugees, asylum seekers, and others in need of protection. Retrieved December 11, 2013, from http://www.migrationpolicy.org/pubs/refugeeprotection-2011.pdf

Office of Refugee Resettlement. (2013). Voluntary agencies. Retrieved December 10, 2013, from http://www.acf.hhs.gov/programs/orr/resource/voluntary-agencies

Office of Refugee Resettlement. (2011). Fiscal year 2009 refugee arrivals. Retrieved March 20, 2011 from http://www.acf.hhs.gov/programs/orr/data/fy2009RA.htm

PhotoVoice (2006). Camp Information. Retrieved December 10, 2013, from http://www.photovoice.org/bhutan/index.php?id=11#organisations.

Rose, L.E. (1977). *Politics of Bhutan.* Ithaca, NY: Cornell University Press.

Rose, L.E. (1994). The role of the monarchy in the current ethnic conflict in Bhutan. In Michael Hutt (ed.), *Bhutan: Perspectives on conflict and dissent* (pp. 183–194). Gartmore, Scotland: Paul Strachan-Kiscadale.

Royal Government of Bhutan. (1991). *Anti-National activities in Southern Bhutan: A terrorist movement.* Thimphu, Bhutan: Department of Information.

Spivak. G. (1988). Can the subaltern speak? In C. Nelson & L. Grossberg (Eds.), *Marxism and the Interpretation of Culture* (pp. 271–313). Urbana, IL: University of Illinois Press.

Strauss A., Corbin J. (1990). *Basics of qualitative research: Grounded theory procedures and techniques.* Thousand Oaks, CA: Sage.

UN General Assembly, Draft Convention relating to the Status of Refugees. 14 December 1950. A/RES/429, available at: http://www.refworld.org/docid/3b00f08a27.html [accessed 20 September 2014]

United Nations High Commissioner for Refugees. (2013). Facts and figures about refugees. Retrieved November 23, 2013, from http://www.unhcr.org.uk/about-us/key-facts-and-figures.html

United States Committee for Refugees and Immigrants. (2013). American Volunteers and Iraqi Refugees Become Friends for Life. Retrieved December 11, 2013, from http://www.refugees.org/refugee-voices/volunteers/american-volunteers-and-iraqi.html

Wood, G. (1997). States without citizens: The problem of the franchise state. In D. Hulme & M. Edwards (Eds.), *NGOs, states and donors: Too close for comfort.* (pp. 79–92). New York: St. Martin's.

Conclusions

Reflections AND New Directions ON Volunteering IN International AND Intercultural Contexts

MICHAEL W. KRAMER
LAURIE K. LEWIS

This book was a natural outgrowth of our previous edited volume, *Volunteering and Communication: Studies from Multiple Contexts* (Kramer, Lewis, & Gossett, 2013). That volume primarily examined the experience of volunteers within the United States. We included only four studies involving volunteering in international or intercultural contexts (Maugh, 2013; McAllum, 2013; Mize-Smith, 2013; Onyx, 2013), despite receiving enough proposals to almost fill an entire volume. Upon completion of that project, the book editor, Mary Savigar of Peter Lang, encouraged us to develop a second volume focused on international and intercultural volunteering. This book is the result of those efforts.

While reading the thirteen original studies included here, it is easy to become engrossed in the individual studies without considering the broader implications and issues the studies collectively raise or the future directions for research that they suggest. In this chapter, we hope to draw attention to broader issues we perceive as important for this line of research while hopefully encouraging others to creatively consider additional options. We divide our observations into five areas: (1) the prevalence of volunteering in international and intercultural contexts; (2) the diversity of volunteering in these contexts; (3) problems facing volunteers in these contexts; (4) problems evaluating volunteering in these contexts; and finally, (5) challenges facing researchers in these contexts.

PREVALENCE OF VOLUNTEERING IN INTERNATIONAL
AND INTERCULTURAL CONTEXTS

The studies in the first section of the book explored how volunteering functions in a variety of countries around the globe. Even from this small sample of studies, it is easy to point to the prevalence of volunteering in international and intercultural contexts. For example, the following countries are represented in the studies as sources or recipients of significant volunteer efforts: Australia, Bhutan, Canada, China, Germany, Haiti, Korea, Mozambique, Namibia, Philippines, Senegal, South Africa, Sub-Saharan Africa, Thailand, Turkey, and Zambia. A variety of other countries are also mentioned in passing comments by one or more volunteer, such as Central African Republic, Egypt, Fiji, Guinea-Bissau, Hong Kong, and Japan. Thus, even this small sample of studies indicates that volunteering is an important activity on all six inhabited continents, even though "no comprehensive, comparative study of world-wide volunteerism exists (United Nations, 2011, p. 3).

More important than the breadth of countries involved in programs involving volunteers, the studies make it quite clear that volunteering is understood differently and functions differently in various international and intercultural settings than it does in the United States. For example, the reluctance of Korean parents to volunteer in their children's schools in the study by Cho and Lee would likely surprise many U.S. parents, especially those known as "helicopter parents." In the study by Kumar and Dutta, it appears that some of the difficulty that Bhutanese refugees have in understanding the difference between a government-agency sponsored refugee camp in Nepal and the volunteers assisting them in settling into the Atlanta area stems from volunteering functioning and being understood differently in the different countries. In fact, the meaning of volunteering is so varied across contexts that individuals who might be considered volunteers by one definition may not even consider themselves volunteers (Butcher, 2010). These differences in understanding of the meaning of volunteering make self-reports of volunteering activity quite unreliable (Lewis, 2013) and likely contribute to the disparate levels of volunteering reported by Gossett across nations in the introductory chapter. Given the variety of other types of international volunteers and the volunteers in many nations not represented here, future research should continue to explore additional international and intercultural contexts in which volunteering occurs to broaden our understanding of the variety of forms and meanings of unpaid, voluntary labor.

The studies in the second section of the book, rather than exploring global forms of volunteering, examined the experiences U.S. citizens working with organizations that promote volunteering in other countries, many of which are easily recognizable. For example, since 1961 when it was founded, the Peace Corps has sent over 215,000 of its individuals as volunteers in 139 countries, including over 7,000 in 65 countries in 2013 (Peace Corps, 2013). Since it is in many ways the marquee example of international volunteering for U.S. citizens, it is not surprising that two studies (Malleus; Hanchey) and a portion of a third (McNamee, Peterson, & Gould) examined volunteer experiences with this organization. Rotary International (Craig & Russo) also promotes and supports major volunteer efforts by both its U.S. affiliates and its international members. Many other organizations promote U.S. volunteers in other countries as well. Mission trips, usually including humanitarian aid, have been a common form of long-term volunteering supported by religious organizations for centuries. The Church of Jesus Christ of Latter-Day Saints is perhaps most well-known for these long-term mission trips (Walch, 2007), although many Christian denominations and other religions also have supported this type of volunteering for centuries (Anheier & Salamon, 1999).

Much more common nowadays are short-term mission trips conducted by groups with religious affiliation which make mission work a core part of service in their faith. These trips involve short-term (1–2 week) service trips arranged by nonprofit organizations, local churches and other religious agencies in which volunteers may teach Vacation Bible School or pour cement for a new facility (Frederick & Mize Smith; McNamee, et al.). These volunteer efforts are much harder to track because of the large number of organizations promoting this type of volunteering.

A plethora of organizations promote other forms of short-term volunteering. This includes recruiting volunteers in the United States (Xu) and from other countries (McAllum & Zahra) for voluntourism. It is estimated that 1.6 million individuals annually participate in this type of short-term volunteer work in which part of the time is spent volunteering and the rest of the time is spent is exploring as tourists (Wearing & McGehee, 2013).

In addition to volunteering across nations and in other countries, intercultural volunteering also occurs when volunteers serve unique cultural populations within their home countries. The studies in the third section of the book provide two examples of this type of volunteering: German citizens volunteering in the Turkish immigrant community (Pfeiffer) and U.S. citizens serving Bhutanese refugees in the Atlanta area (Kumar & Dutta). In addition to examining similar situations, future research could explore whether the same issues these two studies explored, the challenge of participating as equals and importance of giving voice to those being served, affect interethnic volunteering within a country. This could be a productive area of research given that different racial and economic groups understand volunteering differently and have different motives and opportunities for volunteering (Wilson, 2000). An autoethographic study of a youth mentoring program demonstrates that some volunteers experience these issues when they volunteer across racial, ethnic, and economic groups (Douglas & Kim, 2013).

DIVERSITY OF VOLUNTEERING IN INTERNATIONAL AND INTERCULTURAL CONTEXTS

The studies in this volume suggest a wide range of international and intercultural volunteering contexts. Once again, some of the expected examples appear such as the Peace Corps, but the diversity is quite broad. Some of these volunteer efforts are directed as close family members, such as parents volunteering at their children's school (Cho & Lee); others' volunteer efforts are directed at anonymous strangers who have suffered devastating losses due to flooding (Kirdnark & Hale; McDonald, Creber, Sun, & Sonn). Some volunteers are involved in very short term projects such a mission trips (Frederick & Mize Smith) and voluntourism (Xu) while others make long term commitments such as the Peace Corps (Malleus; Hanchey). Some work closely with a large organization such as Rotary International (Craig & Russo) while some work outside of any organization (McDonald et al). And yet, clearly the studies in this volume do not represent the full spectrum of volunteering in intercultural and international contexts. For example, efforts to improve health by providing mosquito nets to prevent malaria or create safe drinking water are often conducted by nonprofit organizations that rely on local or international volunteers to raise money and/or perform the service work.

A common bias in the volunteer literature is to focus only on international volunteering contexts where humanitarian problems are addressed, even though volunteers serve many other purposes. Scant attention has been paid to the volunteering related to sporting and recreational activities, such as the 80,000 volunteers who were recruited for the 2014 Winter Olympics in Sochi, Russia, (Samko, 2013) or the 15,000 volunteers recruited for the World Cup in Brazil in 2014 (FIFA World Cup Brazil, 2014). Volunteers also organize and coach youth sports in many countries around the world. Although there is some research on volunteers in community choirs (Kramer, Meisenbach, & Hansen, 2013) and community theaters (Kramer, 2011) in the U.S., globally volunteering in the fine arts is also often overlooked. Volunteers are often involved in organizing local or international film, art, music, or popular culture festivals. Other volunteers carry out many functions for various occupation-focused organizations such as international professional associations (e.g., International Communication Association), educational associations (e.g., Association of International Education Administrators), historical societies (e.g., World History Association), and artistic cooperatives (e.g., International Arts & Artists). Other volunteers serve as citizen journalists (e.g., see citizen's media in Rodriguez, 2011) and participate in political and advocacy movements of various sorts (e.g., Sierra Club or Amnesty International). Even when there are paid employees in the offices of the nonprofit or nongovernmental organizations involved, the activities are often largely conducted by volunteers.

So in addition to examining volunteers involved in humanitarian assistance, we encourage future scholars to continue to explore the breadth of volunteering experiences to provide a rich understanding of volunteering.

PROBLEMS FACING VOLUNTEERS IN INTERNATIONAL AND INTERCULTURAL CONTEXTS

The studies in this volume point to some of the important problems facing volunteers in international and intercultural settings. Language barriers are an obvious problem. The volunteers teaching English to the Chinese seemed to feel much more successful interacting with Chinese teachers of English whose English language skills were relatively strong compared to many of the students assigned to them; of course, their own lack of understanding of Chinese contributed to this problem (Xu). In some instances the language issues are not so much due to an inability to translate the language but more due to cultural differences in understanding the meanings of words or concepts (Leroux & Saba). Unfortunately, it seems like program managers are faced with a challenging dilemma. If they make language requirements too stringent before sending volunteers into international settings, they severely limit the number of volunteers; however, sending out volunteers with limited local language skills restricts their ability to accomplish meaningful tasks or to feel a sense of accomplishment. Of course, language skills alone are insufficient since knowing the language does not mean that the volunteers and those they serve have a shared understanding of the local meanings of the language. There seems to be no easy answer to managing these language and shared meaning issues; perhaps all volunteers can do is muddle through the situations.

These studies suggest that volunteers face a number of personal issues when volunteering in these contexts. Individuals seemed to be primarily motivated to volunteer by six primary factors: (1) values such as a compassionate desire to serve others; (2) enhancement such as increasing ones self-esteem and feeling of being needed; (3) understanding such as learning about a cause or other people; (4) protection such as escaping from or working through personal problems; (5) social such as being with friends or others who value volunteering; and (6) career such as making career contacts or exploring options (Clary et al., 1998). In some cases, volunteers can become frustrated when their motivations are thwarted because of the bureaucratic procedures involved in many organized volunteer efforts. Many volunteers after the Brisbane floods got frustrated waiting for officials to coordinate their efforts and simply created their own method of volunteering without organizational support using social media to coordinate their efforts (McDonald et al). This pattern of organizing outside official channels has been observed in other disaster settings as well (Johnson, 2012). A more in-depth analysis of individuals involved in various unofficial volunteering efforts may provide additional insights into volunteers' motivations and how they change based on experiences. Examining the voluntary efforts of one family assisting a new immigrant family or elderly couple down the block may provide valuable insight into volunteers' motivations, even though the individuals involved might not classify their efforts as volunteering, but as "just helping out."

Motivations are part of a person's identity when embarking on the volunteer experience. During and after volunteer experiences individuals may experience temporary and/or more permanent changes in their identity depending on their experiences. Sometimes these identity changes may be positive when volunteers feel successful (e.g., Frederick & Mize Smith) which may lead to future volunteering, but in other cases, a sense of frustration in an inability to accomplish goals, such as failing to have a lasting impact, may have a negative effect on individuals (e.g., Craig & Russo) and result in a reduced desire to volunteer. Further examination of how the positive and negative aspects of the volunteer experience influence volunteers' sense of personal identity and self-worth and their future volunteer efforts seem warranted.

Not only may the volunteer experience have an impact on an individual's identity, particularly when it involves a long term commitment, but the volunteer may have to defend their identity in unexpected ways either before and/or after their actual experiences. When others cannot understand why they would give up a job to do mission work in another country or ask them about their "trip" instead of about their work when they return, volunteers may be forced to consider their identity and their definitions of work, particularly volunteer work (McNamee, et al). Volunteers genuinely motivated by their values may be accused of using the volunteer opportunity for personal gain, particularly when they are involved in voluntourism. This suggests the need to explore the communication between volunteers and their network of family and friends in more depth to understand how it has both positive and negative effects on their motivations and identities before and after their volunteer efforts.

It would also be useful to develop a better description of general cultural messages about volunteering around the world. The level of expectation or tolerance for "giving away" labor for free or being rewarded for "volunteering" varies considerably across cultures. As Gossett points out in the first chapter, volunteers may be seen as competitors who take away local jobs or second rate do-gooders who should be replaced by paid employees or government programs. As a result, in some cases volunteers find themselves defending giving free labor rather than being paid for their work; others must defend using a volunteer role to fulfill some personal goal. Overall, additional research is needed to explore messages that volunteers confront about their volunteering and how it impacts their identities and their willingness to engage as volunteers.

PROBLEMS EVALUATING VOLUNTEERING IN INTERNATIONAL AND INTERCULTURAL CONTEXTS

Although understanding the volunteers' experiences and perspectives is important, the studies in the volume indicate that a major challenge in examining volunteering in international and intercultural settings is determining an appropriate way to evaluate such efforts. If individuals are going to continue to do this type of volunteer work and scholars are going to continue to study those efforts, it seems important to assess whether these efforts are "successful." A number of these studies indicate that defining successful is quite challenging, in part, because success is too often defined based on the volunteer perspective without considering the biases of such a definition. For example, Hanchey points out how Peace Corps volunteers often unwittingly reinforce whiteness, masculinity, and national privilege in considering if they were successful volunteers. Kumar and Dutta found that volunteers felt that their own understanding of the needs of refugees was the appropriate way to define success instead of communicating with the refugees and listening to them to allow them to voice their needs. This failure to understand the refugees' perspective seems to have led them to conclude that their efforts were not very successful or appreciated. Similarly, Pfeiffer found that even though a mentoring program focused on treating those being aided by the volunteers as equals, some volunteers continued to assume that they should impart their values to mentees and their families to achieve success; other volunteers attempting to be more egalitarian in their approach had trouble articulating how the relationship was actually mutually beneficial.

Problematic in all of these situations is a sense that volunteers are the ones who impart benefits to the serviceable other in need because of the superiority of the values the volunteers hold (Craig & Russo). As long as this attitude continues, it will be difficult to define success in terms other than by exporting values from the volunteer's country to the others, a post-colonial perspective (Kumar & Dutta). Of course, as Craig and Russo discuss, citing Sampson (1993), the mere positioning of the volunteer as helping the other person reinforces this othering process whereby one individual is viewed as the dominant group by which to evaluate the other. This othering likely applies to many volunteer situations involving service even when it is simply the local volunteer assisting someone of a different socio-economic class or a different race.

One way to perhaps avoid these problems would be to move beyond studying social-service, humanitarian-aid volunteer settings to some of the others mentioned above, such as volunteers involved in athletic and arts activities, or professional associations. In many of those settings, the volunteers are serving not because they have superior values or knowledge to impart to those served. Frequently, they are serving people like themselves because they are also members of the group. They are simply helping to make a situation more pleasant, positive, or efficient. Studying volunteering in such contexts will likely decrease the focus on imparting knowledge or exporting superior values, providing a different perspective on volunteering.

Another way to address these issues would be for future research to take a more systematic, multi-stakeholder perspective on volunteer efforts. Such an approach would consider not only the volunteers and the immediate recipients of their service, but also the broader community. For example, by interviewing community members, McAllum and Zahra found that voluntourists may actually have influenced the long-term success of individuals by instilling in children upward mobility aspirations that enabled them to eventually leave their impoverished community, a positive outcome; however, parents also felt a loss of community as their children left, a negative outcome. A multi-stakeholder perspective would consider both outcomes. Minimally, a multi-stakeholder perspective would include individually collecting responses from the various stakeholders to give them each a voice in the evaluation of volunteer efforts. Ideally, it could include having dialogues among those volunteering, those served, and other community stakeholders to mutually define what a successful effort would be.

Challenges Facing Researchers in International and Intercultural Contexts

There are a number of challenges facing researchers hoping to gain a broader understanding of volunteering in international and intercultural contexts. Of course, there are the obvious problems of language barriers and access. These problems may gradually dissipate as more international collaboration develops through networks of scholars and the number of international students increases access to other countries. Some evidence for this trend is apparent in this volume in collaboration between scholars from different nations (e.g., Cho & Lee; Kirdnark & Hale). However, there are two more difficult challenges that future research should attempt to address.

First, most research on volunteering collects data from the perspective of the volunteer or the volunteer manager. Although we encourage continuation of this type of research, this approach can only provide a partial understanding of the volunteer context because it explores only one perspective, that of the volunteer.

Even a critical critique of volunteering about the possible impact of othering (e.g., Hanchey) or American exceptionalism (e.g., Craig and Russo) does not take the volunteer's perspective. Such critiques still somewhat ironically assume that the researcher's a priori knowledge as an outsider can make an appropriate ideological critique of how specific interests fail to be realized in a given context (Deetz, 2001) without actually gaining the perspective of those whom the volunteers attempt to serve. This is no different than the approach volunteers serving the Bhutanese population took; they assumed they understood what was best for the refugees without actually allowing the refugees to communicate their perspective (Kumar & Dutta). Scholars and volunteers have good intentions but often end up othering those served by volunteers by failing to gain their perspective.

The study by McAllum and Zahra is unique in this volume for studying the perspective of those served by volunteers, although there have occasionally been other studies of the "voluntoured" (e.g., McGehee & Andereck, 2009). Their study of people being attended to by volunteers provides an important perspective on the volunteer context that is rarely studied. Although it may be challenging to identify and study those served by volunteers, additional insight will be gained by studying both the volunteers' perspective and the perspective of those they serve. So for example, linking the studies of voluntourists by Mize-Smith (2013) or Xu with the McAllum and Zahra study of people served by voluntourists provides additional insight that the individual studies cannot provide on their own. Unfortunately, since the studies were conducted in different locations with volunteers from different countries, the insights are somewhat limited. Future research would be even stronger if it collected data from multiple stakeholders of the same volunteer context.

Second, it was not surprising, but disappointing nonetheless, that we were unable to include any broad sample, survey studies of volunteers in international and intercultural contexts in this volume. Although this could be due to an incomplete pool of chapter proposals, this seems to be at least partially related to the challenge of accessing large samples. Most volunteers serving in other countries, whether they are from the U.S. or other countries, function in small groups. Due to this, the challenges of collecting samples large enough for meaningful quantitative analyses are nearly insurmountable for most researchers on their own even though the collective number of volunteers is quite large. Future scholars may be able to develop cooperative relationships with large volunteer agencies like the Peace Corps, Rotary International, or the American Red Cross and its international affiliates so that this type of hypothesis-testing, generalizable research can be conducted.

CONCLUSION

This volume indicates that a range of scholars have begun to examine the many opportunities for research on volunteering in international and intercultural contexts. We have suggested a number of areas where further research should be conducted. However, our suggestions are far from exhaustive. We hope that this volume will encourage other scholars to build on these studies in the years to come.

REFERENCES

Anheier, H. K., & Salamon, L. M. (1999). Volunteering in cross-national perspective: Initial comparisons. *Law and Contemporary Problems, 62*, 43–65.

Butcher, J. (2010). Volunteering. In R. Taylor (Ed.), *Third sector research* (pp. 91–103). San Francisco, CA: Jossey-Bass.

Clary, E. G., Snyder, M., Ridge, R. D., Copeland, J., Stukas, A. A., Haugen, J., & Miene, P. (1998). Understanding and assessing the motivations of volunteers: A functional approach. *Journal of Personality and Social Psychology, 74*, 1516–1530.

Deetz, S. A. (2001). Conceptual foundations. In F. M. Jablin & L. L. Putnam (Eds.), *The new handbook of organizational communication: Advances in theory, research, and methods* (pp. 3–46). Thousand Oaks, CA: Sage.

Douglas, J. C., & Kim, D. K. (2013). What does it mean, "Just be a friend"? Analysis of volunteer uncertainty during the assimilation and socialization process at a youth mentoring organization. In M. W. Kramer, L. K. Lewis, & L. M. Gossett (Eds.), *Volunteering and communication: Studies from multiple contexts* (pp. 169–188). New York, NY: Peter Lang.

FIFA World Cup Brazil. (2014). Information on volunteer programme. Retrieved June 25, from http://www.fifa.com/worldcup/organisation/volunteers/faq/index.html

Johnson, S. (2012). Students vs. the machine: Lessons learned in the student community following the Christchurch earthquakes. *e-vounteerism, V XXII (2)*.

Kramer, M. W. (2011). A study of voluntary organizational membership: The assimilation process in a community choir. *Western Journal of Communication, 75*, 52–74.

Kramer, M. W., Lewis, L. K., & Gossett, L. M. (Eds.). (2013). *Volunteering and communication: Studies from multiple contexts*. New York, NY: Peter Lang.

Kramer, M. W., Meisenbach, R. J., & Hansen, G. J. (2013). Communication, uncertainty, and volunteer membership. *Journal of Applied Communication Research, 41*, 18–39.

Lewis, L. K. (2013). An introduction to volunteers. In M. W. Kramer, L. K. Lewis, & L. M. Gossett (Eds.), *Volunteers and communciation: Studies in multiple contexts* (pp. 1–22). New York, NY: Peter Lang.

Maugh, C. M. (2013). Blogging for peace: Realistic job preview strategies from the 21st century Peace Corps volunteer. In M. W. Kramer, L. K. Lewis, & L. M. Gossett (Eds.), *Volunteering and communication: Studies from multiple contexts* (pp. 25–44). New York, NY: Peter Lang.

McAllum, K. (2013). Challenging nonprofit praxis: Organizational volunteers and the expression of dissent. In M. W. Kramer, L. K. Lewis, & L. M. Gossett (Eds.), *Volunteering and communication: Studies from multiple contexts* (pp. 383–404). New York, NY: Peter Lang.

McGehee, N. G., & Andereck, K. (2009). Volunteer tourism and the "voluntoured": The case of Tijuana, Mexico. *Journal of Sustainable Tourism, 17*, 39–51.

Mize-Smith, J. (2013). Volunteer tourists: The identity and discourse of travelers combining largesse and leisure. In M. W. Kramer, L. K. Lewis, & L. M. Gossett (Eds.), *Volunteering and communication: Studies from multiple contexts* (pp. 189–209). New York, NY: Peter Lang.

Onyx, J. (2013). Breaking the rules: The secret to successful volunteering in a caring role. In M. W. Kramer, L. K. Lewis, & L. M. Gossett (Eds.), *Volunteering and communication: Studies from multiple contexts* (pp. 343–364). New York, NY: Peter Lang.

Peace Corps. (2013). *The Peace Corps Performance and Accountability Report Fiscal Year 2013.* Washington, DC. Retrieved from www.peacecorps.gov.

Rodriguez, C. (2011). *Citizens' media against armed conflict: Disrupting violence in Colombia.* Minneapolis, MN: University of Minnesota Press.

Samko, D. (2013, November 11). Russians put together 2020 road map to develop volunteerism. Retrieved from http://www.upf.org/upf-news/144-europe-eurasia-/5539-russians-put-toge ther-2020-road-map-to-develop-volunteerism

Sampson, E. E. (1993). Identity politics: Challenges to psychology's understanding. *American Psychologist, 48*, 1219–1230.

United Nations. (2011). State of the world's volunteerism report: Universal values for global well-being. New York, NY: United Nations Volunteers.

Walch, T. (2007, June 26). 1 million missionaries for LDS Church–so far. *Deseret News.* Retrieved from http://www.deseretnews.com/article/680194052/1-million-missionaries-for-LDS-Chur ch--so-far.html

Wearing, S., & McGehee, N. G. (2013). Volunteer tourism: A review. *Tourism Management, 38*, 120–130.

Wilson, J. (2000). Volunteering. *Annual Review of Sociology, 26*, 215–240.

Wilson, J., & Musick, M. (1997). Who cares? Toward an integrated theory of volunteer work. *American Sociological Review, 62*, 694–713.

Author Biographies

Jehee Cho (Ph.D., University of Texas at Austin) is an assistant professor in the School of Mass Communication at Chung-Ang University in Seoul, Korea. His research interests include information-sharing, adoptions of information communication technologies (ICTs), and multicultural communication in various organizational and educational settings. Recently, he has conducted multiple research projects exploring motivational factors of adopting health apps on smartphones. He has published peer-reviewed articles in outlets such as *Cyberpsychology, Behavior, and Social Networking*, *Human Communication Research*, *Journal of Applied Communication Research*, and *Journal of Medical Internet Research*. He may be contacted at jcho49@cau.ac.kr.

Melissa Creber (B. in Communications [Public Relations]/B. in Journalism, University of Queensland) is a public relations consultant for a global infrastructure firm. Melissa became interested in the community's response to disaster situations after seeing it first hand as a flood victim in the 2011 Brisbane floods. This led to her involvement in this research project and her current role providing communications and community engagement services for state and local government flood reconstruction and mitigation projects. Melissa aspires to work in disaster and crisis management and would like to conduct further research into community reaction and response during disaster and crises. She may be contacted at: melissa.creber@uqconnect.edu.au.

Brett J. Craig (Ph.D. in communication studies, University of Kansas) is an assistant professor in the Department of Communication in the School of Science & Technology at Nazarbayev University in Astana, Kazakhstan. His research focuses on intergroup communication perspectives in the applied context of health and development, examining the communication of various stakeholders including practitioners, government organizations, NGOs, educational institutions, and the public in developing societies. He may be contacted at bcraig@nu.edu.kz.

Mohan J. Dutta (Ph.D., University of Minnesota) is Provost's Chair Professor and Head of the Department of Communications and New Media at the National University of Singapore and Courtesy Professor of Communication at Purdue University. At NUS, he is the Founding Director of the Center for Culture-Centered Approach to Research and Evaluation (CARE), directing research on culturally-centered, community-based projects of social change. He teaches and conducts research in international health communication, critical cultural theory, poverty in healthcare, health activism in globalization politics, indigenous cosmologies of health, subaltern studies and dialogue, and public policy and social change. Currently, he serves as editor of the Critical Cultural Studies in Global Health Communication Book Series for Left Coast Press and sits on the editorial board of seven journals. At Purdue, he served as the Founding Director of the Center for Poverty and Health Inequities (COPHI). He can be contacted at cnmmohan@nus.edu.sg.

Katelin Frederick (M.A., organizational communication, Western Kentucky University) is a director of sales in the hotel industry. Her academic research focused on volunteer and family communication. She also participated in the Bonner Scholars program where she volunteered with numerous community organizations. She continues to be an active volunteer in her church, particularly in domestic and international mission programs. She may be contacted at katelin.frederick017@topper.wku.edu.

Loril M. Gossett (Ph.D. in organizational communication, University of Colorado at Boulder) is an Associate Professor of Communication Studies and Organizational Science at the University of North Carolina at Charlotte. Her theoretical interests are focused on issues of identification, member voice, and managerial control strategies within organizational settings. In her work, she examines the ways that non-standard work relationships (contingent labor, volunteers, part-time employees, virtual workers, etc.) impact our understanding of what it means to be or communicate as organizational members. Her research has been published in such forums as *Communication Monographs, Management Communication Quarterly, Communication Yearbook,* and *Public Performance and Management Review.* She may be contacted at lgosset1@uncc.edu.

Kelly K. Gould (B.A., Baylor University) is a Master's candidate in the Department of Communication at Baylor University, focusing her studies in family and interpersonal communication. Her undergraduate degree in international studies sparked her early interest in global cultures and service abroad. Kelly's involvement in this research project also stemmed from her own experiences as a missionary in Western China and her ongoing relationships with other international volunteers and their sponsoring organizations. While pursuing her Master's degree in Communication Studies, Kelly works as a senior admissions counselor for Baylor's Office of Admission Services. Contact her at Kelly_Gould@baylor.edu.

Claudia L. Hale (Ph.D., speech communication, University of Illinois) is a professor in the School of Communication Studies at Ohio University. Her research efforts focus on the areas of 1) peace building and community building in societies/cultures that have been affected by violent conflict, 2) interpersonal/intercultural relationships, and 3) organizational conflict. Her research has been published in such forums as *Communication Monographs, Conflict Resolution Quarterly,* and the *International Journal of Cross Cultural Management.* She may be contacted at hale@ohio.edu.

Jenna N. Hanchey (M.A., organizational communication/rhetoric, University of Colorado Boulder) is a doctoral student and William C. Powers Fellow in the Communication Studies Department at the University of Texas at Austin. Her work analyzes Western rhetorics of international aid and assistance, particularly focusing on organizations that work in and with Sub-Saharan Africa. Integrating fieldwork and textual analysis, she also examines the way aid projects are received and responded to by local communities. She is a recent recipient of the Gerard A. Hauser Award from the Rhetoric Society of America, as well as support for dissertation research in Tanzania through the Jesse H. Jones Fellowship from the Moody College of Communication at the University of Texas at Austin. She can be contacted at jenna.hanchey@utexas.edu.

Treepon Kirdnark is the Chairperson of the Journalism Department at Bangkok University, Thailand. He may be contacted at treepon.k@bu.ac.th.

Michael W. Kramer (Ph.D., organizational communication, University of Texas) is professor and chair in the Department of Communication at the University of Oklahoma. His organizational research focuses on employee transitions such as newcomers, exit processes, and corporate mergers. His group research focuses on decision making, membership, and leadership. He has made theoretical contributions in the theory of managing uncertainty and group dialectical theory. His recent research has focused on volunteers rather than paid employees. This led to the edited volume *Volunteering and Communication: Studies from Multiple Contexts* (2013). In addition to various journal articles and book chapters, he has published two other books, *Managing Uncertainty in Organizational Communication* (2004) and *Organizational Socialization: Joining and Leaving Organizations* (2010). He may be contacted at mkramer@ou.edu.

Rati Kumar (Ph.D. in communication, Purdue University) is an assistant professor in the Department of Communication at Central Connecticut State University. Her research focuses primarily on community-based collaborations, critically engaging with communicative practices in the areas of public policy, social justice, health communication and relationship management. Her recent research focuses on minority populations, including the role of communication in health practices and interactions with volunteers assisting in the process. Her current scholarship includes "Relational Tensions in Academic-Community Partnerships in the Culture-Centered Approach (CCA): Negotiating Communication in Creating Spaces for Voices" (2013) in M. J. Dutta & G. Kreps' (Eds.) *Communication interventions addressing health disparities*, and "Activism and Relationships of Social Change: A Culture-centered Approach" (in press) in J. N. Kim (Ed.), *Relationship Management*. She may be contacted at rkumar@ccsu.edu.

H. Erin Lee (Ph.D., radio-TV-film, University of Texas at Austin) is an assistant professor in the Media & Communication Division at Hankuk University of Foreign Studies, Seoul, Korea. Her research focuses on digital media culture, with a particular focus on children/youth and immigrant populations. Her most recent research projects have investigated cyberbullying among teenagers and health app use among college students. She may be contacted at helee@hufs.ac.kr.

Marie-Pierre Leroux (M.A. in project management with a specialization in international development, Université du Québec en Outaouais) is an affiliate member of the Interuniversity Research Centre on Globalization and Work (CRIMT). After graduating in international studies from the University of Montreal, she studied Arabic in Egypt for two years. In 2006, she took on an international volunteer assignment with Oxfam as project officer in the occupied Palestinian territories. She then worked as an independent consultant in project management in West and Central Africa. Her current doctoral research in the School of Industrial Relations at the University of Montreal examines relational factors contributing to capacity building in the context of international technical assistance. Her research fields are international human resources management, expatriate knowledge sharing, and international development project. She may be contacted at marie-pierre. leroux@umontreal.ca.

Laurie K. Lewis (Ph.D., in communication, University of California at Santa Barbara) is professor and chair of the Department of Communication in the Rutgers' School of Communication and Information. Previously she held faculty positions at Pennsylvania State University and the University of Texas at Austin. She teaches and conducts research in areas of organizational change, stakeholder communication, nonprofit organizations, and interorganizational collaboration. A recognized expert in nonprofit settings, her work has appeared in *Communication Monographs, Human Communication Research, Management Communication Quarterly,* and her book, *Organizational Change: Creating Change through Strategic Communication.* She has consulted and done training for various non-profit organizations including Habitat for Humanity, Austin Presbyterian Theological Seminary, the Sharing Network, and Austin's Community Action Network. Prior to her academic career, she worked for the American Red Cross in Human Resource Management. She may be reached at lewisl@rutgers.edu.

Rick Malleus (Ph.D. in intercultural communication, University of Minnesota) is a Zimbabwean serving as an assistant professor in the Communication Department at Seattle University. His research and publishing interests include a focus on mediated communication in the Southern African region, intercultural reentry, and cross-cultural comparison in technology use. He recently published research on travel blogs as potential sources of intercultural communication data. He has also published book chapters on satellite television in Zimbabwe, and the credibility of online news for diaspora populations, with a focus on the Zimbabwean diaspora. He may be contacted at malleusr@seattleu.edu.

Kirstie McAllum (Ph.D., organizational communication, University of Waikato, Hamilton, New Zealand) is an assistant professor in the Département de communication at the Université de Montréal, Canada. Her research focuses on understanding how organizational members who do not interact regularly construct the meanings of their work as well as how persons who occupy hybrid public-private spaces construct organizational and occupational identities. She also investigates how discourses about professionalism combine with organizational control and coordination mechanisms to structure relationality in particular ways, often with the aim of increasing collaboration, and frequently of minimizing or suppressing dissent. Her work on volunteers and volunteering has been published in *Management Communication Quarterly* and *Communication Yearbook*. She may be contacted at kirstie. mcallum@umontreal.ca.

Lynette M. McDonald (Ph.D. in company crisis communication, Griffith University) is an adjunct lecturer in the Australian Centre for Sustainable Business and Development at the University of Southern Queensland. A former public relations consultant, her research examines stakeholder response to corporate social responsibility initiatives, as well as to crisis communication. Her group research examines crises and emergencies. In particular, she is interested in emotion response and its behavioral and attitudinal outcomes. Her publications include book chapters and articles in such journals as *Public Relations Review*, *Journal of Management Education*, and the *International Journal of Bank Marketing*. She may be contacted at lyn.mcdonald@usq.edu. au.

Lacy G. McNamee (Ph.D., University of Texas at Austin) is an assistant professor of Organizational Communication in Baylor University's Department of Communication. Her research focuses on organizational socialization and the negotiation of members' roles, responsibilities, and relationships. Her recent work has more specifically examined the communication dynamics between different member types in nonprofit and faith-based organizational settings, such as paid staff and volunteers. Lacy's work has been published in journals including *Communication Monographs*, *Management Communication Quarterly*, *Journal of Applied Communication Research*, *Health Communication*, and *Human Relations*, and she has served as a board director, advisor, and consultant for several nonprofit and volunteer-based organizations. She may be contacted at Lacy_McNamee@baylor.edu.

Jennifer Mize Smith (Ph.D., organizational communication, Purdue University) is an associate professor in the Department of Communication at Western Kentucky University. Her research focuses on issues of identity and identification, corporate giving, fundraising rhetoric, and other communication processes in and of the nonprofit sector. She explores the ways in which giving and volunteering are socially constructed and in various contexts (e.g., workplace, family, school, leisure) and the extent to which those meanings (re)construct one's philanthropic self. Her work has been published in the *International Journal of Business Communication*, the *Southern Communication Journal*, and *Communication Studies*, as well as the edited volume *Volunteering and Communication: Studies from Multiple Contexts*. She may be contacted at jennifer.mize.smith@wku.edu.

Brittany L. Peterson (Ph.D., University of Texas at Austin) is an assistant professor in the School of Communication Studies and the Coordinator of e-Learning for the Scripps College of Communication at Ohio University. Her research focuses on challenging, deconstructing, and extending traditional constructions of membership in organizations with a specific focus on involuntary membership in and around correctional institutions and voluntary membership in "high stakes" organizations (e.g., volunteer fire departments). Her scholarship is tied to socialization, identification, and structuration processes, and she teaches graduate and undergraduate classes on organizational communication, socialization, membership, and interpretive research methods. Brittany's work has been published in peer-reviewed journals including *Management Communication Quarterly*, *Communication Monographs*, *Communication Quarterly*, *Communication Education*, and *Journal of Applied Social Science* as well as in edited books. She may be contacted at petersob@ohio.edu.

Anna Sarah Pfeiffer (M.A. in organization studies, Lund University, Sweden) is a doctoral student in organization studies at Lund University's School of Economics and Management. Her doctoral research explores the relation between experiences of recognition and individual self-formation in the context of voluntary work. Next to her attention to volunteering, her research interests include subjectivity in organizations, recognition theories, postcolonialism, and critical perspectives on management. She may be contacted at Anna.Pfeiffer@fek.lu.se.

Tracy Russo (Ph.D. in communication studies, University of Kansas) is an associate professor in the Department of Communication Studies at the University of Kansas. Her research focuses on communication behaviors in mediated environments, especially focusing on group member attachments to others in online teams and groups and in online classes and on how these attachments affect organizational outcomes. She may be contacted at trusso@ku.edu.

Tania Saba (Ph. D. in industrial relations, University of Montreal) is professor in the School of Industrial Relations at the University of Montreal and researcher at the Interuniversity Research Centre on Globalization and Work (CRIMT) and the Centre d'études et de recherches internationales de l'Université de Montréal (CÉRIUM). She was the School of Industrial Relations Chair from 2008 to 2010 and Associate Dean of Undergraduate Studies from 2010 until 2012. She is presently the Associate Dean of Graduate Studies and External Relations in the Faculty of Arts and Sciences at the University of Montreal. Since 1996, she teaches HRM with a focus on international dimensions, employee relations and strategic management. Her research interests include international human resource management, knowledge transfer, mobility, new employment relations, older worker's management, intergenerational differences and the organization of the HR function. She may be contacted at tania.saba@umontreal.ca.

Lindsey Sonn (M.A. Lindsey Sonn (M.A. in communication [public relations and professional communications], University of Queensland) became interested in disaster volunteer response while researching the Brisbane floods. Currently, she is employed as the Public Relations and Marketing Manger for Cataldo Ambulance Service in Malden, MA. She may be contacted at lindsey.sonn@uqconnect.edu.

Huichun Sun (M.A. in Communication [public relations and professional communication], University of Queensland) is passionate about spontaneous volunteering behavior and disaster response management. Her Brisbane flood research paid special attention to emotion response during disaster and its impact on helping behavior. She may be contacted at hui.sun1@ uqconnect.edu.au.

Janice Hua Xu (Ph.D. in communication, University of Illinois at Urbana-Champaign) is assistant professor of Communication at Holy Family University, Pennsylvania. Prior to college teaching in the U.S., she worked as lecturer of international communication in Peking University in China, news assistant at New York Times Beijing Bureau, and radio broadcaster at Voice of America, Washington, DC. Her research interests include cross-cultural communication, media globalization, and grassroots activism. She has published journal articles in *Media, Culture, & Society, Journalism Studies, International Journal of Communication*, and *Telematics and Informatics*, and contributed chapters to multiple communication studies books. She may be reached at jxu@holyfamily.edu.

Anne Zahra (Ph.D., University of Waikato, Hamilton, New Zealand) is an Associate Professor in the Department of Tourism and Hospitality Management at the University of Waikato, New Zealand. Her current research areas include volunteer tourism, tourism policy and governance, and critical hospitality and the home. Anne has had a twenty-five year involvement in volunteering, both as a volunteer working with rural and urban poor in less developed countries and as an organizer of development projects for volunteers in Fiji, Tonga, India, and the Philippines. She has also had a long-term governance role with Reledev Australia Limited, a non-governmental organization registered with AusAid, the Australian foreign aid agency, which works with partner NGOs on development projects in South America, Asia, and the Middle East. She may be contacted at a.zahra@waikato.ac.nz.

Author Index

A

Acker, J., 236, 249
Ashforth, B. E., 117, 126, 194, 211

B

Baaz, M. E., 253, 255–256, 267, 269, 270
Barraket, J., 28, 30, 32–33, 41, 44–45
Beamer, L., 173, 190
Beyerlein, K., 28–32, 40–41, 45, 193, 211
Bhabha, H. K., 106, 256, 268, 270
Bochner, S., 133, 151, 174–176, 190–191
Bonache, J., 92, 105
Bonilla-Silva, E., 239–240, 249
Broadfoot, K., 155, 166, 170, 271
Bruno, A., 274, 290

C

Callahan, C., 153, 157, 168, 170
Carlile, P., 102, 104–105
Carlsson, J., 91, 105
Carrera, P., 31, 44, 46
Cheong, F., 28, 33, 46
Cho, J., 21, 67–88, 296, 298, 302, 307
Choden, T., 11, 22, 280, 290
Cialdini, R., 29–30, 41, 46
CIDA, 90, 105, 107
Collier, M., 111, 126
Contu, A., 254–255, 267, 269, 271
Craig, B. J., 21, 213–231, 297–298, 300–301, 303, 308
Creber, M., 20, 27–47, 298–299, 307
Cushner, K., 176, 190

Subject Index